The Narrative Shape of Truth

Literature and Philosophy

A. J. Cascardi, General Editor

This series publishes books in a wide range of subjects in philosophy and literature, including studies of the social and historical issues that relate these two fields. Drawing on the resources of the Anglo-American and Continental traditions, the series is open to philosophically informed scholarship covering the entire range of contemporary critical thought.

ALREADY PUBLISHED:

J. M. Bernstein, *The Fate of Art: Aesthetic Alienation from Kant to Derrida and Adorno*
Peter Bürger, *The Decline of Modernism*
Mary E. Finn, *Writing the Incommensurable: Kierkegaard, Rossetti, and Hopkins*
Reed Way Dasenbrock, ed., *Literary Theory After Davidson*
David P. Haney, *William Wordsworth and the Hermeneutics of Incarnation*
David Jacobson, *Emerson's Pragmatic Vision: The Dance of the Eye*
Gray Kochhar-Lindgren, *Narcissus Transformed: The Textual Subject in Psychoanalysis and Literature*
Robert Steiner, *Toward a Grammar of Abstraction: Modernity, Wittgenstein, and the Paintings of Jackson Pollock*
Sylvia Walsh, *Living Poetically: Kierkegaard's Existential Aesthetics*
Michel Meyer, *Rhetoric, Language, and Reason*
Christie McDonald and Gary Wihl, eds., *Transformations in Personhood and Culture After Theory*
Charles Altieri, *Painterly Abstraction in Modernist American Poetry: The Contemporaneity of Modernism*
John C. O'Neal, *The Authority of Experience: Sensationist Theory in the French Enlightenment*
John O'Neill, ed., *Freud and the Passions*
Sheridan Hough, *Nietzsche's Noontide Friend: The Self as Metaphoric Double*
E. M. Dadlez, *What's Hecuba to Him? Fictional Events and Actual Emotions*
Hugh Roberts, *Shelley and the Chaos of History: A New Politics of Poetry*
Charles Altieri, *Postmodernisms Now: Essays on Contemporaneity in the Arts*
Arabella Lyon, *Intentions: Negotiated, Contested, and Ignored*
Jill Gordon, *Turning Toward Philosophy: Literary Device and Dramatic Structure in Plato's Dialogues*
Michel Meyer, *Philosophy and the Passions: Toward a History of Human Nature.* Translated by Robert F. Barsky
Reed Way Dasenbrock, *Truth and Consequences: Intentions, Conventions, and the New Thematics*
David P. Haney, *The Challenge of Coleridge: Ethics and Interpretation in Romanticism and Modern Philosophy*
Alan Singer, *Aesthetic Reason: Artworks and the Deliberative Ethos*
Tom Huhn, *Imitation and Society: The Persistence of Mimesis in the Aesthetics of Burke, Hogarth, and Kant*
Jennifer Anna Gosetti-Ferenci, *The Ecstatic Quotidian: Phenomenological Sightings in Modern Art and Literature*
Max Statkiewicz, *Rhapsody of Philosophy: Dialogues with Plato in Contemporary Thought*
David N. McNeill, *An Image of the Soul in Speech: Plato and the Problem of Socrates*
Alan Singer, *The Self-Deceiving Muse: Notice and Knowledge in the Work of Art*
Chad Wellmon, *Becoming Human: Romantic Anthropology and the Embodiment of Freedom*

The Narrative Shape of Truth

Veridiction in Modern European Literature

Ilya Kliger

The Pennsylvania State University Press
University Park, Pennsylvania

Library of Congress Cataloging-in-Publication Data

Kliger, Ilya.
The narrative shape of truth : veridiction in modern European literature / Ilya Kliger.
    p. cm. — (Literature and philosophy)
Summary: "Draws on philosophical and novelistic texts from the Western European and Russian canons to explore a crucial moment in the epistemological history of narrative and present a nonreductive way of conjugating the histories of philosophy and the novel"—Provided by publisher.
Includes bibliographical references and index.
ISBN 978-0-271-03798-1 (cloth : alk. paper)
ISBN 978-0-271-05077-5 (pbk. : alk. paper)
1. European fiction—History and criticism.
2. Truth in literature.
3. Fictions, Theory of.
4. Literature—Philosophy.
5. Narration (Rhetoric).
I. Title.

PN3347.K55 2011
809'.93353—dc22
2010041918

Copyright © 2011 The Pennsylvania State University
All rights reserved
Printed in the United States of America
Published by The Pennsylvania State University Press,
University Park, PA 16802–1003

The Pennsylvania State University Press is a member of the Association of American University Presses.

It is the policy of The Pennsylvania State University Press to use acid-free paper. Publications on uncoated stock satisfy the minimum requirements of American National Standard for Information Sciences—Permanence of Paper for Printed Library Material, ANSI Z39.48–1992.

Contents

Acknowledgments   vii

Note on Transliteration   ix

Introduction: The Veridictory Mutation of the Novel   1

1 Precipitant Knowledge in Balzac   43

2 The Whole and the Untrue: Stendhal's Fragile Veridiction   77

3 Enigma and Emplotment in Dostoevsky   114

4 Tolstoy's Plotlines and Truth Shapes   145

Conclusion: Enduring the *Schema* in Modernist Time   177

Notes   207

Bibliography   233

Index   243

Acknowledgments

My early work on the manuscript was done under the direction of Peter Brooks and Michael Holquist. The manuscript benefited greatly from conversations with Peter Brooks, from his encouragement and critique. Michael Holquist read, hurried along, inspired, and influenced this manuscript at every stage of its composition. To both of them I owe much of how I understand narrative and the novel.

This project can be said to have originated in Vladimir Alexandrov's seminar on *Anna Karenina* with some thoughts on the authority of the novel's epigraph. I am very grateful for his thoughtful guidance and example in matters intellectual, professional, and human.

To the many readers of the manuscript at various stages—Thomas Campbell, Katerina Clark, Caryl Emerson, Carol Jacobs, Jeff Love, John Mackay, and Haun Saussy—I am thankful for their comments, criticisms, and suggestions. Special thanks to Masha Salazkina, who read and commented on the manuscript at a very late stage.

I am grateful to Una Belau, Seth Brodsky, Rossen Djagalov, Kate Holland, Itzik Melamed, Yuliya Minkova, Marco Roth, Neta Stahl, Lina Steiner, Katia Vernikov, and David and Alla Vernikov for their unswerving friendship and intellectual companionship over the years.

Irina Paperno, Harsha Ram, and Nancy Ruttenberg offered invaluable help with the publication process and much else. Many thanks to Irina for the many things she taught me and for her attentive critical reading of the manuscript; to Harsha for his friendship, his encouragement, and his insight; and to Nancy for her generous advice and advocacy.

At Penn State University Press, I am extremely grateful to Mary Petrusewicz for the work she has done editing the manuscript and to Tony Cascardi for supporting this project from the start.

Many thanks to Genya Altman, Irina Belodedova, Eliot Borenstein, Jane Burbank, Milan Fryscak, Diana Greene, Anneta Greenlee, Michael Kunichika,

Yanni Kotsonis, and Anne Lounsbery—I could not have asked for a more intellectually stimulating and convivial group of people to work with.

Without my friend and collaborator, Nasser Zakariya, nothing about this book would have been the same, and everything would have been worse. I have come to rely almost unwittingly on his painstaking engagement with my work, his invariably enlightening conversation, and his questions, testing the limits of what I can articulate—for all this I am grateful beyond expression.

To Hiba Hafiz, my closest reader, at once the most demanding and the most enthusiastic, for challenging me to be more detailed, to understand better what I am doing, and to rewrite; but, above all, for being a constant inspiration in big things and small—I am more and more thankful every day.

To my parents, Tanya, Samuel, Marius, and Olga, I am grateful for their support over the years and for the many ways they made working on this book worthwhile; to my no-longer-so-little siblings, Hannah and Daniel, for their friendship, their teasing, and their faith. I would like to dedicate this book to my daughter Sasha, whose radiance was a constant source of strength.

Note on Transliteration

I have used the Library of Congress system of transliteration, except in the case of well-known personal names, where I resorted to –sky and –y, as in "Dostoevsky," "Aglaya," and so on.

Introduction:
The Veridictory Mutation of the Novel

Modernity and the Novel

The novel has often been understood, by its champions as well as detractors, as the genre *par excellence* of truthlessness. However its genealogy is traced—whether it is conceived of as an avatar of the epic, the romance, or the heroic poem; whether it is seen as essentially opposed to tragedy, or history, or the lyric; whether its beginnings are sought after in the Hellenistic world or in early modern Europe—one differential feature consistently emerges as crucial: the novel's formal and thematic alliance with a certain modernity as the condition from which higher truth has withdrawn. The world of the novel is forsaken by God, it is a world in which chance is given free play, a world in which universals no longer find a home and "general truths only exist *post res*," a world of constant flux, in which multiple worldviews and discourses vie for dominance but none ultimately wins, in which the duration of life is victorious over the moment of realization—these are some of the ways in which the fundamental hostility of the novel to truth has been most famously conceived.[1] A hostility that is, to be sure, not merely negative, as if the novel simply lacked at its disposal the means for sustaining universal claims. Rather, the novel is seen as the genre whose very essence is to give voice—with nostalgia or exaltation, defiance or resignation—to a truthless world.

Georg Lukács opposes the novel to the epic, to the world in which meaning is still immanent, in which the very question of truth as the relation between thought and thing has yet to be raised. The epic is the form of the happy age "when the starry sky is the map of all possible paths."[2] The novel belongs to a world and an age in which the starry sky no longer shows the way, in which the division between the sky and the earth, the word and the thing, the thought and the act, is irreparable.

The logic of novelistic polyphony in Mikhail Bakhtin's theory of the novel posits the genre as the best fit for orchestrating multiple, unfinalizable, discursively embodied worldviews, casting out monologic truth, both in its subjectivist lyric and objectivist epic incarnations. The epic presupposes the totality of life immediately available to man, the coincidence of existence and meaning. The lyric assumes the same coincidence, the same immediacy, but achieved on the basis of a solitary consciousness. Only the novel remains resolutely truthless, a ventriloquist of the many voices that can be heard in the metropolitan, multicultural world for which it serves as the most appropriate symbolic form.

Tragedy, with its insistence on absolutes, its ideological intransigence, its reliance on the pivotal event, is the novel's antagonist in, for example, Franco Moretti's essay "The Moment of Truth." By contrast to tragedy, the novel emerges here as dealing in compromises, half-truths, and elusions, obsessed with ceaseless conversations at the expense of sudden enlightenment, and has endlessly multiplying opportunities at the expense of decisive events. For Moretti too, then, the world of the novel is the world of "life" precisely insofar as "life" is opposed to truth.[3]

Higher meaning, authoritative monologue, the conversionary or revelatory moment—each specifies a distinct veridictory mode, a mode of decisive adequation between human being and world, and each is denied to the novel. Intriguingly, these prominent twentieth-century theories of the novel, in elaborating the genre's relation to the authoritative discourse of truth, recapitulate the classical taxonomy of genre into which the European novel had so much difficulty fitting during the seventeenth and eighteenth centuries. They seem to accept a number of classical arguments that were again and again adduced against the novel: that it is cumbersome, that it gives free reign to the imagination, that it fails to edify, that, moreover, it corrupts. But in accepting these criticisms, they turn them upside down, arguing or at least implying that, in being messy, the novel gives us an accurate representation of the bewilderment of the modern world; that, in foregrounding fictionality, it reminds us that truth itself is traversed by invention; that a certain moral and ideological relativism, or at least an appreciation for life's high moral complexity, teaches tolerance and attunement to the voices of those around us.

These arguments sound natural enough today, when, having been elevated by some of its turn-of-the-eighteenth-century theorists to the status of the ultimate genre of modernity, the novel no longer has to prove its worth. But a survey of the rhetoric surrounding one of the novel's most recent mutations in the seventeenth and eighteenth centuries reveals an intense struggle for legitimacy, a struggle in the course of which practitioners and defenders of the novel repeatedly invoked notions of truth within an unstable intellectual environment permeated by a tension between two veridictory discourses—one residual, the other emerging.

To be sure, a closer look at the period does confirm some of the basic assumptions about the novel's hostility to higher truth. This is famously the thesis of Ian Watt's classic account of the rise of the novel in eighteenth-century England. Here the novel's "formal realism" is praised as allowing for "a more immediate imitation of individual experience set in its temporal and spatial environment than do other literary forms."[4] Watt links the rise of the novel during that period to the emergence and spread of empiricist philosophy and the corresponding shift of emphasis from timeless universals to particulars localized in space and time. On this account, the novel is truthless in the sense that it is constructed according to a different and emerging conception of truth, one that demands from it high flexibility and developed mimetic capabilities.

Following Watt, Michael McKeon documents the struggle of "true histories" to distance themselves from the kinds of narrative, both religious and secular, that remain faithful to notions of a higher truth. Throughout the seventeenth and eighteenth centuries, argues McKeon in *The Origins of the English Novel: 1600–1740*, "romance" progressively emerges as a derogatory term, indicating a kind of fantastical narrative that relies on the idealist epistemology of *a priori* traditions and received authorities.[5] The "idealism" of the romance relies on the guarantees, externally given, of absolute conciliation: adventures inevitably culminate in discovery, the worth and purity of the hero is firmly established, and the belief, sustaining the reader throughout, in the ultimate meaningfulness of what comes to pass is confirmed.[6] The truth of romance is the organizing principle of what is the already redeemed best of all possible worlds. It is the kind of truth that relies on something like the presumption behind the medieval ontological proof for the existence of God: that the makeup of the actual world corresponds to our rational conception of it, that insofar as our ideas about the world are clear, the world meekly conforms to them.

Now this presumption begins to emerge as mere fantasy and wish fulfillment in the seventeenth and eighteenth century. An exemplary encounter in this respect is one, notoriously internalized in Voltaire's *Candide* (1759), between a Leibnizian theodicy and the relentlessly lapsarian depiction of the world of human suffering, stupidity, and evil. Here the logic of sufficient reason runs into the obstinacy of hard facts: deception, murder, rape, and natural catastrophe.

And not only does Voltaire make a mockery of philosophical optimism, but together with it he mocks the "optimistic" conventions of romance narrative itself. For Leibniz, human history is a romance (*roman*) "devised in the divine understanding."[7] Voltaire brings the redemptive conventions of this sort of romance idealism to their breaking point, most vividly in the obsessiveness with which the narrative resurrects characters that were previously supposed to have died a violent death.

But of course it is not *contes philosophiques* like *Candide* that come to replace definitively the idealistic optimism of romance. Voltaire's novel itself still relies too much on romance conventions even as it turns romantic assumptions inside out.[8] Rather, "romance idealism" is succeeded, in McKeon's account, by the "naïve empiricism" of "true histories," claiming to provide accurate accounts of what actually happened.[9] Winding, episodic, and "low" in subject matter, these narratives render all preexisting patterns and overarching truths problematic. It is thus—in terms of this struggle waged by new "historical" narratives against the highly conventional lies and fantasies of their suspect forebears—that we might want to understand the claim of the novel's essential truthlessness in the context of the seventeenth and eighteenth centuries. Here, the novel's freedom from the weight of truth is its freedom from the weight of the authoritative past. For "historical" is not meant here primarily as involved with times gone by, but rather the opposite: that the past of these histories is so recent that it is still very much part of the present, while the present itself acquires the features of a newfound flow.

The process whereby modernity's emerging experience of temporal acceleration comes to crystallization is a long one, no doubt. We detect its early traces already with Francis Bacon's celebrated statement in *Novum Organum* (1620): "For rightly is truth called the daughter of time, not of authority. It is no wonder therefore if those enchantments of antiquity and authority and consent have so bound up men's powers that they have been made impotent (like persons bewitched) to accompany with the nature of things."[10] To *accompany with*—that is, at least here, to be in the company or in the presence of. A century and a half later Goethe complains of the constant need to relearn what he has learned. Unlike their ancestors, he says, who could rely on the lessons they had learned as children, his contemporaries have to "relearn things every five years."[11] Thus, Bacon's *to accompany with* has become simply *to accompany*: in order to know things, one must stay abreast of them, keep up, as it were, with their movement through time.

Reinhart Koselleck comments: "The shortening of the time spans necessary for gaining new experiences that the technical-industrial world forces upon us can be described as a historical acceleration. It provides evidence of a history in which time continually seems to overtake itself, as it were, and it is thus conceived as *Neuzeit* in an emphatic sense."[12] The newness of *Neuzeit* is perpetual newness, ceaseless novelty at the very foundation of social life. Truths learned in the past turn out to have been neither eternal nor even lasting. They are constantly being surpassed by more recent truths. Past history can thus no longer be conceived as a depository of exemplary wisdom, the familiarity with which might guide us in our actions. Instead, it will be more and more readily conceived—as it is already in Bacon's statement—as a storehouse of outmoded superstitions, the consultation with which could only lead one deeper into ignorance.[13]

It is not surprising, then, that there is as much agreement about the novel's peculiar attunement to time as about its inability (or rather structural unwillingness) to contain higher truth. "The novel is in nothing so characteristic of our culture," writes Watt, "as in the way that it reflects this characteristic [temporal] orientation of modern thought."[14] For Watt, the novel's truthlessness and its ability to represent time are actually related achievements. The novel breaks with the literary tradition of using conventional forms to illustrate timeless moral truths and thus finds itself in the same situation as history, which is also compelled to renounce recourse to the eternal wisdom of the past and to step into the treacherous stream of an unanchored, accelerating present. Eternity and the past, these sites of higher truth, are renounced by the novel in its capacity as the symbolic form of modernity, that is, the most precise tool for capturing the experience of time as the compulsive experience of the new.

The Narrative Shape of Truth

It would appear simple enough to say, then, that the novel is the genre of human time and empirical truth precisely insofar as it represents and participates in the condition of being severed from a higher timeless truth of romance idealism. But this would be much too one-sided a formulation if we consider how much of the discussion around the novel in seventeenth- and eighteenth-century France and England centered on the capacity of this literary form to provide moral instruction to its readers. Thus, Pierre-Daniel Huet, in his exemplary and influential *Traité de l'origine des romans* (1670), defines the goal of sentimental prose narratives as follows: "The principal End of *Romance,* or at least what ought to be so, and is chiefly to be regarded by the Author, is the Instruction of the Reader; before whom he must present Virtue successful and Vice in Disgrace; but because the Mind of Man naturally hates to be inform'd and (by the influence of Self-Conceit) resists Instruction, 'tis to be deceived by the Blandishments of Pleasure; and the Rigor of Precept is to be subdued by the Allurements of Example."[15] The task of the novel, then, is to promote moral principles through illustration. The novel is here in the service of precisely higher, universal, and presumably timeless moral precepts; it is called upon to illustrate a moral or metaphysical truth that exists prior to and independently of the narrative. Its purpose is to seduce readers into compliance with morality, to make them love the harsh dictates of virtue and hate and fear the enticements of vice. Huet's translator comments in the preface to his 1715 English translation of the treatise:

> Where the mind can't be subdued into virtue by reason and philosophy, nothing can influence it more than to present to it the success and felicity of which crowns the pursuit of what's great and honorable. . . . And since in all the ages there were few instances fit to be proposed for exact patterns of imitation, the ingenious fabulist was forced to supply them out of his own invention. Hence it appears that the original of romance is very ancient since this way of promoting virtue has been received in the earliest ages as is evident from the first records of mankind.[16]

The *roman* is deployed where reason and philosophy fail, where haughty truths must be brought closer, rendered accessible to human beings. And as such it finds very respectable forebears among the ancients themselves, in fables, parables, figures, allegories, in Plato, in the Koran, in the Talmud, and in the teachings of Christ himself.[17] The novel's pedigree, then, is just as noble as that of the epic, or the lyric, or drama. And this nobility comes from the intimate relation the genre bears to the higher truths of religion and philosophy, to teachings that need to be simplified and made more appealing to the uninitiated public. Far from being truthless, then, far from lacking access to higher and ancient wisdom, the novel actively seeks a truth discourse of its own and finds it repeatedly, both in the seventeenth and eighteenth century, in the logic of exemplarity.[18]

Huet's basic arguments survive intact into the eighteenth century. Antoine François Prévost, for example, claims in a preface to *Manon Lescaut* (1731) that his novel is no less than "a moral treatise entertainingly put into practice" for the use of those for whom, as for most people, abstract moral precepts are too vague, too rigorous, and must therefore be elaborated and rendered more appealing through narrative example.[19] And almost one hundred years after the publication of Huet's treatise, Rousseau's second preface to *La Nouvelle Héloïse* (1761) does not appear to go beyond a more nuanced restatement of this principle: "Sublime Authors, bring your models down a bit, if you want people to try to imitate them. To whom do you vaunt purity that has not been sullied? Well! tell us about purity that can be recovered; perhaps at least someone will be able to get your meaning."[20] Instances of this defense of the novel appear no less commonly in eighteenth-century England. Perhaps one of the most telling among them is to be found in the dedication to *Tom Jones,* which states that the purpose of the book is "to recommend goodness and innocence" and adds that "an example is a kind of picture, in which virtue becomes as it were an object of sight, and strikes us with an idea of that loveliness, which Plato asserts there is in her naked charms."[21] Thus, again and again, the novel invokes the specter of a nobler veridictory ancestor, claiming for itself the high, more than merely narrative calling of rendering truth itself (biblical, metaphysical, wise) both comprehensible and attractive.[22]

We can say then that the serious novel's rejection of romance idealism in favor of the empiricist pathos of the actual is complemented, perhaps paradoxically, by a stubborn insistence on its special affinity with the higher truths of morality and religion. The unease with which these tendencies coexisted with each other is perhaps most vividly detectable along the prominent fissure within novelistic discourse between two types of narratives: the picaresque or satirical novel and the philosophical or politico-philosophical tale. In the former we find winding, episodic narratives, treating "low" heroes in "low," everyday settings; here, the emphasis on concrete situations decisively outweighs interest in society or humanity in general. By contrast, philosophical novels pay little attention to empirical detail, unfold in fantastically exotic settings, involve romancelike idealized characters and a heightened interest in elaborating general moral truths. Yuri Lotman comments on the dualism of the novelistic field as it developed in eighteenth-century Russia: "The rationalist novel had only one ideological-stylistic plane—the world of ideas, since everything real, all everyday reality was considered to be extraliterary material. The picaresque novel also unfolded on a single plane—it cast off the ideological, shutting itself into the sphere of the empirically given."[23] The temporality of the former is characterized, appropriately enough, by a kind of stillness or timelessness, while the latter tends to fall apart into episodes, loosely connected with one another in serial time.

On Russian soil this narrative dualism is well represented by two contemporary, and highly derivative, works of fiction, Mikhail Kheraskov's 1768 philosophical *Numa Pompilius or the Flourishing Rome* and the early picaresque by Mikhail Chulkov, *The Comely Cook* (1770). The former novel, set in ancient Rome, consists of discourses on the nature of proper political rule, delivered to the celebrated king and lawgiver Numa by his tutor, the nymph Egera. In order to appreciate the extent to which incidents are here secondary and subordinate to instruction, one brief example will suffice. Having listened to a vestal priestess's heartrending story of injustice and abuse to which she has been subject, Numa and the nymph attempt to lead her out of the dark cave in which she has been condemned to live. At the sight of light, the priestess collapses; Numa and the nymph return her inert body to the cave and leave it there. On the way back to the city, the nymph says: "This encounter has made me extremely pleased . . . ; it will open to us a wide field for useful discussion."[24] Here, the incident is subsumed by the truth with a casual ruthlessness that testifies to the essential insignificance of individual events and characters in themselves. But this logic finds its mirror image in *The Comely Cook*, where the narrator's regular recourse to folk sayings and proverbs as well as her occasional moralizing obviously serve as mere excuse for the breathless report of amusing episodes. Truth, wisdom, goodness are here reduced to the status of legitimizing signposts, anchoring an unruly and salacious narrative by a disreputable tramp.

Less glaringly polarized than these Russian exemplars are their French forebears and inspirations, Fénelon's *Aventures de Télémaque* (1699) and *Manon Lescault*. In the former, episodes, however fabulous, possess a certain independence, are taken more seriously in themselves, even though their ultimate goal is to teach the young prince moral and political lessons. In the latter, weightier and more nuanced (though just as much "for the occasion") moralizing frequently interrupts the account of Des Grieux's misadventures in his pursuit of happiness with the fickle Manon. Less lopsided perhaps, but still conforming to the polarity: the merely episodic, truthless time of low (and frequently immoral) everydayness on the one hand, and the high truth of fabulous antiquity/timelessness on the other.

The polarity persisted well into the eighteenth century and was still operative in what is by many accounts the most perfectly plotted novel of its time, *Tom Jones* (1749). Here again the narrator's discourse vigilantly shadows the narrated events, constantly intruding with its obsessive "to say the truth," displaying a profound lack of trust in the ability of the story to generate truth out of itself. A well-founded mistrust, it would seem, given that the story is from the beginning to the end delivered over to error: initiated in misrepresentation, sustained on mistakes and partial recognitions and, with the arrival of truth, the central truth of Tom's identity, terminated. It is as if truth were to stand outside temporal progression, waiting patiently to show itself and save the day just at the moment when error-ridden time, left to itself, seems destined to carry the hero to scandal and destruction.[25]

Thus when the worthy landlady, Mrs. Miller, exclaims that "time will show all matters in their true and natural colors," the statement does not, within the narrative logic of the novel, function as an indication of the veridictory potential of temporal unfolding itself but points only to the fact that at a certain moment in time, truth will out.[26] One symptom of this separation can be found in the fact that the novel, though its plot is motivated by an error and culminates in discovery, is almost entirely devoid of mystery. Whenever minor revelations and recognitions occur, they surprise but do not work as solutions for persisting puzzles; here, answers are received before questions are even posed. In other words, though truth does occur in time and at the end of time, time itself is not pregnant with truth. And this is the case even with regard to the greatest revelation of all, that of Tom's birth, which is simply assumed to be "low" until it turns out to be noble.[27]

When the truth does come out, time, the time of the story, cannot be sustained. For a moment Sophia seems intent on postponing her marriage to Tom by a year in order to test his prudence and fidelity. But apparently everything that's there to know about him is already known, no ordeal can uncover new characteristics or identities, and so the wedding takes place the very next day. Here, truth is static, singular, and indivisible; it cannot be distended in time.

Tzvetan Todorov's formulation in "The Secret of Narrative" comes to mind as highly apposite: "The presence of truth is possible, but it is incompatible with narrative."[28] Todorov is speaking of the tales of Henry James, whose veridictory poetics might actually be somewhat more complicated,[29] but as a description of the "eighteenth-century" either-truth-or-time dynamic organizing Fielding's great novel, this formula is perfectly on target.[30]

Compatibility of truth with narrative aside, one aspect of Fielding's veridictory poetics that comes out with particular starkness when juxtaposed with that of James pertains to the role of the objective authoritative narrator as a site of truth. Notoriously negligible in James, it is impossible to overlook in

Fielding.[31] One particularly striking example should suffice. Opening book 6 of the novel with some prefatory remarks on love, the author-narrator says, "Examine your heart, my good reader, and resolve whether you do believe these matters with me. If you do, you may now proceed to their exemplification in the following pages; if you do not, you have, I assure you, already read more than you have understood."[32] The logic here is once again one of exemplarity. The novel illustrates only what is already the case. The narrator possesses the truth, the narrative entertains us only with a compelling "view" of it. If you do not believe the truth already, ahead of time, you will learn nothing *in time*. If you believe it, you will be glad to find it pleasantly confirmed.[33]

Commenting on the "additive-episodic" temporality of the early British novel, Patricia Tobin suggests that it should be understood as a symptom of incomplete secularization: "When the authorizing center of order is acknowledged as being outside the theory (or above life), then there exists no need at the level of narrative (or of a life) for a strict coherence between the two terminals of beginning and end (birth and death) to establish the proof of that order."[34] Time, in other words, is not perceived here as possessing within itself the means for its own containment. The access of timeless truth to truthless time is not immanently achieved but granted ahead of time by divine (authorial) decree, which is itself atemporal. The unbound temporality of adventure, one might think, would be unbearable to the "eighteenth-century reader" without prior external guarantees with regard to meaning.

Whether or not this is the proper reading of the intellectual-historical situation of which these narratives were a part, the fact remains that we are confronted by a persistent split, a disjunction between authoritative, coherence-endowing truth and episodic runaway time. But if that is the case, if the dualism in fact describes the state of affairs within the seventeenth- and eighteenth-century practice of prose narrative, then we are justified in questioning the depth of the association between modernity and the rise of the novel at least in one crucial respect. After all, there is nothing particularly modern either about the conception of truth as linked to eternity or about the view of time as too fickle to be trusted with the Idea. Timeless truth and truthless time—the *locus classicus* of this opposition can be found as far back as Plato, with "secondary" *loci* reappearing again and again, in new incarnations, from St. Augustine[35] to Descartes[36] and Milton.[37]

If it is in fact possible to assert that the modern novel registers, in its very form, a change in attitude toward the truth, we would have to look for this change elsewhere than in the old disjunction between the timeless rational concept and time, between essence and existence, the ideal and the empirical. I would suggest, albeit at this point only provisionally, that where the problematics of truth are concerned, the modern novel is at its most innovative while trying precisely to get away from these oppositions. When Rousseau appeals to "sublime authors" to depict fallible creatures rather than produce allegories of pure virtue, he is pleading for a synthesis of the high and the low, the abstract and the concrete. When, in polemicizing with Richardson, Fielding proclaims his refusal to serve as time's amanuensis, preferring to be the kind of historian who hopes to "disclose the revolutions of countries" rather than fill paper "with the detail of months and years in which nothing remarkable happened," he is striving toward the same synthesis as it were from the other side.[38]

In order to teach good morals one must borrow examples from the life that readers would recognize as their own; in order for events to be made available to the reader's generalizing faculties as *exempla*, they must be lifted out of their simple givenness, carefully selected, and coherently organized. When the rational strives to subsume the empirical, when the empirical seeks for itself a general principle, then we are no longer in the realm of romance idealism. And when the romantic principle of virtue rewarded and vice punished is drawn into the realm of the everyday, it becomes vulnerable to refutation or dismissal. In short, the synthetic exigency is prominent in both of these statements: in Rousseau's denial of the educational potential of idealized representations of virtue as well as in Fielding's reference to Plato, who can "assert" the beauty of virtue but who cannot be counted on to make it "an object of sight."

The suggestion here then is that, *pace* many of its most prominent theorists, the modern novel should be understood not so much as reflecting the rift between truth and time, the essential and the actual, but rather as exploring the narrative mechanisms that might be called upon to repair the rift. Rather than deprived of a genuine truth discourse as a consequence of the flagging of "romance idealism," the novel should be regarded as developing a sui generis veridiction, one that can no longer rely on ontological optimism or epistemological trust but must develop an authority of its own, distinct from those of the epic, or tragedy, or romance, but no less authoritative for that. And as a methodological corollary of this approach, the novel would have to be conceived dynamically, as a (frequently compensatory) *response* to—rather than a mere *reflection* of—the experience of accelerated time in modernity.

Paradoxically, it is precisely when regarded as such a response that the novel turns out to be properly "reflective" of the Janus-faced nature of modern temporality itself. It is to this dual dynamic of modern time that Jürgen Habermas calls our attention, for example, when he characterizes Koselleck's vision of *Neuzeit*'s furious forward thrust as somewhat one-sided. Koselleck's conception of modernity, writes Habermas, "overlooks the fact that the notion of progress served not only to render eschatological hopes profane and open up the horizon of expectation in a utopian fashion, but also to close off the future as a source of disruption with the aid of teleological constructions of history."[39] The open future of modernity, the unchaining of time from the eternalistically conceived past of authority, is never absolute. But if through much of the eighteenth century it is primarily complemented by eternal, divinely or naturally guaranteed, and *a priori* knowable principles, then toward the end of the century, time, and historical time in particular, is seen more and more as capable of producing order from within itself.[40]

The production of order from within the historical sequence itself is exactly what is at stake in two contrasting invocations of the generic category of the *roman* (romance or novel, perhaps ambiguously) in relation to the study of history: one at the very beginning of the eighteenth century, the other at the end. We have already seen the first, from Leibniz's *Theodicy*, where human history appears as a romance penned by God. More than seventy years later, in 1784, Immanuel Kant uses the same analogy in his "Idea for a Universal History," but now with a different inflection. "It is strange and apparently silly," he says, "to wish to write a history in accordance with an Idea of how the course of the world must be if it is to lead to certain rational ends. It seems that with such an Idea only a romance [*Roman*] could be written."[41] What is crucial not to overlook here is Kant's specific use of *Idee* to imply the merely provisional, regulative status of history as a coherent whole. The romancelike coherence cannot be presupposed *a priori*, nor is it ever given in experience, but it can regulate our attempts to organize facts and events in such a way as to avoid perceiving history as no more than a "planless conglomeration of human actions." Kant's position here is therefore ambiguous. He is first of all suspicious of those who, like his former student Johann Gottfried Herder, are willing to reinvest historical progression *a priori* with the patterned quality of romance. But at the same time, he is compelled to admit that he, too, is sympathetic to the project. In a review of Herder's *Ideas for a Philosophy of History of Mankind* (1784) published in the same year as his own "Idea for a Universal History," Kant expresses this ambivalence as follows: "To be sure, this attempt [to grasp human history as a totality of interconnected elements] is bold but still natural to the scientific bent of our reason, and it should not pass uncommended. . . .

All the more is it to be wished, therefore, that our gifted author in continuing his work, where there is solid ground before him, should constrain his lively genius."[42]

A certain conception of time underlies the attempt to project order decisively onto historical succession. Hayden White comments: "The spectacle of coming into being and passing away which the historical record displays to consciousness was no occasion for despair to Herder. Time did not threaten him, because he did not take time seriously. Things pass away when *their* time has come, not when Time requires it of them."[43] Perhaps it is overstating things somewhat to say that Herder does not take time seriously. Time is after all the essential medium of historical existence; it is just that in the organic metaphor, he finds the means for taming time, for making it yield significance from within. Time is no longer indifferent to being and hostile to form; rather it is the very condition of the form's ability to accommodate content. Time, in other words, is the medium of formation rather than decomposition.

Thus, the two invocations of romance in relation to history, Leibniz's and Kant's, mark a veritably epochal distance.[44] History as God's romance in Leibniz is, at least in terms of the categories of truth and time, a premodern image, figuring the weighty omnipresence of providential design in human life and in the life of humanity, so that the progress of time is always already bound by the romancelike formula of fall and redemption, of evil bringing forth the good.[45] Time in this conception is altogether eliminated, as is its Enlightenment companion, causality: "For, not to mention the fact that one cannot explain how something can pass from one thing into the substance of another, we have already shown that from the notion of each and every thing follows all of its future states. What we call causes are only concurrent requisites, in metaphysical rigor."[46] In fact, everything is there to begin with—this is what romance means for Leibniz. When, at the end of the century, history and romance come together once again, it is, as it were, from the other side. Now the dominant category is history, and the patterns of romance must be cautiously and with qualifications derived or, more often, imaginatively intuited from historical data. The eternal patterns of higher truth do not preexist and do not transcend temporal unfolding; rather it is this unfolding itself that generates and is shaped by patterns of its own. In the words of Michel Foucault, order mutates into history,[47] and rather than being satisfied with the Enlightenment restatement of the ancient disjunction between truth and time we are confronted with the truly new task of thinking truth and time together.

In what now follows I propose to take a brief look at a number of texts rich in implications for this very task. Both philosophical and novelistic, or novel-theoretical, they will, at least in my presentation here, come together to articulate a formal shift in the veridictory discourse of modernity, a shift that brings philosophical and narrative endeavors perhaps closer together than ever before. Clustering around what I will refer to as the Kantian crisis of truth (not because he brings it about but because he gives it the most vivid and nuanced expression), these texts register its aftershocks in a new kind of narrative theory and practice. They thus help us map out the conceptual field for the rest of our inquiry into the fortunes of veridiction in the nineteenth-century realist novel and beyond. They should also confirm us in the conviction that it is ultimately misleading to think of the novel as simply truthless, that we should think of it instead as prompting us, and giving us the means, to think of truth differently, as immanent in a temporal shape rather than transcendent in a principle, a fact, or a higher order.

The Kantian Synthesis

Foucault suggests in *The Order of Things* that nineteenth-century philosophy "will be Metaphysics . . . only in so far as it is Memory, and it will necessarily lead thought back to the question of knowing what it means for thought to have a history."[48] The statement immediately invokes G. W. F. Hegel, with his historical metaphysics and metaphysical conception of history, pushed onward by "the cunning of reason." But it is actually Kant with whom we must begin if we are to appreciate the force of the modern breakthrough in the relation between truth and time. It is first of all here that we must look for the way in which the new temporality finds a place within the old discourse about the possibility of attaining the truth. We could even say that one of Kant's "world-historical" accomplishments in his *Critique of Pure Reason* (1781) is to give voice to the modern reversal of the Platonic formula for truth. If, for Plato, truth relates discourse to being in *timelessness*,[49] for Kant it relates discourse (the understanding) to being (sensibility) in *time*.

The central question of the *First Critique*, the question how synthetic *a priori* knowledge is possible, can be reformulated as follows: given that there is no divinely guaranteed continuity between reason and experience (such that, as for example in Descartes, our ideas about the world move from being vague and confused in sensation to being clear and distinct in philosophy and mathematics); given, in other words, that we are not justified in positing an *a priori* fit between reason and nature, how can the former apply to the latter? Or, approaching from the opposite direction, as it were, we might put it as follows: given that, as Hume shows with abundant clarity, no general truths can be validly inferred from particular experiences, no matter how numerous and consistent, are we not condemned to radical skepticism?

And yet our experience of the world is coherent, so coherent in fact as to enable natural philosophers like Newton to formulate general laws that govern the behavior of objects as different as planets and billiard balls. What is it that makes this coherent experience possible? This is the question to which *The Critique of Pure Reason* is dedicated. This is also the question that constitutes the basis for Kant's Copernican revolution in philosophy, his inquiry into the transcendental structures of subjectivity that enable knowledge of the world: "All our knowledge falls within the bounds of possible experience, and just in this universal relation to possible experience consists that transcendental truth which precedes all empirical truth and makes it possible."[50]

But for Kant "possible experience" is not limited to *a priori* laws of logic, delimiting the manner in which objects must appear to us. If that were the case, Kant would simply be another rationalist and his conception of truth would remain atemporal. Instead, the concepts as *a priori* laws of the understanding must be complemented by something given in sensibility. It is the specific nature of the relation between the two that constitutes what he calls "transcendental truth" or "possible experience."

In the chapter "The Schematism of the Pure Concepts of Understanding," by elaborating what that relation consists in, Kant finally begins to answer the central question of the *Critique*.[51] The problem that Kant is here confronting pertains to the possibility of a relation between something as abstract as pure concepts of the understanding and something as particular and concrete as sensible intuitions. How can the categories of causality, substance, or magnitude apply to what we intuit through the senses? How, once again, can the intelligible apply to the sensible? Kant proceeds to argue that there must be some "third thing, which is homogeneous on the one hand with the category, and on the other hand with appearance, and which thus makes the application of the former to the latter possible."[52] This third thing, in other words, must be both intelligible and sensible. Now Kant has established, by the beginning of the discussion of schematism, that all sensible experience, whether of external reality or internal states, takes place in time. If it were possible therefore to temporalize the categories, to project them onto the flow of temporal perception, then time would emerge as the substratum of that "third thing," the medium in which the sensible and the intelligible meet and truth happens. Only by way of this third thing as a "transcendental determination of time" does sensible experience become available to the understanding, and can it be studied as a coherent whole, as nature.[53]

It is easy to recognize, behind this philosophical problematic, a generalized version of the problem we encountered in our brief examination of the veridictory dynamic of the seventeenth- and eighteenth-century novel: namely, how, given the decline of "romance idealism" and the unfeasibility of the ontological proof, can we think higher, abstract, timeless principles together with the low, empirical, and successively given material? Kant's answer, then, registers a late development in modernity's conception of time in its relation to truth.

The radical character of this development, the fundamental originality of this notion of truth in the Western philosophical discourse, is eloquently captured by Alexandre Kojève:

> Therefore for us, knowledge—that is the identification of the diverse—can be accomplished only in Time, because the very identification of the diverse is Time. It was always known that the human Concept appears at some moment of Time; and it was known that Man needs time in order to think. But Kant was the first to see that this is not accidental but essential to Man. Hence the World in which Man thinks is necessarily a temporal World. And if human thought is related to what is in time, the Kantian analysis shows that Time is what makes the actual exercise of thought possible. In other words, we can use our eternal Concepts only provided that we relate them to Time as such—that is, provided we "schematize" them.[54]

Thus, the dichotomy between eternal intelligibility and temporal sensibility is, in Kant, both systematically subverted and resolved through the schematization of time, through the conceptual shaping of time and, reciprocally, the distention of concepts in the temporal medium. As a result, time becomes not only an ineluctable element in the relation of truth but an enabling, constitutive element, without which that relation itself would be unthinkable: "All increase in empirical knowledge, and every advance of perception, no matter what the objects may be, whether appearances or pure intuitions, is nothing but an extension of the determination of inner sense, that is, an advance in time. This advance in time determines everything and is not in itself determined through anything further."⁵⁵ Thus, in Kant the historical development implicating time in truth comes to rigorous philosophical consciousness.

Wilhelm Meisters Lehrjahre and Hegelian Narratology

Now once again, for Kant, transcendental idealism presupposes sensible experience and asks only what makes it possible, what constitutes the world in the way in which it gives itself to us. Kant conceives of experience as a relation between self and world, where neither of the two members of the relation remains unchanged in the process of the relation. "Thoughts without content are empty," Kant famously says, "[sensible] intuitions without concepts are blind."⁵⁶ The world is not given to us independently of that relation, and therefore there is always the possibility of it actually being "in-itself" different from the way it is for us. For us, however, the relation is always in time.

In his *Phenomenology of Spirit* (1807), Hegel objects to the "critical" (Kantian) turn in philosophy, focusing precisely on the scandal of this "in-itself," on what he takes to be the preservation of the false dualism of reason and being, of knowledge and its object. After all, if Kant does solve the problem of the relation between universal concepts and particular sensations by means of the schematization of time, it is only a partial solution, for it leaves behind an unknowable surplus, the *noumenon* or the "thing-in-itself." And yet, in order to overcome this "critical" rift between consciousness and the world, Hegel resorts precisely to the Kantian discovery of the schematism. For him, too, temporal succession mediates between subject and object; only now it does so in a more thoroughgoing way. Here, once again, is Kojève:

> Generally speaking, in his theory of the Concept, Hegel merely makes more precise (and consequently transforms) the Kantian theory of the Schematismus. . . . In Hegel as in Kant, therefore, Time is what allows for the application of the Concept to Being. But in Hegel, this Time that mediates conceptual thought is "materialized": it is a movement (Bewegung), and a dialectical "movement"—that is, precisely, it is active— hence it negates, hence it transforms (the given), hence it creates (new things). . . . Therefore: in Kant time is "schema" and passive "intuition"; in Hegel it is "movement" and conscious, voluntary "action." Consequently the Concept or the a priori in Kant is a "notion" which allows Man to conform to given Being, whereas in Hegel the a priori Concept

is a "project" which allows Man to transform given Being and make it conform.[57]

The protoexistentialist overtones of Kojève's interpretation are perhaps somewhat too strong to give an accurate picture of truth as understood in Hegel's *Phenomenology*, but it rightly emphasizes the operation by which Kant's temporal conception of truth is turned inside out in Hegel. If for Kant time is, loosely speaking, "inside" consciousness, for Hegel consciousness is "inside" time. In the Kantian model, truth happens when experience of the world becomes en-formed by temporalized categories; in Hegel, it happens when conscious subjects enter into knowing and acting contact with the world.[58] As for the "thing-in-itself," the static limit of knowledge in Kant, it, too, is projected onto the temporal plane in *Phenomenology*. At each stage on consciousness's way to absolute knowing, it encounters limits, stares dumbly at what, for the moment at least, is utterly opaque to it, its "thing-in-itself." But inevitably the limit is overcome, the relationship between consciousness and the world is reconfigured, and a new limit is posited.

Let us now explore more attentively the structure of temporalized truth in Hegel's *Phenomenology*. To do this it would suffice to examine the difficult paragraphs 81 to 89 of the introduction, where Hegel is explicitly concerned with outlining the dialectical method. Essentially, dialectical truth consists of three moments, the "for-another" or "for-consciousness," the "in-itself," and the "for-us." The first two moments refer to the relationship between consciousness and its object: "Consciousness simultaneously *distinguishes* itself from something, and at the same time *relates* itself to it."[59] By way of this double movement of relating and distinguishing, the object of knowledge is split into two. It is, first of all, the object of knowledge, the object as it exists for consciousness; but it is also what Hegel calls "the standard" of that knowledge, i.e., the object as it exists "in-itself." Thus, "consciousness provides its own criterion from within itself, so that the investigation becomes a comparison of consciousness with itself."[60]

What Hegel calls "experience" (*Erfahrung*) in *Phenomenology* is the repeated discovery by consciousness of the inadequacy of its knowledge, that is, the misfit between the "for-consciousness" and the "in-itself." As Jean Hyppolite explains: "This, precisely, is the result of experience: the *negation* of the preceding object and the *appearance* of a new object, which in turn engenders a new knowledge."[61] The world turns out to have been different from what consciousness imagined it to be. Thus, both the world and its consciousness are posited anew. Consciousness encounters new truths, then rejects them and is itself transformed, educated by this experience.

So far, then, "truth" possesses two meanings: it is the static truth of the "in-itself," the world posited by consciousness as independent of it; and it is the temporal truth of overcoming, where this first truth is revealed to be untrue and the "real" truth emerges. Later in the treatise, it will be said for example that perception (as shape of consciousness) is the truth of sense certainty, understanding the truth of perception, and so on, where each "true" shape of consciousness is subsequent to the untrue (and formerly, the true) one, according to a logic that posits the present as the truth of the past. Thus, Hegel writes in the preface to *Phenomenology*: "The bud disappears in the bursting forth of the blossom, and one might say that the former is refuted by the latter; similarly, when the fruit appears, the blossom is shown up in its turn as a false manifestation of the plant, and the fruit emerges as the truth of it instead."[62]

But there is here a third meaning, or rather "moment," of truth as well. Endowed with unfailing "negative" power, always driven forward toward new subject-object configurations, consciousness does not realize that its trajectory is predetermined: "Facing its future and not its past, it is unable to understand how its past experience was a genesis of what for it is a new object."[63] The emergence of new truths appears to it to be contingent, always a surprise, but *for us*, who are following its trajectory from the perspective of the completed journey, the progress of consciousness is absolutely necessary: "The origination of the new object, that presents itself to consciousness without its [the latter's] understanding how this happens . . . proceeds for us, as it were, behind the back of consciousness."[64]

This last moment of truth, then, is what Hegel refers to when he says in the preface that "the True is the whole."[65] It is the whole of the coherent, completed system, projected back retrospectively from the end of absolute knowledge onto the path of phenomenal consciousness, the path of doubt and despair in which one truth replaces another in seemingly unending contingency.[66] Truth as agreement between consciousness and the world is projected upon the temporal plane, undermined, replaced by other truths and throughout shadowed by the third, the truth of the whole. Hegel expresses this dynamic in a striking extended metaphor: "The True is thus a Bacchanalian revel in which no member is not drunk; yet because each member collapses as soon as he drops out, the revel is just as much transparent and simple repose."[67]

Truth as pure negating action in time is thus complemented by the third moment of the dialectic, the "for-us" that represents the perspective of the completed whole. Left to itself, temporal negation alone would better serve as the principle of a kind of Enlightenment, picaresque temporality, which is surpassed (though preserved) in the move that invests temporal progression with the ordering power of truth. And Hegel's famous pronouncement that "time is . . . the existent Notion [*Begriff*] itself" must be understood as follows: that time, as shaped by truth, flows forward and backward, negates and recuperates, cuts and heals.[68]

It is clear then that Hegel doesn't just radicalize the Kantian understanding of the relation between truth and time. He works out, in the process, a kind of narratology, inspiring many of his interpreters to compare his first treatise to a classical nineteenth-century novelistic form, the *Bildungsroman*. Here, for example, is Jean Hyppolite: "Hegel's *Phenomenology* . . . is the novel of philosophic formation [insofar as] it follows the development of consciousness, which, renouncing its first beliefs, reaches through its experiences the properly philosophic point of view, that of absolute knowledge."[69] In fact, in suggesting a structural affinity between *Phenomenology* and the *Bildungsroman,* Hyppolite and many others (Josiah Royce, Hans-Georg Gadamer, M. H. Abrams) seem to have a very specific novel in mind: Goethe's supremely influential *Wilhelm Meisters Lehrjahre* (*Wilhelm Meister's Apprenticeship,* 1795–1796).

Lehrjahre was written in two stages. First came the six books of *Wilhelm Meisters theatralische Sendung* (*Wilhelm Meister's Theatrical Mission*). These were left unfinished in 1785. Then, in 1794, Goethe went back to the novel, finally completing it in 1796. Between the two novels lie Goethe's travels in Italy and the French Revolution, and, as will become clear from what follows, we can imagine the boundary between the two drafts of the novel as a segment of a larger demarcation line that separates the veridictory dynamics of the "eighteenth-century novel" from its "nineteenth-century" avatar.

Theatrical Mission is essentially an unfinished, straightforward, and forward-looking account of the progress of the eponymous hero from childhood to adolescence to young manhood, centering on his wanderings with a traveling theatre and terminating at the point at which he is about to become the lead actor of a professional theatre group. The novel has the loose structure of a picaresque: it is episodic, filled with accidents, coincidental appearances, mysterious encounters, and sudden reversals of fortune. It presents a "realistic" picture of more or less contemporary life, but, aside from Wilhelm's character and a persistent concern with the theatre, it is largely devoid of unifying mechanisms. In Hegelian terms, then, it could be seen as a narrative of the encounter between the "in-itself" and the "for-consciousness" without the meaning-making, structuring effects of the "for-us." Instead, the novel's episodic structure is complemented by a highly intrusive narrator: his comments, his digressions, his repeated "I cannot fail to observe."

This narrative dualism of serial progression and authorial intrusion (often to introduce new chapters) should remind us of *Tom Jones,* where, except for the frantic ending, the order-making function of the "for-us" is fulfilled only by the narrator, who on occasion reminds the reader of the importance of the whole plot and the impossibility of judging any part of it before the final catastrophe is reached: "First then we must warn thee [reader] not too hastily to condemn any of the incidents in this our history, as impertinent and foreign to our main design, because thou dost not immediately conceive in what manner such incident may conduce to that design."[70] The very existence of the whole has to be posited, guaranteed as if "from above." Without such guarantees the work threatens to fall apart into loosely connected episodes, each of which might be excised at will.

To be sure, this use of the Hegelian veridictory triad is, in this instance, somewhat anachronistic. It presupposes the kind of temporal layout of truth that neither of the novels possesses. After all, in order for the hero-consciousness to *encounter* the "in-itself," he/it must be confronted by resistance, face disappointments, be proven wrong, fail to fulfill a promise, give up his most precious belief. More important still, the novel's ending should shed a retrospective truth-bestowing light on the hero's progress, since the unifying function of the "for-us" is temporal in character, revealing the necessity behind what appear to be contingent developments rather than shadowing events with the transcendent voice of the narrator's authority. Neither *Tom Jones* nor *Theatrical Mission* presents us with a narrative of this sort: in both, resistance has the light quality of instructive misadventure or minor character flaw, the ending is relatively unambitious, and the reins of veridiction are in the hands of the authoritative narrator alone.

But when, after a break of about ten years, Goethe rewrites the novel, the Hegelian terms suddenly become apposite. Particularly striking in this respect is the introduction into the novel of the quasi-Masonic Society of the Tower with its pedagogical mission, a device that allows for an immanently signifying elaboration of the plot. The original episodic narrative of the first draft of the novel is now interspersed with hints and inklings of a higher-order plot, a net woven behind Wilhelm's back, a scheme, sly but not unfriendly. The first such hint appears during an early conversation with "the stranger" (an emissary of the Tower, as we later find out). It is here that Wilhelm realizes, though only for a moment, that something is amiss. The stranger brings up an example of a young man destined to become a good actor but corrupted by a childhood love of the puppet theatre. It is of course Wilhelm himself whose interest in the theatre starts with a few puppets. He is alarmed; he asks the stranger why he had mentioned it. But the stranger redirects the conversation.[71]

The mode in which the Society of the Tower reveals its presence throughout the novel is that of enigma. The appearance and disappearance of its emissaries is enigmatic, their speeches wise, their tricks both playful and portentous. Wilhelm's travels are filled with mysteries and frustrations; the time of his existence is the picaresque time of adventure, the fickle time best instantiated in the behavior of the whimsical Philine, the most vivid of the traveling actors: "When Philine agrees to something, or gives someone a promise, she does so on the unspoken condition that it will suit her when the time comes. She likes to make gifts, but one must always be prepared to give them back."[72] It is this unpredictable "Philinian," modern temporality that Wilhelm occupies in the first five books of the novel. But throughout questions are raised: Where is his grandfather's art collection located? Who played the ghost during the performance of Hamlet? Who was the stranger? Who was the woman with whom he spent the night after the performance? Who is the mysterious Amazon? Who is Mignon? Who is the Harpist? And more pertinent still: What is Wilhelm's true purpose in life? Is it business? Is it the theatre? Is it something else?

It turns out to be something else. And it is here that we finally have the true Hegelian encounter between the "for-consciousness" and the "in-itself." Traveling with the theatre all along, Wilhelm believes himself to be on the path of becoming a great actor and playwright. But actually, he is becoming infinitely more: a harmoniously developed person. All along, unbeknownst to the hero, a plot is being woven by the Society of the Tower, by the function of the "for-us," the "cunning of Reason."

The image of Wilhelm confronted, in the Tower, with the manuscript of his own life resonates with the dualistic structure of the novel itself. It is as if the first five books are all living, while the last two are all reading; first, time pregnant with truth, then truth delivered by time.[73] But this sort of truth is here not merely a matter of knowledge; it is not just about receiving answers to lingering questions. It is also a matter of happiness. To have the truth and to be happy is one and the same condition. This is at bottom a very Hegelian logic, according to which it would be wrong to separate, the way Kant does, knowledge from existence. Here, all increase in knowledge implies the perfection of existence and vice versa. The "for-us," the function of conciliating retrospection, is, for Hegel, also the condition of ontological and ethical perfection.

The conjunction of truth and happiness is a feature common to *Wilhelm Meisters Lehrjahre* and *Tom Jones,* linking them under the generic umbrella of comedy. The overall design, too, appears to bring them close: first a chain of episodes, then, at the end, their linkages and overarching meaning. But if in Fielding's novel this overarching meaning is guaranteed only from above, by the paternal narrator, *Lehrjahre* insinuates it throughout. It is as if Wilhelm's travels constantly raise questions from within, while the narrator, in contrast to his predecessor from the first draft, usually resists the temptation to comment. The time of Goethe's novel, then, is the kind of time that lets truth ripen, while the time of *Tom Jones* is one to which truth is external. And so if Tom turns out to have been a gentleman all along, Wilhelm *becomes* one only at the end, matures into one, and is only then allowed to marry into the nobility. If Tom's identity is stable, outside time and, insofar as it is *in* time, concealed, Wilhelm is not at first who he is in the end; his identity is launched onto a temporal trajectory: he must become who he is. Tom is angelically beautiful throughout, but Wilhelm grows into his beauty, and only at the end of his journey are we granted the perspective of his childhood friend Werner: "I've never seen anything like this . . . and yet I know I am not deceiving myself. Your eyes are more deep-set, your forehead is broader, your nose is more delicate and your mouth is much more pleasant. Look at how you stand! How well everything fits together!"[74] Tom's movement through the narrative is practically devoid of attempts on his part to foresee the future or, in any significant way, make sense of the past; his mind is firmly fixed on Sophia, a motionless ideal, despite the peripeteia of her own life. Tom's wisdom, or rather the Wisdom into which he is allegorically initiated by marrying his beloved, is timeless. But Wilhelm's is bound to time: he recalls, predicts, and makes promises obsessively, and is again and again, like Hegel's hero-consciousness, disappointed in his predictions.

In this connection it is helpful to invoke the function of tutors in the lives of these two protagonists. The ludicrous Square and Thwackum, philosophy and dogmatic religion, can teach Tom nothing. They can hypocritically proclaim universal principles and they can punish, but they can neither improve nor corrupt his essentially noble nature. Tom is throughout, even when this is not recognized, what he is. Wilhelm's "tutors," Jarno and the Abbé, on the other hand, represent two genuine schools of thought about upbringing and education. Jarno believes in interfering with the student's actions in order to guide him along the proper path, to prevent him from making mistakes. The Abbé lets students make mistakes and correct them on their own. According to him, it is only through erring and then freely recognizing one's errors that one can grow.[75] The difference at stake here is central to the veridictory structure of the novel: does truth emerge progressively out of time or is it given *a priori* ahead of time as a set of principles to follow? *Lehrjahre* seems to take the side of the Abbé. In *Tom Jones*, the question is not even raised.[76]

Of course, if there is any direct influence between Goethe's novel, finished in 1796, and Hegel's treatise from 1807, it proceeds from the former to the latter. But influence is not what we are after. Rather, it is the emergence, at a certain point in the history of philosophy and history of the novel, of a logic whereby time and truth can no longer be kept apart. In philosophical discourse, the Kantian solution to the problem of heterogeneity between the understanding and sensibility becomes, in Hegel, the solution to the problem of heterogeneity between subject and object, self, and world. As in Kant, time is here the ally and not the enemy of truth, but in the new Hegelian inflection, this alliance makes full-fledged demands for a new, historical philosophy and a new, narrative discourse of truth.

The structural analogies between *Phenomenology* and *Lehrjahre* testify to the preoccupation with this new alliance, but approximately at the same time, and in response to a number of similar issues, an altogether different narratology is being developed and a rather different sort of novel is being written. Our analysis would remain incomplete without a consideration of this alternative reaction to the crisis of truth implicit in its Kantian elaboration.

Romantic Veridiction

The early Romantic theory of the novel was developed sometime between the publication of *Lehrjahre* and the composition of *Phenomenology*. In fact, just like *Phenomenology*, it can be seen as an attempt to propose a narrative resolution to the Kantian crisis, and for a long time it was thought that Goethe's novel provided the Romantic theorists with the paradigm of what such a narrative should be.[77] There are very good reasons to think, however, that this is not the case. Though in a famous essay on *Lehrjahre*, written in 1798, Friedrich Schlegel praises it for its many fine qualities, and though he does list Goethe's masterpiece, together with Fichte's *Wissenschaftslehre* (*Science of Knowledge*, 1795) and the French Revolution, as one of the greatest tendencies of the age,[78] nowhere does he suggest that Goethe has written the paradigmatic *Romantic* novel. In fact, he states quite explicitly that *Lehrjahre,* if it were to aspire to the status of a perfect novel, would have to be far more "romantic" than it actually is.[79]

The stakes of rejecting Goethe as the novelistic paradigm are higher than might seem at first glance. And they are related to the way in which the novel, within the (antisystematic) system of Jena Romanticism, functions as a sort of solution to the anxieties of Kantian dualism. In order to appreciate the importance of the genre for the Romantics, however, we must make a brief detour through their philosophical hero and Kant's self-proclaimed follower, Johann Gottlieb Fichte.

Kant's schematism is, once again, a solution to a problem: on the one hand we have the understanding, "spontaneity," the mind's active imposition of categories on reality; on the other hand there is sensibility, "receptivity," the passive attunement of the senses to the world. How can the two be reconciled? The meeting of the understanding and sensibility in the medium of schematized time is accomplished by the faculty Kant calls the imagination (*Einbildungskraft*).[80] Fichte, in his *Wissenschaftslehre* (Leipzig, 1794–1795; Tübingen, 1802; Jena and Leipzig, 1802), where he hopes to bring Kantian philosophy to fruition, attributes to the imagination a similarly synthesizing function. Without attempting a full exposition of Fichte's extremely abstruse system, let us focus briefly on those aspects of it that enable a conceptual transition from the Kantian problematic to that of the Jena Romantic poetics.

Fichte's foundational claim, repeated throughout the treatise, is that "the self cannot posit itself otherwise than as determined by the not-self (no object, no subject)." The reverse, however, is also true: "At the same time [the self] posits itself also as determinant; for the limiting factor in the not-self is its own product (no subject, no object)."[81] The subject and the object are unthinkable without each other. Positing one necessarily brings to mind the other. And yet they are distinct. This is the paradox that, in Fichte, constitutes the counterpart to Kant's dualism: how can we think of subject and object, activity and passivity, spontaneity and receptivity together? The name for Fichte's "schematism," effected, as in Kant, by the faculty of the imagination, is wavering or hovering (*Schweben*).

Fichte argues that subject and object, since they are posited only through opposition to each other, are nothing before they are synthesized: "As one makes its appearance, the other is destroyed; but since this one can only appear under the predicate of counterpart of the other, so that along with its concept the concept of the other simultaneously enters and destroys it, even the first cannot make its appearance."[82] In synthesis, on the other hand, subject and object are thought of as one. At the same time, they are still opposed to each other and therefore *cannot* be thought of as one, "and hence there arises a conflict between the incapacity and the demand. The mind lingers in this conflict and wavers between the two.... And in this condition, but only therein, it lays hold on both at once."[83]

This wavering between synthesis and opposition, therefore, paradoxically stands at the very origin of the subject-object distinction and, according to Fichte, "gives us truth, and the only possible truth."[84] Once again therefore, truth is a question of relating subject to object. But here, unlike in Kant, the relation does not depend on the mediating function of time. Rather, it is instantaneous. The two must be *simultaneously* conceived of as identical and different. Without this mechanism, reality as we know it, and time itself, would not exist.

Schlegel's famous *Athenaeum Fragment* 53 reads: "It is equally fatal for the mind [*für den Geist*] to have a system and to have none. It will simply have to decide to combine the two."[85] If we read this statement as a witty paraphrase of the cumbersome paradox with which the *Wissenschaftslehre* confronts us, it will quickly become evident that, in his attempt to present to us the activity of truth as a wavering between synthesis and opposition, Fichte is already operating with the elements of Hegel's later dialectic. What Hegel will soon call, with a similar penchant for paradox, "the identity of identity and nonidentity" is the process whereby absolute identity (the backward-looking perspective of the "for-us") shadows the progression of consciousness (the "for-consciousness") through the world (the "in-itself"), which, as long as there is still progression, persist in nonidentity. Here, time is presupposed. For Fichte, on the other hand, the imagination's wavering "gives us truth" by mediating system (identity of subject and object) and lack of system (nonidentity of subject and object) in *timeless simultaneity.*[86]

In his "Deduction of Presentation," a crucial section of the *Wissenschaftslehre,* Fichte speaks of the synthesis in the imagination of subject and object in terms of the opposition between progression and reflection. He proposes that we conceive of the self as in constant "endlessly outreaching activity ... in which nothing can be distinguished, precisely because it reaches into infinity."[87] Now this outreaching activity, starting, let's say, from point A (the locus of the self), is checked at some point C. "Under the conditions postulated," Fichte writes, "the direction of the self's activity from A to C is reflected from

C to A." In other words, the infinite striving of the self to assert itself without limit is counteracted by the necessary check of reflection. Fichte continues: "And thus we obtain between A and C a twofold direction of the self's activity, at variance with itself, wherein the direction from C to A may be regarded as a passivity, and that from A to C as an activity; both being one and the same state of the self."[88]

Reality, as constituted by a more or less stable tension between subject and object, is "produced" when progression is complemented by reflection, when the two (timeless) activities mutually limit each other. The trajectory of *reflection* corresponds in the above analysis to the demand for synthesis of subject and object, of the ideal and the real, i.e., to the drive for system. *Progression*, on the other hand, presupposes the preservation of the subject-object opposition and thus represents the antisystemic element of the dynamic. But it is only abstractly that we can talk about the two in separation. In actuality, they act *simultaneously,* constituting the very "world" in which we live.

Thus, to have a system and to have none at the same time implies, in dynamic terms, to reach out and to reflect back—all at once. And as it turns out, this is exactly how Schlegel conceives of the task of Romantic poetry in a key *Athenaeum Fragment* worth citing at length:

> Romantic poetry is a progressive universal poetry. . . . It tries to and should mix and fuse poetry and prose, inspiration and criticism, the poetry of art and the poetry of nature; and make poetry lively and sociable, and life and society poetical. . . . [S]o many artists who started out to write only a novel ended up by providing us with a portrait of themselves. It alone can become, like the epic, a mirror of the whole circumambient world, an image of the age. And it can also—more than any other form—hover at the midpoint between the portrayed and the portrayer. . . . Romantic poetry is in the arts what wit is in philosophy, and what society and sociability, friendship and love are in life. . . . The romantic kind of poetry is still in the state of becoming; that, in fact, is its real essence: that it should forever be becoming and never be perfected. . . . It alone is infinite, just as it alone is free; and it recognizes as its first commandment that the will of the poet can tolerate no law above itself.[89]

At the beginning of the fragment, the synthetic ambitions of Romantic poetry emerge with characteristic boldness. Essentially, it is the sought-for system, the synthesis of the subjective (identified in Schlegel with prose, criticism, poetry of art) and the objective (poetry, inspiration, poetry of nature). It is what allows for a lively and sociable poetry as well as a poetic society and life. It is what produces both the novel and the portrait of its author; it is both the age and the mirror image of the age. This, in Fichtean terms, is the demand of *reflection*: to take everything encountered in the world back into the self and, reciprocally, to imbue the real with the form of subjectivity. But the second half of the fragment asserts that its movement is infinite, that it is free, that this drive is located in the will of the subject as poet. Thus, the essence of Romantic poetry is not just *reflection* but also endless *progression*. Not just a circle, but also a straight line going off into infinity. And it is precisely between these two assertions that the mediating element occurs as Fichte's *Schweben,* as hovering "at the midpoint" between reflection and progression, and thus "giving us truth."[90]

Romantic poetry, then, appears to possess the shape of Fichtean truth. But the question remains: what is, for Schlegel and the Jena circle, Romantic poetry proper? By way of what is nearly a tautology in the original German (which turns into a somewhat baffling aphorism in the English translation), the Romantic proper is the *novelistic*. Friedrich Schlegel embraces the wordplay in the "Letter about the Novel" with the notorious: "Ein Roman ist ein romantisches Buch."[91] We are thus back to the novel, which is once again conceived as occupying the space of philosophical truth, of Kantian truth more specifically, and yet the manner in which it does this diverges quite radically from anything we have seen in Hegel or in Goethe. Here, the novel's relation to Kant is mediated via Fichte's militantly atemporal recasting of the activity of the imagination.

Toward the end of "Letter," in a characteristically reflexive gesture, Schlegel suggests that only a novel can serve as an adequate theory of the novel.[92] It is, at least in part, as such a theory that Schlegel's own *Lucinde* (1799) was surely intended. The novel consists of letters, journal entries, dramatic dialogues, an idyll, a character sketch, and a brief narrative, and for the most part it stages a state of inaction, a dreamlike condition of idleness in which perfect simultaneity reigns. At the very opening of the novel the hero has already lost his sense of time, and throughout the novel, except in the narrative passage dedicated to his development, he never regains it. Devoid of narrative link, the segments of the novel fall apart into fragments related to one another as it were in space, without forming a determinate sequence. The only narrative element of the novel is a little narrative of education, entitled "Apprenticeship for Manhood"

(*Lehrjahre der Männlichkeit*) and surely invoking Goethe's exemplary *Lehrjahre*. All the other fragments framing the story represent the hero's reflections and dialogues with his beloved after the completion of his apprenticeship. In fact, it seems that the journey itself has the sole task here of adumbrating the blissfulness of repose. *Lucinde* contains a little *Bildungsroman* in order to bring out all the more clearly the fact that it itself is not one.[93]

Northrop Frye notes in passing that Romanticism can be understood as a "sentimental form of romance."[94] Sentimental, in the vaguely Schillerian sense of subjective, nostalgic, ironic. The idealism of a modern romance like *Lucinde* or Novalis's *Heinrich von Ofterdingen* is no longer naïve; it knows itself as insufficient; it lacks the confidence, the ontological optimism of "objective" romance; it has to re-create such confidence on the shaky grounds of a single, self-reflective, "Fichtean" subject. Hence, the penchant of this sort of narrative for playful irony, a tendency to gesture back again and again to the place of the author-hero, to the act of creation itself. In a sense, the Romantic novel marks with its very structure the impossibility of a modern romance founded on anything more solid than a single self-creating and world-creating consciousness. But at the same time, and as we shall see again and again in the chapters that follow, it marks the persistence of the romantic temptation.

In his lectures on aesthetics, delivered at the University of Berlin during the 1820s, Hegel objects to Romantic poetics precisely on the grounds of its ironic formalism. Romantic theory, he argues, glorifies "absolutely empty forms, which originate from the absoluteness of the abstract ego."[95] For him, the Romantic standpoint remains too formal and too abstract, too subjective in its systematic avoidance of all determinations, an over-quick and empty "for-us," bypassing the difficulties the "for-consciousness" (the hero) encounters in its drive toward final reconciliation with the "in-itself" (the objective world). Later on in the lectures, Hegel will invoke precisely Goethe's *Lehrjahre* in an attempt to characterize the kind of work that does take seriously the objective conditions of the world: "But in the modern world, these fights are nothing more than 'apprenticeship,' the education of the individual into the realities of the present, and thereby they acquire their true significance. For the end of such apprenticeship consists in this, that the subject sows his wild oats, builds himself with his wishes and opinions into harmony with subsisting relationships and their rationality, enters the concatenation of the world, and acquires for himself an appropriate attitude to it."[96] And if *Lehrjahre* and *Phenomenology* are superior, in Hegel's own eyes, to a work like Schlegel's *Lucinde*, it is because they have enough patience to follow the spirit down a long and tortuous journey. They are not afraid to let the concept exist empirically, or put another way, they are not afraid of time.

We have here, then, something like a map of veridictory narrative shapes, crystallizing around the historical and philosophic development embodied in the Kantian alignment of truth with time. On this map, Goethe's early and abandoned *Theatrical Mission* marks the point "farthest" from Schlegel's unfinished *Lucinde*. One is about a traveler whose progress, like that of Tom Jones, is still too episodic to be shaped into an immanent order, while the other is written from the perspective of a traveler who has safely reached his final destination but remembers nothing of the journey. And if both are indeed unfinished, this fact can be read in light of contrasting exigencies. *Lucinde* is incomplete because, before it even begins, duration itself is abandoned in favor of peaceful contemplation, while the time of *Theatrical Mission* is serial and thus possesses only an arbitrary terminus. Somewhere between these two extreme points, one of "blind" time, the other of "empty" truth, we find Goethe's fully accomplished *Bildungsroman* and Hegel's *Phenomenology*. The *Lehrjahre* represents a narrative with a full-blown veridictory drive, where temporal progression turns into the medium of constant inquiry, which is largely (though not entirely) satisfied at the journey's end. Here the picaresque and the philosophical tale find their structural synthesis, while the "atemporal" narrator slowly withdraws into absence.[97]

As for Hegel, he can be seen as presenting us with a formula for an ideal of balance between time and truth, for a steady patience with which the end shadows the beginning and the middle, and knowledge oversees the progress of ignorance. The veridictory ideal of Hegelian closure, of narrative proceeding in the shadow of absolute meaning, this ideal traced out in the introduction to *Phenomenology* is not something even Hegel's treatise itself, with its odd leaps and uneven pace, can live up to. What is important for us is the emergence of this ideal, the historically specific affiliation of truth with immanently achieved closure, the ideal *with* and *against* which the novelistic veridictory shapes analyzed in the rest of the book will work.

It should by now be clear that this map is not meant to be straightforwardly teleological. There is no sense in which we could take, say, Hegelian narrative configurations to replace definitively those that are represented by *Tom Jones* or *Theatrical Mission*. As we shall see in the cases of Stendhal and Tolstoy, the "eighteenth-century" tradition of dissociating higher truth from time is strong in many nineteenth-century novels (and in a different way, as we shall see, in some twentieth-century works as well). Nor can we say that it is the Romantic novel that supplants the picaresque. There is very little in the nineteenth century that looks like *Lucinde* or *Heinrich von Ofterdingen,* though we will be confronted with one pivotal instance of such literary-historical anachronism in Balzac's *Louis Lambert.* In short, the trajectory I am sketching out here is neither linear nor singular. Rather, all that can be said is that a certain powerful configuration—detectable in philosophical, historiographic, and literary discourses—crystallizes and demands to be reckoned with on the level of narrative construction. And such is the force of this demand that for quite some time even those authors who will reject the alliance between truth and time will have to do so via a detour through this very alliance.

I have paused to consider this moment in the history of philosophy and the novel, the moment that reveals that history to be, in fact, a shared one, not merely because of its diverse and wide-ranging effects on the form of the nineteenth-century novel in France and Russia. What interests me here is something other than the more or less direct influence that German philosophy and poetics had on the thought and fiction of the authors I will be treating in the remaining chapters of the book. It is rather that this historically specific constellation of issues brings into a particularly sharp light the problems that arise at the turn of the eighteenth century, when the modern experience of accelerated time emerges as in need of mastery and when narrative, and the novel in particular, emerges in its double task of staging acceleration and confusion along with stabilization and order. No longer given in advance, truth struggles to rise up from within narrative itself; no longer spinning out of control, time strains to make itself accessible to overarching meaning.[98]

Thus, it is only here, and not in the logic of eighteenth-century "true histories" that a real innovation with regard to the relationship between truth and time is in evidence. Only here, in short, do the two become necessarily entangled; narrative, and especially the novel, emerge as a product and a medium of this entanglement. J. M. Bernstein writes: "Truth acquires a wholly novel aspect when becoming is recognized as constitutive of human being, when theory is divorced from its presumptive attachment to eternal (and forever external) objects, thereby overturning optical images of truth and allowing action itself to acquire an interrogative and an assertive character."[99] The preceding analysis should have prepared us to hear the pun, apparently unintended by Bernstein, concealed here in the word "novel."

Realism and the Question of Truth

Michael McKeon's account of the rise of the English novel traces out the following three steps in the process whereby the novel attains full-fledged identity and autonomy: First, during the stage of "romance idealism" romance carries with it an atemporal truth or the truth of the "overarching pattern." Next, "true histories" arise, espousing "naïve empiricism," that is, claiming to give an account of what actually happened without reference to preexisting formulas for the construction of narrative. Finally arrives the age of "radical skepticism," with its increasing suspicion that these new "true histories" are quite as *romantic,* as patterned and artificial, as the romances of old. In the process of this intense questioning, the claim to historicity turns into the claim of being historylike, and truth gives way to verisimilitude. Thus, we witness the rise of literary realism when "true history [i.e., the early novel] must cease to find its justification in the mediation of 'other' truths, whether spiritual or moral, because it will by then have achieved their internalization; at which point it will also cease to need to call itself 'true history.'"[100]

McKeon's analysis thus follows the emergence of verisimilitude out of the struggle between "idealist" and "empiricist" conceptions of truth. The end of the struggle is marked by the following development: "By the end of the eighteenth century, romance idealism will have emerged from the long process of positive revaluation that issues in the romantic movement and in the ascendancy of the secularized, human spirituality of the aesthetic. In the realm of prose fiction, questions of truth will be addressed by reference to a notion of 'history' that is now sufficiently separated from 'literature' to be 'realistically' represented by it."[101] The need to legitimize its existence by deferring to an empirical standard of truth disappears with the rise of autonomous aesthetics. We can no longer demand from narrative, in other words, an account of what actually happened, but only of what can happen, what typically or characteristically happens. We are no longer interested in getting a story about particular people and events, but rather about people and events that are somehow representative. A truthful narrative will from now on be one that captures what is essential about the world it represents. A synthesis of romance idealism and naïve empiricism, it will serve as a Kantian inquiry into *possible* rather than actual experience. And insofar as both the realist novel and Kant's philosophy seek truth on the level of possible experience alone, it might perhaps be more accurate to say that this synthesis finds its philosophical counterpart not, *pace* McKeon, in "radical skepticism," but in transcendental idealism.

For Kant, in order to specify the conditions for experience, we must resolve the problem of how synthetic *a priori* judgments are possible, that is, how concepts and sensations relate to each other. It is to this last question, to the question of the truth of truth, so to speak, that the temporal schematism is called upon to serve as an answer: the deep-structural conditions for the possibility of experience involve meaningful organization of events in time. Translating this into the language of novel criticism, we recover an important difference between asking, What do we find out from the novel about the essential characteristics of the world depicted in it? and asking, What do we find out about what it means to find out anything at all in or about the world that is being depicted in the novel? More simply perhaps, inquiry into novelistic veridiction is an inquiry not into the truth of a novel, but into the conditions for the possibility of truth in that novel, into the novel's implicit understanding of what truth is, of what it might mean to strive for it or to have it.

These two sets of questions—What is the truth *of* the story? What is truth *for* the story?—though they are obviously distinct, are also related. It would not have been possible to pose the latter question without posing the former. When truth in narrative is a matter of fidelity to a preexisting pattern, or when it is a matter of reporting precisely and exhaustively the events supposed to have actually happened, we can be sure of the operative veridictory standard. In the first case, it is, roughly speaking, idealist, and in the second, just as roughly, empiricist. But when at stake are a series of attempts to *represent* the world "realistically," the question of what "realistic" means, what the standard of realism is, must arise again and again. And in each case, though the particular veridictory configurations vary from novel to novel, their "location" is the same: in the internal narrative dynamics that correspond to a certain temporal understanding of truth. How is truth to be told in time? What is the truthful arrangement of events in time? These are questions that each realistic narrative tacitly answers in an attempt to speak truthfully about the world.[102]

We have arrived from the other side, so to speak, at an understanding of realism implicit here: that animating the realist practice is an alliance—rigorously articulated in Kant, elaborated into a full-fledged novelistic narratology by Hegel, and consequentially evaded in the Jena Romantic theory of the novel—between truth and time. The realist novels to which we will soon turn will never come close to the "ideal type" of veridictory balance we have elaborated in connection with Hegel and Goethe. Rather, they will tend to deviate from it, drawn to the "eighteenth-century" picaresque pole of "true histories" or to the Romantic limit of timeless, form-giving truth. What differentiates these narratives from their predecessors, however, is their inability to avoid a serious confrontation—*on the level of narrative form itself*—with the essential mutation in the veridictory makeup of the novel and the resulting (historical) unsustainability of the older forms in their one-sidedness.

It is now possible to specify the sense, or rather the senses, in which I am here using the term "veridiction." First, the term points to a distinction between claims of truth proper and those of its representation. To characterize a statement as truthful is to say that it adequately refers to a certain kind of reality; to characterize a claim as veridictory is to say only that it *aspires* to refer in this way. In other words, the study of veridiction brackets the question of the actual truthfulness of a statement or a story and inquires only into the standards or "images" of truth on which the statement or story more or less explicitly relies. For example, truth might be represented as eternal or emerging in time, best achievable in solitude or in communication with others, singular or multiple. It is as a further formal-historical specification of this broad sense of veridiction, then, that the narrower understanding of it as naming the association between truth and time is intended. The "veridictory mutation" of the title can thus be understood in two ways: broadly, as positing a change in the dominant novelistic truth discourse, occurring around the turn of the eighteenth century; and narrowly, as a transition to the kind of truth discourse best captured by the processual and temporal connotations of the term. It has been the task of this introduction to trace the emergence of precisely this, *temporal,* instantiation of veridiction.

Nonsynchronous Contexts

So far, then, the "nineteenth-century" veridictory mutation of the novel and a certain modernity that sets for itself the task of mastering its own experience of temporal acceleration have been shown to converge in the conception of a truth immanent to a shape of time. Along this trajectory, the novel, which searches for a truth discourse of its own throughout the seventeenth and eighteenth centuries and finds it in rational (timeless) moral principles as much as in empirical (time-bound) historicity, achieves sometime at the turn of the eighteenth century a problematic (and merely regulative) fusion of the two. But having come this far, we have exhausted neither the consequences of the accelerated time of modernity nor the wealth of novelistic innovations in relation to the question of truth.

If we look closely at the section on Spirit from Hegel's *Phenomenology*—the section in which dialectical stages appear to recapitulate the history of Western culture from ancient Greece to the present—we will find a striking asymmetry. It turns out that the number of stages covered by Spirit in the first twenty-two centuries of European history, from the Greek city-state to the age of Enlightenment, is six; and then, in the last one hundred years, from the age of Enlightenment to the end of the eighteenth century—six more. Such is the intensity of acceleration here that, at a certain point, the very principle of successive stages is no longer sustainable.[103] Successive stages become simultaneous, acceleration reaches the point at which the "supplanted" stage no longer has time to vanish from the scene before its successor, too, is in danger of becoming obsolete. The experience of temporal acceleration culminates in what has, in the twentieth-century philosophy of history, come to be known as *Ungleichzeitigkeit,* or nonsynchronicity.[104]

If in Hegel this consequence is merely implicit in the structure of his account of Spirit's progress, in someone like Herder it is already an explicit historical category. Human history as a whole is for him a totality of independent and interacting parts, each of which (both on the level of a single human being and an entire nation) operates according to a clock of its own: some aging, some mature, some fast or slow, incipient or recurring: "Each age is different, but each has the center of happiness within itself."[105] Here, different temporalities coexist simultaneously, contributing their own rhythms to the all-encompassing movement of the whole.

Surely, when Herder attacks "the philosopher [who] is never more of an ass than when he ... pronounces on the perfection of the world, wholly convinced that everything moves just so, in a nice straight line," he anticipates by more than thirty years an objection to Hegel's conception of time as a singular medium for the unfolding of the ultimately singular Concept.[106] But we can also say that Hegel's *Phenomenology,* with its narrative growing significantly denser at the approach of the end, gives us the means to historicize Herder's temporal pluralism. What we get then is a formula according to which there comes a time when time is no longer singular; and this time, as Hegel's section on Spirit testifies, is the time of modernity.[107]

If it was accurate to say, therefore, that in the course of the dialectic of modernity, at a particular moment in it time and truth enter into an alliance, then how do we evaluate the consequences for this alliance of extreme temporal condensation and the resulting condition of nonsynchronicity? Must truth-time configurations be conceived of as multiple as well? And if yes, then what about the novel? Will the problem of establishing a particular novel's veridictory stance involve at least in part uncovering the simultaneity of co-present truth discourses?

Indeed, if the accelerating rhythms of modernity ensure that there comes a time when time becomes multiple, and if time is indeed to be conceived of as the modern medium of truth, then the genre appropriate to modernity is one capable of internalizing temporal and thus veridictory multiplicity. In other words, truth discourse in the "realist" novel—that is, in the novel structured by the modern exigency of thinking truth and time together—does not yield to the kind of analysis that would disregard the simultaneity of nonsynchronous veridictory mechanisms organizing the text.[108] And since the novel itself does not merely represent but also intervenes in the discursive multiplicity of the world, the proper question to pose in analyzing it is twofold: First, what sorts of veridictory shapes are available to the particular novel? And second, which of them, or which configuration of them, does it appear to privilege? What kind of time must one occupy in order to be in—or to speak—the truth?

The novels to which we are about to turn can be seen precisely as such interventions in contexts of intensified modernity. Intensified because the ages of the Bourbon Restoration (Balzac, Stendhal) and of the so-called Great Reforms in Russia (Dostoevsky, Tolstoy) present us with veritable explosions in ideologically charged temporal multiplicity. The condensation of time characteristic of modernity is raised to a higher power during the period of the Restoration. Here, the *ancien régime,* the Revolution, the Terror, the Empire, the return of the monarchy, the Hundred Days, the White Terror—each leaves on the sociohistorical surface ideological and temporal sediments that don't have time to stratify and thus appear in simultaneity to the naked eye. Here, one is confronted with many possibilities: in order to speak the truth must one deny the significance of passing time altogether, or try to stick faithfully with the fleeting present, or leap into a radically different future, or master that future through careful planning, or look for answers in the energy of a very distant past? These are some of the options that both Balzac and Stendhal will consider.

In Russia, the university reforms and the relaxation of censorship in the late fifties, as well as the emancipation of the serfs and the introduction of provincial councils in the early sixties, contribute to growing social displacement and to the kind of ideological and discursive diversity not seen there at least since the first decade of the nineteenth century. The period that later came to be know as the age of the Great Reforms is one of the highest points in imperial Russia's fitful modernity; the experience of a precipitously accelerated time produces a temporal condensation, after a thirty-year repression of a vast array of ideological positions, the public sphere bursts open and myriad opinions, hopes, interests, projects, histories, and utopias surge forth, providing the novel with a wealth of discursive material for polyphonic treatment.[109] Again, multiple temporalities enter into contest and become visible in their most condensed and vivid form in the novels of the period. The serial, mechanical temporality of industrialization, the cyclical premodern time of the land, the step-by-step time of career, the leap of sudden enrichment, the time of harmonious personal development or of personal ordeal, the quasi-magical stillness of the time of exile—each presents an option, each is the temporality of a certain insight.

Two sets of novels, then, and two exemplary modernities. I spend some time, in each of the four chapters that follow, discussing the author's explicit engagement with the historical moment in order to bring to light the various veridictory possibilities available to him. In each case, however, a close analysis of the author's representative fiction will yield a determinate truth-time configuration, a specific story shape capable of containing the truth.[110]

The first chapter, dedicated to the workings of veridiction in the novels of Balzac, focuses especially on two of his *Études philosophiques*: *Louis Lambert* and *La Peau de chagrin* (*The Magic Skin*). *Louis Lambert*, as a fictional biography of the most prominent philosopher of the *Comédie humaine*, represents a particularly fruitful point of departure insofar as the narrator of the biography is, in stylistic and narratological terms, the philosopher's disciple. This means that his story is shaped by the privileged trope of Louis Lambert's own represented writings, the veridictory metaphor, establishing (true) identities where only (illusory) differences are in evidence and protecting archaic stability from the threat of modern acceleration. Transferred onto the temporal plane of narrative, this metaphoric truth discourse confuses diachronic succession and transfixes the narrative in fragmentary simultaneity. I suggest that this novel, fractured by its own truth discourse, stages the simultaneous desire for and despair of having things both ways—telling the story step-by-step and grasping its truth all at once. Read in this way, *Louis Lambert* fits into the tradition of the Romantic novel (as do the aforementioned *Lucinde* and *Heinrich von Ofterdingen*), and as such presents an instance of what has been called "sentimental romance," honestly displaying the dire formal consequences for narrative of the ascendancy of metaphoric truth discourse.

Unlike *Louis Lambert*, *La Peau de chagrin* resembles in its narrative shape what later comes to be known as the "realist novel." And yet, paradoxically, its entanglement with romance is all the more *naïve*. The magic skin itself—granting the hero the dubious privilege of constantly possessing before his eyes the entire shape of his life—serves as the key figure of such romance naïveté. The paradox emerges as yet more poignant when we realize that, throughout the novel, the "archaic" magic skin is heavily associated with the accelerated rhythms of modernity. And yet I argue that it is precisely the temporality of the magic skin, the prominence of "magic time"—combining the *now* with the *always*, embroidering the truth of the whole onto blind step-by-step progression—that allows the novel to dissolve the ironies and contradictions tearing at *Louis Lambert*. I suggest furthermore that this same logic dominates the *Comédie* as a whole, which repeatedly relies on figurations of accelerated time to articulate the truth of situations and events through their emplotment in a totalizing narrative.

While for Balzac the truth of events is revealed in their relation to the whole of the narrative, for Stendhal truth is produced in the act of subverting that whole. And while "magic time" names the *Comédie*'s penchant for veridictory *emplotment*, "dutiful action" in Stendhal produces moments of *disemplotment* capable of hosting the truth. Thus, in the second chapter, I focus on Stendhal's Restoration novels, especially *Armance* and *Le Rouge et le noir* (*The Red and the Black*) with a view to elaborating what may be called "the time of duty." To begin with, the time of duty is haste—this Stendhal shares with his seventeenth-century neoclassicist forebears. However, what separates Stendhalian duty from that of say, Pierre Corneille, is its radically subjective inflection. It is no longer duty to one's "name," to one's place in the social order, but rather the reverse: duty calls the ambitious hero to act in accordance with an inner impulse and an inner conception of honor and thus not only against his own calculable interests but also, more important, counter to societal expectations.

I suggest that this recasting of duty can be understood as an intervention in the Restoration debates about the relationship between social norms and individual freedom. In order to situate *Rouge* in its historical context, I spend some time analyzing Benjamin Constant's important psychological novel *Adolphe* in light of his conception of modern freedom as private rather than political. I contrast the veridictory conditions underlying Constant's novel with those adhered to by the conservative ideologues of the Restoration—de Bonald, de Maistre, Chateaubriand—whose conception of truth is both eternalist and social-traditionalist. In direct opposition to this atavistic veridiction stands

Constant's and Stendhal's resolutely modernizing notion that truth has been uprooted from the past and launched on an incalculable trajectory of the individual's inner life. As such, truth is linked to intimacy and sincerity; it is extrahistorical and asocial or even antisocial.

Adolphe stages a struggle between the competing conceptions of truth, but here (as arguably befits a narrative by the theorist of modern, private liberty) social and timeless veridiction for the most part remains behind the scenes while the intimate fleeting truth of inner life occupies center stage. In *Le Rouge et le noir* (1830), a novel which by many accounts inaugurates the practice of historical realism, the intimate sphere can no longer occupy the foreground to the exclusion of social conditions. It is here that impetuous dutiful action becomes central as a narrative and thematic loophole through which fluid, incalculable inner life bursts—however weakly and momentarily—onto the heavily regimented social scene and the calculating, compromising plot of ambition. Momentarily and weakly, it belies social hierarchies and conventions, and reveals the hero's "authentic self" beneath the hypocritical mask of a careerist. Thus, here too, as in Balzac, veridiction emerges as parasitic on the accelerated pace of modern life. But the function of Stendhalian truthful haste is not to synthesize but to break apart, to produce flashes of the unexpected, moments of disemplotment in which the truth of the hero fleetingly debunks social objectivity and rigid romancelike plot structures.

If for Balzac veridiction subsists in "magic time" and for Stendhal in "the time of dutiful action," then for Dostoevsky its habitat is "the time of the accident." The third chapter begins with a consideration of Dostoevsky's journalistic interventions in debates about the future of Russia and argues that his post-Great Reforms novelistic obsession with the enigmatic hero is readable as an effect of a fictional, biographical recasting of the question, What is Russia?—what (now that it has been emancipated) is the narrative shape adequate to its distinctiveness, its particularity? Dostoevsky's post-Reform novels, then, in their preoccupation with the truth of the enigmatic self, can be understood as testing grounds for various modes of veridictory emplotment, as zones of narrative experimentation, where the proper veridictory plot(s) can be identified among a number of historically available possibilities.

A close examination of *Crime and Punishment,* along with Dostoevsky's other novels and shorter works from the post-Reform period, establishes the thematic and narratological prominence of the accident in his veridictory poetics. I show that the accident functions in his narratives as an intersection point between (at minimum) two plots, allowing one to establish a position and apply the power of interpretative outsideness in relation to the other. Accidental, unpremeditated events repeatedly produce enigmatic gaps in the hero's biography, soliciting reemplotment by the hero himself and by other characters in the novel. What results is a novelistic structure in which the authority of the end has been radically undermined and veridictory power has been transferred into the seams of emplotment, where multiple genres and temporalities (those of a career, a *Bildungsroman,* a conversion narrative, a narrative of ordeal, etc.) intersect and compete with one another for the right to serve as the hero's true story.

The fourth chapter adds to these veridictory shapes another; in fact, it adds two. Focusing on Tolstoy's great novel set in contemporary Russia, I argue that here, as well as throughout much of his fiction, one is confronted with an essentially dualistic narrative shape. The plotlines of *Anna Karenina*'s two heroes (Anna and Levin) are constructed according to different principles and represent two distinct veridictory configurations. The truth of Anna's narrative is the truth of the whole, an unfolding of a foretold fate; a kind of naïve romance, shot through with prophetic dreams, ominous forebodings, ill omens, and literary allusions. It is best figured by the all-important motif of the railway, with its capacity for temporal condensation; as soon as one boards the train one feels that one is already at the point of destination ("The Kreutzer Sonata"). Levin's story on the other hand relies on an altogether different—though no less modern—veridictory framework, one in which time emerges in its function to dissolve, negate, and critique. This negation and dispersal, incarnated in the picaresque motif of the country road, constitutes the mechanism of veridiction within the parameters of Levin's plot.

The meandering "time of the country road" (which is placed in the novel between the railway and the peasant idyll) and the collapsed "time of the railway"—these two key truth shapes of modernity are at war. One emphasizes the centrifugal ideals of self-consciousness, freedom, and the ceaseless dynamism of experience; the other figures the self-containment of modern acceleration in city life, in social convention, and in "literary" emplotment.[111] Tolstoy sides with the former, positing a disjunction between emplotment and truth. In this, as in many other respects, he reveals a kinship with Stendhal and a disaffinity with Dostoevsky and Balzac. But over and above Stendhal's momentary outbursts of truth, instantly shut down by centripetal social forces, Tolstoy appears capable of representing an entire trajectory of a truthful life.

The relations, then, between particular truth discourses and their historical conditions of possibility within the differently configured modernities of

Restoration France and Emancipation Russia are complex and highly mediated. The veridictory shapes of more or less contemporary novels differ from one another and gravitate instead to their counterparts from another period, in another country. Balzac and Stendhal, while responding to a similar historical moment, will produce truth discourses that in many respects oppose one another and instead display affinities with, respectively, Dostoevsky and Tolstoy. The Russian novelists in turn, writing in circumstances very different from those of their French predecessors, will nevertheless repeat some of their fundamental veridictory gestures. In short, it will become clear that we are dealing with two diverging veridictory trajectories: one, anchoring Balzac and Dostoevsky and relying on a fundamental affinity between truth and narrative emplotment; the other, uniting Stendhal with Tolstoy and casting truth as an enemy of plot. Each of these trajectories, foregrounding veridictory emplotment and disemplotment respectively, will be shown to possess a long tradition of its own, reaching back to the eighteenth century and beyond. Each will appear within a constellation of prominent formal and thematic corollaries, pertaining to narrative discourse and the shape of the plot, to generic proclivities, the function of beginnings and endings, the place of the epigraph, as well as conceptions of socialization, transgression, career, the family, passion, duty, etc.

And yet this is not to say that the pressures of the "historical moment" did not leave a mark on the work of these authors, bringing contemporaries and compatriots together in significant formal consonance. In the case of Balzac and Stendhal, a kind of "Restoration" narratology promotes temporal-ideological closure and thus—without determining whether a particular novel will rely on an alliance (Balzac) or a disjunction (Stendhal) between emplotment and truth—delimits the fictional shape this alliance or disjunction will take. Balzac's emplotment veridiction is thus reinforced by the deadly decisiveness of the ending, while Stendhal's truthful outbursts of disemplotment are shut down just as decisively and to similarly mortal effect. By contrast, in post-Reform Russia, we find potent a kind of "emancipatory" temporality, which once again does not overdetermine specific structures of truth discourse, but, by rendering closure problematic, ensures that, whether truth-bearing (Dostoevsky) or falsifying (Tolstoy), final emplotment is outside the reach and beyond the power of the narrative's end. Thus, by having a say over the ultimate fate of truth "in the world," historico-narratological conditions also influence the shape this truth takes in particular novels. The simultaneous sway of "veridictory tradition" (linking Balzac and Dostoevsky, Stendhal and Tolstoy) and historical situation (aligning Balzac with Stendhal and Dostoevsky with Tolstoy) is what accounts for the structure of crisscrossing formal resemblances between the four narrative truth discourses at issue in the book.

It would be impossible to treat both veridictory trajectories exhaustively. Together with Balzac and Dostoevsky one would have to talk of Rousseau, Wilkie Collins, and Henry James; to Stendhal and Tolstoy one would have to add Pushkin, George Eliot, and Chekhov. And yet it seemed to me important to read the chosen novels closely and as wholes because it is precisely in the relations between parts and their (regulative) completion that veridictory strategies are most vivid—at least during the period in question. Thus, what follows is by no means exhaustive but only—in line with the new "realist" conception of verisimilitude—representative. In picking prominent novels from two literary traditions and two historical moments, my hope is to provide a map of reading, with the help of which further research into the veridictory dimensions of narrative could be conducted on other material, in other national literatures and historical periods. It is an attempt to chart two key trajectories of novelistic veridiction in light of which it might be possible to understand the truth discourses of other novels belonging to the veridictory mutation, whose prehistory and beginnings it has been the purpose of this introduction to present and whose outer bounds within the philosophical and novelistic discourses of modernism are delineated in the conclusion.

I

Precipitant Knowledge in Balzac

The True Is the Whole

In an 1840 review of Stendhal's *La Chartreuse de Parme,* Balzac displays an awareness of the condition of *nonsynchronicity* permeating the literary field in post-Restoration France. According to him, a proper classification of contemporary French letters would have to be tripartite, a literary *triplicité,* including works that privilege ideas, those that display a penchant for images, and those that combine both tendencies in a kind of eclecticism. The literature of ideas persists as a residue of the seventeenth and eighteenth centuries and is characterized by an emphasis on action, speed, movement, and dramatic collision. It has experienced its flowering in the works of Montesquieu, Pascal, Lesage, Prévost, Voltaire, and Rousseau, but it is still quite energetic, producing such brilliant practitioners of the novel as Stendhal himself, the subject of the review. A movement with more contemporary roots—one that appeals in particular to the elegiac constitution, is contemplative and attuned to higher spiritual domains—produces the literature of images, whose masters include Hugo, Sainte-Beuve, Chateaubriand, and, once again, Rousseau. Finally, representing an emergent but powerful trend headed by Balzac himself, there are those who strive to synthesize the two methods in the literature of eclecticism: "Finally, certain complete persons, certain two-sided minds embrace everything, want both lyricism and action, both drama and the ode, believing that perfection demands a total view of things."[1] These writers, according to Balzac, want to represent the world as it is, "the images and the ideas, the idea in the image or the image in the idea, the movement and the reverie."[2] Which of these schools is the best, asks Balzac, and answers, coyly, that he does not know. But the rhetoric of reconciliation, of artistic perfection and the total embrace of what is, leaves little room for doubt: the future belongs to eclecticism.

Balzac borrows the term "eclecticism" from the philosopher Victor Cousin, who used it to name what he took to be the only kind of philosophical system tenable in the nineteenth century, one that strives to achieve "the living harmony of all truths, even when they appear opposed."[3] According to Cousin, the philosophy of eclecticism is particularly appropriate for the historical moment of the Restoration because it can ground a reconciliation between the two opposing political principles of democracy and the monarchy. It can consequently legitimize the reigning order in France under the constitutional charter as well as the concomitant ideology of peaceful coexistence between former implacable enemies. But of course eclecticism is called upon to do more: to unify all contradictions tearing at thought and existence alike, to bring together finitude and infinity, contingency and necessity, selfhood and otherness, idealism and sensualism—and thus to achieve a comprehensive vision of reality.[4]

For Balzac, the more comprehensive the better, of course. But in addition to clarifying the stakes of his "realism," the invocation of this philosophical term sheds light on the nature of the two lesser literary methods. Apparently, the "classical" literature of ideas with its "heap of events and ideas"[5] stands to its more modern contemplative, "Romantic" counterpart as philosophical sensualism stands to idealism. One privileges experience: matter-of-fact, condensed depiction of (fictional or historical) facts; the other strives to intuit essences and, in the process, poeticizes language and perfects style.

It does not seem to matter that under each literary school Balzac gathers authors distant from one another in time and diverse in genre; nor does it matter that Rousseau, for instance, appears to belong to both schools, or that poetry, prose (picaresque, "psychological," philosophical), history, and politico-theological polemics are carelessly lumped together. Balzacian synthesis, his eclecticism retrospectively produces the thesis and antithesis it claims to have reconciled, and we find ourselves in the presence of a number of familiar oppositions: experience and thought, action and contemplation, keen observation and stylistic elegance, prosaic (i.e. forward-directed) movement and elegiac or poetic (that is, inturned) stillness. The oppositions should sound familiar to us, invoking the dualism of truthless time and timeless truth organizing much of the thought and narration prior to the turn of the century. And just as Hegel (following Kant) sought mediation between the two terms of the dualism, so Balzac, with his Cousin-inspired eclecticism, believes himself to be practicing the kind of novelistic sublation that affirms "le mouvement" together with "la rêverie."

It was not just Cousin, a scholar of Kant and a friend of Hegel, whose synthesizing impulse informed Balzac's understanding of his work. More unequivocally a hero for Balzac was the naturalist Étienne Geoffroy Saint-Hilaire, whose name was (for better and for worse) linked in the minds of his colleagues and admirers to the tradition of German *Naturphilosophie* from Schelling and Hegel to Goethe. Geoffroy's conception of nature as a self-forming totality seems to have won him as many critics among naturalists as admirers among novelists and historians. Jules Michelet, George Sand, and, perhaps most consequentially, Balzac believed his doctrine of the unity of composition to be a major characteristic discovery of the age. In a funeral oration for Geoffroy, the historian Edgar Quinet proclaimed: "The idea to which he has given birth is, in many respects, at the heart of our time. The desire, the presentiment, the necessity for a vast unity—that is what the world is working toward. M. Geoffroy Saint-Hilaire, a true prophetic genius, has established in nature and in science that harmonious principle that we still seek in the civil, political and religious world."[6] This in 1844.

In 1842, in the *Avant-propos* to the *Comédie humaine,* Balzac is already applying Geoffroy's unity of composition precisely to an understanding of the "the civil, political and religious world." The principle, argues Balzac, applies to society as much as to nature. And just as in nature the single animal appears in different forms depending on the environment in which it has to develop, so society modifies man "according to the conditions in which he lives and acts, into men as manifold as the species in Zoology."[7] Beneath apparent diversity there is thus unity, and science is called upon to unify phenomena rather than allow itself to be fractured under the pressure of illusory differences. Hence there is one science and not many; and underlying the multiplicity of Balzac's narrative output, there is the unity of the *Comédie humaine.*[8]

"Balzac's world," writes Georg Lukács, "is, like Hegel's, a circle consisting entirely of circles."[9] No less explicitly Hegelian is Hippolyte Taine's significantly earlier formulation, according to which Balzac has grasped the truth precisely because he has grasped the whole.[10] The parallels between Balzac and Hegel are indeed compelling, not so much for establishing lines of influence but for identifying analogous formal responses to the post-Kantian veridictory demand that truth be conjugated with time. Thus, Hegel unfolds his system as a narrative, and Balzac gathers narrative into a system. Or, to put it in terms of Balzacian literary history, Hegel makes abstract reverie yield movement, while Balzac's own "eclecticism" contains movement within the totalizing horizon of reverie.

What are the structural correlates of this sort of literary eclecticism for Balzac's narrative? Or, to put the question differently: what is the medium, in narrative, of the "eclectic" synthesis between movement and reverie? To begin with, it is certainly not authorial discourse. This is not to say that the Balzacian narrator, like the narrator in Goethe's *Lehrjahre*, is reserved, allowing narrative to speak for itself. But nor is it any longer the case, as in *Tom Jones* and many other seventeenth- and eighteenth-century novels, that the narrator is a legitimate purveyor of truth. Rather, we have a strangely transitional situation, where the narrator sounds less and less convincing and yet is still (and even *increasingly*) incapable of keeping quiet. What results is a rearticulation of the place of authoritative discourse within the total dynamic of the narrative. Gérard Genette comments: "As we know, Balzac has 'theories about everything,' but these theories are not there for the sole pleasure of theorizing; first and foremost, they are in the service of narration: at every instant they serve as its guarantor, its justification, its *captatio benevolentiae*, they fill all of its cracks and mark all of its crossroads."[11]

Elements of authorial discourse, aspiring to the status of moral, psychological, and sociological truths for all time, turn out to have little value in themselves. They appear primarily to grease the workings of narrative, to make it run smoothly. Thus, for example, if *La Cousine Bette*'s Wenceslas Steinbock, who adores his wife, must, for the purposes of the story, become infatuated with the vulgar Mme Marneffe, it is because he happens to be Polish. A long meditation on the history of Poland and the psychology of Poles comes to the rescue, smoothing the way of narrative progress. Not so much a revelation of true cause as reassuring causal rhetoric, the universal principle does not generate or justify the particular event but is rather produced as the event's discursive epiphenomenon.

Genette himself takes the relationship between discourse and narrative in Balzac to be one of relative balance. But his insight into the *ad hoc* nature of discursive psychomoralizing in the *Comédie humaine* is taken further by Franco Moretti. Invoking Harald Weinrich's view that in modern narrative, narration is progressively severed from wisdom-purveying commentary, he casts the subordination of discourse to narrative in Balzac as the most radical break to date between story and knowledge: "The goal of the *Comédie Humaine*," Moretti writes, "is not 'knowledge'. . . . It is instead a form of perception, which will become firmly rooted in modern culture, sustained by a consuming desire for the new *as such*, regardless of all else."[12] Rather than balance, what we apparently have is a reversal of eighteenth-century hierarchies, placing authorial discourse at the service of the story itself. Knowledge of the world, the kind of knowledge that is conveyed through discursive authorial commentary is, in Balzac, reduced to an enabling device of obsessive narrativity; it is not an end of narrative but a means to keep it going. It is this, according to Moretti, that marks the *Comédie* as a specific response to capitalism's frenzied advent in post-Napoleonic France.[13]

It appears then that rather than allowing itself to be balanced out by discourse, Balzac's narrative completely overwhelms it. And the discursive *"background* idéologique" of which Genette speaks, or the gnomic code, which notoriously nauseates Roland Barthes in *S/Z*, is a manifestation of a feeble and outdated veridiction. Still, to say that the Balzacian narrative is not about knowledge would require overlooking a great deal. In a chapter of *S/Z* entitled "The Voice of Truth," Barthes proposes to enumerate the morphemes of what he calls the hermeneutic sentence of Balzac's short tale *Sarrasine*. The long list renders vivid the extent to which the question of truth is a singular obsession of the story.[14] And it would be wrong to argue, as Moretti does, that *Sarrasine* is atypical in this respect.[15] *La Cousine Bette,* for instance, which is distant from the earlier story in genre, time of composition, and explicit preoccupations, nevertheless displays symptoms of comparable epistemophilia. Here, it is not so much that the narrative as a whole is called upon to enlighten the narratee with regard to a particular mystery; such was the case in *Sarrasine*. Instead, the larger novel is invaded and propelled by a veridictory drive that is nearly indistinguishable from the narrative itself. Occasionally, this drive will rise to the surface in narratorial interjections: "How then had the Baron raised the thirty thousand francs that he had just brought? As follows."[16] Or: "How had Valérie managed to keep Crevel and Hulot side by side in her house, while the vindictive Mayor was all for open triumph over Hulot?"[17] Or, again, tautologically baring the stakes all the way: "The secret of this profound secret was as follows."[18]

This movement from fact to secret, to the secret of the secret, is the very grammar of Balzac's narrative, placing it in the veridictory paradigm we have developed with reference to Goethe's *Lehrjahre* and Hegel's *Phenomenology,* investing progression with the function of inquiry, rendering time mysterious. Meanwhile, the narrator's relative veridictory weakness as a source of authoritative discourse is compensated by the urgency with which he directs the reader's attention along the path of narrative discovery. The site of the narrator serves as a kind of index, directing the reader to the revelatory narrative that is about to unfold. Thus, in *Eugénie Grandet*: "It is impossible to understand fully what these words mean to the local people unless you are told the story of Monsieur Grandet's life."[19] The meaning behind a word, a situation, or an event is to be found in a story; an element in that story needs another story to explain it—on and on, the narrative is impelled forward by questioning. Forward or, more precisely, inward, moving from surface to depth, from appearance to reality, pursuing "the secret of the secret" to its very core. And conversely, in *Le Père Goriot*: "Without [Rastignac's] careful observations, and skill at making his way into Parisian society, this tale could not have been colored in these truthful hues which, without any doubt, it owes to his shrewdness, as well as to his interest in deciphering the secrets of a shocking situation, concealed just as carefully by those who had created it as by the man whom it crushed."[20] That is to say, truth itself depends on a particular type of narration; in this instance, one of social ambition.

A vivid illustration of what is meant by a rigorous connection between truth and narrative can be found in two alternative readings of Balzac's *La Recherche de l'Absolu*. Balthazar Claës's discovery of the substance "common to all created things" would enable him to make anything out of anything else. In order to keep his quest alive, to purchase the appropriate materials and equipment for his alchemical experiments, he must sell his family possessions, accumulated over many generations. As he lies on his deathbed, having failed to achieve his goal, his son-in-law picks up a newspaper and reads about the "bargain concluded by a celebrated Polish mathematician for the secret of the Absolute, which he had discovered."[21] At this point, Balthazar sits up in bed, raises his fist, cries out "*Eureka!*" and dies.

There is of course a way to interpret this ending as implying that the Absolute is somehow altogether incommunicable, that whoever has found it is paralyzed and struck dumb. On this reading the truth of the narrative is discovered only at the end. It could in principle be contained in an esoteric aphorism, a mystic formula, a sacred name, but the person who has finally reached it is rendered speechless or incomprehensible. But then what should we make of the Polish mathematician who succeeds not only in communicating the Absolute but even in selling it? It appears then that the more interesting and more consistent reading of the novel would suggest that the chemist's final "*Eureka!*" marks the discovery that the substance common to everything, the medium into which everything (even the Absolute itself) can be decomposed and out of which anything can be made, is money itself. Then the story of Balthazar's life—insofar as it is a story of converting family property into laboratory materials and equipment through the mediation of money—would be nothing if not a confirmation or, better, an acting out of this truth. Then, also, one of the novelistic pillars of the more fantastic *Études philosophiques* would be revealed as elaborating a crucial thematic and formal feature of the properly "realist" *Études de moeurs,* namely, the function of money as a connecting tissue of narrative and as "the secret of the secret" beneath the surface of represented situations and events.

The first reading, though it casts the truth as ineffable, nevertheless thinks of it as an object, a goal. As such, it is consonant with Todorov's view of narrative veridiction: so far as the narrative lasts, the truth is unavailable; once it is available, the narrative must stop. Truth is there at the end of time or, all along, outside it. But, more important, this reading collapses the veridictory structure of Balzacian narrative back onto one that we have identified in *Tom Jones,* in which the secret of the hero's identity is external to and even proscribed for narrative. The second reading, meanwhile, gives credence precisely to the veridictory mutation of the novel (of which Balzac may be the first grand attestor) by insisting that truth is to be found neither at the end of narrative nor in the discourse of its author, that is, neither at the end nor outside time, but rather in the structure of the narrative itself, shaping it.

If the truth must be named, then, it must name a process: exchange in *La Recherche de l'Absolu,* financial and cultural circulation in *Illusions perdues,* signification in *Le Père Goriot,* desire in *La Cousine Bette,* which also makes this explicit: "The next day these three existences, so variously and so really unhappy, that of a desperate mother, that of the Marneffe home, and that of the unfortunate exile, were all to be affected by Hortense's naïve passion, and by the singular outcome of the Baron's unfortunate passion for Josépha."[22] But in fact, in all of these cases, desire, exchange, signification, etc. flow into one another in an irreducible dynamism, a *mouvement* underlying all apparently distinct things, tracing "a pattern in which separation gives way to connection"[23] and thus serving as the kind of veridictory object that requires precisely narrative for its elaboration.[24]

It appears therefore—and the following analyses will develop this claim—that the veridictory drive, while vacating the space of the enfeebled, henceforth almost laughable, narratorial authority, does not vanish altogether but rather migrates into the structure of narrative itself, becomes one with it, visible only in its interstices, but omnipresent. Truth is no longer to be found in timeless discourse, delivering temporality over to falsehood. Rather, it is now to be found in narrative itself—this is the significance of Balzac's self-proclaimed eclecticism, his effort to represent the modern world by combining eighteenth-century *mouvement* with Romantic *rêverie.* And it should come as no surprise that Balzac himself, in *Louis Lambert*—a relatively neglected novel that may have been dearer to his heart than any other he wrote—would propose a striking figure for this veridictory mutation, the two-headed (*bifront*) creature of *Poète-et-Pythagore*.

Pythagore: Metaphoric Structures of Truth

Louis Lambert, written in 1832, does not merely belong to what Balzac will three years later call *Études philosophiques*, it also represents the most properly "philosophical" of all the novels and stories grouped under that title. This is not only because it presents itself as a biographical account of a philosopher's life and contains extended passages dedicated to elaborating metaphysical problems. More important, the novel attempts to integrate a robust philosophical impulse with more conventionally narrative (biographical) elements, thus foregrounding for us the very problem of novelistic veridiction. "Philosophy," in other words, does not remain isolated as a mere theme within the novel but enters into a more significant structural relation with narration. *Louis Lambert*, then, is not simply a novel about philosophy; it is, truly, a philosophical novel. As such, however, it is unlike its eighteenth-century forebears insofar as it is no longer structured by the principle of exemplarity, whereby narrative is called upon to illustrate the timeless truth of (explicit or implicit) discourse. Rather, as we shall see, it stages narrative's more modern complicity with the veridictory impulse in the same gesture as it establishes truth's inextricability from narration.

Pointing to the complex relationship between philosophical theme and narrative structure in this novel is the immediately apparent difficulty of disentangling the narrative voice of the biographer from the philosophical inquiries of his hero. Hence, we can say that the most appropriate articulation of the problem of authorship in *Louis Lambert* is unwittingly achieved by the children at the college of Vendôme in the formula *Poète-et-Pythagore*, meant to mock the close friendship between the little philosopher and his classmate and future biographer, presumably Balzac himself. A newcomer at the school, Louis is nicknamed "Pythagoras" when he remains calm and silent in response to his new classmates' jeering welcome. His future biographer is well known for his bad poetry. The double nickname sticks so well that it is used even when only one of them is being called.

The novel, in other words, is the result of an inextricable collaboration. Passages composed by the philosopher Lambert exist alongside those written by his biographer, the author. The philosopher's insights are mediated in the narrative of the biographer, who collects, reshapes, and re-presents them. More important, this re-presentation is itself influenced by the ideas and style of the philosopher and thus can be analyzed as an instance of "philosophical" representation. In short, it would probably be difficult to find, in the whole reservoir of the nineteenth-century European novel, a better figural condensation for the problematic of novelistic veridiction than this grotesque figure of Poet-and-Pythagoras.

Louis Lambert appears to us for the first time while expounding his philosophy of language. He tells the narrator of his etymological adventures, following a single word from Greece to Rome and then traversing with it the entire extent of the modern ages. To be sure, he pays attention to the differences that changes of time and place produced, but he derives special joy from contemplating continuity, from being able to perceive in the word "the exact reflection, in accordance with the character of each nation, of the unknown beings whose traces survive in us."[25] Just as, in accordance with Geoffroy's doctrine of the unity of composition, there is originally only one Animal, just as, according to Balzac's *Avant-propos,* the original Man is changed in accordance with the milieu in which he or she is compelled to develop, so Louis Lambert appears to believe that there is only a single Language, manifesting itself in different ways according to the character of the nation it must serve.

But what is the origin of this language? Louis Lambert offers an insight into this mystery as well. The progression he traces is as follows: from sensation to thought, from thought to the word, from the word to its hieroglyphic expression, from the hieroglyph to the alphabet, and from the alphabet to written eloquence, producing images that are in turn none other than "the hieroglyphs of thought" (147). The distance from original, preverbal, prelinguistic sensation to rhetorical mastery of the written word is great. Humanity must traverse many stages of development, each lasting centuries, and yet, when it has reached the last stage of development, having traveled so far, it can reclaim the immediacy of its origins. The key word here is, not accidentally, the hieroglyph. Though the novel was composed in the year of Jean-François Champollion's death, and the hieroglyphic writing system had already become known as combining logographic and alphabetic elements, Lambert appears to understand the hieroglyph in a somewhat older, more mystical mode as a pictogram, standing in an iconic relation to objects in Nature, which is itself understood as a hieroglyph, that is, an analogy of the archaic-Spiritual realm.[26] Thus, according to him, written eloquence grants us access to that "remnant of the primitive speech of nations, a majestic and solemn tongue whose grandeur and solemnity decrease as communities grow old" (148).

For Lambert, all words, insofar as they preserve traces of their origins in sensation, are hieroglyphs. They do not merely indicate their referents, they also serve as analogues of them. By the terms of post-Saussurean linguistics, their relationship to concepts and things is not arbitrary but natural. Thus, the word *vrai,* through its very sound, invokes the chastity and simplicity of truth, while the word *vol* directly implores one to flee: "Thus, by their mere physiognomy, words call to life in our brain the beings which they serve to clothe" (148).

Lambert's philosophy of language links words to things in a relation that is essentially metaphoric, a relation that establishes a similarity where differences are evident. For him, differences are superficial; similarity, essential. Later in life, he works out a metaphysics based on the same principle. In the concluding chapters he appears to have crossed over entirely into the sphere of pure thought. Transfixed in cataleptic stillness, he nevertheless occasionally speaks. His fiancée, Pauline de Villenoix, writes down what he says, producing two sets of metaphysical fragments. Each set begins with the same construction: "Everything here on earth [*ici-bas*] is produced by an ethereal Substance" and "Everything on earth [*ici-bas*] exits solely by Motion [*le Mouvement*] and Number" (249, 255). At stake is the explanation for everything, an explanation that functions therefore through the reduction of variety to unity. Instincts are products of the will, passions are actually electricity, colors are light, sounds are air, until finally the universe in its variety becomes Movement and Number, where—significantly—Movement emerges as still more primordial. Lambert proceeds from one term to the next by establishing equivalences between them. These equivalences once again function like metaphors; one term—the deeper, truer expression of reality, the cause, the first principle—always subsuming the more profane other as its inferior synonym.

Strikingly, Lambert's fate and character display a similar predilection for the metaphoric construction of identities. As a child, he possesses an extraordinary memory that allows him not only to recall any object at will but also to see it in his mind, situated and lit just as he had originally seen it (149). Recollection introduces no further distance vis-à-vis perception. To recall is the same as to see the actual thing. His imagination is apparently capable of a similar feat: "the image [of objects] stamped on his mind could not have been clearer if he had actually seen them, whether this was by process of analogy or that he was gifted with a sort of second sight by which he could command all nature" (150). Here, too, absolute identity is established between mental processes and sensations.

In short, Louis is a veritable mechanism for overcoming distance and mediation, for collapsing distinctions and assimilating differences. But it is this very tendency, this dubious gift, that drives him toward what "ici-bas" must be considered a tragic end. First, it is surely in light of the drive to collapse distinctions and overcome distances that his attempted self-castration should be understood. In his view, the main condition for union with his fiancée is a kind of preexisting and unmediated identity. What he does not want to do, what induces unbearable anxiety in him, is to have to interpret her words, gestures, facial expressions. Interpretation is already the result of distance. Castration is a symbolic act eliminating the difference between them. She is a woman and she is pure—these are her two most pronounced features in the novel. Thus, by following Origen's example, Louis can hope to become one with his Pauline—a oneness as paradoxically erotic as it is mystical.

Still more decisively, the drive to identity is responsible for the manner in which he ends his life. His paralysis and eventual death appear to enact his favorite formula, reversing the direction of the teaching of St. John, "And the Word became flesh" (John 1:14). Indeed, *Et Verbum caro factum est*—Lambert's dream that flesh will one day become the Word is apparently realized at least in his own person. "The life of the soul has perhaps subdued that of the body," says the narrator, confronted with the mortal, still breathing husk of his old friend (247). And if it is true, as Felix Davin claims in his introduction to the first edition of *Études philosophiques,* that *Louis Lambert* shows how the thought can kill the thinker (329), it is specifically in the sense that the thinker can become the thought and thus cease to exist physically.

Rhetorically and, as we shall see, narratologically, Louis Lambert's life and thought are dominated by the workings of the veridictory metaphor.[27] Truth is approached through a process of establishing similarities where only differences are initially visible: between cause and effect, woman and man, word and flesh. But similarities alone are not enough; there is a further sense that one of the terms is anterior and superior to the other, that truthful discourse must ultimately proceed by way of subsumption: the flesh in the word, the man in the woman, the effect in the cause, and all worldly phenomena in movement.

Poète: Metonymic Exigencies of Modernity

Thus far we have dealt with the philosopher, with the veridictory style of Louis Lambert. But to what extent does the narrator himself, as Lambert's biographer, assimilate this style? Is the poet indeed the philosopher's disciple? Are the two actually inseparable?

Throughout the narrative, the "philosophical" Lambertian elements of style are evident. More generally, of course, the desire to establish a close link between various effects and their causes is the impulse behind the conception of *Études philosophiques*. But in *Louis Lambert* perhaps more than anywhere else, the placement of effects back into the domain of causes is at stake. The story is told under the pressure of the demand that causes be directly perceivable in the effects.

It is in this metaphorical mode that Lambert's personality, his actions, his writings become objects for the narrator's interpretation. The narrator constantly inquires into the deeper meaning, the truth, behind details, events, and words. Frequently, the deeper meaning behind a description is inserted directly into a sentence in the form of a modifier: "the distinction of his prophetic brow" (162). More frequently still, the hidden cause is revealed in a direct statement, which often altogether obviates the mention of the actual effect or the detail that signifies: "His countenance, which was full of expression, revealed his sweet nature" (199). Finally, at times a detail's real significance lurks in the motiflike consistency with which it is invoked at various points in the narrative. We learn, for example, that white is the color of angels, and so the whiteness of Lambert's skin at the end of his life begins to signify the victory of the angelic in him over the animal.

Peter Brooks has argued that the metaphoric impulse, probing the surfaces of reality to reach the depths of signification, is felt as much in the *Études de moeurs* as in the *Études philosophiques*.[28] But in *Louis Lambert* the metaphor is all too often turned upside down, as it were, presenting the hidden term immediately, bypassing outer appearance altogether. The probing of the surfaces of reality achieves such intensity here that the hidden essence rises to the surface, overwhelming the representation of physical detail. The veridictory metaphor obviates the particular, renders it invisible under ontologically primary universals. We don't know anything about Lambert's brow but that it is prophetic. His face, however it might actually look, reflects the deeper reality of the goodness of his character. What are the consequences of this sort of metaphor-heavy representation for narrative?

To be sure, story in Balzac tends to function as a link between the top and the bottom terms of the veridictory metaphor. Something appears to us, demands explanation: the sad demeanor of Josephine Claës in *La Recherche de l'absolu*, the wealth of de Lanty in *Sarrasine*, the mysterious visitors received by Père Goriot, the suicidal intentions of Raphael de Valentin in *La Peau de chagrin*. Next comes the story that contextualizes the isolated enigmatic descriptions, presenting us with the whole (narrative) truth beneath mere appearance. But what happens when, as in *Louis Lambert*, the narrator pressures the surface of appearances so resolutely that the surface actually yields to the depths, that description becomes immediately translatable into concepts? When the metaphor collapses, is the story still needed? Is it still possible?

One is tempted to reply in the negative. But in *Louis Lambert* we do have a story, and quite a traditional one, it would seem, a biography. What is it then that makes it possible? Most immediately, it is the biographer's reconstruction. The Poet compensates for the Philosopher's iconic incoherence and ultimate silence. Almost everything we hear of his philosophy has gone through the biographer's mediating reconstruction. Even his letters to Pauline and his uncle stand in need of deciphering. They, too, tend toward iconic representation, become hieroglyphs (once again) of a stenography invented by the impatience of his passion. The narrator is called upon to restore their meaning (222).

What we get in the end is thus, most directly, the result not of the Philosopher's genius but of the narrator's patience. In fact, there is something paradoxical about the Philosopher writing at all. Schoolmates give Louis his mocking nickname because he is silent. The writer, on the other hand, is framed as inadequate: his poetry is simply bad (160). In this conception, there is something about philosophy that induces it, in the end, to silence and requires that somebody else, the poet, speak for it. There is something about writing, conversely, that makes it always in some sense bad writing insofar as it is never adequate to the philosopher's profound tranquility.

Inadequate indeed, for along with unambiguous examples of the narrator's metaphoric drive to make appearances yield their truths, we discover, in his writing, a number of instances when this tendency is complicated and even subverted. At times the narrator seems to vacillate, not knowing what has caused a particular effect. Trying to pinpoint the source of Lambert's extraordinary imagination, the biographer wonders, for example, whether the vividness of his mental images was due to the power of analogy or to second sight (150). He doubts also whether Lambert's precocious development was caused by a disease or a perfection of his organs (203). This vacillation between two codes, between the metaphysically fabulous and the physiologically profane, renders him incapable of performing the ultimate Lambertian task of folding effects back onto causes and marks him as belonging, at least in part, to the fallen world of criticism and doubt.

In an 1830 review of Frederic Ancillon's "Essai sur la science et sur la foi philosophiques," Balzac makes the standard Saint-Simonist distinction between organic and critical epochs in the history of humanity. The present age is one dominated by individualism and reason. Here, the circle of firm belief and systematic thinking has been broken, "the thought marches in freedom . . . , a man cannot receive the law from the intelligence of his fellow man except through proof or science."[29] Living in the midst of this epoch, the poet is compelled to make concessions to skepticism. To a lesser extent, this is also true of his philosophical double. In fact, just as it is possible to attribute elements of what we have called "the philosophical style" to the narrator, so, under certain circumstances, the philosopher appears to us as more of a poet. It is important, in other words, not to hypostasize the stylistic and narrative functions "Poète" and "Pythagore" by attaching them definitively to particular characters. The significance of the appellation itself lies precisely in the difficulty of disentangling one from the other. It appears, moreover, that one tendency or the other may be activated as much by the specific field of representation confronting the novel as with the "character zones" of Lambert and the biographer.[30]

Thus, one of the occasions on which Lambert is referred to as a poet is particularly marked. It immediately precedes the only fragment of the novel authored by Lambert that is presented to us directly, without the narrator's reconstruction. This is Lambert's letter from Paris to his uncle. Unlike the majority of his intellectual endeavors, this one focuses on depicting the triumph of effect over cause, matter over spirit. The *poet* Lambert, confronted with Paris, is no longer able to perform the sublating operations of which he is capable as a philosopher. The veridictory metaphor breaks down against the profoundly unphilosophical dynamism of the city. Examining it, he reaches melancholy conclusions and begins, perhaps for the first time in his life, to doubt. He complains about the dominance of money, the overabundance of harmful external (most dangerous, sexual) stimuli, the lack of unity in scientific work, division everywhere, the reign of the moment, the anarchy of social factions. "The activity of the universe," he writes, "is not absurd; it must tend to an end, and that end is surely not a social body constituted as ours is!" (214).

The experience of modern Parisian society makes Lambert doubt even the supreme principle of historical continuity. Compare the earlier passages on the history of language to the following ruminations: "No development of politics has hindered civilization . . . from moving from Memphis to Tyre to Baalbek, from Tadmor to Carthage, from Carthage to Rome, from Rome to Constantinople, from Constantinople to Venice, from Venice to Spain, from Spain to England—while no trace is left of Memphis, of Tyre, of Carthage, of Rome, of Venice, or Madrid" (211). Nothing is permanent, no civilization lasts. Worse, the movement from one civilization to the next does not in the least resemble the continuous progression from Greece and Rome to modernity or from primordial sensation to written eloquence. It is rather a series of leaps, a disjunctive movement, resembling less Geoffroy's conception of continuous development than his opponent Cuvier's "catastrophism." In the course of this movement, the past is not preserved in the present but is decisively annihilated. It is here that he formulates one of his most memorable axioms: "When the effect produced ceases to be in [relation] to its cause, disorganization follows" (211).

What then are the causes of the terrible disorganization that makes Lambert doubt the applicability of his veridictory metaphor to history? Is it not perhaps history itself? In his 1830 "Satirical Complaints About the Mores of the Present Times," Balzac writes: "We don't have mores if by that word we understand the habits specific to a people, a physiognomy of a nation. We draw our clothes from the Revolution, our boots from the Empire, our carriages from England, our cooking from the Restoration."[31] Confusion, division, and disorganization result from a condensation of a series of apparently radical historical breaks into the short time span of forty years: Revolution, Empire, Restoration, Immigration—the present is filled with disjointed shards of the past. What can we say about proper social organization, complains Louis Lambert, when governments supposedly derived directly from God have perished, when the rule of aristocracy is past and the power of priesthood is disappearing, when the monarchy is dying and democracy has turned out to be a lie? History, and, specifically, history conceived as chaotic, disjointed, meaningless change, in the course of which effects are severed from their causes—this is precisely what produces the kind of Babelian disorganization that so distresses Balzac's metaphysician. And Balzac himself: "It is high time however for a comic poet to arrive and put things in their place, and bring order to this tower of Babel-like language which we have been speaking for the past fifteen years."[32] No longer do we have a single Language, persisting in all the diverse languages of the nations. Rather, a single nation is torn apart by an irreducible multiplicity of languages.

Louis Lambert's metaphoric truth discourse shuts down when confronted with Parisian life in the times when, to invoke Balzac's review of Ancillon's essay once again, "the true mingles with the absurd, and the work of progress is latent in the labor of destruction."[33] In what is probably the most striking and the densest description of Paris in Balzac's oeuvre, the opening chapter of *La Fille aux yeaux d'or* (1835), the city is represented as first and foremost uncontrollably fast moving. In Paris feelings fail to withstand the frantic movement of the current of life: love is turned into desire and hatred into whim. The city is ceaselessly in motion, its dwellers are devastated, broken by the swiftness of the pace; they must "devour time, hasten time, find more than four-and-twenty hours in the day and night, waste themselves, slay themselves."[34] "Time is their tyrant: it fails them, it escapes them; they can neither expand it nor cut it short."[35] Again, it is the accelerated time of modern city life, the kind of time that can accommodate only whims and desires, but never weighty, lasting feelings and eternal truths. Paris is the city from which Charles Grandet writes to the ever-faithful Eugénie: "I know from my own experience that nothing resists the passage of time."[36] Paris is the place where old Baron Hulot's desire shifts freely and with grotesque insatiability from Joséjpha to Mme Marneffe, to Olympe, to Atala, to Agathe, all along avoiding its only legitimate and true object, his all-suffering wife.

Philosophical time and the time of modernity, then, emerge as differently structured. One is organic, continuous, and, insofar as the past persists in the present, conservative; the other is critical, catastrophist, and, insofar as the link between cause (the past) and effect (the present) is broken, disorganized and revolutionary. And once again, in tropological terms, if philosophical time is metaphoric, connecting moment to moment in similarity, then the accelerated time of modernity is metonymic, with one event linking up to the other through mere contiguity. Thus, Pythagoras and the Poet each contribute what Roman Jakobson would have called a constitutive axis of narrative.[37] Similarity, repetition, continuity, subsumption—the complete triumph of one would give us a kind of cataleptic silence, the silence of the Absolute, achieved in ecstasy or madness by a number of Balzac's seekers and of course by Louis Lambert himself. Contiguity, catastrophism, seriality, elusion—the purification of the other would produce paratactic incoherence. Instead of pure *rêverie* or pure *mouvement*, we have an intimate alliance between them, producing the specific overall structure of *Louis Lambert*.

Poète-et-Pythagore: Simultaneity

What is this overall structure? At first glance, the novel appears to be a rather straightforward biography, invoking the movement of a kind of Hegelian *Bildungsroman*, dividing Louis Lambert's life into three phases, three distinct modes of relating to the world. As if to reinforce this expectation, the biographer casts himself as occupying the place of the *for-us,* a kind of mature immobility from which the entire progression can be traced as a whole. Thus: "it was time alone that initiated me into the meaning of the events and facts that were crowded into that obscure life." And: "my memory is now able to coordinate them" (164). With the passage of time, from the place of retrospection events are connected into a whole, facts are made available to meaning, revealing their truth.

Still, it soon becomes clear that nothing like the Hegelian triad is here being offered. The first stage of Lambert's development, we are told, consists in learning to reduce things to their simplest expression and to study them in their essence. In this, Lambert is precocious: what other thinkers achieve after years of painstaking study, he possesses to begin with. The next stage is precipitated by Lambert's unhappiness at school. Here, the biographer perceives "the struggle of the Mind reacting on itself, and trying to detect the secrets of its own nature" (204). The period of self-reflection is followed by the third phase, during which the philosopher encounters Paris and recoils in horror. His experiences there seem to impel him toward a lifestyle of ascetic ecstasy, a temptation, comments his biographer, of all noble souls during periods of social upheaval and renewal.

Instantly evident, then, is precisely the nonprogressive nature of Lambert's life. If anything, his life appears to proceed backward or, at it were, inward. He begins with an uncanny ability to perceive essences, is pushed further upon himself in self-reflection and, finally, further still into mystical ecstasy. There is no talk here of Hegelian maturity wherein the outer world would finally present itself to the hero as a friendly medium for his activity. Quite to the contrary: Paris appears to Lambert in a shape so alien to him that all he can do is flee. This failure echoes through the remainder of the novel in his failure to actualize his love for Pauline. A paradigmatic corollary of successful *Bildung,* marriage likewise turns out to be impossible for Lambert, and his eventual madness or ecstasy forecloses the possibility that his development might resume in a spiral narrative movement. In the end, the world is left altogether behind; Lambert transcends his humanity to ventriloquize pure abstractions from the Beyond.

What would be an adequate narrative form for a life such as this? Or, in other words—and here we come to the crucial question—what would be the adequate narrative form for a story told about (and from the perspective of) someone whose fate and thought are dominated by the veridictory metaphor? As it turns out, it is a form we have already glimpsed. Let us briefly review some of the novel's most prominent organizing principles.

First, we notice that philosophical passages constantly interrupt biographical ones. The narrator excuses himself: "Already in spite of myself I have reversed the order in which I ought to tell the history of this man, who transferred all his activities to thinking, as others throw all their life into action" (150). The biographer is caught in a mimetic relationship with his subject. In an attempt to remain faithful to the logic of his friend's life, he must repeatedly interrupt his account of it with philosophical interpolations. He must not just tell Lambert's story but give reasons, reestablish connections between causes and effects, even at the expense of chronology. If a particular theory that Lambert develops later in his life can illuminate an event that occurs earlier, the narrator does not hesitate to insert it. Veridictory considerations interfere with biographical ones. The passage of time, while preserved as the organizing principle of the whole (the movement from the hero's birth to his death), is locally spurned again and again.

Further, this fragmentary character of the novel is complemented by an obvious generic multiplicity. Here we have a biography, a Balzacian-realist description of the college of Vendôme, a retelling of Swedenborg's theories and of Lambert's own unfinished *Treatise on the Will,* which itself consists of numerous anecdotes; a meditation on the stages of Lambert's life; two sets of letters, one in the form of a journal, containing a description and analysis of Parisian life, the other a fragment of an epistolary romance; and finally two sets of Lambert's philosophical fragments, written down by Pauline.

All of this adds up to what we have referred to, in the discussion of Friedrich Schlegel's *Lucinde* and the Romantic novel, as the structure of simultaneity. And if we remember that the characterological corollary of this structure consists in Lambert's progressive withdrawal into the self, then Hegel's earlier cited words about the predilection of Romantic theory for "absolutely empty forms, which originate from the absoluteness of the abstract ego" would appear to be relevant as well. The metaphoric "Pythagorean" ascendancy over metonymic ("Poetic") progression produces a narrative dominated by what Balzac would call *rêverie,* the ability, in the words of Schlegel's hero, to "look and delight in everything at the same time."[38] The truth drive of the Philosopher, who hopes to do just that, misshapes, breaks up the narrative of the tale told by the Poet. The biographer who imitates the philosopher tells a story that fails to add up to a coherent temporal progression, a story transfixed and fractured by the veridictory metaphor into generic and narrative fragments. Rather than leave temporal succession to falsehood or subordinate it to exemplarity in the manner of earlier narratives, veridiction awkwardly attempts to graft itself onto temporal succession and fractures it in the process. This fracturing can be read as a sign of an appreciation for the difficulty of having things both ways— of telling the story step-by-step and grasping it all at once. Read in this way, *Louis Lambert* would join *Lucinde* as a kind of *sentimental*, that is, self-critical romance, honestly displaying the formal consequences for narrative of the ascendancy of metaphor at the service of identity and subjective withdrawal.

The Veridictory Fragment

The Romanticism of *Louis Lambert* can be characterized as sentimental in large part due to its knowledge of itself as merely subjective. The dominance of the veridictory metaphor, the valorization of unity and totality, the philosophical pretensions—nothing can cover up (in fact, everything betrays) the gaps in the biographer's knowledge of his subject or the difficulties of casting the philosopher's life into a coherent whole. The novel breaks up into fragments under the double pressure of metaphoric veridiction and subjective limitation; *Poète* is inadequate, *Pythagore* is ultimately silent. But if it is somewhat uncanny to encounter a *sentimental* romance among the novels of the *Comédie*, then how much more surprising would it be to discover, at the foundations of the novel that was destined to inaugurate Balzacian realism, a thematics and a structure of romance in its *naïve* instantiation? And yet this is in fact what we find in *La Peau de chagrin*.

In a curious passage in *Louis Lambert*, Balzac renders the connection between these two novels explicit: "It was in memory of the disaster that befell Louis' book that, in the tale which comes first in these Études, I adopted the title invented by Lambert for a work of fiction, and gave the name of a woman who was dear to him to a girl characterized by her self-devotion; but this is not all I have borrowed from him: his character and occupations were of great value to me in writing that book, and the subject arose from some reminiscences of our youthful meditations" (183–84). This gesture obviously anticipates the project of the *Comédie humaine*, the celebrated *retour des personages*.

But the novels of the *Comédie* are usually linked up on the same fictional plane. In *Illusions perdues,* for example, Louis Lambert's death is mourned by his friends, the true geniuses of their age.[39] The philosopher, it is implied, lived and worked among them during his brief stay in Paris. In *Louis Lambert,* however, something more is taking place. The events depicted in the philosophical novel are presented as possessing a higher ontological status, as somehow more "real" than the fictional events depicted in other novels. Not only more real, though, but also causally prior. The relationship between *Louis Lambert* and the rest of the *Études* (especially *La Peau de chagrin*) is once again metaphoric, metaphoric moreover in just the way in which the veridictory metaphor functions in *Louis Lambert* itself: the real, the original, the essential rises up from the bottom to the surface of what is merely secondary, apparent, or, in this particular case, fictional. I would argue that if *La Peau de chagrin* or, indeed, much of the *Comédie humaine,* is more "fictional" than *Louis Lambert* it is at least in part because the veridictory drive is neutralized in it, allowing for the narrative to proceed more smoothly. Neutralized, or perhaps honed, perfected—we will return to this shortly.

For now it is crucial not to overlook another, a complementary, interpretation. According to it, the fragmentary structure of *Louis Lambert* is also a testimony to its self-consciousness as a narrative from a limited point of view. No biography, no "life," is ever complete; it can never be told to the full, its narration is always a matter of an arrangement of fragments. It is due to this honesty then that the later novel is not merely "truer" (on the plane of veridiction) but also more "realistic" (on the plane of verisimilitude) than its earlier counterpart.

La Peau de chagrin, then, is fictional twice over. And yet there is little doubt that, with its unified plot, objective narrator, and thematic preoccupations, it bears a much more striking resemblance to what we have come to know as "the realist novel" than does the more realistic *Louis Lambert*. And this despite the significantly less skeptical stance of its narrator. Lambert's biographer, we recall, equivocates throughout between the materialistic and the mystical, and even at the end refuses to take sides on the question of whether his friend has simply gone mad or is communing with the angels. The narrator of *La Peau de chagrin* on the other hand appears to have no doubts as to the miraculous powers of its focal object, the magic skin. The novel is not merely shot through with mystical yearnings and forebodings, it is constructed upon the core premise of explicit and undeniable magic. What do we make, then, of the persistent temptation to think of this novel—by many accounts the first fully realized novel Balzac wrote[40]—as inaugurating nineteenth-century novelistic (and of course, especially, Balzacian) realism? How do we understand its ambiguous literary-historical position as a naïve romance, apparently lacking even the minimal skepticism of *Louis Lambert,* and at the same time as a direct forebear, if not one of the earliest representatives, of the realist novel?

It will not come as a surprise that answers to these questions bear directly on what we have referred to as the veridictory mutation of the novel. And so, to begin with, it would be useful to inquire into the conception of truth implicit in the narrative of the novel here at issue.

Our first encounter with truth discourse in *La Peau de chagrin* will be familiar in structure to readers of *Louis Lambert.* The hero enters a gambling house and is asked to give up his hat. The narrator wonders why. In the words of Peter Brooks, "the narrator [pressures] the surface of reality . . . in order to make it yield the full, true terms of his story."[41] Metaphoric veridiction is at work once again. Thus, the little old man who takes Raphael's hat casts on him a dull glance "in which a philosopher might have seen wretchedness lying in the hospital, the vagrant lives of ruined folk, inquests on numberless suicides, life-long penal servitude and transportations to Guazacoalco."[42] A philosopher sees through surfaces; and what he sees there, in the eyes of an old man, is suffering on a mass scale. Images of grand agony break through and overwhelm the apparent meaninglessness of a chance look of dull eyes. Mere appearance is singular, static, and dull; the hidden truth is multiple, dynamic, and sublime.

So far then, what we see conforms to the veridictory principles derived from *Louis Lambert.* Metaphor is still the trope of truth, and that to which metaphor gives voice, the hidden, still threatens to fracture the surface of the narrative. But not far into the novel, as we follow forlorn, suicidal Raphael into an antiques shop, we encounter a conception of truth that is, at least at first glance, new. The locus of this truth is the shop itself. Here, there is everything: every epoch, every civilization, every possible human experience appears simultaneously in this wonder cabinet with a multilayered, labyrinthine topography. Ancient Greece, imperial Rome, Christian Rome, India, China, the Renaissance—every facet of humanity finds its place in the store, represented by various artifacts: paintings, sculptures, furniture, scrolls, even ruins.

The ancient shopkeeper comments: "What are all the disasters that wait on your erratic whims, compared with the magnificent power of conjuring up the whole world within your soul, compared with the immeasurable joys of movement unstrangled by the cords of time, unclogged by the fetters of space; the joys of beholding all things, of comprehending all things, of leaning over the parapet of the world to question the other spheres, to hearken to the voice of God?" (31). True knowledge and true pleasure lie beyond desire. Desire brings with it disasters, but pure contemplation of the whole is a pleasure as delightful as it is harmless and conducive to a long life. What can compare to the pleasure of movement outside time and space, the sort of movement that allows one to be everywhere at once, to behold and embrace in thought the entirety of the world. But these pleasures are given only to those who have managed to escape the relentless trajectory of desire (*vouloir*) and satisfaction (*pouvoir*). Only then will knowledge of the whole be possible.

This conception of knowledge may indeed appear unfamiliar, but only at first glance. In fact the totality of the antiques shop is constituted in a manner that readers of *Louis Lambert* should find recognizable. The Whole is not there as such; rather, it is represented synecdochally by shards, souvenirs, relics, remnants. That which serves as a structuring principle in the philosopher's biography appears as an allegory in *La Peau de chagrin*. Once again, the Jena Romantics come to mind, this time for their theorization of the genre of the fragment: "The feeling for projects—which one might call fragments of the future—is distinguishable from the feeling for fragments of the past only by its direction: progressive in the former, regressive in the latter. What is essential is to be able to idealize and realize objects *immediately and simultaneously*: to complete them and in part carry them out within oneself."[43]

The fragment then is paradoxically the immediate and simultaneous co-presence of the future and the past; it is time collapsed into an instant. But it is also, of course, the whole, collapsed into a part. Thus, "a fragment, like a miniature work of art, has to be entirely isolated from the surrounding world and be complete in itself like a porcupine."[44] Lacoue-Labarthe and Nancy provide a gloss: "Fragmentary totality, in keeping with what should be called the logic of [the porcupine], cannot be situated in any single point: it is simultaneously in the whole and in each part."[45] Again: "simultaneously." Parts don't come together into a mechanical whole; they contain the whole immediately. Each part is itself part and whole, pointing to the whole beyond it—the whole whose fragment it is—and thus, paradoxically, revealing its own incompleteness.

What is necessary for the fragment to stand for the whole is precisely what accounts for its form, namely, the weakening of contextual relations with other parts of the whole. The fragment is essentially *decontextualized*. Its relation to other fragments is one of structural equivalence rather than contiguity. This is indeed what we have seen on the formal level in *Louis Lambert*. There, fragmentary structure was precisely the consequence of metaphoric domination;

but it was also—very much in tune with the Romantic theory of the fragment—a sign of imperfection, an index of a limited point of view. In *La Peau de chagrin,* this conception of truth as an instantaneous, timeless whole reappears in allegorical form. The narrative shape of the novel itself is relatively free from fragmentation, and there is little evidence of the narrator's limitations. And yet here, too, this simultaneous whole undergoes an ironic twist. Raphael leaves in possession of the magic skin, one of the fragments on display in the shop. The magic skin will fulfill his every desire at the expense of his life: the greater the fulfilled desire the more time is subtracted from Raphael's total lifespan. Stepping out the door, he wishes that the old man fall in love with an opera dancer and spend all of his (and thus, in a sense, the world's) riches on her. Toward the end of the novel, Raphael indeed encounters the old shopkeeper arm-in-arm with a young courtesan. The old man is happy. He produces a new maxim, which sounds like a parody of his one-time organic wisdom: "One hour of love has a whole life in it" (165). Thus, the whole leaks through one of its parts. The absolute, timeless, imperturbable subject of synthesis falls into the devastating stream of desire and satisfaction; knowledge itself is now at the service of the ravenous will.

The old antiques dealer has been seen as a fictional incarnation of the all-knowing Balzacian narrator, and in this respect he merits comparison with the still more monumental figure of the usurer Gobseck, who brags that his gaze is like God's. Like Gobseck, the shopkeeper remains motionless as human passions parade before him in a kind of total spectacle. Like Gobseck, he represents the perspective from which the whole can be seen. They are both subjects of synthesis, both attempting to take hold of the totality of existence all at once. And, ultimately, both fail through similar mechanisms. Obeying Raphael's now imperious command, the antiques dealer succumbs to desire and, powdered and painted next to his young lover, switches codes from the oracular to the grotesque, and is himself rendered antiquated. Gobseck dies, and we are presented with a revolting picture of decomposition among some of his hoarded possessions, complete with swarming insects and maggots. They succumb then to the very power they hope to contain, the power of time. The antiques dealer, ageless and, indeed, immortal amidst his sacred fragments, finally bends under the weight of his age next to the young courtesan. As for Gobseck, not only are we presented upon his death with a vivid picture of putrification, but his fortune itself arrives *too late,* in *Splendeurs et misères des courtisanes,* to save the star-crossed Esther and Lucien from suicide.

Thus, even the demigods of the *Comédie* must eventually grapple with time, and if the formula holds and the true in Balzac is indeed the whole, this whole cannot ultimately be conceived as one of fragmentary simultaneity. In other words, while it is important to recognize essential continuity in the passing of the figural baton, the transition from the figure of the antiques shop to that of the magic skin, we must also keep in mind that, as the narrative proceeds, the former fades away, yielding precedence to the latter. Simultaneously, the all-embracing ontological and world-historical Whole of the shop gives way to its schematized version as *biographical* whole, the totality of a single life.

The Time of a Wager

Raphael is brought up by his father in strict discipline. Installed in a room next to his father's study, he has to rise at five o'clock in the morning and go to bed before nine. All of his time is supposed to be spent in study. At dinner, he is expected to give a strict account of his doings. "To have swerved from the straight course which my father had mapped out for me," he says, "would have drawn down his wrath upon me; at my first delinquency, he threatened to ship me off as a cabin boy to the Antilles" (64). But what is the nature of this *route uniforme*? Raphael does not find out until later. At twenty, he has only a meager allowance, no mistress, a very limited knowledge of worldly conventions. He lives day-to-day, relying entirely on his father's benevolent authority, until, one evening, he transgresses against it.

That evening, at a ball, M. de Valentin dumbfounds his son by handing him his purse and keys and disappearing into the crowd. The gambling table in the adjacent room tempts Raphael. He takes two twenty-franc pieces out of the purse, wagers them, and wins. It is worth lingering here on two curious observations framing the episode of the wager. First, before placing the two twenty-franc pieces on the table, Raphael notices that the dates on the coins have been erased. Only Napoleon's simpering face remains on them. Then, once he has staked the money, Raphael walks away from the table and stands with his back to it. Here, he realizes that somehow, "by a gift accorded to the passions which enables them to annihilate time and space" he is able to see and hear everything that takes place on the table (66). This, he says, is the first observation of a physiological kind, to which he owes insight into certain mysteries of human nature.

This second observation framing the moment of Raphael's transgression is common to the concerns of *Études philosophiques*. It is a matter of immediate spiritual insight, with the help of which Louis Lambert appears to have seen the Château de Rochambeau in his dream the night before he was actually able to visit it, the same insight that enables Mme De Dey (in "Le Réquisitionnaire") to die at the very hour when her son is shot far away from (and unbeknownst to) her. What is particularly important here for us is the extratemporal and nonspatial character of this knowledge. It is essentially a leap over time and space that, under usual circumstances, must be traversed moment-by-moment and step-by-step.

The first observation, apparently unrelated to the second one, contains nevertheless a related element. Here too time is annihilated, but in this instance it is historical time. The date on the coin has been worn off to invisibility: historical time has been suspended or, more properly—taking account of Napoleon's significance for Balzac as a figure of energy—time has been overleapt. The appearance of Napoleon here bears yet another import. It is to him, to the period of the Empire, that M. de Valentin owes his fortune. His financial troubles begin with the emperor's downfall; he never recovers from them and passes them onto his son. We might say, then, that Raphael is ruined by accelerated historical change, which reverberates in the lives of individuals with dramatic rises in fortune and tragic reversals. It is in the shadow of this historical shape that Raphael is condemned to live out his life.

His wager, then, can be understood as an act of mimicry, imitating history's impulsive bounds in hopes of gaining everything, trembling at the thought of losing what he has. Still, why is gambling in the end *the* transgression for Raphael? The framing images provide a hint. As a disruption of the retarded course he had been forced to follow by his father, gambling represents the temporal mode diametrically opposed to the one in the shadow of which Raphael has been forced to live. Not surprisingly, then, it is associated with an attempt, at last, to envision a future: himself "well dressed, in a carriage, with a pretty woman by my side, playing the great lord" (65).

More than to envision, in fact, but to force. And, in a certain sense, this forcing proves to be successful. Up until the day of the forbidden wager, Raphael must leave the care of his future to his father. But that very night, convinced that his son has resisted the temptation of staking the money and has thus withstood the ordeal, M. de Valentin suddenly promotes him to the position of his associate and friend. In accordance with this position, Raphael must learn what it was his father has all along been preparing him for (the career of a statesman). Moreover, he now finds out exactly how his life fits into the larger historical context. The story of the ups and downs of his father's life, rising and falling with the changing political circumstances in the country, becomes available to him at last. He understands who he is and comes to embrace his responsibilities, redoubling his efforts at work in an attempt to rescue his family fortune.

Raphael's little *Bildungsroman* is now complete: he understands that his entire past has not been in vain, that all along he has been blindly working toward the goal he now sees clearly and accepts as his own: "But lately I would have stolen a paltry sum from [my father] with secret delight; but now that I shared the burden of his affairs, of his name and of his house, I would secretly have given up my fortune and my hopes for him, as I was sacrificing my pleasures, and even have been glad of the sacrifice!" (69).

Louis Lambert finds it difficult or, rather, perhaps unnecessary (dishonest?) to present us with the kind of progression that would be redeemable to truth. What we have instead is, as we have seen, fragmentation in which simultaneous grasp of the timeless whole is ironized by a presentation of the obviously limited perspective of the one who grasps. *La Peau de chagrin* introduces the problem of time and appears to demand that the whole be conceived of not in simultaneity but in succession. Thus, it is only here that the formula identifying the true with the whole acquires a properly Hegelian import and brings with it the possibility of the Hegelian genre, the *Bildungsroman*.

But a troubling question remains. How is it that step-by-step progression reaches the point at which retrospection can begin? Something like Zeno's paradox is operative here: covering distance in parts, it appears that one never reaches one's goal. And indeed, Raphael's transition from childhood to manhood is sudden and precipitated by his wager, which is itself a figure less for progress than for a leap: from a coin to a fortune, from part to whole, from the present and into the future. A gap opens up between progression and retrospection, between time and truth—a gap that cannot be bridged but must be overleapt. In the microcosmic narrative of Raphael's upbringing, this feat is accomplished by means of a wager.[46] And insofar as we can read the gambling incident as assimilating the historical trajectory of acceleration, that acceleration itself would be revealed as something like a historical condition for the possibility of the suturing of time to truth.

Foedora, *Fabula*

But let us step back from this early sequence and look at the structure of the novel globally. *La Peau de chagrin* starts off as an enigma, at the moment when despairing Raphael enters the gaming house, loses his last remaining money and is about to commit suicide. "What is it that explains the hero's despair?" we are meant to inquire. The explanation is deferred. Raphael decides to postpone the hour of his death until dark and enters the antiques shop, where he acquires the magic skin, capable of satisfying his every wish at the price of shortening his life. On leaving the shop he meets his friends, who are just then looking for him and who take him to a party during which he tells his story to one of them from the beginning. It is here, in the section entitled "La Femme Sans Coeur," that we finally learn the reason behind the pitiful condition in which we find him at the start of the novel. The movement of the narrative is suspended while Raphael provides a chronological account of the events leading up to his decision to commit suicide. He begins: "Perhaps it is an effect of the fumes of the punch—I really cannot tell—this clearness of mind that enables me *to comprise my whole life in a single picture*. . . . Seen from afar my life appears to contract by some mental process. That long, slow agony of ten years' duration can be brought to memory today in some few phrases, in which pain is resolved into a mere idea, and pleasure becomes a philosophical reflection" (63, emphasis added). The relation between the first two parts of the novel is analogous to the shape of Raphael's early education: first progression in ignorance, then illumination in an instant. And just as there the transition between the two was precipitated by the wager, so here it coincides with the acquisition of the magic skin. In narratological terms what happens in both cases can be described as emplotment, as a process or procedure whereby *fabula* becomes *sjuzhet*.

The well-known distinction between these two categories of narrative goes back to the early work of Russian Formalists, especially Viktor Shklovsky and Boris Tomashevsky. In its initial articulation, *fabula* was associated with the way "things actually happened" or at least with the chronological or causal organization of events. *Sjuzhet*, in turn, was understood as the manner in which that actual or chronological chain is meaningfully distorted into the shape of a thematically signifying narrative whole. Critics of the early formulation of this dichotomy soon remarked that, to be sure, all narrative is essentially organized, and that, furthermore, the very "actual happening" of events is never free from the meaning-giving energy of *sjuzhet*. It would be more precise then to conceive of *sjuzhet* and *fabula* as poles of narrative organization and to think of all narratives as constituted in some ratio of the two.[47] Thus, the clearness of mind allowing Raphael to embrace his life in an instant as a single picture is a classical instance of the workings of *sjuzhet*, while the long, slow agony of the ten years being embraced designates the difficult path of *fabula*. Raphael's initial appearance in the novel tends narratologically toward *fabula* while his narration of his story is characterized by the retrospective insight of *sjuzhet*.

Truth discourse in *Louis Lambert* appeared to lend itself more easily to analysis in terms of veridictory ("Pythagorean") metaphor and falsifying ("Poetic") metonymy. There, the intrusion of deeper truth into the surface of the narrative transfixed it into fragments whose relations to one another tended toward simultaneity. Ultimately, the whole as the vessel and vehicle of truth was atemporally conceived. It has by now become clear that *La Peau de chagrin* is structured around a different conception of veridiction, one that relies on the construction of the whole *in time*. What becomes relevant narratologically then is not segmentation but emplotment, the becoming *sjuzhet* of *fabula*. Thus, we have traveled a long way—and in fact as long as will be necessary for the purposes of the entire argument of the book—from the initial narratological distinction between discourse and narrative. At least as it appears in Genette's historical poetics, the distinction fails to allow for a conception of truth that would radically rely on temporal sequence—truth as parasitic on narrative alone.[48] We have seen that the distinction is therefore obviated by the logic of the Balzacian novel. Obviated, in the case of the Romantic *Louis Lambert,* in favor of the veridictory metaphor inhabiting and fracturing sequential narrative. This latter dichotomy in turn has now been complemented by one that better accommodates the more radical aspects of Balzac's veridictory poetics in *La Peau de chagrin* and in much of the *Comédie* as a whole: *sjuzhet* and *fabula*.

Returning to the novel, then, the solution to the enigma of Raphael's condition is contained in the story of his involvement with Foedora. But this solution is itself an enigma. The truth behind Raphael's condition is itself in need of a truth. Foedora, "the woman without a heart" who drives him to the brink of death, is constituted for him as a metaphor. "Your beautiful face," he says to her, "is for me a promise of a soul yet more beautiful" (128). Foedora's beautiful appearance promises beautiful essence. But however hard Raphael probes the smooth social polish of her words and actions, searching for signs of true feeling, he discovers nothing. Foedora seems to possess no interiority, "no heart." Driven to despair, Raphael hides in her bedroom and watches her as she is being undressed by her maid, hoping to discover a secret blemish on her body, a material substitute for the mystery she does not appear to possess. He discovers no such blemish, but does not leave entirely unrewarded. Listening to her toss and sigh in her bed, he overhears her exclaim: "Mon Dieu!" This exclamation once again gives Raphael hope that Foedora might be hiding something behind the perfect surface: "The mystery that lurked beneath this fair semblance of womanhood grew afresh; there were so many ways of explaining Foedora, that she became inexplicable. A certain language seemed to flow from between her lips. I put thoughts and feelings into the accidents of her breathing, whether weak or regular, gentle or labored" (124).

Let us keep in mind that Raphael is a philosopher, the author of the *Treatise on the Will,* Louis Lambert's ("more fictional") double. He, too, is a master—and a victim—of the veridictory metaphor. His love for Foedora is also philosophical love, a love of truth. But this love is perpetually frustrated, and soon enough we find out that Foedora's exclamation, too, had little significance. "I was thinking of my stockbroker," she explains, "I had forgotten to tell him to convert my five per cent stock into threes, and the three per cents had fallen during the day" (129). Instead of solid essence—spiritual suffering, earnest hopes, urgent desires—we have once again exasperating fluidity, the ceaseless *mouvement* of the stock market, with which even Foedora herself can hardly keep up. Beneath, behind, beyond, in short, anywhere truth is to be looked for, there is nothing but more of the same, more surfaces and fleeting appearances.

"If only you knew my story!" exclaims Raphael. This, as Raphael's friend Emile points out, is a hackneyed remark. Everyone claims to have suffered as no other ever did. And yet we can now agree with Raphael that his story is indeed a special kind of *story.* Though it possesses all the necessary conditions for a meaningful narrative, it yields no truth. Foedora as flat, uninterpretable surface stands in the way of Raphael's development as a man and a thinker. And Raphael, who seems to be able to look back at his life in a condensed, idealized form, in the mode of *sjuzhet,* nevertheless fails to grasp and hold on to it. His backward emplotment fails him. Just as in the case of the old antiques dealer and Gobseck, *fabula* leaks out, escapes the veridictory grasp of *sjuzhet.*

Pauline, *Sjuzhet*

As it turns out, the aperture through which it escapes is the place in the narrative occupied by the other female character in the novel, Raphael's loyal pupil, the daughter of his landlady, and, ultimately, his true love, Pauline. Pauline is out of focus throughout the central narrative of the novel, which is dedicated instead to Foedora. She is, as it were, too close to notice, always around, always available. She is not the kind of woman, he tells Émile during the narrative of "A Woman Without a Heart," who could bring him the love that is death.

And yet this is precisely what she does. In a playful palm-reading session, Pauline herself foretells Raphael that the woman he marries will kill him.[49] At the moment, both of them are thinking of Foedora, and yet it is in the end Pauline herself who brings about his death: "'What do you want?'" she asks, holding Raphael's lifeless body in her arms, "'He is mine, I have killed him. Did I not foresee how it would be?'" (234).

The story of the heartless woman then is a detour. It is a detour from Pauline (who is already there, living under the same roof with Raphael) by way of Foedora and back to Pauline (now under erasure, a forbidden, death-dealing Pauline). It is also a detour from a *fabula*-like narrative by way of a narrative organized and projected from the end as *sjuzhet* but leaking final veri-diction, and finally back to the *fabula* of an altogether different sort, one that suffocates as it were in the grips of the weightiest *sjuzhet* yet, the deadly contract, the visible contraction of the skin.

Let us go back for a moment to the place in the novel when Raphael's first-person account of his life switches back to third-person narrative. The transition takes place midsentence: "However, I at last found myself alone with a twenty-franc piece; I bethought me then of Rastignac's luck—'Eh, eh!'—Raphael exclaimed, interrupting himself, as he remembered the talisman and drew it from his pocket" (143). Instead of giving the account of his third and final wager, the one, incidentally, with which the novel begins, Raphael remembers the magic skin. Once again we seem to be present at a passing of the baton. The first time it was the magic skin as it were "taking over" for the atemporal, fragmentary whole of the antiques shop. Now, it is at the crucial moment when Raphael's retrospective, *sjuzhet*-tending account links up to the *fabulaic*, forward-looking narrative that follows. How do we make sense of this sudden thematic shift?

We have seen that, in its first instance, gambling represents a leap of impatience, the desire for (and, here, success of) immediate movement from part to whole. An instant fortune in a coin—narratologically this is the figure for *sjuzhet* itself, for the integration of part in the whole. As such it is the very opposite of the paternal injunction of *fabulaic* patience, of step-by-step progression in ignorance of the future. Accompanied with imagery of mystical immediacy and historical acceleration, the first gambling episode was a glorious Napoleonic success, propelling Raphael to instant truth-dealing maturity. The third and last gambling episode, however, fails. And it is not by chance that the only unsuccessful wager in the novel reappears precisely here and in the mode of elision, covered up as it were by the magic skin. Gambling fails precisely when emplotment fails, when questions remain and *fabula* evades *sjuzhet*'s veridictory finalization. Foedora does not yield satisfaction; the end is still not in sight. And for this failure, for the havoc wreaked upon the story of his life by the collapsed metaphor, the insistent *fabula* of Foedora, Raphael is compensated with the dubious gift of the magic skin. If in part two he was unable after all to bring his life together into a whole, the agony of part three will consist in possessing his life as a whole to begin with. In part three we have, on the one hand, a forward progression practically devoid of recapitulation, and, on the other, a progression with an unthinkably clear perception of the workings of the end.

The terror and paralysis that overcome Raphael upon realization that the skin, in shrinking, does indeed enable the immediate transition from desire to satisfaction can be understood as an affect of a particular kind of knowledge. This knowledge is not unlike the one Raphael refers to in beginning the account of his life. It is not unlike, in other words, the knowledge of one's own life story, the retrospective contraction of events into a veridictory sequence, where pain resolves into idea and pleasure into philosophical reflection. And yet the difference is here crucial. The fearful aberration of the skin consists in bestowing this knowledge not retrospectively but immediately, it represents the radical immanence of *sjuzhet* in *fabula,* of truth in time.

If gambling is a violation of the paternal prohibition, if it is an illicit attempt to short-circuit the path from part to whole—a short circuit whose example has been provided by the radical acceleration of historical time itself—then how much more so is the magic skin? In it, *fabulaic* progression, the slow, step-by-step movement of desire and ambition is altogether obviated: desire and satisfaction collapse onto each other, while time—the distance between the two—shrivels up. That the skin contracts, Raphael says, is a paradox: after all, desires are supposed to distend (144). Indeed they do, but he must have forgotten for the moment that the skin does not just represent desire but desire together with satisfaction. Thus, contraction, figuring the shriveling up of time, is just the thing for it to do.

At the beginning of the third part of the novel, Raphael, living in the dark shadow of the magic skin, goes to the opera. Sitting in his box, he observes Foedora. She seems happy at the thought of being the most beautiful woman in the theatre. Then she meets Raphael's eyes and turns pale. He alone is proof against her charms: "The delicious thought, 'I am the most beautiful,' the thought that at all times had soothed every mortification, had turned into a lie" (166). In the very next sentence, another woman walks into the box next to his. From the public's reaction, he knows that she has supplanted Foedora as the greatest beauty in Paris. He resists looking at her for fear of being caught off guard by desire. At last, the two glance at each other, and Raphael recognizes his former pupil Pauline.

In a sense, while Raphael was chasing after Foedora, Pauline was there all along, hidden through her proximity. Her prediction concerning the woman who will be the death of Raphael was taken to invoke Foedora, while it in fact referred to Pauline herself. In the scene at the opera, this logic reaches its natural culmination: Pauline substitutes for Foedora, emerges as her truth. What Foedora has been hiding all along was not some sincere sentiment, some interiority filled with feelings, a beautiful soul behind a beautiful face, but another woman, Pauline. The truth about Foedora does not break out metaphorically but unfolds metonymically, in the workings of plot. In the workings of plot, the *fabulaic* pursuit of Foedora finds its resolution in the *sjuzhet*-forming veridictory discovery of Pauline. Pauline is what Foedora has been hiding "all along."

The Pivotal Genre

Pragmatically, the magic skin effects the transition from the pursuit of Foedora, the evasive object of desire that allegorizes, as we find out in the epilogue, "Parisian Society," to Pauline, a paradigm of provincial and motherly purity and fidelity, a Eugénie Grandet who finds herself in Paris as if by accident. If Foedora, the perfect surface, sustaining desire, is *fabula,* then Pauline—who is there all along, who connects the beginning and the end, who emplots Raphael with her palm reading insight—Pauline does the work of truth-dealing *sjuzhet.* As a figure for the precipitation of *fabula* onto *sjuzhet,* the talisman is a kind of aberration, smuggling completion into temporal movement. *Mouvement* itself becomes *rêverie.*

When in part three of the novel, Raphael visits Planchette, a celebrated professor of mechanics, in hopes of extending the surface of the skin and with it the duration of his life, the scientist gives him a brief lecture on metaphysics: "Everything is movement, thought itself is a movement, upon movement nature is based. . . . If God is eternal be sure that he moves perpetually; perhaps God is movement. That is why movement, like God, is inexplicable, unfathomable, unlimited, incomprehensible, intangible" (185).

We have already heard something like this from Louis Lambert. More important, we have seen that movement is a constant preoccupation of Balzac's fiction: movement as desire, as ambition, as money. In Balzac, everything is indeed movement; movement is God. Specifically, it is the God of the modern world, where, as Balzac complains, every man strives to rise above the condition of his father.[50] Movement is the basis of Parisian life in *La Fille aux yeaux d'or,* in *Illusions perdues,* everywhere in the *Comédie.* But here, it is called upon to do its unfathomable work upon the magic talisman, and, to the scientist's embarrassment, it fails to produce the desired effect. In fact, the very formidable machine bursts at the seams when applied to the skin. How is it that modernity, this unquenchable, intractable, wild movement, the movement that is God and that overwhelms and breaks through everything in the Balzacian universe—how could it fail to distend a piece of onager hide? But once again, what is this hide?

Another scientist, this time a naturalist, tells Raphael of the creature from whose skin the talisman is made: "The rapidity of its movements can only be compared with the flight of birds. . . . In the East he is the king of beasts. Turkish and Persian superstition even credits him. . . . Our myth of the winged horse, our Pegasus had its origins doubtless in these countries where the shepherds could see the onager springing from one rock to another" (182). The talisman arrives in the novel carrying with it a dense aura of romance. Bringing with it visions of the Orient, mysterious origins and magic effects, it instantly transforms Raphael into the hero of a romance, an all-powerful man, distinguishable from the gods only by his mortality.[51] But mortality here is precisely the issue. The talisman's most terrifying gift after all is a premature, illicit vision of his life as a whole. No longer the static whole—beyond *fabula* and desire—of the antiques shop, but the whole that stages the self-overcoming of desire and succession in radical impatience, in the imploded time of *sjuzhet.* It should not come as a surprise then that the skin is associated with something wondrously fast. And it becomes clear as well that the one thing that can resist modernity's movement is denser movement still, *mouvement* so frantic it overshoots itself, its formidable momentum carrying it over into *rêverie.* What *fabulaic* modernity cannot disrupt in Balzac is its own condensation in *sjuzhet.* What scientific "realism" fails to exorcise is romance idealism at its very core.[52]

La Peau de chagrin, then, makes it exceedingly vivid that truth insists in Balzac's narrative not despite but precisely in proportion to the intensity of what Franco Moretti terms its "syntagmatic fascination."[53] Its particular sort of "realism," founded as it is on the metaphysics and narratology of movement, is thus not opposed to but rather implicated in its romance idealism. Perhaps for the very first time in the history of the novel, the accelerated time of modernity provides the proper habitat for truth. And thus the literary-historical paradox of *La Peau de chagrin,* its ambivalent position between naïve romance and realist novel, turns out to provide an exemplary pivot. The Balzacian novel, insofar as it internalizes temporal acceleration, stages the creative, shaping insistence of truth in time and concurrently registers the importation of romance idealism into modernity itself.

2

The Whole and the Untrue: Stendhal's Fragile Veridiction

Comparative Interlude I: *Poète*-ou-*Pythagore* (Balzac)

When Raphael appears to the reader of *La Peau de chagrin* on the verge of committing suicide, the reasons for his despair are hidden. They are hidden in such a way as to tempt us into asking: why? The answer is soon enough provided. The entire part two of the novel, the story of Raphael's involvement with a heartless woman, emerges as the truth of his pitiful condition. In order to get at the truth of the present, we must seek causes in the past. In order to get at the truth of appearance, we must find essence in a well-told story. The way to knowledge lies via the detour of narrative. In Balzac, the poet must come to the aid of the philosopher's silence.

Stendhal's texts give us a sense that truth and narrative coherence stand in a disjunctive relation to each other. Not that the philosopher is forever mute and his truth necessarily instantaneous, but rather that the philosopher is working subversively from within the domain of poetry. Either the poem is pretty or the philosopher has his way with it and it contains some truth.

Early on in *Le Rouge et le noir*, Julien suddenly grows pale. We are not asked to inquire; nothing insists that we treat the incident as an enigma. We move on. Julien asks Mme de Rênal to go up to his room, take a box with a portrait from under his mattress, and bring it to him without opening the box. We follow her to the room; we are given access to her worries, suspicions, conjectures. Her guess is, we know, off the mark. She is jealous; she thinks it is a portrait of Julien's lover. When we find out what the fuss is all about, it is almost by accident, as an aside. The truth is not addressed to us, nor to Mme de Rênal; it is something Julien happens to think: "The portrait of Napoleon, he said to himself, shaking his head; and found on a man who professes such hatred for the usurper!"[1]

On the diegetic level, a series of actions is set into motion in order to conceal the truth. Julien burns the portrait; no one inside the story finds out. We do, but the story did nothing in the way of revelation. It only distracted us. It concealed the truth: from the other characters in the novel, forever, and from us, for a time. We could have easily done without it. The truth stands still and waits patiently while the story is being told. And when the story ends, the truth is nonchalantly revealed—in the mode of a character's thoughts, with no communication or narration involved. The story is neither a direct path to the truth nor a labyrinthine detour to it; the truth remains outside the story and the story outside the truth. We might say that in Stendhal, Balzac's veridictory formula is reversed: Poet *or* Pythagoras.

Restoration Historiography

In 1824, Balzac writes an essay on primogeniture, where he says, referring to the period between the Revolution and the Restoration: "Twenty-five years are nothing when it comes to destroying the customs of a nation."[2] Stendhal begins the preface to the 1823 version of his pamphlet *Racine et Shakespeare* with a spirited statement to the contrary: "Nothing resembles less than we do those *marquis* in embroidered coats and big periwigs costing a thousand *écus* who, about 1670, judged the plays of Racine and Molière."[3] In making his case for the *droit d'ainesse,* Balzac gestures not so much at the insignificance of the revolutionary years as at the persisting weightiness of the monarchical past. Stendhal, on the contrary, invokes the days of Louis XIV in order to emphasize the distance that the Republic and the Empire opened up between the *ancien régime* and its present reincarnation. Stendhal's statement, tearing the fabric of history into a past and a present utterly unlike each other, addresses itself explicitly to those "classicists" and "academicians" who believe that contemporary drama should follow conventions current during the reign of Louis XIV. But underneath this polemic on art, it is not difficult to discern an attack on the underlying historiographic principles that ground the classicism of Stendhal's contemporaries.

The Constitutional Charter of 1814, granted to the French by Louis XVIII, announced the policy of *oubli,* of forgetting and amnesty, forbidding both courts and citizens to inquire into "opinions and votes expressed before the Restoration." In fact, at least after the disturbing interlude of the Hundred Days, this policy was intended not so much to protect those who continued to sympathize with Napoleon or with the Republic as to promote a forgetting of the prolonged interregnum between 1793 and 1814. Forgetting was to be active: in addition to the strict ban on public representation of any political symbols other than those of the Bourbon monarchy, public officials all over France were ordered in 1815 to gather and destroy all the remainders of revolutionary turmoil. Citizens were required to make public oaths, swearing unwavering fidelity to the Bourbons. Elaborate *mise-en-place* ceremonies were staged across the country, featuring the destruction of the many "unnatural" symbols of the Revolution and Empire, the tricolor flags and cockades, the busts of Napoleon. Liberty trees were cut down; mission crosses and churches were erected in their place.[4] The preamble to the charter made sure to emphasize the unbroken character of Bourbon rule: "Given in Paris, in the year of Our Lord 1814, and of our reign *the nineteenth*" (emphasis added).[5]

A popular caricature at the time depicted a writer presenting the king with a weighty, beautiful volume entitled "History of the Nineteen Glorious Years of the Reign of Louis XVIII." The pages of the book were blank.[6] Stendhal's opening statement in *Racine et Shakespeare* should be read in this spirit, as intent on marking the wound in the body politic of the monarchy. But still deeper implications of this position arise if we consider that claims for historical continuity were not only politically but also ethically and ontologically charged.

In the thought of the philosophers and ideologues of the Restoration, the discontinuous is unnatural; moreover, it is impious and immoral. Thus, one of Balzac's favorite contemporary philosophers, Louis de Bonald, writes in his treatise on divorce: "This divine and natural legislation [i.e., marriage], outside of which there is only misery for man, never develops better than when men, delivering themselves to the march of time and the irresistible course of things, do not disturb it with their preconceived operations."[7] Breaks, pauses, sudden turns in the march of time and the course of things are, by implication, unnatural and demonic: nothing good can come of them. Stendhal seems to take mischievous pleasure in striking the traditionalists where it hurts most. Thus, proclaiming that his contemporaries resemble their ancestors not at all, he invokes the disconcerting possibility that history itself should not be conceived of as continuous. Rather than merely posit a difference between the old monarchy and the new within a single historical continuum, rather than posit a distinction between one time and another on a single timeline, he rejects here a particular historiography and, with it, an aesthetics and a metaphysics.

Further: the conception of history Stendhal is proposing in the context of debates about classical and Romantic drama is one that explicitly denies the authority of the past over the present. In the thought of Balzac's Louis Lambert—who can be seen in this respect as a representative philosopher of the Restoration[8]—continuity and hence ontological order relies on the weighty persistence of the past in the present: "When the effect produced ceases to be in [relation] to its cause, disorganization follows." When the past ceases to anchor the present, then time is out of joint, and we are surely in the presence of a monstrosity. Stendhal tirelessly proclaims throughout *Racine et Shakespeare,* and without visible signs of anxiety, that such is indeed the predicament of his contemporaries. History is no longer held together in identity, nor even in resemblance (as in the resemblance between "our ancestors" and "us"). Instead, it has spun out of control in pure difference.

In the second installment of *Racine et Shakespeare* (1825), Stendhal writes: "I have the utmost respect for classicists [in whom the idea of a tragedy in prose arouses an overwhelming feeling of repugnance], and I pity them for having been born in an age when sons are so little like their fathers. What a change there was between 1785 and 1824! There has probably never been such an abrupt revolution in habits, ideas, and beliefs in the two thousand years since we have known the history of the world."[9] The transition from 1785 to 1824 is not so much historical as it is epochal; *before* and *after* are no longer part of the same timeline; they belong to two different ages.

This is not to say, of course, that history had always been plagued so insistently by difference and temporal dispersal. On the contrary, "there has probably never been such an abrupt revolution." We are here confronted with a certain conception of modernity, then, a sense that our present is separated from our past more decisively than any other present has ever been cut off from what came before it. We are once again, then, witnessing the coming-to-consciousness of the experience of temporal acceleration.

Hans Robert Jauss situates the view of history in *Racine et Shakespeare* as marking one significant turning point in the course that the concept of modernity took from late antiquity to Baudelaire. With Stendhal, Jauss argues, modernity is for the first time understood as the condition of being irrevocably and repeatedly cut off from the past:

> For Stendhal, history since 1789 stands in complete contrast to its entire course heretofore. He finds in the revolution an event separating the Français de 1785 from his generation as though by an abyss. . . . The knowledge that the course of history has become utterly different since 1789 stands at the beginning of an epochal consciousness that perceives

the step from old to new as a total rupture in time; the revolution has cut the cords between past and present. . . . The romantic is no longer the allure of that which transcends the present, the remote and the bygone, which stand, as though in a field of tension, over against the real and the everyday. The romantic is rather the latest trend, whatever is beautiful now—which, once outmoded, will have to forfeit its immediate allure, capable then of arousing merely historical interest.[10]

The emphasis on the now, the latest trend, the fear of the outmoded—these are indeed everywhere in *Racine et Shakespeare,* which speaks to the classicists with the same ironic condescension with which a man of fashion addresses those who fail to keep abreast of the world. Thus, "Romanticism is the art of presenting to different peoples those literary works which, in the existing state of their habits and beliefs, are capable of giving them the greatest possible pleasure. Classicism, on the contrary, presents to them that literature which gave the greatest possible pleasure to their great-grandfathers."[11]

And yet fashion is altogether futureless. Its future is by definition impossible to conceive. Fashion is a radical commitment to the now. In Stendhal's thought, however, a conception of the future does figure prominently. Just as the present is not only different from the past but also somehow "better," so the future carries with it a number of promises. In *Souvenirs d'égotisme* (1832–?), for instance: "Since saying something improper is much more fatal to a young man than it is to his advantage to say something well, *posterity—less inane than the present probably—*won't be able to conceive how insipid good society was." Or a little further in the text: "Likewise, *as people will be much less deceived by 'Kings,' nobles and priests around 1870 than they are today,* I'm tempted by the idea of exaggerating certain characteristics against those vermin of the human race."[12]

What we have, then, is not just difference and discontinuity but something like improvement. The present is no longer weighed down by the past—true, but perhaps it is projected toward a better future. This aspect of Stendhal's philosophy of history, left unmentioned in Jauss's discussion, invokes the Enlightenment conception of the present as a field of contention between the past, as the age of superstition and tyranny, and the future, as inaugurating the reign of reason, freedom, and unity of the human race.[13] Still, Jauss is for the most part justified in passing over the role of the future in Stendhal's conception of history, not only because it doesn't figure prominently in either version of *Racine et Shakespeare* with which Jauss is working but also because the residues of Enlightenment historical optimism that might be found in Stendhal reappear in his writings in a highly attenuated form. Addressing himself to a prosaic, not-so-distant future, largely devoid of an eschatological dimension and, as we shall see, not even properly *historical,* Stendhal does not find there any guarantees: "I regard our books as being so many lottery tickets; they really have little more value than that. Posterity, by forgetting some of them and reprinting others, will declare the winning tickets."[14]

The proper relation to the future, then, is that of a wager. But, unlike in Balzac, where the result of a gamble is instantly known, here this result is deferred to a distant future. Rather than figuring *sjuzhet* as the binding of time into an instant, the Stendhalian wager figures *fabula* as blind and risky progress through time. The former ties past, present, and future into a kairotic knot; the latter stretches the distance between them. For a predictable, calculable future is no more than an avatar of the past. A *telos* entangles and stabilizes the present with the help of meanings projected from the end of time; it treats the present as a past. To have liberated modernity from the weight of tradition but not from a predictable future is thus a somewhat paradoxical achievement.

The future and the past, then, are not symmetrically distributed in relation to the present. The past—that is, the past to which Restoration ideology appeals—is dark and contemptible, and it is located safely outside the present, separated from it by the chasm opened up by the Revolution. The future in the meantime is light and unimposing, and it is located *within* the present as no more than "hope." But as such, it volatilizes the present, affording Stendhal a leverage point outside the conventionalized, repetitive, present masquerading as the past, whereby he could catapult himself out of this historical position and into the real present of the incalculable day-to-day, the present that, under the conditions of the Restoration (and later, in *Souvenirs d'égotisme,* of the July Monarchy) can only be personal, intimate.

This explains the prominence, in Stendhal's writings, of the sort of future that is figured by a reader or an interlocutor who will understand him, as might a friend or a lover. This future is embodied, in a manner counter to all ostentation, in a child ("I calculate that my future readers are ten or twelve years old"[15]) who will one day grow up to become a reader. As such, it serves as a loophole out of historical and into personal time. It is also a loophole out of the present dominated by conventions, reiterations, recitations, and lies into the domain of sincerity and truth.

And so if *Racine et Shakespeare* presents us with a version of modernity, it is a paradoxical version. We are asked to strive, against all odds, to be our own contemporaries, to inhabit the present resolutely, to be up-to-date in history, and yet this history falls apart before our very eyes into numberless private presences, fleeting and antisocial: "Every human being, if he thought about it very hard, would have a different *ideal beauty*."[16] To be modern, it turns out, one must be original, unlike everyone else. Linked, through the categories of repetition, convention, and inertia to the past we are supposed to have left behind, the social turns out to be hostile to modernity itself.

Again and again, Stendhal complains of this condition in his letters, often to comic effect: "When he draws his handkerchief from the left pocket of his tail-coat, the poor Frenchman, especially if he is a nobleman and rich, is assaulted by the terror of breaking nineteen rules concerning the manner of blowing one's nose. What makes him despair is that many of these rules are or seem contradictory."[17] Here, the structural alliance between social conventions and the work of *sjuzhet* emerges as evident. There is a significant and signifying logic according to which everything, even the minutest of events, must happen. Each next step is known ahead of time; each event is caught in the suffocating grip of its numberless precedents.[18] We are in the world of the Hegelian *for-us,* in the world where time's acceleration is thoroughly neutralized. To be modern then, to be true to the new experience of secularized, accelerated time, one must disentangle oneself from the grasp of the social, of the past, and, in the language of narrative, of *sjuzhet*.

Of course, the link between modernity and desocialization is by no means Stendhal's alone. His contemporary and fellow liberal Benjamin Constant renders it vivid in his celebrated lecture "On the Liberty of the Ancients Compared to That of the Moderns" (1819).[19] Constant famously argues that in contrast to ancient liberty, which involved active participation of citizens in government but implied no protection of the private rights of individuals, its modern counterpart demands precisely such protection—without, however, demanding that citizens take an active role in government. Modern freedom is personal and not political; it amounts to being able to pursue one's interests and desires—commercial, intellectual, personal—with minimal interference from the society and the state.[20] Tzvetan Todorov isolates the leitmotiv of Constant's political philosophy: "The territory of the individual is not subject to societal sovereignty, whatever form that may take."[21]

What Stendhal contributes, however, is a mechanism whereby this distinction acquires a temporal dimension. Revealed here is the link between the principle of social fragmentation or individuation and a philosophy of history and time that privileges the conception of the present as unhinged from the past and launched toward a personal, intimate, and incalculable future. Here, the interests of free commerce, which, in Constant's essay, serve as a legitimizing principle for the guarantees of modern liberty, are rendered irrelevant. In fact, Stendhal appears to reject (not as unviable but as unworthy) the very conditions for the possibility of commerce: a calculable future and a calculating life.

The Time of Truth and the Addressee

George Poulet writes: "A fleeting moment in which one feels strongly, that is what Stendhalian temporality reduces to."[22] How is one to be truthful under these temporal conditions? Or, in other words, how is one to be truthful in a way that would be distinctly modern? In *Souvenirs d'égotisme,* Stendhal describes his method:

> So as to try not to lie and hide my faults I've imposed on myself the task of writing these memoires at the rate of twenty pages a sitting, like a letter. After my decease, they'll publish them from the original manuscript. In this way I will perhaps achieve truthfulness, but I will also have to beg the reader (perhaps born this morning in the house next door) to forgive me for these dreadful digressions.[23]

The veridiction of modernity relies on possessing the swiftness to stay abreast of the fleeting moment. One must be quick in order not to fall into a lie; one must strive to forestall the temptation to cover up the truth out of fear of ridicule, out of vanity, or out of habitual hypocrisy. It does not seem even to occur to Stendhal that in writing quickly one might put oneself in danger of succumbing to triviality and cliché. Unlike Flaubert, who incidentally did not think highly of his style, Stendhal does not fear that the way to truth and sincerity might be one, paradoxically, of painstaking avoidance (or, for that matter, orchestration) of ubiquitous sociolects and *idées reçues.* Together with Rousseau and Tolstoy, he seems to believe that truth is the easiest thing of all. Its difficulty lies only in our having unlearned this ease. Its demands are the demands, as it were, of relaxation.

Thus, the technology of truthful writing, necessitated by the condition of modernity as resolutely cut off from the past and launched upon an incalculable future, involves speed. It also, as the above passage testifies, involves an addressee and at least a fantasy of the epistolary. Notoriously, those of his works that Stendhal cannot finish quickly, he does not finish at all. Both the finished and the unfinished are addressed to "the happy few." In the second preface to *De l'Amour*, he says: "I only write for about a hundred readers, and about those unhappy, amiable, simple, non-moral beings who I want to please; I only know one or two."[24] Or: "I confess that I wouldn't have any motive for writing if I didn't imagine that one day these pages will be printed, and read by someone I love, a person such as Mme. Roland or M. Gros, the geometrician."[25]

Stendhal conceives of his readers in an intimate mode, as near-epistolary addressees, people like the idealized heroine of the Revolution or the old mathematics teacher, the "one or two," or, projected onto the entire course of future history, "the hundred" who will understand him. There is always a gesture excluding the public as a whole. Stendhal's represented attitude toward his readers could be heard in the words of Octave from the early novel *Armance* (1827): "Ah, it is friends that I need, and not society."[26]

One particularly intriguing passage, invoking the public in its relation to truth and time, appears in *Racine et Shakespeare*:

> I am setting forth in clear and imprudent terms what seems to me to be the truth. If I am mistaken, the public will have forgotten me. But whatever abuses the classicists may heap upon me, I am safe from contempt because I have been frank. At the very most, it will perhaps be said that I attach too much importance to all this. An hour from now I myself will laugh at the sentence I have just written: it betrays the man who has just reread [Werner's] Luther with enthusiasm. But I probably will not delete that sentence. It seemed true to me when I wrote it.[27]

It is instructive to follow the logic of this statement sequentially. "If I am mistaken the public will have forgotten me"—this implies a conception of truth as both social and timeless. Mistakes and lies are forgotten, but the truth persists through the ages. This again, invokes the ideology of the Restoration as stated, for example, by Joseph de Maistre: "Man may have covered over and encrusted the truth with errors he has loaded onto it, but these errors are local, and universal truth will always show itself."[28] But then, within the space of several sentences, Stendhal appears to take it all back, turning the relation between truth and time inside out. Even without reference to the public, even to himself his statement will soon seem laughable and false, but that no longer makes it any less true. Truthfulness, inhabiting a *fabulaic* temporality, does not have to survive the moment of its enunciation. Truth does not have to persist in time even for the self, let alone for the public or the academicians.

Or would it be more accurate to say that it is precisely for the self that truth does not persist? The passage stages the desocialization of truth, its withdrawal from history and into the self, isolated not only from the social world but also from its own past and future. Truth moves from being aligned with eternity to being shut into an instant. The alliance of truth with timelessness is warranted by the "public," the stabilizing social force, which remembers only the truths that are eternal, the kinds of "intuitive" truths of which de Maistre writes that they are constituted by "the sentiments of all men . . . before which all rationalist sophistries fade away."[29] For truth to split off from timelessness, figured by tradition with its beginnings in the inscrutable past, it has to be addressed either to one's own self, or to an intimate circle whose function it is to stand for what is not a public. As such, particular truths tend to lose their force with the passage of time. Stendhal worries in *Souvenirs d'égotisme*: "Let's see whether, examining my conscience with pen in hand, I will reach any *positive* conclusions that will remain *true* in my eyes *for a long time*. What will I think about the things I feel inclined to write when I re-read them about 1835, if I live?"[30]

Again, Stendhal is not alone in opposing intimate-fleeting to public-timeless truth discourses. It is perhaps not by chance that the same dichotomy organizes a novel by the theorist of modern liberty himself. In a personal letter, Constant writes: "The intimacy of the present moment is all that I desire."[31] His short and highly influential novel *Adolphe* (completed 1810, published 1816), with its relatively simple veridictory dynamics, affords an illuminating transition from Stendhal's conceptions of truth and time to his own more complex novelistic from.

Dual Veridiction in *Adolphe*

Adolphe, the hero and narrator of the eponymous novel, is, from early youth, tormented by timidity, a distaste for society, a love of solitude: "The astonishment of early youth at the sight of so artificial and so complicated a society reveals a natural heart rather than an evil disposition. In any case, society has nothing to fear. It weighs so heavily upon us, its hidden influence is so powerful, that it very soon shapes us into the universal mould. . . . If some escape this universal fate, they keep their hidden dissent for themselves."[32] Following this brief sociopsychological introduction, and in an apparent non sequitur, Adolphe recounts the story of his love affair with Ellénore, a beautiful Polish émigré and companion of his friend Count de P***. What preoccupies him throughout the account is the way his feelings for Ellénore constantly change, first as he pursues her out of vanity, then passionately in love, then growing colder, then in love again, then burdened by her presence, overcome by pity, and, after her death, mortally burdened by the freedom he has newly acquired. In these sections of the novel, time is marked primarily by the expression "no longer" (*ne . . . plus*): "Little by little, my feelings quickened, I had risen that same day no longer thinking about Ellénore; an hour after receiving the news of her arrival . . . I was in a fever of anxiety lest I might not see her . . . I no longer felt in a hurry to arrive. . . . No longer was my mind full of calculations and schemes. . . . No longer was it the hope of success that governed my behavior" (19–21). But this intimate, psychological temporality of ever-changing affects, this inner time with which it is almost impossible to catch up in writing, is complemented by an utterly static time of the unchanging situation, as Adolphe is straining to find within himself the strength to break with his lover: "The first year of our stay in Caden had come to an end without any change occurring in our situation" (46). In the preface to the third edition of *Adolphe,* Constant himself characterizes the novel as one "where the characters are reduced to two, and the situation is always the same" (3).

Subjectively then, there is only temporal flux: thoughts come to replace thoughts, feelings rush to supplant other feelings. But objectively, years go by and nothing changes: Adolphe and Ellénore stay together. Toward the end of the novel, Adolphe is resolved to break with his lover but on a number of occasions is unable to tell her what he calls "the truth." The reason for his failure is not merely—not so much—his fear of hurting her feelings. He does enough of that along the way. What makes it impossible for him to speak the truth is that his feelings for Ellénore change with disorienting frequency. Again and again, he gives in to changing moods until, at the very moment of crisis, suddenly he finds himself quite reconciled with his situation: "I rejoiced in her expressions of love, formerly unwelcome, now precious because each might be the last" (68).

Under such circumstances, with qualitative distinctions between one change and another erased, the narrative lacks the means for a decisive denouement. Nothing can change from within because the intimate sphere in which Adolphe and Ellénore are installed does not appear to allow for change on the level of the "situation," just as it ceaselessly stimulates change on the level of feelings and thoughts. And indeed, when it comes, the catastrophe is precipitated from the outside, from the realm of what, after brief introductory remarks, has been left out of the frame of the main narrative: the realm of ambition, career, and socialization.

Throughout the novel, the social imperative is periodically voiced by Adolphe's father and then by his father's friend, Baron de T***, a French diplomat in Warsaw, where Adolphe and Ellénore have in the meantime moved. Both urge him to give up his hapless liaison and enter on the path of a career. At some point, Adolphe gives Baron de T*** his word that he will break with Ellénore within three days. Then, as is his wont, he goes back on his promise; he writes a long letter to the Baron in which he repeats his promises but asks for more time. The crisis is brought about when Baron de T*** forwards this very letter to Ellénore, and adds to it a letter of his own. Ellénore falls ill and does not recover.

The career plot, dormant throughout most of the novel, intrudes into the amorous plot and destroys it in a kind of moment of truth. All is, in a sense, as should be expected, except that, in a final peripety, we find out that Ellénore had known the truth all along. After her death, Adolphe unseals a letter she had written to him some months before but decided not to send. In it, Ellénore bemoans her lover's weakness, his inability to break with her decisively, which, as she can plainly see, is what he wants to do. The moment of truth turns out to be belated; the truth is already known when it is revealed. The novel confronts us with something mysterious, then, something that cannot be accounted for in purely psychological terms. Why is it that the truth of the Baron's letter precipitates the moment of crisis while Ellénore's sober knowledge of the situation changes nothing? How, given Ellénore's knowledge of the truth "all along," can we account for the capacity of that same truth coming from the Baron to produce the decisive blow, the catastrophe in the plot?

We seem to have here one and the same truth delivered from different sources. Coming from within the intimate, psychologically inflected love plot, where veridiction relies on staying abreast of the fleeting, changeable present, truth can have no transformative effect. It does not persist; it fails to subsume a long enough period of time for a *sjuzhet*-like whole to emerge as an epoch, and is merely a stage on one's way, a time that is no more. Intruding from the public world of a career, from the social domain that weighs so heavily and threatens to shape us "into the universal mould," this kind of truth is timeless and decisive. Unlike the truth of inner states, public veridiction will not vary from moment to moment, and thus it has strength and stability enough to demand that the situation itself change irreversibly, destroying its participants along the way.

The conservative ideologues of the Restoration—de Bonald, de Maistre, Chateaubriand—all seem to agree on a conception of truth that draws its strength from an alliance between social obligation and timelessness, merging into the concept of continuous tradition. In other words, for them, truth is timeless not because it is rationally deducible (as in Idealist philosophy), nor because it is deposited in eternal forms (Platonism), but because it has been believed "always, everywhere, by all."[33] In direct opposition to this atavistic conception of truth and its expression as repetitiveness, inertia, and boredom stands Stendhal's notion, underlying both *Racine et Shakespeare* and *Souvenirs d'égotisme,* that truth has been uprooted from the past and launched toward an incalculable and ahistorical, that is, intimate, future. *Adolphe* stages a struggle between these veridictory poles. This struggle is mostly hidden from view because, appropriately enough for the proponent of modern liberty, social and timeless veridiction remain behind the scenes while intimate fleeting truth discourse occupies center stage.

In an essay on *La Cousine Bette,* Fredric Jameson points out that the modern psychological novel, beginning with *Adolphe,* "presupposes that consciousness, the personality, is a stable unit, comprehensible in itself; in other words that the individual life has a certain unity about it, can stand alone as a complete thing, is no longer felt as a mere part that must be seen in the light of the whole to have any meaning."[34] In this respect, Constant's method is surely to be contrasted with Balzac's. Furthermore, this anti-Balzacian realism is also evident in Stendhal, whose more complex and more sociohistorical novelistic form can be seen as struggling both to preserve Constant's intimate, isolatable veridiction and to sublate it in his own particular version of the realist novel. Thus, Balzac subordinates his characters to the social situation in which they appear, making it impossible for their biographies to unfold fully outside the principle of the *retour des personnages.* For him, characters are only comprehensible in light of the whole and as parts of it. Stendhal, on the contrary, "always tries to crowd the essential features of a whole epoch into the personal biography of some individual type."[35] An individual type, we should add, who, unlike Adolphe, does not merely retreat from but both inhabits and abhors the epoch, both sees through and is seduced by its falsehoods.

Dutiful Haste

In *Adolphe*, the thematics of career are entirely external, social, objective. Having a career implies submitting to a demand to be useful to society, serving it according to one's distinct social status and natural gifts. Adolphe is neglecting a "career for which [he is] destined" (50). In *Le Rouge et le noir*, the thematics and narratology of a career plot are internalized in the hero as ambition. Julien Sorel, a plebeian, is destined for nothing, and so for him having a career means rising above his station. He is first and foremost ambitious: he would "die a thousand deaths rather than fail to make his fortune" (19). His choice of career is secondary to ambition; it depends on calculations regarding the most efficient way of making a fortune in a given society at a given historical moment. Thus, having witnessed the construction of a magnificent church at Verrières, having come to appreciate the importance of the church in Restoration society, he decides on a career of a priest.

Here lies the root of Julien's notorious hypocrisy. It is not simply that he must conceal his love of Napoleon from the people he works for—that is true, but secondary. Making possible every specific act of pretense and concealment is the essential split within him into a private and a public self, that which falls out of the social world he inhabits and that which seamlessly fits in. The split itself is socially conditioned; it is only in a stratified, hierarchical society that hypocrisy feeds off of ambition: "except in well-organized republics, the ambitious are always a little hypocritical."[36]

This inversion and interiorization of the public career plot has radical consequences for Julien's employment of the word "duty" (*devoir*). Using it quite in earnest to invoke the demands placed on him by his inner sense of honor, Julien travesties the neoclassical notion of duty as fidelity to one's station in life and allegiance to the existing social order. Adolphe is indeed neglecting his duty when he fails to break with his lover; his duty demands that he occupy his proper place in society and be useful to it. Julien's duty, on the other hand, is duty to himself alone. It is duty he assigns to himself, and it repeatedly compels him to perform acts that traduce social boundaries. Duty demands that he hold the hand of Mme de Rênal; it demands that he come to her bedroom. It demands that he make Mathilde de La Mole his lover, and it demands that he insult his own jurors during his trial. The usually oblivious M. de Rênal makes à propos of Julien a sharp observation worthy of de Bonald: "Sure, sure, I know; he makes me hateful to my children. . . . Everything in this century works to make *legitimate* authority odious. Ah, poor France!" (116). Again and again, duty works to delegitimize hierarchy and authority. Toward the end of the novel, Julien has progressed so far down the road mapped out for him by his "unnatural," thoroughly unclassical sense of duty that, in order to naturalize his new position, he must acquire a new name. Julien Sorel must become Julien Sorel de La Vernaye, retroactively acquiring a new father to replace the one he had always hated.[37]

But it is precisely because duty gets him so far so quickly that it must not be confused with ambitious hypocrisy. Hypocrisy, like the society that fosters it, relies on repetition and recitation. Julien is at his most hypocritical when, to the slightly condescending astonishment of his superiors, he recites whole chapters of the New Testament. He is at his most hypocritical when he behaves exactly the way a future priest is expected to behave, when he fits perfectly within his superiors' conception of what he should be. Duty, on the other hand, breaks with such expectations. It makes him do what from the point of view of his own calculable advantage is unthinkable. It is duty, and not ambition, that compels him to take Mme de Rênal's hand, then to kiss her, then to come to her room. It is also duty that makes him lash out at his employer, M. de Rênal, when the latter attempts to rebuke him for neglecting the children. Each of these acts could have easily gotten him dismissed, could have ruined his reputation, but he does whatever duty demands, without thinking of the consequences. Duty, then, is the very opposite of ambitious hypocrisy: it does not calculate, does not prepare for the future; it is immediate and inconsequentialist.

The most common temporal marker linked to duty, both in *Rouge* and elsewhere in Stendhal, is that of haste. This is most starkly thematized in *Armance*: "She did not say it to herself, she felt (to express it in detail would have been tantamount to doubting it), she felt this truth: 'From the moment when I perceived my *duty*, not to follow it immediately, blindly, without argument, is to act in a vulgar spirit, is to be unworthy of Octave.'"[38] But while *Armance* focuses primarily on what might be called the inner experience of duty, the more properly realist *Rouge* is concerned with the socially visible, objective effects of dutiful action. Thus, here dutiful haste is internalized in plot itself, disturbing the smooth, gradual progression of narrative.

Julien's first experience of duty in the novel occurs when he accidentally touches the hand of Mme Rênal: "The hand was swiftly withdrawn; but Julien thought it was his *duty* to make sure that the hand was not withdrawn when he touched it" (42). ("Cette main se retira bien vite; mais Julien pensa qu'il était de son *devoir* d'obtenir que l'on ne retirât pas cette main quand il la touchait."³⁹) The hand must be his not merely "when," some time in the future, he touches it again, but also "whenever" he attempts to do so. Duty's commands are once and for all; they make no distinctions between past, present, and future. Or rather, when duty speaks, past, present, and future are bound together into a timeless instant.

On another occasion, Julien encounters the man who had stared at him too intently in a café: "To see him, drag him from his high seat by the tails of his long coat, and set to lashing him with his own whip was the work of an instant" (216). The work of an instant, yes, but it has far-reaching consequences. Julien's "dutiful" outburst leads to a duel with the diplomat de Beauvoisis, who, finding out that he has fought a mere secretary of Marquis de La Mole and in order to avoid seeming ridiculous, spreads the rumor that Julien is an illegitimate son of a nobleman. In order to naturalize the "unnatural" events precipitated by Julien's strong sense of duty, he is—here only in public opinion—promoted to nobility.

Paradoxically, then, far from sabotaging his career, Julien's dutiful acts advance it. Ambitious hypocrisy with its resolute conformism would have gotten him nowhere. Or rather, it would have gotten him, slowly and painfully, a certain distance along the linear path of the dreary career he had chosen. Duty, on the other hand, breaking through conventional boundaries, is a series of knight's moves that land him not at all where he was going, but rather in a better place, and faster. The fact that dutiful action reroutes Julien from the gloomy career in church to the glorious military career and an aristocratic title corresponds to the logic of immediacy inherent in Stendhalian duty. Julien occupies the social position that finally corresponds to who he was at heart to begin with: honorable, valiant, proud, noble.

Dutiful acts, then, breaking through hypocrisy, introducing a more *fabula*-like, unpremeditated quality into narrative, possess two veridictory functions. First, they give us a glimpse into the "true" Julien. They represent moments of authentic, disinterested self-expression, in which calculation is reduced to a mere "how-to," or "when," but not "for the sake of." Second, duty loosens the static *sjuzhet*-centered structure of conventional social relations. It unmasks as mere prejudice the "natural" hierarchical principle according to which a tutor must behave deferentially toward his employer or be dismissed. When, forgetting to be hypocritical—and thus, in accordance with his social position, humble—Julien scornfully rebukes M. de Rênal, the latter, instead of dismissing his tutor, gives him a raise. Julien is stupefied: "I didn't despise this animal sufficiently, he [says] to himself. No doubt he's just made the best apology of which his degraded mind is capable" (49).⁴⁰

It is worth pausing briefly on this episode. Julien is happy to have been given a raise despite having acted out of duty. He tells himself he has won a battle. But he does not suspect to what he owes his victory. The narrator informs us behind his back: it is to M. de Rênal's fear that Julien might leave his service for that of his rival, M. Valenod, and then people will say that Valenod, and not Rênal, has hired a tutor for his children. Julien's dutiful, disinterested, uncalculating actions win him a victory because he is already a commodity, an object of *interested calculation.*

More generally, while duty flouts social conventions and leads to radical acts of nonconformism, the social order proves flexible enough to neutralize duty's subversive effects. The veridictory opening produced by an act in accordance with duty almost immediately shuts down. The more progress Julien makes—the higher he rises—the more hypocritical he becomes. And at the end, with some surprise but without a consistently guilty conscience, he finds himself serving as a messenger in an ultraconservative conspiracy. In short, the social fabric finds it easy to heal the truth wounds delivered to it by Julien's dutiful acts. He is simply promoted, reemplotted into the social network in such a way as to occupy the objective place to which his acts correspond. If he fights a duel with a nobleman, he is given, at least in public opinion, the status of a nobleman; if he is about to marry the daughter of one of the most prominent aristocrats in Paris, he becomes lieutenant of the hussars, acquiring a sonorous name and an aristocratic lineage in the process.

The pernicious principle emerging here turns out to guide much of the veridictory dynamic of the novel. Local flashes of truth, sincere and unpredictable, are drawn into the movement whereby they become incorporated into a wider network of stasis and hypocrisy. With difficulty, *fabula* disentangles itself from *sjuzhet* and is almost immediately knotted back in. Narrative precipitation relies on and fosters narrative coherence. There is a haunting sense here that, in Guy Debord's desolate inversion of the Hegelian formula, "the true is a moment of the false."⁴¹

Dutiful action in *Rouge*, as a device and a figure for a kind of truthful haste, should remind us of the similar device and figure in *La Peau de chagrin*: the wager. Both speed up the trajectory of the hero, both figure modernity's temporal acceleration. But if in Balzac condensed temporality serves the goals of truth as allied with emplotment, in Stendhal the situation is more complicated. Here, we can distinguish two stages: first duty functions as a principle of veridictory disemplotment, debunking prepackaged official narratives of both self and world; but in the process it calls upon itself the avenging forces of societal and novelistic reemplotment, propelling the hero forward in the story and upward on the social ladder. We are confronted here with a kind of fragile, momentary truth, a flash of genuine and energetic interiority illuminating for an instant the arbitrariness of the supposedly natural and traditional order, an order, which in the very flexibility and ease with which it swallows up the hero's veridictory acts, exposes its own conventionality, its own transience and falsehood. Thus, the above formula is in this context also readable with different emphases. The true is a moment (now, a moment in time) of (pointing at something and saying) "the false."

Late in the novel, when rumors spread that Julien is an illegitimate son of a nobleman, he himself begins to believe them. The force of societal falsification reaches far into the hero's (usually robust) sense of self. This equivocation about origins raises several intriguing possibilities. If, for example, at the end of the novel it turned out that Julien was in fact a nobleman's son, then we would find ourselves confronted by an essentially comic narrative like *Tom Jones*. In such a world, there would be sure ways of telling the difference between a nobleman and a commoner, and we could say that the only way for the hero to be able to act like a nobleman is to be one (and to be able to marry one: Sophia). The key veridictory principle here would be essentially static: truth is there all along; Sophia is waiting from the beginning. If, on the other hand, our hero were, in the course of the novel, to actually *become* a nobleman, to develop into one (and thus to ascend to the position of being able to marry one), then we would of course be confronted with a *Bildungsroman* like Goethe's *Lehrjahre,* and nobility would be less a matter of blood than of cultivation. Here, truth would be understood as gradually unfolding: Natalie is at first not there at all, then she appears to Wilhelm when he is semiconscious, then he sees her in a dream, then hopes for her, and finally she is attained. Neither of these possibilities is available to Balzac and Stendhal. Lucien de Rubempré cannot marry Clotilde de Grandlieu before he purchases the old Rubempré lands and thus ascends to aristocracy—his truth, his end (his wife) is defined by the place he holds in the social whole and is emplotted (by Vautrin) in an elaborate intrigue. The failure of the intrigue leads to the (self-)annihilation of the hero. In Stendhal, it's the other way around: a carpenter's son, Julien is about to be married to, and have a child by, the glamorous daughter of Marquis de La Mole. Dodging travesty, the social world must catch up to this fact, and Julien becomes (and is pronounced to have always been) a member of the nobility. But the fact that he comes to occupy a specific place in the whole, far from defining him, belies that very whole. And the fact that, in a final suicidal reversal, he ultimately refuses that place belies (at least provisionally) the veridictory authority of plot over him.

How the Pastoral is Made

The narrative function of duty changes significantly from the sentimental *Armance* to the historical-realist *Rouge*. In the earlier novel, the notion that one must begin acting in accordance with duty as soon as one hears its call does not—perhaps surprisingly—lead to an intensification of action, a tightening of plot. On the contrary, it appears to function as restraint, as a mechanism of narrative braking. Both Armance and Octave take it to be their duty not to marry each other. Armance is fearful of compromising her honor by marrying her more aristocratic beloved, who in turn promises himself, for reasons that are not revealed, never to marry. Here we already have two distinct notions of duty. One, to which Armance is particularly attuned, is still sociocentric, supported by fear of gossip, ridicule, dishonor, and disgrace. This is still neoclassical duty understood as fidelity to one's symbolic position in the social order. Octave's duty, on the other hand, emerges as obligation to a mystery. Mystery—rumored by some readers of *Armance* to be related to impotence—is indeed a perfect site of duty subjectively conceived. Says Octave: "Instead of making my behavior conform to the incidents which I encountered in life, I had made myself an *a priori* rule anterior to all experience."[42] Whether intended or not, the Kantian language here is highly apposite, since the agency that can make itself an *a priori* rule anterior to all experience is properly transcendental, empty, mysterious. Thus, though Margaret Cohen is indeed correct in saying that *Armance* "[evacuates] all authority from the term [duty]," I would suggest that this is not because duty here has become "a moving target," but because the narrative strains to conceive of duty in a subjective, asocial, and even antisocial mode.[43] Evacuated then is all *external* authority, all compulsion, except when it emanates from within the mysterious inner self.

There are thus two opposing versions of duty in *Armance,* and yet they both lead their adherers in the same direction: to diffidence, hesitation, and passivity, allowing the two lovers to sustain a kind of idyllic friendship, interrupted now and then by misunderstandings, but on the whole blissful in its intimacy, restraint, and, for quite some time, ignorance of the true nature of their feelings for each other. Octave, though he sees Armance virtually every day, remains unconscious of his love for her during the first half of the novel. Armance dreams of staying in just this state for another six years, until, according to her calculations, Octave is going to marry someone else:

> It never occurred to either of these two young hearts to admit that they were enjoying one of the rarest forms of happiness that is to be met with here below; on the contrary they supposed that they had still many unsatisfied desires. Having no experience of life, they did not see that these fortunate moments could only be of very brief duration. At most, this happiness, wholly sentimental and deriving nothing from vanity or ambition, might have survived in the bosom of some poor family who never saw any strangers. But they were living in society. . . . [Society] was bound to have its revenge.[44]

Visible here are some key pastoral motifs: obstacles (here, psychosociologically conceived) on the way to consummation, consequent extolling of the spiritual aspects of love, and even something like the archetypical "Fountain of Love's Truth," ensuring that the lovers remain ignorant of the fact that their love is requited.[45]

At first glance, something similar is being staged early on in *Rouge*. Here, the two inflections of duty are similarly distributed: as societal obligation in the female character (Mme de Rênal) and as subjective duty, duty to the self, in the male (Julien). And during the blissful days they spend together at Vergy, they seem to experience a similar pastoral happiness:

> In Paris, Julien's position with regard to Mme de Rênal would quickly have been simplified; but in Paris, love is the child of novels. . . . The novels would have outlined for them the roles to be played, provided them with a model to imitate; and this model, sooner or later, though without the least pleasure and perhaps even reluctantly, vanity would have forced Julien to follow. In a little village of the Aveyron or the Pyrenees, the slightest incident would have been rendered decisive by the heat of the climate. Under our darker skies a poor young man who is ambitious only because the delicacy of his heart makes absolutely necessary for him some of those pleasures that money bestows can see every day a woman of thirty, sincerely virtuous, devoted to her children and who

never thinks of looking in novels for examples of conduct. Everything progresses slowly, things are done gradually in the provinces, behavior is more natural. (30)

The passage provides a curious classification of the temporalities of love in France, but in the process it appears to misrepresent both the character of Julien and the nature of his relationship with Mme de Rênal. Julien is here given to us in a distinctly pastoral mode, as a young man with a delicate heart whose ambition amounts to nothing more than enjoying, one day, some material comforts. It is clear even this early in the novel that Julien, who would "die a thousand deaths rather than fail to make a fortune," does not resemble this young man in the least. His desires have little to do with the petty pleasures that money bestows; they are quite explicitly Napoleonic.

Just as this pastoral image of Julien does not get at what is essential about him, so the temporality of provincial love does not appear to obtain in his relations with Mme. de Rênal. Things develop rather quickly after all. This is perhaps because not everyone living in the provinces is a good provincial. Julien, though he reads no novels and has never been to Paris, is, at Vergy, a kind of Parisian. Paris is taken here as a name for a kind of time, and Julien carries within himself the dynamism of Parisian temporality. He does have models to imitate; he has martial metaphors that push him onward; he has stories told to him by his more experienced friend Fouqué. Of course, Mme de Rênal fits well into the pastoral tone and description of the passage, and where she alone is concerned things could have progressed gradually indeed. Were it not for Julien's "Parisian" impatience, the slowness of her provincial love might not have warranted a plot at all.

But unlike Adolphe and Octave (as well as Armance and Mme de Rênal), Julien is not a member of the nobility. He does not have at his disposal the kind of *fabulaic*, day-to-day, pastoral narrative potential that leisure affords his richer and less energetic counterparts. His narrative force lies in ambition, in mobility and impatience, and he therefore cannot comfortably occupy the *longue-durée*. To be sure, having promised to come to Mme de Rênal's room at two o'clock in the morning and having received a harsh rebuke, Julien does consider giving up his plans "and living *from day to day* with Mme de Rênal in the childish happiness each hour would bring him" (68, emphasis added). The pastoral tempts him, but he has a strong sense of duty; he cannot go back on his word.

So when, following the dictates of duty, he makes his way into Mme de Rênal's room, two temporalities intersect: the "natural," pastoral time of her provincial love and the impatient duty time of his "Parisian" one. The intersection between them produces the experience of the unexpected. This is the "Southern" temporality of the decisive incident, the moment of confusion when vain projects are forgotten and what could least be counted on to procure success does just that. The narrator comments: "Actually he owed to the love he had previously inspired, and to the unexpected impression produced on him by her feminine charms, a victory to which all of his clumsy subtleties would never have conducted him" (69).

Once again, dutiful action precipitates a certain stripping down, a disclosure of the real and the true. But this time, the butt of its dynamic critique is not social convention but its obverse side: the natural, pastorally conceived. Julien's impetuous actions crack the pastoral into its constitutive parts, passion and guilt: "She spurned Julien from her presence with genuine indignation, and the next instant flung herself into his arms" (69). This is the same indignation with which she met his promise to be in her room that night, and which made Julien wish they could continue their day-to-day happiness. It is in the shadow of this potential indignation that their happiness had thrived all along. But Julien forces the issue, exposing the very structure of the pastoral as an unthinkingly resigned acceptance of socially repressive duty. Still very much a simple substance in the sentimentalist *Armance*, in realist *Rouge* it is—under the veridictory pressure of the new dynamic concept of duty—dereified as the site of struggle between passion and social constraints.

Stendhal himself appears to accept the pastoral, intimate temporality of the day-to-day as the temporality of truth and happiness. The trouble seems to consist in the fact that such a temporality is simply not available to the kind of (modern, realist) narrative that gives voice to the conditions of "temporal concentration."[46] The day-to-day is the thoroughly disemplotted; it is naked *fabula*, and as such, it has no place either in the *sjuzhet*-centered world of the Restoration or in the narrative intent on representing the tempos of that world. In *Armance*, we are told that the pastoral will eventually break down because "society will take its revenge." Here, in *Rouge*, society can be said to be taking its revenge all along, and the simplicity of the pastoral itself is revealed to be imposter simplicity. The question then can be formulated as follows: Given that the *fabulaic* pastoral is not available in *Rouge*, given that the historical-realist hero cannot live day-to-day, what takes its place as the purveyor of truth? We have seen that this is precisely the narrative function of duty, but we can now also appreciate the extent to which dutiful truth is a problematic truth, the extent to which its *fabulaization* is fragile and fleeting, subject to instant resocializing co-optation.[47] And if we look closer, we will see that the veridictory powers of dutiful action are threatened not only from the side of the world but from the side of the subject as well.

Duty and Historical Transcendence

At the end of the novel, in prison, Julien reminisces: "I am isolated here in this dungeon; but I have not *lived in isolation* on the earth; I had the powerful idea of *duty*. The duty I assigned myself, whether wrong or right . . . has been like the trunk of a solid tree, on which I supported myself during the storm; I wavered, I was shaken. After all, I was only a man. . . . But I was not carried away" (402). There is something strange here at first glance. How is it that the possession of an idea of duty, the kind of duty that one assigns to oneself, can forestall the suspicion that one has led an isolated life? Certainly, duty understood as a subjective *a priori* could not produce such guarantees.

But the difficulty disappears once we recognize that self-imposed duty is represented in *Rouge* as only *impurely* subjective to begin with. This fact can already be glimpsed from Julien's thoughts framing the scene in Mme de Rênal's bedroom. Bracing himself before the risky foray, he thinks: "I may be inexperienced and boorish like the son of a peasant. . . . But at least I shan't be a weakling" (68). Once in the room, he no longer strikes a valiant figure. When Mme de Rênal greets him with genuine anger, he "[forgets] his empty projects and [recovers] his natural self" (68). His "natural self" falls at her feet and bursts into tears. But when, after he "has nothing further to desire," he returns to his room, Julien is again in dutiful mode: "Like a soldier just back from review, Julien was intent on examining all the details of his conduct" (69). The true, disemplotted, Julien flashes before our eyes for no more than an instant before falling back into a plot of his own making, before relapsing into a role.

Thus, duty feeds off of models and metaphors that are not difficult to identify. The role out of which Julien occasionally falls and into which he relapses is quite explicitly Napoleonic. The precipitation that he introduces into narrative consistently invokes the imperial rhetoric of glory, valor, conquest, and military strategy. But this imperial, Napoleonic temporality, in the world of the Restoration, has gone underground, has been internalized in the figure of a latecomer, and is condemned to receive its expression not in objective institutional structures but in the subversive efforts of the subject to leap over temporal and social constraints.[48] Julien's transcendence, in other words, is *historical,* invoking sometimes a name, sometimes an act, sometimes an aura of a different epoch.

Julien thinks primarily of Napoleon. Mathilde de La Mole, the only other duty-bound character in *Rouge,* dreams of glamorous Marguerite de Navarre, of her distant ancestor, the tragic Boniface de La Mole and, more generally, of the heroic age of the Wars of Religion. By a logic that will be traced out shortly, this does not prevent her from thinking with sympathy of such an implacable class enemy and martyr of the Revolution as Danton.

Other characters in the novel, when they think of history at all, conceive of it in terms of a dichotomy between uninterrupted tradition on the one hand and scandalous rupture on the other. Synchronically, this dichotomy is instantiated in the distinction between the socially acceptable on the one hand and the ridiculous, the scandalous, the unconventional on the other. Only Julien and Mathilde are inspired by history as a depository of beautiful acts performed by heroic individuals, worthy of being emulated in the present.[49] And they serve as reminders that the obsessive *mise-en-place* rituals staged during the Restoration were called upon to effect historical forgetting precisely in the face of so many contradictory memories permeating the historical moment that claimed for itself consistency and universality.

Stendhalian duty, then, presupposes precisely such a noncontinuous conception of history, the co-presence and simultaneity of multiple historical forms of life within a single temporal cross section. This cross section bears traces of the radical condensation of history between 1789 and 1815, with the *ancien régime,* the early days of the Revolution, the Terror, the Directory, the Consulate, the Empire, the return of the monarchy with a charter, the Hundred Days, the White Terror—all of these historical forms with their own deep historical models, traditions, and canons, passing before the eyes of a single generation, all firmly lodged within the collective memory of Restoration society. The work of duty in *Rouge* is thus indeed the work of isolation and attachment: isolation from the dominant social values of the day and attachment or fidelity to residual and alternative historical forms. Julien and Mathilde are ultimately threatening because, in setting these forms to work, they belie the naturalized present in its pretensions to be the only possible one.

Thus, with the help of the logic of duty elaborated here, we can complicate Hans Robert Jauss's conception of Stendhalian modernity. A decisive severing of the link with the past does not merely launch the moderns toward an ever-receding future. Cut off from an essential tradition and placed in the domain of *nonsynchronicity*, we are, instead, given a chance to mobilize a past that would be our own and yet would not utterly isolate us from historical life.

What then is left of the intimate truthful time delineated in *Souvenirs d'égotisme* and, somewhat more problematically, in *Armance?* On the territory of Stendhalian realism, it can no longer be confined to the sphere of mere interiority. It is no longer the case that the pure isolated subject stands on the side of fleeting truth, while the social world is entirely delivered into the grips of stasis and falsehood. Rather, in Stendhal, intimate, *fabulaic* and truth-bearing time intrudes into the predictable, regulated, *sjuzhet*-centered temporality of the social through the dutiful acts of a subject and thus loses its *a priori* nature and acquires a historical content that is not entirely foreign to the social world itself. The subject becomes an effect of condensed historical time, serving as a loophole that grants various residual values veridictory (that is, here, critical) access to the world that tries to suppress them; and in the process runs the risk of becoming a parody.[50] In narratological terms, then, in order to produce a spark of truthful *fabulaic* disemplotment, the *sjuzhet*-centered, conventional world of the novel must shudder from the force of a "transcendental" *sjuzhet* enlisted by the subject of truth from the archive of preexisting historical models.

The Narrative Pattern of the Unforeseen

The dutiful character in *Rouge* is not merely attached to transcendent models of a different age. He or she becomes a host to a differently flowing time. From the perspective of this different temporality, the social world seems to stand still. Mathilde de La Mole is profoundly dissatisfied with the aristocratic society that surrounds her precisely because it is dominated by the principle of identity. Identity between people first of all; everyone strives to resemble everyone else. But also identity in time, where nothing surprising or out of the ordinary ever happens, where time is uniform and repetitive, where, in short, as in a tightly woven plot, "everything is known beforehand" (265).

"France has great need of repose," writes Chateaubriand shortly after the Restoration, "it is the part of every one who truly loves his country to endeavor to pour oil into her wounds, and not increase and inflame them."[51] As we have seen, Victor Cousin works out a philosophy of reconciliation, particularly fitting, according to him, to the historical moment of the Restoration. The salons of the day seem to heed to these appeals, organize themselves around the ideals of "clement mediation," "conciliation," "planned harmony." Pacification, healing, balance, civility—all were highly prized by those who frequented Restoration salons as the proper cure for the wounds inflicted on French society by the Revolution.[52] Stendhal allows Mathilde to echo the complaints he himself repeatedly voices in letters and diaries: "If by chance [the unexpected] appears among our ideas, there are not epigrams enough to drive it away; if it appears in the form of actions, no act of cowardice can properly express our terror.... What a dull, degenerate century!" (266).

Mathilde takes an interest in Julien because she intuits in him a rare capacity for the unexpected (267). As for Julien, he is exposed, in his relations with Mathilde, to a temporality previously unknown to him. With Mme de Rênal he experiences, however briefly, the joys of pastoral "day-to-day." In the seminary at Besançon he learns the slow time of drudgery and suffering, of hard work and extreme alienation, the slow time of a hateful career, where a quarter of an hour can seem like a whole day (135). He is tempted, early on, by his childhood friend Fouqué to make his fortune as a wood merchant: in several years, having saved up some money, he might be able to embark upon a surer career. In response to this last temptation, Julien thinks: "What! to squander in base pursuits seven or eight years! In that way I should reach the age of twenty-eight; and by that age Bonaparte had already performed his finest actions" (59). Each of these trajectories is, in the end, too slow for Julien. With Mathilde, for the first time in his life, time flows too fast.

Observing Mathilde in her most recent posture of haughty indifference toward him, Julien thinks: "It's like the fall of a favorite in a court" (295). In *Racine et Shakespeare,* Stendhal compares the court of Louis XIV to a game of faro. In matters of favor and gambling, one cannot rely on the future. The logic of favor—whether that of the monarch, the lover, or fortune—is incalculable. Mathilde appears to Julien as maddening unpredictability, as the unexpected itself, raised to a principle. Her impulsiveness, the ease with which she can turn from passion to contempt, drives Julien to despair, and when she makes her last turnabout, once again appearing to be in love, he asks: "What guarantee, what god will assure me that the position you now seem inclined to restore me to will last more than two days?" (340). In fact, with Mathilde, Julien appears to have found himself in an utterly godless, modern temporality, a time so fluid that every next instant annihilates the content of the instant immediately preceding it.[53]

If for Mme de Rênal Julien is too Parisian, his plots too impetuous, with Mathilde, he decisively emerges as a provincial, unable to stay abreast of her frantic pace.⁵⁴ But in essence her inconstancy has the same sources as his earlier restlessness. And paradoxically, both draw their power to loosen preexisting plots from a predilection for emplotment. Here is Mathilde: "Yes, it's love with all its wonders that must come to command my heart; I feel it in the fire that stirs within me. . . . My new joys will be worthy of me. Each of my days will not pass, a frigid imitation of the one before. Already there is some splendor and boldness in my daring to love a man placed so far beneath me on the social scale" (251). And then, on the down swing: "When she reflected on the matter at leisure, she decided that this was a being, if not altogether common, at least not sufficiently out of the ordinary to deserve all the strange follies she had ventured to commit for him" (294). Passion and emplotment go together; disemplotment, on the other hand, a sense that there is no story to tell here, that nothing extraordinary is happening, corresponds, in a kind of narrative-desiring entropy, to a cooling off. Passion and emplotment invoke heroic, antisocial duty; cooling off, Mathilde thinks of her position in society. Duty is only once brought up in connection with her social position, and even then as "*devoirs vulgaires,*" and at the moment that marks "her last effort at vulgar prudence and at deference to conventional ideas" (265). Duty is fidelity to the transcendent model, to the chosen plot. Common obligation is loyalty to the order of things, a sense of propriety, measure, and good taste. Dutiful action assaults that which obligatory repetition and imitation hope to protect: prejudice, convention, the status quo. "It is his right," she writes to her father concerning her pregnancy, "it is my *duty,* he is the father of my child" (349).

What emerges with clarity in the case of Mathilde (and what we have already glimpsed in Julien as well) is the extent to which veridictory disemplotment itself relies on plot. Mathilde finds inspiration for emplotment and dutiful behavior everywhere: in an operatic aria, in the simple fact that a sketch she was unthinkingly drawing turned out to resemble Julien, in Julien's prolonged conversation with the revolutionary Count Altamira. But undoubtedly the most prominent and most constant of her models is the story of Boniface de La Mole, friend of the future Henry IV, lover of Mathilde-Marguerite of Navarre and of Mathilde's distant ancestor, beheaded in 1574 for an attempted insurrection. More generally, she refers us again and again to the heroic age of the Wars of Religion, to the adventurous time when "men showed themselves great by character as well as by birth" (265), to the time as well that preceded the consolidation of royal power and the formation of absolute monarchy. This is the tumultuous age of Charles IX, Henry III, and Henry IV, the age of wars, insurrections, assassinations, and dynastic change. It is, for Mathilde, the age of adventure and the unexpected, the age in which the unforeseen and the extraordinary were the order of the day.

The second half of the sixteenth century is also extolled by the Romantics of the 1820s as the time when the dreary triumph of political absolutism and aesthetic classicism was far from a foregone conclusion. Mathilde's hatred of her own society, which hoped to reconstitute the neoclassical past of the seventeenth century, makes her sympathies with sixteenth-century upheaval natural. It also makes it easy for Stendhal to combine within her character zone allusions to the Wars of the League with allusions to the Revolution, leading Mathilde to think of Julien now as Boniface de La Mole and the next moment as Danton. The two chapters most explicitly devoted to the delineation of her character are entitled "Queen Marguerite" and "A Girl's Empire," turning her into a kind of monstrous but, in the contemporary context, compelling mixture of Marguerite de Navarre and the Emperor Napoleon.

The difficult and unnatural task of re-creating the conditions of an adventurous life in the midst of Restoration boredom finds its analogue in the novel in the paradox of Mathilde's narrative imagination: the obstinacy with which she plans for, consciously enacts, and expects to achieve the unexpected. Embarking on an affair with Julien, Mathilde tells herself: "Between Julien and me there is no contract to be signed, no lawyer, everything is heroic, everything is up to the free play of chance" (252). But what she experiences is something else, something indeed altogether unexpected, the complete absence of what she had been hoping to find: "There was nothing unexpected for her in all the events of the night, except the misery and shame she had discovered instead of those divine raptures that novels (*les romans*) talk about" (278).

The unexpected, then, is revealed as a construction principle of novels or romances. More specifically, of Romantic historical novels or, conversely, of novelistic histories. The distinction is not at this point particularly clear. Prosper de Barante writes histories that are self-consciously novelistic. Prosper Mérimée publishes *1572. Chronique du règne de Charles IX* (1829), Alfred de Vigny writes *Cinq-Mars* (1826), Victor Hugo comes out with *Notre-Dame de Paris* (1831). Walter Scott's historical novels enjoy immense popularity and influence historical writing itself, specifically the writing of Augustin Thierry. In fact, between 1815 and 1832, a very large proportion of all new novels in France are historical.[55] Stendhal himself, in *Racine et Shakespeare,* advocates for the creation of historical tragedies in prose that would teach French history to the French. And of course, *Rouge* itself is so intriguingly subtitled *Chronique de*

1830. In short, the novels that teach Mathilde to recognize and, paradoxically, to plan for the unexpected are the same historical novels that teach her to fantasize about the Wars of the League.

The veridiction of the unexpected emerges as a generic residue of the Romantic historical novel imported into *Rouge* via the character of Mathilde, and as such, it forms a coherent, all-too-predictable strain within the novel. When Mathilde finds nothing unexpected in what she has plotted, she discovers that the unexpected is always in excess of plot, even of the plot of the unexpected itself. On the other side of the Romantic plot, she finds prosaic reality, the misery and shame that recall her to her proper place in the world. Disemplotment, the breakdown of adventure, finds its sociopsychological correlate in renewed attention to social obligations. The loosening of the Romantic plot resolves into the plot of social conformism: "I have given myself a master! . . . He is the soul of honor, well, maybe so; but if I strain his vanity, he'll take revenge by making our relations known" (279).

Mathilde's Parisian temporality is thus closely allied to romance. In fact what we seem to have in her is Stendhal's own *onager*, the figure for the speed that overtakes itself, for the magic time of modernity that is always elsewhere, fleeting, but also, paradoxically, always there as a whole, standing still. Confronted with this sort of temporality, Julien begins to function as a conservative, retarding force. The word *devoir* as applied to him begins increasingly to shift its semantic valence, tending more and more toward an alliance with calculation, prudence, and self-interest. Simultaneously he cedes to Mathilde the privileged position in the novel of the agent of truth. When Mathilde informs Julien that she is pregnant, the lovers have the following exchange:

> —I want to write a note to my father . . . ; he has been more than a father to me, he has been a friend: as such, I should think it unworthy of you and me to try to deceive him even for a moment.
> —Good God! What are you going to do? Julien asked in disquiet.
> —My duty, she replied, her eyes glittering with joy.
> She sensed that she was being more magnanimous than her lover.
> —But he will dismiss me from the house in disgrace!
> —That's his privilege, we must respect it. I shall give you my arm, and we will go out the front door together, in the full light of day.
> Julien, staggered by this turn, begged her to wait a week.
> —I cannot, she told him; honor calls, I have seen my duty, I must do it, and right away. (347)

Much comes together in this exchange. We have an explicit, now thematized, link between truth telling and doing one's duty; we have duty's own impetuous temporality, the demand that it be fulfilled without delay; we have the sense of the shocking veridictory effect that dutiful action can have; we have also a new Julien, prudent, conservative, mindful of the future, and deferential to social proprieties. He is here perhaps at his worst, on the verge of becoming what Mme de Rênal's fateful letter will soon enough say that he is, an amoral ambitious hypocrite, no more.[56]

A particular character's truth-producing potential then is not, in *Rouge*, inherent in his or her essential psychological traits.[57] Rather, it depends on the position the character occupies vis-à-vis the represented social world. Julien progressively loses his veridictory capacity as he advances in the world. In the case of Mathilde, the sociohistorical conditions for the plot of ambition are absent. It would seem that nothing could make her lose the ability to effect the unexpected. And yet in the process she lapses into a kind of falsifying predictability of her own, into the timelessness of romance idealism. Here, everything is known ahead of time not because action follows strict social norms (after all, she has no patience for them) but because it obeys the logic of a preexisting historically transcendent, but no less predictable, model. If, locally, Mathilde achieves veridictory effects by precipitating the unexpected, in the long run, from the perspective of the novel as a whole, her fate (and Julien's as well) conforms to rigid emplotment mechanisms of her own. As Julien is swallowed up by social life, Mathilde loses herself in high romance.

Prison and Endings

Throughout the novel Julien dreams of isolation. Early on, having climbed to the top of a mountain outside of Verrières, he follows with his gaze the flight of a solitary eagle: "Its calm powerful movements struck him; he envied this power, he envied this isolation. Such had been the destiny of Napoleon; would it some day be his?" (51). There is wide agreement among critics that the day does indeed come, at the end of the novel, when Julien is in prison.[58] His sudden, apparently unexplained crime, his attempt on the life of Mme de Rênal, dislodges him from the falsifying grip of success and places him in isolation. Addressing Mathilde and Fouqué in response to their attempts to inform him of certain rumors that might raise his hopes of acquittal, he says: "Leave me my ideal life. Your little tricks and details from real life, all more or less irritating to me, would drag me out of heaven. One dies as one can: I want to think about death only in my own personal way. What do *other people* matter? My relations with *other people* are going to be severed abruptly" (382).

Imprisonment and lofty isolation come together with a final affirmation of the split between the ideal and the real. Julien seems determined to have nothing to do with life as he knew it throughout the novel. He renounces vanity, ambition, and, with them, hypocrisy; he promises to stand trial in contemptuous silence; he spends his time looking "straight into his soul" or, when Mme de Rênal is present, speaking sincerely about his love for her; he retreats into a stance that is resolutely "philosophical"; at last, he is able to inhabit the temporality of the day-to-day. In other words, we seem to have finally arrived at the place of veridiction proper, a place that is intimate enough, pure enough from stratifying social falsification to allow for clear conception and sincere expression of the ever-changing truth of one's inner being.[59]

Indeed, this reading of the place and function of the prison in the novel is tempting, but there is too much here to make us skeptical. Julien himself complains, producing one of his most brilliant maxims along the way: "The worst thing about a prison is that you can't shut your door" (397). And if we look closely, he goes back on just about every self-isolating resolution he makes. He breaks the Shakespearean promise he had given to Mathilde: "From this time forth I never will speak word" (365). He fails in his resolution to "stand mute" at the trial. A young priest installs himself by the gates of the prison and attracts crowds with promises to convert Julien. Julien has no choice but to admit him. Worse, his peace is disturbed by thoughts of how he would behave at the execution, of what people would think if he gives the slightest indication of fear or gloom. He promises to Fouqué: "I shall never *be seen* to grow pale" (407, emphasis added).

While imprisoned in the upper story of a gothic tower, Julien passes his days walking back and forth on the narrow terrace, admiring the magnificent view, smoking expensive cigars, reveling in a sense of freedom and newly acquired inner calm. What he does not know is that all the while he is enjoying his isolation, he is being observed from every telescope in town. Though Julien feels himself to be isolated from the world, the world is in fact engaged in the most intense and variegated involvement with Julien. All the major strains of narrative in which Julien was at one time or another involved come together now, when the protagonist has been thoroughly immobilized, to form the densest network of emplotments yet. The priest, installing himself humbly under the rain in the hope of gaining fame for converting a criminal celebrity, traces out the trajectory of religious hypocrisy, of unapologetic Tartufferie that characterized the spirit of the Besançon seminary. Mme de Rênal's appearance reintroduces the tempting possibilities of the pastoral. Fouqué's successful machinations display the power of the prosaic occupation of a merchant. And of course Mathilde is endlessly scheming on his behalf while persisting in her romantic heroics. All of these trajectories, now rendered ghostly, come to haunt Julien. After all, he had at one time or another considered or pursued them. Julien's isolation, freedom, truthfulness, and, in the face of death, plotlessness are indeed ideal. As such they are the obverse of his real condition, which is characterized by extreme exposure, radical determination, persisting vanity, and the thickest texture of emplotment to date.

What is still more disturbing is the way in which so many of these plots converge on Julien's execution. After the trial, thinking back to his outburst in the courtroom, Julien thinks proudly: "I was improvising, and for the first time in my life" (390). His ruthlessly honest and ultimately self-destructive speech is indeed unprepared and unpremeditated. It is his final dutiful act in the novel. But it is difficult to read as a *triumph* of dutiful veridiction over calculation, hypocrisy, and lies. In getting himself condemned to death, Julien unknowingly colludes with his enemies; in speaking the truth, he buttresses lies. His self-sacrifice is belated and superfluous; he is being sacrificed as it is.

First, as if to emphasize the participation of the entire social world of the Restoration in the execution of Julien, the novel stages a behind-the-scenes intrigue determining the outcome of the trial and involving characters that cover the spectrum of French society: M. de Frilair, M. de Valenod, Mme de Fervaque, and even the bishop of _____. Second, Julien's improvised, disinterested speech casts him in the role of a Danton, the executed source of rebellious truth and one of Mathilde's favorite models for emplotting her lover. Third, this same Danton opens the novel itself with the apocryphal words of the epigraph: "Truth, bitter truth!" Julien's dutiful, disemplotting pursuit of truth throughout the novel, a pursuit that for the most part proceeds against his own explicit will, is thus itself parodied and falsified through emplotment. Just as Mathilde's casting of Julien in the role of Danton or Boniface de La Mole is doubly bent on his decapitation, so is the plot of *Rouge* itself. In being executed for shooting Mme de Rênal, Julien fulfills the destiny that has been foreshadowed at the beginning of the novel in the famous incident in the church of Verrières. It is there that he finds a scrap of printed paper left on the lectern "as if for him to read." He reads about an execution of Louis Jenrel, recognizing that the last three letters of Jenrel's name are the same as his own, and not recognizing it as a full-fledged anagram of Julien Sorel. On the other side of the paper, he reads: "The first step . . ." The church of Verrières is of course the very same church that inspires him to embark on a career as a priest. It also happens to serve as the stage for his crime: this is where he shoots Mme de Rênal. Julien comes full circle; the first step he takes in the world makes the footprint into which his last step perfectly falls.

Julien's attempt on the life of Mme de Rênal is frequently adduced as the most unexpected, unmotivated, and precipitous act in the novel. And taken as a local response to a delimited situation it indeed strikes one as excessive, as carrying with it a dose of dutiful madness. But on the level of the whole, it is of course precisely what we have been awaiting all along. The most unexpected act in the novel is one that is also most forcefully foretold.

Julien's speech at the trial is indeed an improvisation, but once again, only locally. On the level of larger plot structures, it is overdetermined. In casting himself explicitly as a rebel and thus advancing the cause of his condemnation, Julien for the last time bares the device whereby local disturbance is co-opted into global coherence, local acts of veridictory rebellion are taken into a narrative the conclusion of which is triply foregone: through societal, Romantic-historical, and novelistic emplotment. He is executed, then, at the convergence of three plots, at the moment of a grand comic reconciliation of those tendencies within the novel that, throughout, appeared to be entwined in a struggle. Never before had he been traversed by so many determinations: "Never had that head been so poetic as at the moment when it was about to fall" (407).

The Novel's Poetry and the Truth

In light of the preceding, the word "poetic" acquires here an ambiguous ring. The ambiguity permeates the entire novel. If truth is a function of intimate, fleeting, modern time as it penetrates the inevitably social texture of the realist novel, if, in other words, truth is a function of disemplotment, then how can it be contained in a novel? Or, how should a novel be plotted and narrated to be truthful?

The poetry of the novel threatens its truth because it maintains a structural loyalty to the past. Repetition, recapitulation, foreshadowing—all of these are "restorative" modes of preserving the past in the present, of endowing the fleeting now with the weightiness of what can be observed, registered, understood. The logic of *sjuzhet,* of that temporal organization of events for which the passage of time is all along neutralized, is eternalist. Restoration ideology, with its *oubli* of the passage of time, with its obsessive *mise-en-place* of the present as "natural," is also an ideology of narrative, an ideology that even hasty, adventurous acts fail to escape for longer than an instant. Again and again, *Rouge* displays for us the mechanism whereby adventure turns into adventurism, where—through social co-optation of subjective motivations and through the sublation of *fabula* into *sjuzhet*—results of disinterested, spontaneous acts belie their origins, pervert them, make them appear as carefully calculated risks. And so the behind-the-scenes reconciliation of the romantic and the conventional, of duty and career, of adventure and calculation, should come as no surprise.

Truth, as it is conceived in this novel, can never take root in it because, according to this very conception, one of its functions is to debunk the artifice of the novelistic. It is only through the intensifications of plot, only through dutiful action that veridictory disemplotment can be momentarily produced. But ultimately, even this adventurous temporality is revealed as too poetic and thus not adventurous enough. *Fabula*-producing truth is caught in the cross fire between two kinds of falsifying *sjuzhet*, between two sets of conventions, two modes of rigidity: societal and poetic.

The dilemma in which this novel finds itself is generalizable to all narratives that, under the exigency of the veridictory mutation of the novel form, posit a disjunction between emplotment and truth. It can be formulated as follows: how can a coherent story allow for fleeting, irreducibly temporal truth, given that coherence itself is a product of an eternalist falsification? In the case of *Rouge*, the question has received a more specified historical thematization: how can liberating, natural, and open-ended truth be staged within a coherent narrative, given that coherence is always a kind of "restoration"? This is the specific way in which the novel stages the paradox of modernity, the contentious coexistence and codependence of eternalist and temporal veridiction.

The fault line of this paradox traverses the entire narrative structure of *Rouge*, splitting it into the global and the local, the whole and the part. The overarching plot of the novel stages the determining persistence of the past in the present. The eternalist *sjuzhet*-like tendencies of the novel itself reaffirm the lie of the social world that is depicted in the novel. Locally, however, the plotting is self-consciously awkward, stubbornly undramatic. Gérard Genette diagnoses this as a "systematic displacement of the narrative in relation to action, which results both in the elision of the principle events and in the accentuation of the incidental circumstance."[60] Again and again dramatic buildup on the level of narration culminates in nearly nothing. Julien's first nocturnal visit to Mathilde's room, his conversation with the priest in prison, and the execution itself are all crucial events passed over in contemptuous near silence. The effect of this suspension of narrative momentum evokes Julien's condition of helplessness when confronted by the maddening whimsy of Mathilde's temporality. The reader of *Rouge*, too, has no guarantees that the story will continue to be told the way it has been told up to now. On the other hand, he or she has no doubts about the shape of the whole, and can be sure, for example, that Julien will be executed in the end.[61] Global coherence and narrative overdetermination coexists here with local unpredictability, the occasionally frustrating adventure of reading.

Stendhal's novel models a world in which there is no truth of the whole, in which, moreover, the whole is precisely untrue.[62] Totality, taken either synchronically, as static social structure, or diachronically, as rigid narrative configuration, is essentially a mode of falsification. Only the part, the local, can anchor truth; only the subject, in a moment of dutiful action against his or her own calculable interests, can serve as the host of momentary veridiction, unmasking the world s/he inhabits. This paradox, setting the part and the whole against each other as the true and the false, this anti-Hegelian and anti-Balzacian metaphysics nevertheless constitutes Stendhal's solution, within the parameters of the realist novel, to the difficult problem of imbuing the rigid sociohistoric specificity of Restoration society with the intimate, truth-bearing temporality of modern life.

Comparative Interlude II: The Right Woman (Balzac)

The plots of *Rouge* and *La Peau de chagrin* resemble each other in one intriguing respect. In both of them the hero's trajectory leads him first away from the "right woman" and then back to her, via the detour of her false counterpart. Pauline and Mme de Rênal constitute departure points for Raphael and Julien. Both are mother figures, both modest, natural, loving, and both are retrospectively constituted as the proper objects of the heroes' desire. Mathilde and Foedora are mistakes, detours from the truth; they lead the heroes astray. They are wealthy Parisian salonnières, vain, proud, infinitely elusive.

The parallel helps bring out an important contrast: Raphael is emplotted through/by the right woman, Pauline; Julien is emplotted through/by the wrong woman, Mathilde. It is Pauline who foresees Raphael's future while reading his palm. In her embrace, he dies strangled by the Absolute, by identity, by pure *sjuzhet*. With her, he reaches both the truth and the end at the same time. With Julien, things are otherwise. For him, the right woman represents the *fabulaic* temporality of the day-to-day, the ideal (though unreachable) state of utter plotlessness. The wrong woman, on the other hand, is the agent of emplotment. It is Mathilde who foretells that he will get himself condemned to death. She casts him as Boniface de La Mole up to, and beyond, his execution. Here, the woman who holds the truth and the woman who carries with her the plot do not coincide. Again, the relation between plot and truth is disjunctive. Balzac's *Poète-et-Pythagore* becomes *Poète-ou-Pythagore* in Stendhal.

Thematically, at least in this regard, the novels appear to agree. The truths *of* these novels converge in the message: it is better to stick with the provinces, better never to have experienced the rhythms of "Parisian" modernity, better never to have taken the detour away from innocent, faithful, maternal love. But the truths *for* these novels, their implicit veridictory structures—their answers to the question, *how must a story be shaped to be able to contain the truth?*—part ways.

Something else becomes clear from this juxtaposition as well: that each novel contains its obverse veridictory principle and must pass through it, either, as in Balzac, by way of immanent containment and shaping of *fabulaic* temporal acceleration or, as in Stendhal, by way of difficult, hopeless, but resolute cracking open of the eternalist *sjuzhet* organizing both contemporary life and attempts to escape it.

Franco Moretti distinguishes between two ways of conceiving of capitalist society. On the one hand, it is intensely vigorous, highly energetic, constantly productive of narrative—in short, entrepreneurial. On the other hand, it is tedious, petty, repetitive, thrifty—in short, bourgeois: "On the one hand, the turbulent and impassioned civil society of the *Comédie humaine*—on the other, Stendhal's identification of the 'bourgeois' and 'tedious.'"[63] But we seem to have arrived at the conclusion that, in fact, both of these principles are inherent in both Balzacian and Stendhalian narrative. In Balzac, the extreme turbulence of impassioned civil society immanently organizes itself into shapes the horizon of which is more boring than boredom itself, is death. In Stendhal, the pettiness and tedium of contemporary life acquires titanic proportions in its encounter with and defeat of the turbulent, energetic, and impassioned individual. In Balzac, the heroic corners itself and turns, at least structurally, bourgeois; the hero dies in the arms of the woman who rendered truth timeless. In Stendhal, the tedious bourgeois is energized into an indomitable force, allowing the hero no more than glimpses of truth, too fleeting to hold on to or to die in. The veridictory wound inflicted on this world by the hero's death is instantaneously healed; his severed head in the hands of the eternally romantic Mathilde is a figure for the victorious falsehood of heroic ("entrepreneurial") predictability.

3

Enigma and Emplotment in Dostoevsky

> Time demands the truth . . . calls the truth to light and so on,
> so that it would be clear that *Time* and *Truth* are one and the same.[1]
> —Fyodor Dostoevsky (from a letter to his brother Mikhail)

Who Is He Really?

Nowhere in Dostoevsky's fiction does the word "truth" [*pravda*] occur with such obsessive frequency as in his short story "The Meek One" (*Krotkaia*). The narrative—interpolated in his regularly published and primarily journalistic *Diary of a Writer* (November 1876)—is written from the perspective of a just-widowed nameless hero who tells his story in the course of a night, in the presence of his wife's dead body: "Imagine to yourself a husband whose wife is lying on the table, a suicide, who a few hours earlier threw herself out the window. . . . He paces his rooms and tries to make sense of what has happened, 'to collect his thoughts to a point.'. . . Little by little he actually *figures out* the matter and collects his 'thoughts to a point.' A series of memories he calls up brings him irresistibly to the *truth*; the truth irresistibly elevates his mind and heart."[2] The truth first and foremost at stake, then, is the truth behind a certain event, the suicide of the narrator's wife. The first enigma here is the dead body itself, and, as in Balzac, the story is called upon for explanation. But as the story unfolds, we begin to realize that it is itself structured by a veridictory puzzle; the answer to the question, *why this dead body?* turns out to consist of another question: *how is a person to be known?*

A former officer forced, some years ago, to resign from his regiment for refusing to fight a duel, the narrator-hero of the story decides to "take revenge on society" by setting up a pawnshop, thus assuming the disgrace to which he has been subjected by others. Soon enough, however, this manner of vengeance proves to be insufficient. He has been dishonored in the eyes of others, and yet he feels all along that "the very most truthful truth" [*samaia pravdinskaia pravda*] about him is that at bottom he is "the noblest of men." All he lacks is someone to recognize this, to intuit beneath his rough-mannered, curmudgeonly appearance the pure heart of an unjustly suffering outcast. And so the narrator marries a high-minded, strong-willed but gentle girl in order to set her up in the position from which the enigma of his true identity could be solved and the disgrace hanging over him lifted. In order to be solved, however, the enigma must first be sustained. The narrator resolutely avoids direct heart-to-heart communication with his wife and intentionally hides behind the mask of a scoundrel. All along, he imagines, his wife must be watching him, trying to fathom the hidden motivations behind his coldness, cruelty, and stinginess: "Because, you must agree, if I myself had begun explaining and prompting, shuffling and begging for respect—it would have been as if I were begging alms" (262).[3]

As the story nears its conclusion, it becomes increasingly obvious that the meek one has failed to gain insight into her husband's supposedly pure essence. At some point, she seems to have stopped watching, to have given up on him altogether. As soon as the hero recognizes this, he panics and radically switches veridictory strategies. It is not immediate metaphoric insight but full-blown confession that is now supposed to carry the truth about him: "I hurried too much, too much, but a confession was needed, was necessary—yes, and much more than a confession! . . . I told her all about me and about her" (287–88).

Confession, the organization of feelings and events into a meaningful sequence, is motivated here by the failure of the metaphoric transition from appearance to the truth. Narrative rushes in when immediate insight fails. But the text of the confession is absent from the story; all we know is that he tells her *all*. "All" [*vsio*] refers us back to the story itself. What he tells her is what he later tells us in the presence of her dead body: "Here is how it was. I'll simply put it in order (order!)" (250). The truth beneath appearances can only be revealed by means of a plot after all, by means of a telling of *all* "in order."[4]

Overwhelmed by the hero's confession, the meek one commits suicide. She cannot love the man who is telling the story, the vile pawnbroker who has been nasty to her for many months, and yet she *must* love the man about whom the story is told, the unfortunate victim of injustice, disgraced and proud, in the grips of an irresistible desire to be understood against all odds. It is this dilemma that she finds unbearable, one moment promising the hero to be a faithful wife and the next, leaping to her death. But in the presence of her dead body—or, less literally, upon it—veridictory "order" is constructed. The story (not the one told to the meek one but the one told to the imagined listeners after her death) heals the split: to the listeners, he is both men throughout, appearance and essence in one. Here we finally have "everything," everything, that is, minus the meek one herself, plus her dead body, the reminder of what has been sacrificed.

It appears, then, that we have begun elaborating something like a Dostoevskian inflection of the familiar veridictory pair, *Poète* and *Pythagore*. The meek one is called upon to do the work of immediate, metaphoric truth, reading essence behind appearance. She is the new, sacrificial, Pythagoras, infusing the Poet's (the narrator's) work with truth; vanishing, but leaving a trace. The key question is, as before, what is this trace? What is it that remains to remind us of the philosophical or mystical truth at the core of the constructed narrative order? In *Louis Lambert,* it was fragmentary structure; in *La Peau de chagrin,* the shriveling movement of the magic skin: desires may distend, but metaphors inevitably contract. In *Le Rouge et le noir,* it was a certain dutiful haste driving a wedge of uncompromising interiority into the world of socialized repetition, producing flashes of *fabulaization,* the unexpected. Here, in "The Meek One," as in Balzac, the trace of truth is also related to death; it is in fact quite explicitly the dead body itself. But in narratological terms, it is also something else, it is death as the "insensateness" [*kosnost'*] of accident: "Above all, the pity is that it was all chance—simple, barbaric, insensate chance. That's the pity of it! Five minutes is all, I was only five minutes late! If I'd come five minutes earlier—the moment would have flown over like a cloud, and would never have entered her head afterward. . . . And now again empty rooms, again I am alone. There's the pendulum ticking, it doesn't care, it's not sorry for anything. No one's here—that's the trouble!" (293).

The meek one's death, then, is a matter of mere accident; it is utterly meaningless, it both results in and signifies the fact that "no one's here." "No one" resonates with ambiguity: now that the meek one is dead, the hero is alone without her, but he is also alone together with everyone else, alone in the godless world. Accident as insensateness is opposed to (the meek one's) premeditation or (divine) Providence. Only if her suicide is not, strictly speaking, deliberate, a matter of conscious decision on her part, only then is it no more than "barbaric, insensate chance." But on another, grander scale, only if there is no God can such accidents happen: "People are alone on the earth—that's the trouble! 'Is there a living man on the field?' the Russian warrior cries. I, too, though not a warrior, cry out, and no one answers. . . . Everything is dead and the dead are everywhere. Only people, and around them silence—that's the earth! 'People, love one another'—who said that? whose testament is it? The pendulum ticks insensibly, disgustingly. . . . No, seriously, when she's taken away tomorrow, what about me then?" (295).

The equivocation between these two absences (of the meek one and of God) is constant and irresolvable, and irresolvable with it is the equivocation between Providence and plan. According to the narrator, his wife's death is meaningless twice over—not premeditated, not thought-through, "a moment, an unaccountable moment"; *nor* is it, nor could it be, predestined by a benevolent God. But positing this double absence is for the narrator an arduous task, one that is only imperfectly accomplished. He protests too much and, as a result, the questions persist: *not providential? not thought-through?* With regard to the former, there is obvious vacillation: on the one hand "only people, and around them silence," but on the other, vague recollections of Christ's testament of love. As for the supposedly unpremeditated nature of his wife's suicide, the hero's arguments (she didn't leave a note) are no stronger than the counter-arguments he adduces and fails convincingly to dispel (the apparently deliberate gesture of taking the icon with her in her leap).

In a typically Dostoevskian manner, the hero is represented from within his own consciousness and in his own words as having intimations of something he is explicitly denying. Here, what is denied and affirmed at once is the possibility of another's plot coming into contact with his own, the possibility that the accident is not merely a sign of ontological intransigence but also evidence for the existence of other stories, radically or only relatively transcending his own.

The trace of Pythagoras in the Poet, of the meek one in her husband's self-revelatory narrative, can be seen as marking it in several ways, all more or less immanent to the hero's consciousness. The trace is death itself, her dead body motivating and organizing the confessional ordering of feelings and events. It is also the accident as blind chance, as sheer meaninglessness, signifying the profound loneliness of the hero confronted with the truth about himself. And finally, it is accident as a hint of an opening, a kind of coincidence, marking the impingement of other plots upon the plot of the hero, and even perhaps—though this will have to stay merely conjectural for now—the possibility of regeneration in another('s) plot.

Much of this chapter is dedicated to exploring the consequences of this intriguing and distinctly Dostoevskian blend of *Poète* and *Pythagore* (plot and truth, narrative and metaphor) for the veridictory shape of *Crime and Punishment*. But the importance of one particular aspect of the story, having been implied, has not as yet been sufficiently stressed. What we see in "The Meek One" more vividly than anywhere else in Dostoevsky is that the truth most centrally at stake in much of his narrative output is the truth about the hero. For Dostoevsky the novelist, knowledge is primarily knowledge of a self.

It is possible to see, through the prism of this short story, that the question, who is s/he? structures all of Dostoevsky's major novels from the post-Reform era. In *The Idiot,* who is Nastasya Filippovna? who is Aglaya? In *The Brothers Karamazov,* who is Ivan and who is Dmitry? In *The Possessed,* primarily, who is the mysterious Stavrogin? Who is the elusive Versilov in *The Adolescent?* And, of course, in *Crime and Punishment* itself, who is Raskolnikov? Dostoevsky's enigmatic heroes are often uncannily aware of their predicament as objects of knowledge. Thus Ivan Karamazov to his brother Alyosha: "What task are you and I faced with now? My task is to explain to you as quickly as possible my essence, that is, what sort of a man I am, what I believe in and what I hope for, is that right?"[5] What matters, then, is not Ivan's truth against Alyosha's; rather, it is the truth *about* Ivan *to* Alyosha.

But if some major characters in Dostoevsky consistently posit the enigma of their inner, deeper selves, then others function as detectives, called upon to discover or at least obsessively to inquire into the essence of others. The meek one herself is the martyr of such a mission, but there are also the more or less successful Prince Myshkin, Alyosha Karamazov, Father Zosima, Arkady Dolgoruky, the narrator of *The Possessed,* and of course the great forefather of latter-day detectives, investigator by profession Porfiry Petrovich. Some of them, in fact most of them, are nearly as gifted at understanding selves as their counterparts are at presenting selves that mystify. Zosima and Myshkin possess uncanny insight into their interlocutors' minds, hearts, and even destinies. The less saintly figures of Alyosha and Porfiry Petrovich come close.[6]

The narrative dynamic of "The Meek One" sets up this confrontation between the knower and the "to be known" in skeletal form. How does one get at the truth about a person? Instantly, immediately, or through a detour of narration? Is paradigmatic truth available to Father Zosima, who, with uncanny insight, bows to Dmitry Karamazov, marking him out for great future suffering? Or is it more properly granted to Arkady Dolgoruky, desperately ignorant about his father, except when helped out by partial narrative accounts? Put another way, is metaphor alone sufficient or do we need the mediation of story? And if we do, then, once again, in what specific ways does the former shape the latter?

In short, then, the key veridictory question for Dostoevsky's post-Reform novelistic output is: within the parameters of what kind of story is the truth about the hero tellable?[7] But looking beyond the novels to Dostoevsky's journalistic work as well, it becomes clear that this very question persistently reappears in it with a different object of inquiry. To the question, *who is the hero?*

corresponds the question *what is Russia?* within the parameters of what kind of story should we attempt to fathom it?[8]

Nonsynchronicity and the Narrative Shapes of Russia

As soon as it became obvious, after the ascension to the throne of Alexander II in 1855 and the end of the Crimean War in 1856, that the course of Russian history was inevitably going to undergo major shifts, the public sphere began to swarm with possible answers. Unlike Restoration France, Russia in the period of Great Reforms cannot be said to have *undergone* a great number of cataclysmic political and ideological shifts in the course of a very short period of time. Rather, what can be said is that it had intensely *witnessed* them. In France, each new social order, from the Revolution to the Second Empire, conceives of itself as having surpassed and supplanted what has come before. The novels of Balzac and Stendhal stage the conflicts of worldview and narrative pace in historical perspective, maintaining and even symbolically adumbrating distinctions between past and present, the residual and the dominant. The situation in Russia is different. Here, by the late 1850s and after a period of prolonged "stagnation," we find the conditions for what might be called a metahistorical stance, one that surveys all historically unfolding ideological positions simultaneously as competing trajectories for future development.

The search for the proper story of Russia culminates in a number of prominent possibilities. Confronted by defeat in the Crimean War, some argue that Russia has fallen far behind Western Europe and must to be brought up to date at a moderate pace by means of liberalizing reforms. Others, less mainstream and less patient, hope to incite a great peasant revolution that would destroy every foundation of the existing order. There are those as well who believe that such a revolution, though desirable, is as yet impossible and can be realized only after a relatively prolonged period of education and preparation of the masses. Some believe it is necessary to oppose all change, all progressive movement, and instead to defend traditional Russian values: Autocracy, Nationality, Orthodoxy. Still others accept the need for progress but conceive of it in organic terms, as internal development rather than a consequence of the imposition of external principles, a forced Westernization.[9]

Soon after returning to St. Petersburg from political exile, Dostoevsky joined with his brother Mikhail to found a journal "of literature and politics" and became one of its editors. *Time* (*Vremia*, 1861–1863) brought together a number of like-minded writers and thinkers, united by their rejection of the abstract universalism—liberal, radical, and conservative alike—that took Russia to be confined to the universal-historical path traveled by the countries of Western Europe. In fact, much that is published in *Time* presupposes a philosophy of history that altogether rejects historical universalism, claiming instead that histories are multiple, and that Russia should follow its own unique path and keep its own time. Thus, one regular contributor to the journal explains the meaning of freedom (in general and of the former serfs in particular) as follows: "Freedom consists not in the capacity for development as such, but in the capacity for active development, i.e., in complete originality [*samobytnost'*]: in self-rule [*samoupravlenie*], self-activity [*samodeiatel'nost'*], self-sufficiency, [*samodostatochnost'*], and, most important, self-reliance [*samoupovanie*]."[10]

The incantatory repetition of the prefix "self" (*samo*) renders vivid one of the key shared philosophical assumptions of the journal: the emancipated peasants are not to be treated as objects; the bureaucratic question, what is to be done with . . . ? is absolutely inapplicable to them. Instead, they—and, with them, Russia itself—should be posited as an enigma, one that is not unlike the enigma of the living *self*, which must reveal itself through its own independent activity.

To the list of nouns prefixed by "self," Dostoevsky himself soon adds another, the most important one of all: self-historicity. "We are distinct," he writes in an 1865 notice announcing the publication of his second journal *Epoch* (*Epokha*, 1864–1865), "we are peculiar, *self-historical* [*svoeistorichny*]."[11] And while the story of many Western civilizations may have already ended, Russia's story is, in many ways, only just beginning. For many years Russia has lain asleep; now it is waking, ready to embark upon a trajectory. But this trajectory, "our own story" (*nasha sobstvennaiia povest'*)[12] is still a mystery, a puzzle (*zagadka*).[13] Russia's course must be puzzled out; it must be intuited or guessed.[14] This is the task that Dostoevsky sets for the journal: to find the right story for Russia, a story that would be adequate to its self-historicity, that would be uniquely and organically its own.[15]

We can suggest now that Dostoevsky's novelistic preoccupation with the question, who is s/he?—what is the unique and truthful story of his/her life?—is readable as a fictional recasting of the question, What is Russia?—what is the narrative shape adequate to its enigmatic particularity?[16] It would then be possible to understand his post-Reform novels as testing grounds for various modes of veridictory emplotment, as zones of narrative experimentation where the proper veridictory plot or configuration of plots can be identified among a number of historically available possibilities.[17]

Crime and Punishment, as an idiosyncratic protodetective novel, renders the quest for the identity of the hero explicit and delineates its parameters. Critics have noticed that though we know the criminal's name, his whereabouts, and even the minute circumstances of the murder he committed, we are still denied essential knowledge about him.[18] The whodunit is here to be understood as follows: What is the deeper underlying essence of this man, this former student Raskolnikov, who killed the old pawnbroker and took her money? As it turns out, to inquire thus is to ask to which of the many competing stories he most properly belongs.

Early Narrative Options

Early on in the novel Raskolnikov is presented with two alternative visions of advancement in the world: a crime or a career. The narrative trajectory of the crime is formulated as follows: "Kill [the old pawnbroker] and take her money, so that afterwards with its help you can devote yourself to the service of all mankind."[19] This, in the end, is the trajectory he chooses. And here is the one he rejects: "Oh yes, of course, [my] happiness can be arranged; [I] can be kept at the university, made a partner in the office, [my] whole fate can be secured; maybe later [I'll] be rich, honored, respected, and perhaps [I'll] even end [my] life a famous man" (44).

To this bifurcation of ambition, whose *locus classicus* within the realist novel is surely Rastignac's "Mandarin" dilemma in *Père Goriot,* Dostoevsky adds a characteristic twist, casting the alternatives not merely as moral choices but also as modes of self-knowledge. On a higher level of self-consciousness, the question, what is the better, more desirable alternative, crime or career? turns into the transcendental inquiry: will I be defined as someone who transcended ordinary morality and became a great benefactor of humanity or as someone who became a lawyer and a respectable bourgeois?" In Dostoevsky, wealth, success, and the paths to them are only material upon which a mysterious self weaves its self-identifying pattern.

Thus, Raskolnikov's chosen plot, the plot of the crime, must be understood as bearing a generic resemblance to the traditional (e.g., hagiographic) narratives of ordeal.[20] An ordeal is intended to establish the hero's identity in the course of an extraordinary trial. Every time the hero successfully undergoes the trial, his identity is confirmed: he is a loyal knight, a faithful lover, a saintly monk, a true savior. Throughout the novel Dostoevsky repeatedly plays with the Russian word for crime, *prestuplenie,* baring its etymological makeup. *Prestuplenie* is a kind of "overstepping," most explicitly, of course, the overstepping of legal and moral limitations. The word also resonates with the Napoleonic stepping over of dead bodies on the path to glory. Less readily noticed, however, and possibly more fundamental, is the temporal dimension of the metaphor: stepping over stages in time, leaping into the future not merely for the sake of quick success but also for the sake of immediate ordeal-like self-knowledge that would obviate the need to live out one's life, step-by-step, to the end. The particular relevance of this last meaning of *prestuplenie* finds confirmation in Dostoevsky's journalistic polemic with the radical intelligentsia.

In an 1861 essay published in *Vremia,* Dostoevsky addresses his impatient opponents half ironically with the following proposal: "You yearn for enormous activity; would you like us to give you one, one that will exceed all of your expectations? . . . Here it is: sacrifice all of your giantness for the sake of the universal good; instead of seven-mile steps, take inch-long ones; accept the idea that if it is impossible to step farther, then an inch is after all more than nothing."[21] According to Dostoevsky the radicals are too impatient in their desire to transform Russia once and for all according to preexisting models developed in the West. For them the future is not far ahead, not something that must await fruition; it is already upon us, not temporally, but geographically and culturally displaced. To them, Russia's identity must be forced, precipitated in the timeframe of an ordeal: a popular uprising that would overturn the current order of things and allow the people to become who they are, or a coup by a minority of intellectuals to tell the people who they should be—something fast, some overstepping is the method.

This, for better or for worse, is the historiographic "content" of the narrative shape Raskolnikov chooses. But what about the one he explicitly rejects, the significantly slower path of career and accumulation, associated with the unattractive figure of the arriviste Pyotr Luzhin? Luzhin is an "intelligent man" [*umnyi chelovek*], intelligent in the sense that he knows how to look out for his own advantage. "To make a fortune and to have as many things as possible"— this would be Luzhin's motto. But it is not to be found in *Crime and Punishment* itself. Instead, this formula appears again and again in Dostoevsky's reminiscences about his visit to Paris, published in the third volume of *Vremia* for 1863.[22] According to Dostoevsky, these words express no less than the highest moral principle, the very catechism, of the Paris bourgeois.

Still more to the point here is his description in *Winter Notes on Summer Impressions* (*Zimnie zapiski o letnikh vpechatleniiakh*, 1863), of the temporality associated with bourgeois accumulation. This temporality is twofold. First, on the level of human history, time has ended. The petit bourgeois considers himself to be the pinnacle of existence, the crown of creation. The entire course of history leads up to him and, with him, stops. But once history has ended, what is one to do? One is to "*faire fortune*" and to accumulate as many things as possible—this and this alone is now "the duty of nature and humanity" (*dolg prirody i chelovechestva*).²³ And so the second temporal dimension is described as follows: "So, I'll do a little business today in the shop and, tomorrow, God willing, I'll do some more, and maybe the day after tomorrow, too, with God's great mercy. Well, and then, then, only to have saved up a tiny bit as quickly as possible, and *après moi le déluge*."²⁴

The comic insertions of phrases like "God willing" or "with God's mercy," insertions that would in another context invoke the uncertainty of the future, the hopeful and slightly apprehensive look ahead, here emphasize precisely the absence of any weighty conception of the future at all. The time of accumulation, the time of a career, is meaningless repetition, homogeneous, merely quantitative advancement.²⁵

Raskolnikov's early choices would seem to be limited to two narrative trajectories: petit bourgeois career and revolutionary murder ordeal. But they are not. From the very start, another possibility is there, located on the very margins of his consciousness and linked to the character of his fellow student Razumikhin. While wandering through St. Petersburg in a daze of murderous preoccupation, Raskolnikov realizes that he is unconsciously walking in the direction of Razumikhin's lodgings. He is surprised. "So did I really mean to straighten things out with Razumikhin alone? To find the solution for everything in Razumikhin?" he asks himself. The answer, mysteriously enough, appears to be yes, and yet he doesn't go. "I will go to him . . . the next day, after *that*, once *that* is already finished and everything has taken a new course" (52).

Of course, "after *that*" it is already too late, but increasingly it becomes clear that had he gone to Razumikhin then, *that*, the crime, may not have happened at all. Razumikhin, it turns out, presents Raskolnikov with yet another narrative shape. It is not immediately clear what it is, but we have hints of it early on. In order to support himself at the university, Razumikhin works as a tutor and translator. When Raskolnikov does come to visit him, Razumikhin suggests that he take translations as well. The play on the difference between "crime" (*prestuplenie*) and "translation" (*perevod*) is audible in Russian. To step over, to transgress on the one hand and to lead to the other side, to *translate*, on the other.

This of course would not have been enough, but we have better clues in Razumikhin's explicitly formulated historiography. At a crucial point in the novel, apparently by way of a digression, Razumikhin explodes with a diatribe against "the socialists": "With them it's not mankind developing all along in a historical, living way that will finally turn by itself into a normal society, but, on the contrary, a social system coming out of some mathematical head, will at once organize the whole mankind and instantly make it righteous and sinless, sooner than any living process, without any historical and living way! That's why they have such an instinctive hatred of history.... That's why they so dislike the living process of life.... You can't overleap nature with logic alone" (256). Note the stress on "living process," on organic historical development, on the rejection of "mathematical," pregiven formulas for social organization—and all this in contrast to the desire to "overleap," to find a shortcut to perfection. Note also the association between theory and radical temporal precipitation. Much of this could have been taken verbatim from any of the numerous polemical and historico-philosophical passages from *Time* or *Epoch*.[26] Razumikhin's proposed temporality moves step-by-step; it translates, "leads over" (*perevodit*) rather than transgresses, oversteps (*prestupaet*), and, in the process, gives lessons, educates.[27]

It is this last qualification that helps us distinguish between two kinds of step-by-step progression: Luzhin's bourgeois accumulation and Razumikhin's conservative historiography. For Luzhin, temporality is, as we have said, merely serial: the distinction between one moment and the next is quantitative—first this much (profit), then more of the same, then still more, and so on. The trajectory advocated by Razumikhin is one in which every following moment contributes something essentially new; it is the trajectory of development. Earlier we have had a chance to look at a passage in Goethe's *Lehrjahre,* where, toward the end of the novel, Wilhelm is confronted with his childhood friend Werner. All the while Wilhelm was undergoing his "apprenticeship," Werner was making money as a merchant. When they meet after a long separation, Werner comments: "Look at how you stand! How well everything fits together! Indolence makes one prosper, whereas I, poor wretch..., if I had not spent my time earning a mint of money, there wouldn't be anything to say for me."[28]

Though Goethe is not nearly as unfriendly to his "bourgeois" as Dostoevsky is to his, the narrative shape they represent is much the same—mere serial accumulation in time, and this sort of time appears to be narratively unrepresentable. Neither Luzhin nor Werner has a history of his own; each stands for the route untaken by the truly historical (rather than posthistorical) hero. The difference between the trajectories offered by Luzhin and Razumikhin can thus be understood as the difference between the narrative of a career and a narrative of genuine formation, a *Bildungsroman.*

In light of what has been said, then, it is tempting to introduce a corrective to Mikhail Bakhtin's influential account in *Problems of Dostoevsky's Art* (*Problemy tvorchestva Dostoevskogo*, 1929) of Dostoevsky's polyphonic novel. For Bakhtin, who underplays the finalizing, truth-speaking function of plot in Dostoevsky, the polyphony at stake is one of characters' discourses and the worldviews embodied in them. But as we have seen, particular worldviews are reflected not only in characters' speech but also in their manner of plotting. A polyphony of discourses in *Crime and Punishment,* reflecting the multiplicity ("heteroglossia") of social dialects of the time, is thus complemented by a polyphony of emplotments, representing some of the most prominent temporal shapes competing for dominance over the historical moment. The two polyphonies should in fact be impossible to tell apart, and what Bakhtin refers to as discursive character zones are also zones of emplotment.[29] So far, we have seen three such zones: Raskolnikov's own, compelling him to stake everything on a single act; Luzhin's bourgeois, careerist option, relying on homogeneous, serial time; and Razumikhin's model of *Bildungsroman* apprenticeship. Soon, to these will be added narrative trajectories associated with Sonya, Porfiry Petrovich, and Svidrigailov. But before we move on to discuss them in their capacity as carriers of plots of completion, the central veridictory dynamic of enigma and deciphering should be addressed in greater detail.

Comparative Interlude I: Intertexts (Balzac)

It has become a common place of Dostoevsky criticism that if *Crime and Punishment* should be thought of together with any novel by Balzac, that novel is *Le Père Goriot* (1835). There are indeed striking thematic parallels between the two novels. The most prominent of them is surely the question of whether or not it is acceptable to found one's success or happiness on the suffering of another. And considered in light of the problematic here at stake, the two novels also share something; namely, a structure of bifurcating possibilities. Like Raskolnikov, Rastignac has the choice between trajectories of leap and progression. He can struggle to make his way in Paris by more or less dishonest means; or he can follow the demonic Vautrin, become an accomplice to a crime, and make his whole fortune at once.

But throughout the novel, with Vautrin's offer constantly in the background, Rastignac is occupied with making his career in Paris. He makes mistakes, they are corrected, he learns—a kind of Restoration *Bildungsroman* sets in, an apprenticeship to social mores, an attempt to master the social codes of modern city life. And if he never, for himself, decisively rejects Vautrin's plan, still the novel is not concerned with the consequences of narrative leap but, at most, with its temptations. And in the final version of the novel at least, this option is rejected: Rastignac chooses to make his way by other, more "sociable," though perhaps no less unethical, means.

To be sure, the first Russian edition of the novel, which would surely have been familiar to an admirer such as Dostoevsky, ended differently. Here, having buried old Goriot and guided by "Vautrin's shadow," Rastignac goes directly to pay a visit to Mme Couture. In other words, at the novel's conclusion, he appears to accept the criminal offer.[30] Still, even in this version, the transgressive leap takes place at the outer edge of the narrative, while the main body of the novel is organized according to the gradualist logic of education. Yet, as we have seen, this education itself is founded upon the kernel of metaphoric precipitous emplotment that emerges as the central concern of the *Études philosophiques* and of *La Peau de chagrin* in particular. Balzac's philosophical narratives intensify and actualize the veridictory logic of his *Études de moeurs*, and as such they present what is structurally a more appropriate analogy to Dostoevsky's novels and specifically to *Crime and Punishment*. Raphael de Valentin does not hesitate, he gambles; he rejects step-by-step progression, rejects both education and accumulation (possibilities that are invoked but remain unactualized); like Raskolnikov, he chooses to leap and pays the price. Thus, Rastignac may be behind some of Raskolnikov's explicit thoughts, but it is the logic of Raphael's life to which he owes his underlying narrative trajectory.

The "Accidental" Crime and the Constitution of the Enigma

Raskolnikov's crime is plotted as a step, or rather a leap, on the way of a great man's life: kill the old woman, take her money, and become the benefactor of humanity. But unfortunately the crime must also be plotted as an act; it must be planned. It is here, between the two plots of life and event, that Raskolnikov begins to vacillate: "But these were still trifles he had not even begun to think about, nor did he have time. He had thought about the main thing, and put the trifles off until he himself was convinced of everything. But this last seemed decidedly unrealizable. . . . He could in no way imagine, for example, that one day he would finish thinking, get up, and—simply go there" (70). The problem here presented has often been understood as that of mediating between theory and action, the abstract and the concrete. But, more accurately, Raskolnikov's condition is delimited by the need and the difficulty of weaving two plots into each other—the plot of a life (the "abstract") and the plot of an act (the "concrete"). Raskolnikov's impasse is predicated upon the fact that the two plots are inextricably linked but mutually undermining. The more clearly he visualizes the details of the murder, the less convincing the conclusions of the theory become. The more compelling the biographical pattern, the more appalling the particulars of the crime. What fails Raskolnikov is the double plotting constitutive of biographical coherence. He is unable to embed the forward-looking, "intentional" plan of an act into the more encompassing plot that perceives the act in light of an already accomplished life.

Yet despite Raskolnikov's reluctance, the event does take place: "He went on believing least of all in his final decisions, and when the hour struck, everything came out . . . somehow accidentally, even almost unexpectedly" (71). Indeed, numberless accidents, little chance occurrences, and "friendly" coincidences gravitate to the moment of the crime. Both leading up to and away from it, these events carry the hero, protect him, and ensure his success. They surround the crime with an aura of mystery, a sense of design surpassing that of the hero himself. One such encounter takes place on the day before the crime.

Returning home by an unusual route, preoccupied with his murderous plans, but still indecisive, Raskolnikov overhears a conversation between his future victim's sister, Lizaveta, and two tradesmen. He finds out that the very next evening Lizaveta will not be at home between the hours of six and seven and therefore the old pawnbroker will be alone. Quite accidentally, then, the precise time of the murder is established. Raskolnikov knows that such an opportunity may not present itself again. He wonders in retrospect: "But why . . . had such an important, decisive and at the same time highly accidental encounter in the Haymarket (where he did not even have any reason to go) come just then, at such an hour and such a moment in his life, to meet him precisely in such a state of mind and precisely in such circumstances as alone would enable it, this encounter, to produce the most decisive and final effect on his entire fate?" (60). We are confronted here with an implicit theory of the accident in *Crime and Punishment*. The mode of retrospection in which the sentence appears enables it to combine two points of view on the encounter. First, it is "important" and "decisive"; it has weighty consequences, determines what happens later. But it is just as much "highly accidental," unforeseen and unforeseeable, utterly beyond Raskolnikov's horizon of expectations at the time. The encounter is thus shown as falling out of the hero's forward-looking plot and fitting into a pattern that becomes discernable only with the passage of time. It bears with it a veridictory vector, addresses a question to the future and receives from it a reply.[31]

Paradigmatic here is yet another series of chance occurrences in connection with the murder. Raskolnikov has planned to take his weapon, an axe, from his landlady's kitchen. According to his calculations, Nastasya, the landlady's servant, should be out that evening. When he comes down the stairs, however, he sees her in the kitchen and realizes that his plan has failed. From the perspective of his plot, this is a devastating accident. And yet it is remedied all-too-easily and all-too-soon. Lingering indecisively in the gateway, he glimpses an axe in the caretaker's room. "If not reason," he mutters, "then the devil" (72).

From the point of view of conventional plotting, this failure-success sequence is difficult to justify. Here, a potentially smooth, causally solid relation between events leading to the murder is replaced by a jerky sequence of mutually negating accidents: the axe is taken away only, almost instantaneously, to be returned. What happens here surely does not advance the action. Rather, it subtly switches plots on the hero. The second axe is not Raskolnikov's, is not, unlike the first one, part of his plan. It arrives to him from elsewhere, from *another* plot. No wonder then that when he finally delivers the blow, "his own strength seem[s] to have no part in it" (76).[32]

The murder weapon functions here as a figure for the dissecting power of the accident vis-à-vis plot. The accident cuts through plot in such a way as to reveal within it its constitutive parts: *fabula* and *sjuzhet*. What had seemed to Raskolnikov to be a coherent plan turns out to be mere groping in the dark. His plot breaks down against the accidental inaccessibility of the axe; it is revealed as mere *fabula*, as a hodgepodge of unpremeditated actions and random events. Simultaneously, however, this very same axe is found elsewhere, indicating that somewhere, beyond the consciousness of the hero, *sjuzhet* is once again in place; the hero is in the grips of design.

The aura of the accidental surrounding the crime positions it, then, as the place of the enigma, a mysterious event, soliciting veridictory reemplotment. Who was it, after all, who killed the old pawnbroker? And how exactly did it happen? We know the answers to both, and yet, on a deeper level, both are still a puzzle. If in more conventional detective fiction, the endpoint of the narrative is reached when we retrace the criminal's steps all the way up to the moment of the crime, here the logic is reversed. The criminal's ways to the crime, traced in detail, is the very mystery itself, not the solution. Who did it? How? We don't quite know, and neither does the hero. The accident both poses the question and invites a response. Raskolnikov himself is the first to heed the invitation.

Days after the crime, in a state of delirium, having just fainted at the police station and thus attracted the attention of suspicious investigators, he rushes home, gathers up everything he has taken from the old pawnbroker, and runs out. He walks through the city, frantically, not knowing what to do with the loot. At a certain point he even considers throwing it all in the river. But minutes later, he wonders: "If indeed this whole thing was done consciously ..., then how is it that so far you haven't even looked into the purse and do not know what you've actually gained ... ? Weren't you going to throw it into the water just now, this purse, along with all the other things which you also haven't seen yet?" (110). Raskolnikov is confronted with the task of making the crime his own; he is astonished at not being able to do so. He has become a mystery to himself.[33]

Much of his behavior in the aftermath of the murder can be understood as the work of self-detection, an attempt to emplot retroactively the accident that has rendered him enigmatic, to link *fabula* back to *sjuzhet*. But this is not all. Like the narrator-hero of "The Meek One," Raskolnikov is also counting on the attentive eyes of others. Indeed, the problem of weaving together the biography of a great man and the life of a criminal is only exacerbated once the crime has been committed. Raskolnikov is now pulled in two opposite directions. As "the noblest of men," he must live his life in the open. It is an essential part of the successful ordeal that it be integrated into a public narrative, a narrative *for others*. Raskolnikov's "extraordinary man" is a social, even a political, man: his "new word" is supposed to revolutionize humanity's very forms of life. But at the same time, the murder must, at least for the time being, remain secret. Otherwise, in the terms in which Raskolnikov understands his success, the ordeal will be a failed one.

His endless provocations in the wake of the crime, his challenges (both conscious and unconscious) to be found out, should be understood precisely in these terms. Like the hero of "The Meek One" and like Dostoevsky's other enigmatic types, he is not merely himself a riddle, someone others must understand; he actively "sets riddles" [*zagadyvaet zagadki*] for others, counts on their attention, on their veridictory participation.³⁴ In Raskolnikov's case and in many others, these riddles are set "suddenly," "unexpectedly," "accidentally." In the conversation with the policeman Zamyotov, he finds himself saying: "And what if it was I who killed the old woman and Lizaveta?" Having been summoned to the police station, he faints at the mention of the recent crime (his own), and those present exchange meaningful glances. Walking through the city, he "suddenly" finds himself back at the scene of the murder, comes in, asks strange questions and arouses the suspicions of bystanders. With the main investigator Porfiry Petrovich, he accidentally pales, blushes, and trembles with rage. The chance event, the unpremeditated act, serves as a site for the posing of the riddle, an invitation to emplotment. His interlocutors are allowed to make sense of the clues as best they can. Zamyotov takes him to be a madman; Razumikhin believes that he is a revolutionary; most of the tradesmen who witness his distraught wanderings in and around *"that* house" take him for a drunk; one of them suspects that he is the murderer. Porfiry Petrovich, who, at least by the end of the novel, knows the most, knows also the manner in which he knows: "And for me personally, it began by *accident,* a quite *accidental accident (sovershenno sluchainaia sluchainost'),* something which in the highest degree might or might not have happened—and what was it? Hm, I think there's no need to say" (451, emphasis added).³⁵

As it happens, Porfiry Petrovich lists several candidates. By accident, he hears the story of Raskolnikov's fainting spell at the police station. By accident, he discovers and, at the right moment, remembers Raskolnikov's old article on the ethics of crime. By accident, he is prepared to interpret Raskolnikov's staged fit of laughter in a manner directly contrary to its intentions: "And that laughter, that laughter of yours as you walked in then, remember? I saw through it all at once, like a pane of glass, but if I hadn't been waiting for you in such a special way, I wouldn't have noticed anything in your laughter" (453).

Raskolnikov walks into the investigator's room laughing in order to mislead him into thinking that he must be innocent. But waiting in "a special way," Porfiry Petrovich recognizes the laughter precisely as a ruse and is thus only reinforced in his suspicions. Once again, *accidentally,* the hero's plot collides with the plot of another; the hero's plot is cracked open; a riddle is constituted, a question raised, inviting the work of veridiction, allowing one plot to establish a position and apply the power of interpretative outsideness in relation to the other.³⁶

In "The Meek One," the accident invokes "blind force," ontological intransigence, the absence of others and of grand design. There, the accident marks the boundary of the hero's plot, the boundary beyond which "everything is dead." There, only glimpses and intimations of possible other functions for the accident can be gleaned. But in *Crime and Punishment*, accidental, unpremeditated events are again and again revealed as seams of reemplotment, stitching the hero's progress to multiple zones of interpretation, sustaining the work of the veridictory metaphor in narrative.

Comparative Interlude II: Truth and the Unexpected (Stendhal)

For Stendhal, duty; for Dostoevsky, the accident—these are motifs most closely allied with truth. Each opens up the space of the unexpected; each punctures plotted coherence; each ends up functioning as a nexus of multiple emplotments. And yet, duty in Stendhal and accident in Dostoevsky should not be seen as two different thematizations for one and the same veridictory operation. Rather, they represent the obverse sides of truth. In Stendhal, duty is the energy of disemplotment; it demands the subjective act that momentarily stands outside stifling conventions and illuminates the falsehood of the existing world. The accident in Dostoevsky is a moment of passive openness; the incapacitation of the hero and a solicitation of emplotment. In duty, truth and narrative coherence stand in a disjunctive relation; in accident, they are pulled together. Duty figures the intrusion of the defeated values of the energetic past into the stifling world of the present, while accident affirms the power of the present by inviting the future to en-form the momentary enigmatic openness it creates. And in a longer historical perspective, veridiction in Stendhal hearkens back to the eighteenth-century rearticulation of social into subjective duty, while the accident, as we are about to see, represents a secularized version of immediate insight into timeless truth.

The Raising of Lazarus: Gospel Truth in *Crime and Punishment*

Accident as a matter of faith, as metaphor, as immediate insight—we know this from the key passages in the novel dealing with the biblical story of the resurrection of Lazarus. After committing the murder, Raskolnikov repeatedly finds himself in, and seeks, the company of the saintly prostitute Sonya. Their acquaintance culminates in a gothic scene during which, at his request, she reads to him the Gospel story of the raising of Lazarus. Ostensibly, Sonya reads aloud the entire story from the eleventh chapter of the Gospel of John. But the passages that are cited in the novel focus only on a certain segment of the original story. The segment begins with Jesus arriving in Bethany and learning that Lazarus has died and has been in the tomb for four days. Before proceeding to resurrect the dead man, Jesus holds several meaningful conversations, the most dramatic of which involves Lazarus's sister Martha: "'Jesus saith unto her, Thy brother shall rise again. Martha saith unto him, I know that he shall rise again in the resurrection at the last day. Jesus said unto her, I am the resurrection and the life: he that believeth in me, though he were dead, yet shall he live: and whosoever liveth and believeth in me shall never die'" (327).

Among other things, the passage presents us with a narratological scandal. The claim that "the last day" is no longer needed implies that the end has lost its power to pronounce upon the beginning and the middle, to judge and reconcile, to endow the preceding with meaning. It is no longer from the end that truth shines on history and individual life. It is no longer, as in Hegel or Goethe, from the perspective of the completion of the journey that every stage of it begins to make sense. To say that the truth is already upon us, to reckon with the damage that incarnated eternity does to temporal order, is not unlike being in the presence of the talisman in *La Peau de chagrin*. It is, once again, to imply that no story at all is needed (that immediate insight is enough) or that what's needed is a very differently shaped story in which veridictory authority and meaning would radiate, somehow, from the midst.

But of course our reading of the novel so far would lead us to conclude that we have here precisely such a truth-bearing middle, the accident as a gap in the narrative, mysterious, soliciting emplotment; and the carrier of this accident, the mysterious hero, demanding attention, interpretation, insight. Thus, two crucial features of the novel—the veridictory centrality of the accident as well as the characterological emphasis on the enigma—acquire a Christological thematization. Like Christ's history-ending incarnation, the accident is the violent intrusion of mystery into the smooth progress of time. And in the very manner in which he demands faith—a metaphoric operation, à la Louis Lambert, whereby an external sign or a miracle points unambiguously to the divine essence of the man—Christ emerges as Raskolnikov's sacred prototype, and the prototype of all other heroes in Dostoevsky who command the interpretative attention of others. Recall the hero-narrator in "The Meek One" proclaiming that "the very most truthful truth about him" is that, deep down, he is "the noblest of men."

This final, characterological, claim receives further support once we turn to the parts of the Lazarus story that are not explicitly cited in the novel. When news of the illness of Lazarus reaches Jesus, he refuses to come to the rescue, claiming that this is not an illness unto death but unto the greater glory of God and the Son of God. Two days later, he nevertheless starts off for Judea, informing his students that Lazarus has in fact died but that his death will eventually contribute to the dissemination of faith among the people. Left out of the text of the novel, then, is the essentially *preplanned* nature of the story. What happens to Lazarus is part of a tightly plotted ordeal, a provisional sacrifice of Lazarus's life for the eventual dramatic revelation or confirmation of Christ's true identity as the Son of God.

Zones of Emplotment and the Transcendent Plot

Why then is all this left out of the text of the novel? One way to answer this question is to realize that the scene unfolds within Sonya's zone of emplotment. The narrator comments on her manner of reading: "At the last verse: 'Could not this man, which opened the eyes of the blind . . . ' she lowered her voice, conveying ardently and passionately the doubt, reproach, and reviling of the blind, unbelieving Jews, who in another moment, as if thunderstruck, would fall down and weep and believe . . . 'And he, he who is also blinded and unbelieving, he too will now hear, he, too, will believe—yes, yes! right now, this minute'" (327). Sonya's thinking tends to reject mediation. To her, what happened once nearly two thousand years ago is happening eternally, still, "right now, this minute." She makes no difference between reading and witnessing, narrating something and testifying to it. It is this kind of reading that allows her to draw a parallel between Raskolnikov and the unbelieving Jews, making her hope that her listener, too, will come to have faith in Christ as soon as he hears about (or witnesses—again, for her there is little difference) the great miracle of resurrection.

When Sonya finds out that Raskolnikov has killed the old pawnbroker and Lizaveta, she has the following to suggest: "Go now, this minute, stand at the crossroads, bow down, and first kiss the earth you have defiled, then bow to the whole world, on all four sides, and say aloud to everyone: 'I have killed!' Then God will send you life again" (420). The narrative into which she emplots Raskolnikov is filled with symbolic acts, stressing the now, this very moment, the crossroads, the four corners of the world. The sequence of actions she suggests is organized with an emphasis on metaphoric significance rather than on diachronic arrangement. At work here is something like the hagiographic genre memory, where at the moment of conversion chronology comes to an end.

Thus, Sonya emplots Raskolnikov as a blind Jew, about to be converted to faith. But this is not the only possible reading of the hero in terms of the inserted narrative of Lazarus. Another crystallizes within the emplotment zone of the investigator Porfiry Petrovich, who invokes Lazarus earlier in the novel, during his first meeting with Raskolnikov. "And . . . and do you believe in the resurrection of Lazarus?" he asks. Raskolnikov replies that he does. "Do you believe literally?" Porfiry insists. "Literally," says Raskolnikov (261).

One wonders, however, what Porfiry Petrovich has in mind in invoking the Gospel story. To begin with, it is clear that his emplotment strategy radically diverges from Sonya's model of conversionary immediacy. In fact, Porfiry's main concern during their conversations is precisely that Raskolnikov is such an "impatient young man" as it is. During their last interview, he argues that Raskolnikov should turn himself in: "God has prepared a life for you (though, who knows, maybe it will also pass like smoke and nothing will happen). What matter that you'll be passing into a different category of people? You're not going to miss your comforts, will you, with a heart like yours? What matter if no one will see you for a long time?" (460). In other words, Porfiry situates Raskolnikov's confession and the punishment that would follow within a vaster plot of a biography. "Just give yourself directly to life, without reasoning," he says, "don't worry—it will carry you straight to the shore and set you on your feet" (460). Again and again, he emphasizes the need to relinquish control, to be more patient and passive, to suffer (things done to one), to spend some time on the periphery.

But the investigator's emplotment techniques are not limited to exhortations of this kind. He does more than simply tempt Raskolnikov with the temporal shape of a better life. He interpolates the very logic of that life, the logic of passivity and extended duration, into the hero's experience. Visiting Porfiry at his office, Raskolnikov is surprised to discover that his appearance makes no impression. He is made to wait for a long time, whereas he thought they would have "pounced on him at once" (331). As the conversation between them begins, Raskolnikov is impatient to get to the point, but Porfiry talks of seemingly unrelated matters, digresses, repeats: "it will keep, it will keep." This deliberate braking of Raskolnikov's impetuous movement, the injection of the criminal's trajectory with patience and duration—to be sure, these are techniques intended to throw the criminal off balance and trap him. But more profoundly, they subtly reroute Raskolnikov's trajectory, launch him on another path and thus provide a resolution for the deeper, intransigent mystery of the hero, a mystery that can stay unresolved even after the identity of the criminal has been established.

It is from the perspective of this temporal shape that we can appreciate Porfiry's invocation of Lazarus. After all, passive suffering (things done to one)—this is what Lazarus undergoes: death and resurrection at the hands of another. The most important event of his life is part of another design, a design of which he is presumably unaware but which he presumably discovers with joy. In this, we should also be able to recognize the very logic that Raskolnikov almost unconsciously rejects at the beginning of the novel, the logic that was at that point in time represented not by Porfiry but by his relative Razumikhin. Suffering, passivity, letting the course of one's life take care of itself—all invoke the *Bildungsroman,* the temporal dimensions of which are strikingly different from Raskolnikov's plot of ordeal as much as from Sonya's conversion plot. Using terms that are particularly apposite for our discussion, Franco Moretti writes: "The 'trial' that the protagonist of the *Bildungsroman* must overcome consists . . . in accepting the deferment of the ultimate meaning of his existence."[37]

His explicit purpose aside, Porfiry Petrovich functions here as a kind of investigator tutor, like Goethe's Abbé, interested less in punishing his charge than in facilitating his development. And the assumption is that, like the Society of the Tower, "life," or "organic, natural and gradual necessity"[38] will take care of the hero if the hero would only let it.

For Porfiry, then, Raskolnikov's confession, trial, and punishment are only the middle of his story. For Raskolnikov himself, however, they are absolutely the end. During his first encounter with the investigator, he outlines his conception of crime according to which extraordinary men are permitted to eliminate the obstacles standing between them and a genuine breakthrough in the history of mankind, even if according to conventional standards, this leads them to commit illegal or amoral acts. Porfiry Petrovich ironically worries:

> But tell me this: how does one manage to distinguish these extraordinary ones from the ordinary? Are they somehow marked at birth, or what [*pri rozhdenii, chto l' znaki takie est'*]? What I am getting at is that one could do with more accuracy here, more outward certainty, so to speak: excuse the natural uneasiness of a practical and law-abiding man, but wouldn't it be possible in this case, for example, to introduce some special clothing, the wearing of some insignia, or whatever? . . . Because,

you must agree, if there is some sort of mix-up, and a person from one category imagines he belongs to the other category and starts "removing all obstacles," as you quite happily put it, well then . . . (262)

The investigator's question evokes the widespread contemporary complaint, rendered classic in Balzac's *Physiologie de la toilette,* that it is no longer possible to distinguish people belonging to particular social classes by the way they dress.[39] The great social volatilization of modern life does not allow for external signs to be unambiguously indicative of identity. In Russia's specific case, modern life and especially post-Reform life in the city increasingly witnesses the coming together of people from all social classes into the category of *raznochintsy* ("persons of miscellaneous ranks"). Teachers, tutors, students, journalists, educated children of priests, poor or impoverished noblemen—it is impossible to tell who is who. An example from Dostoevsky's own work instantly suggests itself. Indigent Prince Myshkin, having just arrived in St. Petersburg, is radically mistaken by Nastasya Filippovna: "Prince? He's a prince? Imagine, and just now, in the front hall, I took him for a lackey and sent him to announce me!" (104). In short, the world of rigid visible distinctions is gone and with it a certain way of getting at the truth of who one is. From now on, one must wait to find out how it all ends: a prince might lose his fortune; a low-born provincial might rise to prominence and fame; a "Napoleon" might end up in prison; a murderer might turn out to be a genius or a savior.

In replying to the investigator's sly question, Raskolnikov takes this into account. Of course, such archaic indicators of extraordinariness as portents at birth (Jesus?) or special clothing (Joseph?) are no longer available. Instead, he argues, in order to determine whether someone is truly exceptional, we must wait and see how things turn out. If a person who takes himself to be extraordinary tests himself by committing a crime, but soon enough regrets his actions, confesses, and seeks penance, then it becomes retrospectively evident that he has made a mistake, and his identity is reestablished on a ground more solid than that of mere fantasy. In other words, not given *a priori,* the truth about the new enigmatic man finds its proper medium in the narrative shape of a story.

In the early chapters of the novel Raskolnikov rejects the gradual progression of the *Bildungsroman* in favor of the leap of the ordeal. He chooses a shortcut, immediate knowledge over knowledge deferred. And this choice now makes it impossible for him to think of the crime as a "stage on life's way," even as a mistake or a sin, redeemable in wisdom or repentance. Within the logic of ordeal, formulated by Raskolnikov himself in his article on crime, confession means decisive failure: he has simply "misbehaved" and needs to be punished like a schoolboy.

The Authority of the Fragment

It is telling of Dostoevsky's veridictory poetics that he likes his "absolute truths" to be already, explicitly, stories. Even when, as in *The Brothers Karamazov* or in *The Possessed,* the biblical verses appear "outside" the novel as its epigraph, still they confront us not so much with the true principle of the narrative as with the true narrative itself, the story in light of which everything should be understood. An overarching "eternal" narrative imbues the novelistic world with transcendent meaning. For Dostoevsky, the moral of the story is already itself a story. "Verily, verily, I say unto you," reads the biblical epigraph to *The Brothers Karamazov,* "Except a corn of wheat fall into the ground and die, it abideth alone: but if it die, it bringeth forth much fruit" (John 12:24). And so we know that the story to live out, the right and true narrative shape, is one that ties into a knot: redemption with death.

The story of Lazarus serves as the dense, truth-radiating kernel of *Crime and Punishment.* It is not an epigraph, does not possess a natural, authoritative externality. Its externality must be wrested from the text. And in fact, much rhetorical energy goes into extricating the scene of Sonya's reading from the narrative of the rest of the novel. The frame of the scene is insistently and meticulously constructed. The narrator opens and concludes it with the worlds "suddenly" [*vdrug*] and "strange" [*strannyi*], as it were extracting it from the regular causal chain. It is further separated from the rest of the novel through the excessively long period of silence ("five minutes or more") following the reading. These mechanisms of decontextualization combine to heighten the scene, casting the Lazarus story as something like the essence behind the appearance of the narrative of the novel as a whole.[40]

What we have here then is a familiar mode, a Romantic fragment, analogous and, as it were, "metaphorically applicable" to the rest of the novel. We have seen that Raskolnikov is, throughout the novel, emplotted as any number of characters from the story of Lazarus. He is—at least in his own eyes and potentially—a Jesus, the grand plotter, a master over life, death, and redemption, inhabiting the narrative of a successful ordeal.[41] He is, to Porfiry Petrovich, a Lazarus, the passive sufferer of (spiritual and civic) death and resurrection, the hero of a *Bildungsroman*. To Sonya he is one of the Jews, an astounded witness (perhaps of Sonya's own self-sacrifice), capable at last of faith and deeper insight, the hero of a conversion narrative.[42]

More than an instance of Romantic fragmentariness, then, the Lazarus story introduces into the novel the generic element of romance proper. Just as the magic skin lifts Raphael out of the realm of the ordinary and, setting him apart in power and in wealth, "elevates" him to the position of a romance hero, so the story of Lazarus, inviting comparisons and contrasts with Christ, produces a similar elevation in the figure of Raskolnikov. Whether a Jew, a Lazarus, or a Jesus, the hero half belongs to a world more archaic and more sacred than that of nineteenth-century St. Petersburg *raznochintsy*. And, like so many other heroes in Dostoevsky, he can also be said to serve as the ambassador of that world, bringing its aura with him and rendering the logic of Christian romance immanent in the profane realms of the modern novel.

But the Lazarus narrative is not unique in its reliance on fragmentary, metaphoric and romance-oriented truth discourse. Rather, it renders vivid the veridictory principle that is always active but often more difficult to discern in the rest of the novel. The *suddenly*s framing the scene of the reading are far from atypical,[43] and from a certain perspective, the novel reveals itself to be made up of mutually external segments. Much less obviously than in *Lucinde* and *Louis Lambert*, but nevertheless unmistakably, we are dealing here with a fragmentary novel, consisting of parts related to one another in quasi-synchronic equivalence and thus particularly predisposed for mutual veridictory inflection. Sudden events, accidents, and chance occurrences mark the seams of such inflection, the paradoxical sites of distinction and mutual access among multiple zones of emplotment.

The Lazarus narrative should thus be seen as representative rather than exceptional with respect to the novel's reliance on a certain "romance idealism." For, as we have seen, the insistence on maintaining the alliance between truth and emplotment is as evident in *Crime and Punishment* as in *La Peau de chagrin*.[44] Transcendent emplotment as the imposition of preexisting narrative paradigms on novelistic characters is not only the function of the story of Lazarus but the veridictory principle of the novel as a whole. Throughout the novel, the truth of Raskolnikov's identity—the "who is he?"—is addressed (by other characters as well as by himself) via precisely such transcendent emplotment. Here, as in Balzac, however, this transcendence is not absolute but relative and, paradoxically, immanent, rooted not in a preexisting pattern to which the narrative has to conform, but in internally generated principles of shaping. In *La Peau de chagrin* this internal shaping is achieved through precipitant narrative and evoked in motifs of self-overtaking speed. Here, it is the accident and its bearer the hero as the point of intersection between multiple competing and historically specific emplotments.

The Hero's End and the Contours of Truth Beyond the Novel

If the proper site of veridiction in *Crime and Punishment* is indeed not the end but the middle or, still better, the midst, then it might be interesting to ask: what happens at the end? Spurred on by Sonya's entreaties and cornered by Porfiry Petrovich, Raskolnikov turns himself in at the police station:

> "It was I . . ." Raskolnikov tried to begin.
> "Drink some water."
> Raskolnikov pushed the water aside with his hand and said softly, with some pauses, but distinctly:
> "It was I who killed the official's old widow and her sister Lizaveta with an axe and robbed them." (531)

Raskolnikov's "It is I . . ." (*eto ia* . . .)[45]—his ostensibly final coincidence with himself, the moment when the original gap between biography and the act is finally bridged—continues to resound with ambiguity. Is it the *I* of Sonya's plot in the moment of conversion? (After all, moments before he does fall on his knees on the square and kiss the earth.) Or is it the *I* of the resuscitated *Bildungsroman*? (He does turn himself in, mitigating the punishment, just as Porfiry Petrovich had recommended.) Does it belong to the great man who has successfully withstood the ordeal? (To all appearances, not.) Or to the criminal who failed to get away with the crime? (So it seems.)

Raskolnikov says "I" twice in this scene. The second statement is unambiguous: from this moment on, he is for others what he is, by now, also for himself: no more than a murderer. The plot of the crime is finished, and with it, the ordeal. But the echo of the initial, unfinished "it is I . . ." persists, as do the possibilities that Sonya, Porfiry Petrovich, and Raskolnikov himself elaborate. In other words, the end itself proves to be a kind of middle, a point of convergence among a number of plots. In a striking reversal of the Hegelian narrative paradigm, it is the middle, with its density of projecting (forward-looking) emplotments, that represents the repertoire of meanings for the end. And so the novel has a difficult time ending. The remaining completion plots persist, and their inertia carries us into the epilogue.

As it turns out, the epilogue briefly recapitulates some of the dominant emplotment trajectories of the novel, imbuing them with a more or less subtle parodic tinge. The discourse of the trial, for one, continues and travesties the criminal plot of the novel. It retells the crime in chronological and logical sequence, providing the relevant information about the motivation as well as the moral and psychological makeup of the criminal. Raskolnikov himself does his best to avoid reintroducing even a hint of mystery into the way in which the straightforward criminal narrative identifies him. Certain evidence points to the fact that Raskolnikov is not a common criminal, but he does his best to contradict it, doing his best to impart to his crime an air of decisive banality. All in all, the trial takes the criminal plot to its extreme, to the point at which there is "something almost crude about it all" (536).

Alongside this obviously simplistic account of Raskolnikov as an ordinary criminal, we have a travesty of the plot of the extraordinary man. Here, Raskolnikov's ambitions are at last realized, albeit in his mother's fawning and disturbed imagination: "As for his future career, to her it also seemed unquestionable and brilliant . . . ; she assured Razumikhin that in time her son would even be a statesman, as was proved by his article and his brilliant literary talent" (538). To her, Raskolnikov's life is wrapped in mystery, a life transcending common understanding, unfolding in the realm far above the ordinary. And yet Raskolnikov's hopes are here rendered somewhat more prosaic, as if muddied by Luzhinian, petit bourgeois plotting, the kind of plotting that fails to go beyond ordinary notions of success even in dreams. Thus, Pulcheria Alexandrovna's early, ill-informed wishes for an alliance between her son and Luzhin are echoed here, adding a false note of careerism to Raskolnikov's heroic plot.

We even glimpse something relatively new here, a remnant of an emplotment zone crystallizing late in the novel around the figure of the depraved landowner Svidrigailov: "And [Raskolnikov] suffered from another thought: why had he not killed himself [as soon as he realized that he was no more than a criminal]? Was there really such a force in this desire to live, and was it so difficult to overcome it? Had not Svidrigailov, who was afraid of death, overcome it?" (545).

Svidrigailov's suicide scenario heavily shadows Raskolnikov's last hours of freedom, which he spends wandering the Neva's bridges, looking down at the river. And even at the last moment, already at the police station, as soon as he hears of Svidrigailov's suicide, he rushes out, only to be pushed back in by Sonya's wild stare. What is to be made of Svidrigailov, then—as yet another, a final, zone of emplotment for the hero?

Briefly, Svidrigailov is perhaps best understood in his capacity as the only bona fide landowner in the novel. Mysterious, brooding, lovelorn, depraved, hopeless, and transcendentally homeless, he is moreover a very late version of the Byronic type that was once so important in the Russian literary imagination. And in the Russian context itself, he follows in the long line of Byron-inspired aristocratic misfits from Pushkin's to Lermontov's to Herzen's to Turgenev's—morally dubious but psychologically fascinating.

Literary critical debates starting in the late 1850s about the place of the so-called "superfluous man" in the liberalized environment of the Great Reforms coincided with the retreat of the type from novelistic center stage, giving way to the positively, negatively, or, in Dostoevsky's case, enigmatically construed figure of the more proactive *raznochinets*. Svidrigailov's suicide, then, is readable as a declaration of a kind of literary-historical dead end. But it is also, on the diegetic plane, an early instance of the motif of aristocratic degeneration, soon to become more prevalent with the increasing popularity in Russia of Zola's naturalist novel. Whatever the case, the *raznochinets* Raskolnikov proves more vital (Porfiry Petrovich might say, more open to life) both as a literary-historical phenomenon and as a represented character, and manages to escape the aristocrat's futureless lot. And of course, resisting Svidrigailov's option, he manages to escape as well his temporal shape, the shape that is, perhaps paradoxically, analogous to that of the petit bourgeois Luzhin.

Indeed, as for Luzhin, so for Svidrigailov: time possesses no genuinely veridictory dimension. It is empty serial time; not of career and accumulation, to be sure, since Svidrigailov already has everything he needs, but the serial time of depravity and boredom. And if, as the novel suggests, Svidrigailov is indeed a criminal (among other things he killed his wife), it is of a very different kind from Raskolnikov. Raskolnikov's crime is a manner of testing himself; it possesses the features of a question, a risk. Svidrigailov's crimes are senseless, guided by the needs of the moment and no more. From this point of view, too, suicide is a natural death for Svidrigailov, the death of a man any moment of whose life is indistinguishable from any other. It is no wonder then that suicide becomes such an attractive option for Raskolnikov precisely in exile, after the ordeal is finished; the test has been failed and nothing but monotony remains.

All of these options, then—the crime story, the story of the great man, the story of career, and the story of depravity and suicide—are dismissed at last, and the final scenes of the novel take place in the ambiguous shadow of the remaining two.

The first of these unfolds within Sonya's emplotment zone, narrating Raskolnikov's "conversion." The moment is carefully prepared: "There, on the boundless, sun-bathed steppe, nomadic yurts could be seen, like barely visible black specks. There was freedom, there a different people lived, quite unlike those here, there time itself seemed to stop, as if the centuries of Abraham and his flocks had not passed. Raskolnikov sat and stared fixedly, not tearing his eyes away" (549). We are transported into an archaic space and a time that stands still. Nothing of St. Petersburg modernity remains. We can tell that we are in the vicinity of Sonya. And indeed, "suddenly," she appears. "How it happen[s], he himself [does] not know," but he falls at her feet, bursts into tears, and embraces her knees. A new life opens up before him, a life of hope, love, and perhaps even faith: "Seven years, only seven years! At the beginning of their happiness there were moments when they were both ready to look at those seven years as if they were seven days. He did not even know that a new life would not be given him for nothing, that it still had to be dearly bought, to be paid for with a great future deed" (551). The conflation of seven years with seven days, the treatment of time as everlasting *kairos*, the persistence of the miraculous—these are of course characteristic of Sonya's emplotment temporality.[46] This is once again an experience of a break in the normal state of affairs, a revelatory or redemptive event, a grand "accident" inaugurating a saintly life and retroactively redeeming the life of a sinner.

But this is not the end. The very end, the final paragraph, gestures beyond the novel, where yet another story is about to begin: "the account of a man's gradual renewal, the account of his gradual regeneration, his gradual transition from one world to another, his acquaintance with a new, hitherto completely unknown reality" (551). Contrary to the sacralizing impetuousness of conversion, we have a triple insistence on the gradual. The narrative shape at which the novel gestures beyond itself once again looks strikingly like the narrative Raskolnikov has rejected at the start, the slow biographical story of development, given voice to, early on, by Razumikhin, and later, still more forcefully, by Porfiry Petrovich.

The novel vacillates, then, but perhaps the fact that at the end (and beyond) we are confronted with something other than a *Bildungsroman* and something other than a saint's life is not altogether surprising. To begin with, the *Bildungsroman*, insofar as it is an emplotment possibility for Raskolnikov throughout the novel, departs in significant ways from its classical Western European models. While appearing to adopt this subgenre's "gradualist" temporal shape as well as its faith in the hero's eventual formation and ascent into meaning, it rejects the assumptions about what that formation would amount to and what that meaning would endorse. It rejects, in other words, the genre's tendency to posit the goal of the hero's *Bildung* in socialization, adaptation to the exigencies of modernity or of life in the capital. Its central organizing category is not, as in Goethe, the aristocratic, philanthropic "Society of the Tower"; nor, as in Balzac, Restoration-era Paris; nor even the more abstractly conceived "modern age," as in Ivan Goncharov's *A Common Story* (*Obyknovennaiia istoriia*, 1846). Rather, it is the significantly wider "life," characterized simply by a certain vague benevolence, something verging on grace.

Meanwhile, the hagiographic mode of emplotment, though prominent throughout the novel, emerges as dangerously resonant with the narrative impatience of the radical intelligentsia, and of Raskolnikov's own impatience, compelling him to commit the inaugural crime. A saint's life, like the life of a radical or a great man, hinges on precipitant acts, ready results, and immediate knowledge. This, on its own terms, too, is thus inadequate to the task, and so the narrator must intervene, disabusing the protagonists and the readers of their hopes for an imminent resolution.[47]

A saint's life in *Bildung*-time, then—this is the shape of the story beyond *Crime and Punishment*, transcending it and constituting its regulative ideal. An odd, paradoxical synthesis, it is a narrative shape for which there is perhaps no name and of which there might not be an example.[48] Whatever the case may be, at the point at which the novel ends and the imaginary narrative beyond it begins, at this final locus of veridictory emplotment, Raskolnikov is about to cross over into a new kind of story. This story casts back upon the novel the shadow of an altogether differently shaped truth, confirming one last time the central injunction underlying the veridictory structure of the novel: that truth be given through emplotment as the becoming *sjuzhet* of *fabula*, at the intersection point and moment of metaphoric encounter between plot and plot, the point that registers the momentary becoming *fabula* of *sjuzhet* and whose privileged name in the novel is the accident.[49]

Veridiction and the Moral of the Story

If it is indeed possible to read *Crime and Punishment* as a kind of experimental novelistic testing ground for Russia's veridictory emplotment, then what would the true narrative of Russia be? The answer to this question hinges on the already familiar distinction between thematic or didactic conceptions of truth and the conception that is structural and more properly veridictory. If we are concerned with the former, with what has been called the truth *of* the novel, then, clearly, this is the hybrid form of saintly *Bildung*. But this is not of course the narrative of *Crime and Punishment*; this is not, in fact, the narrative of any novel Dostoevsky writes, though it is the narrative that can sometimes be found on the horizon of his novels. What he does write possesses a rather different veridictory structure, one that relies precisely on the logic of ordeal and posits the hero's precipitous trajectory as repeatedly cut open, traversed by multiple temporalities, always ready to shift, to be realigned. The truth *of* Russia for Dostoevsky, what Russia needs and strains to be, may thus be realized in the paradoxical utopian rhythms of a gradualist saintliness, but the truth *for* it, that which underlies the manner in which truths are registered and evaluated, can be found only in its status as "accidental," open—one is tempted to say *emancipated*—to multiple, though historically delimited, emplotments.

4

Tolstoy's Plotlines and Truth Shapes

Against the World as a Whole

In the decades around the composition of *Anna Karenina* (1873–1877), starting perhaps in the late fifties and early sixties, Tolstoy is consistently preoccupied with problems in historiography. Infected by an intensified awareness of historical movement characterizing what came to be known as the period of the Great Reforms, Tolstoy speaks out on the topic again and again, in his diaries, his letters, his journalism, and his fiction. As is so often the case with him, interest takes the form of rejection. While everyone around him—journalists, novelists, and friends—attempts an account of what history is or should be, Tolstoy spends an extravagant amount of time and effort dismissing the question itself. Particularly blistering and insistent are his attacks on the dominant, *sine qua non* conceptual cluster of historical thinking of the time: development, perfectibility, progress. These are of course already the subjects of the narrator's fixation in *War and Peace* (1865–1869), but the offensive continues well into the seventies and past the composition of *Anna Karenina*. As late as 1878, in a letter to his friend and main philosophical interlocutor at the time, Nikolai Strakhov, Tolstoy objects to Ernest Renan's historical treatment of the figure of Christ:

> Progress to my mind is a logarithm of time, that is, nothing, a mere statement of the fact that we live in time, and suddenly it becomes the arbiter of the highest truth we know. . . . Christian truth, that is, the highest expression of absolute goodness, is an expression of essence itself, outside the forms of time, etc. In the meantime, people like Renan mix up [Christian truth's] absolute expression with its historical expression, reduce it to a temporal manifestation and then discuss it. If Christian truth is high and deep, it is only because it is subjectively absolute. If we consider its

objective manifestation, it's on the same level as the Code Napoléon and the like.¹

The passage contains a number of resonant and complexly interconnected claims. Most important, progress emerges as a *presumed* arbiter of truth, a veridictory imposter. No more than a hypostatization of a certain experience of time, it claims to endow mere succession with a significance and depth it does not merit. Time, as such, is essentially truthless. Truth, the absolute truth of Christianity, is not only timeless but also subjective; that is, it should not be understood as a series of historically determinate doctrinal and institutional instantiations capable of realizing the teachings of Christ (truth) in history (time). Taken together as the key conceptual alliance of historical thinking, truth and time form an unlikely monstrosity.

That Strakhov should be the addressee of this polemical *profession de foi* is not surprising. It was Strakhov, after all, whose book *The World as a Whole* (*Mir kak tseloe*, 1872) explicitly defends the Hegelian category of objective spirit, conceiving of all essential human activity precisely in its objectified—that is, socialized, institutional—aspect. Shortly after the publication of the book (some parts of which were first serialized in the 1860s), Tolstoy writes Strakhov a letter, praising many of its accomplishments, but criticizing some of its basic presuppositions. Especially under attack are Strakhov's avowedly Hegelian appeals to the category of *spirit* (*dukh*): "Everything goes wonderfully. But in the fifth letter, on pages 73 and 74, the author speaks of spirit, of the fact that comprehension must begin with spirit. Why? In my eyes, man differs from the rest of the world not because of spirit, which I don't understand at all, but because when he reflects on human beings in general he reflects on himself, and when he reflects on other things, he reflects on not himself" (61:346). Tolstoy's irritable incomprehension of the concept of spirit is doubtless no more than a rhetorical gesture, a pose. Only several lines later, he gives ample evidence of an adequate grasp of the term's meaning and implications. According to him, the trouble with spirit is that it names an object of faith, an unverifiable and unfalsifiable force of constant and universal perfectibility (*sovershenstvovanie*), historiographically inflected precisely as a *religion* of progress. Perfectibility is indeed the point, the Hegelian crux of Strakhov's inquiry, the foundational assumption that the passage of time is not merely change and surely not degeneration but development and improvement.²

In the introduction to the volume, Strakhov complains: "Since we have called the world *whole,* then, referring to this expression, we can say that man constantly seeks an exit from this whole, strives to break the links connecting him with this world, to tear the umbilical cord. Hardly ever has this been as clear as in our sad time, a time that is very interesting but horribly difficult. People rush about, looking for the exit; they look for suffering and consider it shameful to be content with this life the way it is."[3] Thus, the presumption of the wholeness of the world renders those who express dissatisfaction with it simply immature. To say that the world is whole is to say that it is essentially complete, finished, perfected. To say that it is whole is also to say that nobody can have legitimate reasons to complain. In his reply, Tolstoy objects directly to this point: "The contention that the purpose of human life consists in perfectibility which coincides with the perfectibility of an organism diminishes the value of human life. And the fact of dissatisfaction with life . . . is a fact that cannot be explained away as confusion. It has a most legitimate root. It has as its basis the essence of life" (61:347). "Unreasonable" protest, a childish wish to stand outside the world as a whole, even if that outsideness leads to suffering—according to Tolstoy, this is the very essence of life. The childlike and the immature are for him valid principles, not merely justifiable, but vital, life-affirming.

The uses to which Tolstoy puts figures of the childlike, the naïve, and the inexperienced in his fiction and journalism are of course well-documented. It is this stance—strongly associated since the eighteenth century with what is natural and therefore true—that again and again provides him with the leverage point to launch his radical critique of the world as it is. Natasha Rostova's incomprehension of the opera in *War and Peace,* the horse Strider's "critique" of private property in *Strider,* Konstantin Levin's confusion at the provincial elections in *Anna Karenina*—all testify to the capacity of consciousness unreconciled with reality to shed truthful light on the world.[4] The bearer of such consciousness must be marked by a certain externality and disinterestedness vis-à-vis the given situation, a lack of investment in the status quo, and a resistance, whether conscious or unconscious, to being co-opted into the acceptance of what is. Hence, one could say that, *pace* Strakhov, a child is the best, the most perfected subject of all.

Pace Strakhov, then, Tolstoy rejects the Hegelian world as a whole in favor of free, dynamic, and reflexive subjectivity. And yet, despite what Tolstoy himself might think, this does not amount to a rejection of Hegel *tout court*. Thus, one remark in his diary from 1860 reads as follows: "Who said to someone that progress is good? It is only an absence of faith, and the need for conscious action posing as faith. A human being needs a breakthrough, *Spannung*—yes" (48:25).

Breakthrough (*proryv*) and *Spannung,* tension, can be read here as naming a certain conception of dynamic, reflexive subjectivity, the kind of subjectivity that proudly recognizes itself as separate and independent from the world it inhabits and that serves as the very engine of Hegel's phenomenological dialectics. To be sure, this conception of the subject constitutes Hegel's precious conceptual inheritance from eighteenth-century Enlightenment philosophy, and especially from Kant, for whom subjectivity, autonomy, and critique had become synonymous and who repeatedly debunked notions of totality, whether natural or historical, as at best useful fictions. Insofar as he insists on these dynamic, critical principles of modernity, Tolstoy—whose affinity with eighteenth-century philosophy and whose admiration for Kant have often been attested—finds himself aligned with the other side of Hegel, precisely the side Strakhov appears to neglect. Conversely, what Tolstoy objects to in Hegel is precisely what Strakhov finds most indispensable, namely, the German philosopher's belief that "a modernity without models [can] stabilize itself on the basis of the very diremptions it had wrought."[5] Spirit, as Strakhov uses this word, is the name of the paradoxical end result of this self-stabilization. It is movement, yes, but contained, guaranteed, bent into the predictable shape of development. Moreover, it is the sort of movement that in all of its essential features has come to a stop, flowing into "the world as a whole," and no longer capable either of *proryv* or of genuine *Spannung.* In his 1886 book-length essay *What Then Must We Do?* (*Tak chto zhe nam delat'?*), Tolstoy finds all that unacceptable: "The conclusions of [Hegel's] philosophical theory indulged people's weaknesses. These conclusions came down to the fact that everything is rational, everything is fine, nobody is to blame for anything" (25:331–32).

Tolstoy's subjectivist ethics and epistemology, his critique of the modern "world as a whole," and his views on the proper trajectory of a life come together into a single figure in his writings on one of the most pressing issues of the post-Emancipation era, the people's education. In June 1874, while already at work on *Anna Karenina,* Tolstoy publishes an article intended to clarify his position in the debate. He begins by questioning the assumption, common to contemporary pedagogues, that the task of education is not limited to teaching peasants and peasant children to read, write, and count but consists primarily in helping them "develop." Tolstoy asks: In what does this development consist? His answer, more or less explicit throughout the essay, is that what is called "development" amounts to bringing the "little savages" up-to-date with the modern world, teaching them to follow the rules of proper behavior in society and to respect order (17:78).[6] Thus, to bring up, to educate, to develop peasants in accordance with contemporary pedagogical principles means, for Tolstoy, essentially to bring them into harmony with Strakhov's "world as a whole," to give them a place in what those who believe in progress take to be the perfected order of things, but what Tolstoy sees as a historically determined and therefore transient moment.

But Tolstoy's critique of contemporary education does not stop with these revelations. On the basis of his analysis of *upbringing* and *development*, he accuses modern pedagogy of not having traveled very far from the sort of education purveyed under the aegis of the Orthodox Church. According to Tolstoy, the old church school and the contemporary school based on the most recent discoveries of German pedagogy bear a striking resemblance to each other: "In one exactly as much as in the other method, the mechanical side of education dominates over the intellectual side. As in church schools, so in these, students stand out for good handwriting and for an absolutely precise pronunciation while reading, that is, they pronounce words not as they are spoken but as they are written. In one exactly as much as in the other method, constant external order reigns in the school, and children are constantly in fear and can be controlled only with the greatest strictness" (17:101). An episode from *Anna Karenina* here suggests itself, in which Seryozha is asked by his father to repeat some verses from the Bible. Seryozha is distracted and makes a mistake. His father takes this as a sign that the boy doesn't understand what he is saying: "He frowned and began to explain what Seryozha had already heard many times, and could never remember because he understood it all too clearly—the same sort of thing as 'thus' being an adverbial modifier of manner."[7] Religious and secular education are thus brought together and revealed as comparable in their dogmatic reliance on memorization and on the routine sublation of the specific and the simple into an obfuscating system.

Neither in methods, then, nor in results do contemporary pedagogues transcend the supposedly antiquated traditions of church education. Tolstoy's rhetoric hits the modernizing pedagogues where they are most sensitive; it shows that their new theories and techniques repeat rather than depart from what they themselves take to be outdated principles and practices. More generally, Tolstoy perceives in the underlying logic of the new pedagogy an essential tendency of the age: to reinsert new content into an old frame, or rather to fold newness back upon itself, to contain it in the shape that strikingly resembles the old. Most broadly understood, then, the logic of contemporary pedagogues is one where—to invoke Habermas on Hegel—"reason has now taken over the place of fate and knows that every event of essential significance has *already* been decided."⁸

What then is the proper criterion of education, according to Tolstoy, and what are its proper methods? His answer is simple and, once again, polemically charged: the proper criterion of education is freedom; the proper method is experience. Tolstoy relies on the two key principles of enlightened modernization and makes it clear that, in sticking to their theories, his opponents betray these very principles and, in the interests of "development," revert to such abhorrent barbarisms of the past as corporal punishment.

Tolstoy's struggle with the pedagogues is a struggle between two conceptions of modernity: one that emphasizes the centrifugal ideals of reflection, freedom, and the ceaseless dynamism of experience, and the other that relies on the centripetal forces of containment implicit in notions of maturity, development, and perfectibility as adequation to the socially objective order of things. Associated with these two conceptions of modernity are two veridictory figures: on the one hand, the truth of childlike incomprehension and refusal underlying the method of estrangement and its historical links to eighteenth-century Enlightenment literature and philosophy,⁹ and on the other hand, the truth of a maturity, reconciled to the objective world and capable of casting its own pacification into the shape of a unified system. It is clear from his writings of the time that Tolstoy is on the side of the former. Thus, in a note from 1870, he launches an attack on systematic thinking, with its Hegelian assumption that the true is the whole: "A system, a philosophical system, carries within itself, in addition to the errors of thinking, the errors of a system. . . . In order to say clearly what you have to say, speak sincerely, and in order to speak sincerely, speak in the way that the thought came to you. . . . Truth is repulsive because it is disjointed, incomprehensible, while error is coherent and consistent" (48:344–45).¹⁰

Truth as a function of sincerity tends to take the form of fragmentariness and incoherence, while coherence (*sviaznost'*) and consistency (*posledovatel'nost'*) are, in their artificial objectivity, sure harbingers of falsehood. We have already encountered something that resembles this dichotomy in Stendhal: on the one hand, truth as keeping up with minute subjective processes, with a self in constant flux, and, on the other, the falsehood and merely conventional stasis of a warranted social whole. In both cases sincere and thus fragmentary registering of subjective change emerges as the proper veridictory mechanism, while fidelity to the objective order, expressed through narratives of teleological predictability, covers up, or even produces, falsehood. What is figured as tradition and old-regime conventionality in Stendhal reappears in Tolstoy in the guise of Hegelian, progressive conceptions of historical and individual development, presumed by a whole spectrum of political and philosophical positions from moderate conservatism (as in Strakhov) to moderate liberalism (as in Boris Chicherin).[11]

Stendhal and Tolstoy have frequently been read as brilliant analysts of the human soul and as comparable precisely on this account. Reviewing the early parts of *Anna Karenina*, one contemporary critic makes this connection explicit. Tolstoy, he claims, is everywhere an original analyst of the diverse instances of the inner life of a human being and as such he should be compared to the other great psychologist, Stendhal.[12] Since then, critics from Boris Eikhenbaum to Boris Reizov and Isabelle Naginskii have addressed themselves to the distinct artistic affinity between the two novelists.[13] Yet these comparative studies tend to bypass discussion of the overall veridictory constellation of the novels and thus frequently fail to appreciate that minute depiction of dynamic subjectivity is not an end in itself, but rather one pole organizing the narrative field and powerfully counteracted by the threatening and falsifying work of totalizing mechanisms. If, as Eikhenbaum and others suggest, Stendhal and Tolstoy turn to the philosophical and novelistic traditions of the eighteenth century, it is because they are seeking alliances, within modernity itself, to combat what they see as the oppressive totality of the world around them.[14] And if, to some extent, they resuscitate "eighteenth-century" veridictory methods, positing a new disjunction between truth and time, it is no longer innocently. Rather, their novels resolutely internalize, on the level of form, the cultural forces of totalizing emplotment. Thus, situations and feelings broken up into their constitutive parts are not merely objects of representation in their novels. They imply a certain kind of work, the hard labor of narrative disassembly of the teleological superstitions of the modern world: coherence, maturity, convention.

Comparative Interlude I: The Whole (Balzac)

Nikolai Strakhov attempts to do for post-Emancipation Russia what Victor Cousin hoped to do for Restoration France: to produce a philosophical defense of the present order of things, to hypostasize a reconciled, pacified whole as the truth of an evidently volatile social world around him. For Balzac, this was of course a congenial project. For Tolstoy, it is something to reject outright. And yet in some contexts, the two novelists seem to agree on the value of preserving wholes from disintegration. Balzac's early essay on primogeniture, for instance, echoes Tolstoy's concerns about the division of estates and peasant landholdings. Both authors are of course notorious for their anxiety-ridden portrayal of familial dissolution.

It would seem then that Balzac and Tolstoy don't so much disagree on the value of holistic existence as on its proper place vis-à-vis the social reality around them. Like Strakhov and Hegel, Balzac appears willing—in fact, seeks—to posit the whole as temporal and social. For Tolstoy, on the other hand, the social world is a phony totality, glued together through institutional repression, bureaucratic administration, and behavioral convention. Tolstoy's desirable whole is posited elsewhere, outside society proper, in the imagery and thematics of the peasant idyll, in a moment of radically transcendent insight, in patriarchal family life on the land, or in a utopian community of brotherly love. And just as this whole is asocial, it is also explicitly timeless. A single instant takes in Ivan Golovin's enlightened realization, in *The Death of Ivan Ilych* (1886), that compassion (that is, thoroughgoing relatedness to others) trumps death, and though for the outside world his death agony lasts, for the dying man himself, "the meaning of that instant [does] not change."[15] Konstantin Levin loses all awareness of time as he is mowing with the peasants; he begins to feel that some universal force is doing its work through him (251). The atemporal and asocial, or marginally social, totality that is thus posited is the only kind acceptable to Tolstoy. The other kind, hypostasized onto social life and informing its imaginative comprehension in certain dominant strains of literary realism—the very whole-in-motion with which Balzac operates—is for Tolstoy a great and dangerous falsehood.

Plotlines

Early on in the reception history of *Anna Karenina*, Tolstoy is charged with having insufficiently linked its two storylines. In an 1878 letter to Tolstoy, botanist, educator, and friend Sergei Rachinsky writes: "It is undoubtedly your best work. The last part produced a cooling impression, not because it was weaker than the others . . . , but because of a basic lack in the structure of the novel as a whole. There is no architecture in it. In it, two themes are developed, and beautifully developed, next to each other, but there is no link between them."[16]

Rachinsky is diagnosing here an apparent discord between the two narrative lines of the novel, one dedicated to the affair between Anna and Vronsky, the other telling the story of Levin's spiritual quest and his love for Kitty. The two lines proceed independently; the two main characters, Anna and Levin, meet only once, late in the novel, almost by accident and with few consequences. The explicit thematic concerns of the two plotlines differ: one focuses on passion, adultery, jealousy, while the other on happy marriage, agriculture, life in the country, and the search for meaning. All this is true, to be sure, but in his reply to Rachinsky, Tolstoy intimates that his early reader has read too superficially. It is precisely the architecture of the whole, he says, the inner links between the various parts of the novel that make him proud of the work he has done (62:377). He doesn't elaborate on the nature of these inner links, but it is not difficult to guess what he means. On closer reading, one finds numberless situation rhymes,[17] motifs appearing across plotlines, and transitions strategically arranged to punctuate the narrative at significant moments.[18] There is little doubt, in other words, that the Levin-Kitty and Anna-Vronsky storylines come together into a whole at least as harmonious as it is unstable. And yet I would argue that Rachinsky's misguided insight should not be too quickly dismissed.

In fact, it is possible to reconcile Rachinsky's perspective with Tolstoy's by saying that the unity of *Anna Karenina* is irreconcilably dualistic. It is a unity, in other words, that acquires its distinctiveness precisely as a tension between two narratives that function according to different and even mutually exclusive principles. If it is true that, as many critics have suggested, themes and situational echoes bind the novel together, it is no less true that the bifurcation of the narrative is decisive, irreducible, and that the shapes of the two storylines are impossible to conflate.

The difference between these storylines is rendered vivid already in the ways the two protagonists are introduced. Levin appears at his old friend Stiva's department utterly unexpected, as "some man," who is, moreover, "bashful," "cross," and "uneasy" in the environment in which he now finds himself. We meet him, further, as someone who has just entered "a new phase": only recently a provincial council (*zemstvo*) activist, he is now convinced that *zemstvo* activity is useless. Anna's appearance, by contrast, is well-prepared, and in such a way as to adumbrate a major aspect of her story: she comes as a mediator in a house thrown into disarray by adultery. Her arrival at the train station not only prefigures her death under the train but also marks a thickening of emplotment; Stiva and Vronsky wait for two women (one for his sister, the other for his mother) who turn out to have traveled in the very same compartment. In short, Levin's appearance is *fabulaically* narrated: something happens, then something else, and something else, but none of it comes together into a whole. Anna, on the other hand, is from the very beginning caught in a tight network of *sjuzhet,* a pivotal figure, connecting, reconciling, and coinciding.

Generically, the two storylines also diverge. Anna's is reminiscent of more conventional European adultery novels, densely plotted narratives of illicit passion and death. Tolstoy repeatedly calls attention to this fact when Anna's female acquaintances refer to her as a heroine of a novel/romance (*geroinia romana*). Long passages are dedicated to the painting of Anna's portrait and, later, to the description of that portrait. Throughout the novel, Anna constantly reads and, toward the end, becomes a writer herself. It is perhaps the aura of novelistic and aesthetic conventionality surrounding Anna that allows Tolstoy to insist in a letter to Strakhov that in *Anna Karenina* he is writing *a novel* [*roman*], and the very first one of his life (62:25).

As a heroine of her particular sort of *roman,* Anna also carries with herself traces of "romance idealism." Prophetic dreams, premonitions, omens—all testify to the debt of the Anna-Vronsky plotline to the kind of story whose coherence and significance is never in doubt, whose world, in Strakhov's terms, is a whole. "Superior in degree to other characters and to nature,"[19] she is uncannily (though still imperfectly) attuned to the "higher powers" emplotting her life. Her prophesies can be said to be self-fulfilling, but only insofar as her story is one in which the hero and the plot are so tightly entwined that there is no telling which is which. Thus we are compelled to notice that by the end of the novel almost everyone in Anna's immediate surrounding carries a name that is derivative of her own. Her maid is called Annushka; her daughter's name is Annie; the name of the English girl whom Anna takes as her ward is Ganna (Tolstoy's Russian derivative of "Hannah"). The name "Anna" is echoed through the novel, and, as a palindrome—readable, like the perfect figure of *sjuzhet,* both forward and back—it echoes itself.

In her capacity as the bearer of the generic memory of romance idealism, Anna is in fact reminiscent of Mathilde de La Mole. A similar figure of binding passion and romance emplotment, the impetuous girl-emperor generates so much narrative energy through her appeal to the glorious past of the Wars of the League that she is dislodged from the social boredom of Restoration aristocracy to which she belongs. Though in Tolstoy's novel, romantic discourse is already decisively located on the side of society itself, and sundry *salonnières* identify Anna's affair as properly "novelistic," Anna's high passion also catapults her out of her social environment. As (updated) heroes of romance, both women find themselves above social constraints; and insofar as contemporary society is cast by both authors as pretending to the status of "nature," both Anna and Mathilde rise above "nature" as well.

If Anna, then, is a heroine of a kind of romance, Levin is something of a comic hero. He is, no less than Anna, preoccupied with the future. But unlike her, he is altogether incompetent when it comes to foreknowledge. His trajectory is that of a metaphysical drifter, now believing this, now that, now disappointed, now once again inspired. Compared to Anna's impetuous romance with Vronsky, Levin's personal life is a halting series of comic missteps. To begin with, he is in love with the entire Shcherbatsky household. His interest is initially centered on the oldest sister, Dolly. But Dolly marries his friend Stiva, and Levin is compelled to redirect his attentions to Natalie. When Natalie in turn marries L'vov, Kitty is the last unmarried daughter in the house and, sure enough, Levin falls in love with her. But, having realized that he is in love, he unexpectedly and almost scandalously flees. When at last he comes back, he has reasons to suspect that he has been upstaged by the brilliant Vronsky. Nevertheless, he proposes and is rejected. "It could not have been otherwise," he remarks in a manner reminiscent of Anna's fatalism. Except that, about a third into the novel, when he is reunited with Kitty, he once again believes himself to have foreseen how things would turn out. With surprising consistency, the narrative winding persists: when they are married, the novel is barely halfway through.

Levin's story meanders, repeatedly undermines his projects and the reader's conventional expectations. Even his final illumination, treated in the final chapters of the novel, can be seen as privileged only insofar as here he comprehends at last the narrative pattern within the confines of which he has proceeded all along. Levin's truly new realization in the end is irreducible to his rather incoherent discovery of Orthodox Christianity. Such a discovery would not differ significantly from all the previous realizations he has had: that the *zemstvo* is useful, for instance; or that the *zemstvo* is useless; that time has come to die; or that he should marry a peasant. What is distinctive about the final discovery is an understanding that the universal will never subsume the particular, an understanding that by no means implies the necessity or even the possibility of giving up on one or the other.[20] Hence, the last paragraph of the novel: "I'll get angry in the same way at the coachman Ivan, argue in the same way, speak my mind inappropriately, there will be the same wall between my soul's holy of holies and other people . . .—but my life now, my whole life, regardless of all that may happen to me, every minute of it, is not only not meaningless, as it was before, but has the unquestionable meaning of the good which it is in my power to put into it!" (817).

Levin's story, then, is not as tightly plotted as Anna's. But, just as in her case it is impossible to assign to her full responsibility for what happens, so the events of Levin's narrative are not unilaterally caused by his temperamental makeup. Rather, the novel eloquently testifies precisely to the inseparability of character from plot. Just as Anna and Vronsky are functions of and, at the same time, provide psychological grounds for their tightly woven narrative, so Levin and Kitty shape and are shaped by their looser tale.[21]

Truth Shapes

One of Tolstoy's favorite devices in his fiction before and after *Anna Karenina* is to tell the same story twice: the way it really happened, and the way it is disfigured by conventional expectations. The narrator and the ingénue—these paradigmatic Tolstoian witnesses of truth—know neither how the story will end nor where its ultimate significance lies. The better-socialized types suffuse their tales (both the ones they tell and the ones that happen to them) with stable, preexisting meanings, drawing on a vast depository of situational clichés.

Here is a memorable example from *War and Peace*. Nikolai Rostov's first battle exploits are nothing special. In brief, he falls from a horse; instead of shooting, throws his gun at a Frenchman; and runs for the bushes "like a hare." About seventy pages later, he tells the story in the company of officers. The narrator comments:

> He began with the intention of relating everything exactly as it happened, but imperceptibly, unconsciously and inevitably, he slipped into falsehood. . . . He could not tell them simply that everyone had set out at a trot, that he had fallen from his horse, sprained his arm, and then had run from a Frenchman into the woods as fast as his legs could carry him. . . . His listeners expected to hear how, fired with excitement and beside himself, he had swept down on the enemy's square like a tempest, cut his way in, slashing right and left, and how his saber had tasted blood and he had fallen exhausted and so on. And these are the things he told them. (298)

The first kind of story, the one that "really" happened, is *fabulaic*, told from the forward-looking perspective of the character encountering a situation for the first time. The second kind tends toward the narrative pole of *sjuzhet*, with its teleological, that is, retrospective reorganization and its reliance on prior models and expectations. Now what is striking about *Anna Karenina* is that here Tolstoy's preoccupation with narrative doubling finds a powerful expression in the distinct narrative shapes of the novel's two major plotlines. Anna's story is *sjuzhet*-centered, heavily emplotted with the help of forebodings, premonitions, repetitions, literary models, a portentous epigraph, and greater temporal density.[22] Levin's progress through the novel possesses a more irregular, *fabulaic*, unpremeditated quality and a looser, more cavernous, temporal framework.

But just as Nikolai's two stories present us with two conceptions of what it means to tell the truth in narrative, so the plotlines of Anna and Levin represent two distinct veridictory shapes. The truth of Anna's narrative is the truth of the whole, an unfolding of a foretold fate. In Hegelian terms, this is the truth of the Absolute, where the "anticipation of retrospection" dominates, thickens into a foreknowledge of the end. This truth presupposes an essential harmony between self and world, and a cumulative, formative conception of time.

Levin's story, in the meantime, relies on an altogether different veridictory framework. Here, time emerges in its function to dissolve, decompose, negate. During the night he spends in the field, for example, Levin radically reevaluates his views on what constitutes the good life, deciding to renounce his old habits and start on a new course, a simpler one, perhaps even to marry a peasant woman. He looks up at the sky, at a shell of clouds forming over his head, and thinks: "And when did that shell have time to form? A moment ago I looked at the sky and there was nothing there—only two white strips. Yes, and in the same imperceptible way my views of life have also changed" (276).

But only several minutes later, having glimpsed Kitty in a passing carriage and having realized that he cannot "go back" to this life of simplicity, he looks up once again: "He looked at the sky hoping to find there the shell he had admired, which had embodied for him the whole train of thoughts and feelings of the past night. There was no longer anything resembling a shell in the sky. There, in the inaccessible heights, a mysterious change had already been accomplished" (277–78). As unnoticeably as time decomposes forms, the events of Levin's life frustrate his attempts to bind them together into a coherent, meaningful whole. Slow, imperceptible progress of time, the time of *fabula*, is the medium of deformation and dispersal, the medium that underlies the veridictory principles within Levin's plotline. Here, veridiction relies on the negative work of disemplotment. It is, to invoke Hegel once again, the truth of experience, the moment when consciousness (the *for-itself*) encounters the *in-itself* and recognizes its previous construction as error.

The two plotlines of the novel can thus be read as a polemical thought experiment, a fictional reply to Strakhov. Here, the novel appears to say, pointing to Anna's story, is what "the world as a whole" looks like. And here, by way of contrast, is the story of a man who is constantly spurred on by dissatisfaction with life. Yet Strakhov's "world as a whole," like the alliance between truth and time, cannot be simply dismissed. It stands for a basic socioontological condition of modernity, and unless it is actively resisted or evaded, it will inevitably inscribe itself into the trajectory of the hero's life. As in Stendhal, so here, work must be done, the hard work of disemplotment, in order to hold truth and time apart even for an instant.

Endings

On the train back from Moscow to St. Petersburg, having brought about a reconciliation between Stiva and Dolly, Anna reads a novel by the light of a candle lantern. While reading, she identifies with the characters of the English novel so intensely that she can no longer distinguish between herself and the protagonist. And when a sudden feeling of shame arises in her, this shame is shared: it is both her own and the protagonist's. Already here, the boundary between reading and life is porous.

The scene of reading on the train takes place toward the beginning of the novel. It is immediately adjacent to Vronsky's declaration of love and thus serves as a kind of overture to Anna's romance, to the passionate course of the remainder of her life. Rounding off or epanaleptically framing the plotline, the book and the candle reappear at the very end. Thus, as Anna throws herself under the passing train, the narrator comments: "The candle [lantern], by the light of which she had been reading that book filled with anxieties, deceptions, grief and evil, flared up with a brighter light than before, lit up for her all that had before been dark, flickered, began to grow dim, and went out for ever" (768). The heroine's entire trajectory, then, unfolds between two scenes of reading. Her life seems to have been a book; and the book she has been reading all along has been the book of her life. The ultimate and fatal metaphor ties the knot so tightly that, at any point in her story, it is difficult to tell which is which. This is a figure for the veridiction of near-absolute *sjuzhet*.

Anna's end is overdetermined. Everything suggests that her story will terminate with death. The accident at the railroad station, the repeated portentous dreams, Frou-Frou's collapse at the races, an overabundance of death imagery toward the end of part seven—all prepare the end. But, given the imagery of conflation between reading and living, between consciousness and existence, it is also no wonder that when death does come, it is by suicide, staging the usurpation by the character of ultimate authority over plot, of control over the narrative's end.

At the end of his apprenticeship, Wilhelm Meister gets a chance to read the story of his life as it has been narrated by the Society of the Tower. Here, too, (staged) narration loops back upon (narrated) experience. Yet confronted with the scroll of his life, Wilhelm does not quite recognize himself; or rather, he recognizes himself not as in a mirror but as in a "portrait painted by the masterful hand of a superior talent."[23] His life and its account originate from different sources: life and experience (full of missteps) are Wilhelm's; the account, its truth, are bestowed upon him from the outside, from above, from the end. We have seen Raskolnikov provide a coherent, *sjuzhet*-centered account of the delirious and *fabulaic* act of hiding his loot under a rock. Here, experience and meaning are produced by one and the same agent, but at different points in time. In Anna's case, however, life and the book of life weave into each other constantly: we might say that she does not just read at the end, but all along.

As for Levin, his story is reminiscent, rather, of Wilhelm's prior to his arrival at the Tower, a trajectory that, in its rambling movement, runs over marriage and death (not his own, to be sure, but his brother Nikolai's), destroying faith in the decisiveness of the end and in the robust "world as a whole." Indeed, if for Anna everything—death, understanding, the realization of a destiny—converges at the end, in Levin's case all conventional endpoints are transferred to the middle. Marriage and death follow quickly upon each other (both making an appearance in part five of the novel), but the story does not end.[24]

Within Levin's trajectory, death appears externalized in the horrifyingly halting description of Nikolai's agony. Watching by his brother's bed, he strains to grasp the mystery of life and death:

> Levin involuntarily thought with [Nikolai] about what was now being accomplished in him, but, despite all his mental efforts to go with him, he saw from the expression of that calm, stern face and the play of a muscle over one eyebrow, that for the dying man something was becoming increasingly clearer which for him remained as dark as ever.

"Yes, yes, it's so," the dying man said slowly, distinctly. "Wait." Again he was silent. "So!" (501)

Levin fails to follow Nikolai all the way to ultimate illumination and is soon distracted by unrelated thoughts. But even for the dying man himself, the moment of final realization does not, as it does for Ivan Ilych, coincide with death. Having gotten to the truth, Nikolai lives on and on, eats soup, asks for another doctor, entertains hopes and complains. Whatever it was that he understood and affirmed with his "So!" fails to transform him, to imbue his life (past or future) with nobler meaning. The ultimate truth is overrun, lost beneath meaningless, irrecuperable suffering. Death is here understood not as delivering veridictory finality, but rather as the process of temporally decomposing meaning.

From the time consumptive, moribund Nikolai visits Levin at his estate, death becomes immanent to Levin's story: it is the end that does not coincide with the actual termination of narrative but inheres in it both as the content of the character's thoughts and as the organizing principle of the story he inhabits. Death persists for Levin as a kind of negation, annulling all positive content and, if not paralyzing activity, at least depriving it of inherent meaning. Thus, for him, death is the very opposite of what it is for Anna: it is the gap between thought and life, the universal and the particular; it is the crack through which meaning leaks.

In the concluding chapters of the novel, the thought of death continues to obsess Levin. For him, too, suicide is an option. But within the logic of his narrative, with the logic that spurns all finality, this would be an impossible end. Levin does not take his life. He is saved, instead, by a conversation with the peasant Fyodor. During the conversation, Fyodor mentions another peasant, Fokanych, characterizing him as a truthful old man who lives for the sake of his soul and remembers God. Levin does not immediately understand what it means to live for the sake of one's soul; he wants to know what it means and how it is possible. The peasant clarifies: "'Everybody knows how—by the truth [*po pravde*], by God's way. People are different. Now take you even, you wouldn't offend anybody either . . .'" (794).

The explanation contains a curious use of the word "truth." Truth is not a matter of accurate knowledge here but of a certain condition. Fokanych is "truthful" not because he consistently tells the truth but because he leads a truthful life, lives by the truth. How? By looking beyond this life, by caring for his soul, remembering God, acting kindly and fairly toward others. And as far as Fyodor is concerned, the same can be said of Levin.

Levin rushes off in confusion and for the remainder of the novel tries to make sense of these words. His eventual acceptance of the truths of Orthodox Christianity is condensed into a telling formula: "In place of each of the Church's beliefs, there could be put the belief in serving the good (*sluzhenie pravde*) instead of one's needs" (799).[25] The good or, more properly, the truth (*pravda*) is here pointing beyond needs; it is transcendence, urged precisely by that "dissatisfaction with life" that Tolstoy defends against Strakhov's self-satisfied "world as a whole." Living in truth means continuing to experience, as Levin does at the very end of the novel, the disjunction between the ideal of goodness and the reality of experience. Living in truth presupposes death as that which marks the limit of the world as a whole and generates the need to transcend it.

Both plotlines end with the affirmation of a certain truth. Anna's suicide completes the tragic totality of her life, posits truth as the truth of the whole, the veridiction of *sjuzhet*. Levin's internalization of death reveals the precondition of the structuring principle of his life, the truth of the unexpected, the veridiction of *fabula* as deformation, decomposition, negation. Once again, if "remembering God" and "living for one's soul" are taken to refer to an ideological content, then it is no different from Levin's conviction that he should serve in the *zemstvo*, or quit it, or marry a peasant girl, or commit suicide.[26] The real revelation is structural: Levin is granted insight into the nature of the narrative he has inhabited from the very beginning—he recognizes and sanctions his own partial externality in relation to existence.[27]

Timeless Truth: Narrative Discourse

We have seen that the narrator's discourse, which, throughout the eighteenth century and before, has served as the privileged site of atemporal truth, is, in the novels of Balzac, radically demoted. In Dostoevsky this decline is even more apparent. Here, the objective narrator has a number of equally unglamorous options: he can stay out of the narrative altogether (as in *Notes from the Underground*, *The Adolescent*), he can occasionally appear in the guise of the hero's belated retrospection (as in *Crime and Punishment*), or he can report mere rumors and gossip (as in *The Idiot*, *The Possessed*). Whatever the case may be, he, too, is consistently placed at the service of narrative unfolding. Truth, now that it has become so tightly linked to time, can do without him. It should not come as a surprise, however, that novelists such as Stendhal and Tolstoy, working against the grain of the novel's veridictory mutation, would present us with more respectable narratorial figures. Sober, analytical, ironic, they are in fact nothing like their degraded, clownish counterparts from the opposite camp. Of course, there are significant differences between them. Stendhal's is often lightly palpable, a good-natured, generous ironist, occasionally referring to himself in the first person. Tolstoy's is always distant, authoritative, often sarcastic, never playful or tongue-in-cheek. But despite their differences, it is clear that neither of them is there to prop up the plot, to render the sequence of events believable, or to present it (as Dostoevsky's narrators often do) in the mode of self-conscious incredulity. They are there, instead, to comment, to assess, and to judge.

Recall, for example, this interpolation early on in *Le Rouge et le noir*: "In a word, what made Julien a superior being was precisely the quality that prevented him from seizing a pleasure that lay directly in his path."[28] Or the more one-sidedly disparaging statement in *Anna Karenina*, declaring that Anna held her husband "guilty for everything bad she could find in him and [forgave] him nothing, on account of the terrible fault for which she stood guilty before him" (189). In neither case is the story in need of patching up; it is simply there, such as it is. But hovering above it is a loose evaluative superstructure, a site from which timeless truths can be pronounced upon temporally arranged sequences of events. We seem to be closer here to eighteenth-century novelistic truth discourse than to one that obeys the more modern veridictory imperative. But upon closer inspection, it is easy to see that we are by no means all the way back.

Anna Karenina opens with an instance of what looks like a militantly archaist device, a universalizing statement of truth by the narrator, aspiring to speak for all times and to subsume all particular situations: "All happy families are alike; each unhappy family is unhappy in its own way" (1). One might think we are in the presence of the earlier novelistic discourse of exemplarity: first a maxim, then its illustration in a story; or, first a story, and then its lesson, its moral. And yet this doesn't quite work. First, it is difficult to say exactly how the happy families in the novel—the Levins, the L'vovs, the old Shcherbat-skys—are similar. As for the unhappy ones—the Karenins, the Oblonskys, the Levins (when they *are* unhappy)—their unhappiness, predicated as it is on jealousy and adultery, could not be more alike. One gets the sense, in short, that the veridictory rhetoric of the maxim is here misplaced, that all the opening sentence is supposed to do is draw the reader's attention to the story that follows. Here is a story of an unhappy family, the narrator seems to be saying; it's worth reading because stories about unhappy families are all unusual, unique. As such the statement possesses neither inductive nor properly deductive authority. It is rather something like a preamble, authoritative but impotent, somewhere between the ancillary narratorial discourse in Balzac and its genuinely truth-purveying forebear from the eighteenth century.

This is even more obviously the case with the narrator's other "objective" claim about family, one that appears toward the end of the novel. It reads: "In order to undertake anything in family life, it is necessary that there be either complete discord between the spouses or loving harmony" (739). The immediate pretext for this statement is Anna and Vronsky's indecision about leaving Moscow. Here, indeed, there is neither radical disagreement nor loving harmony, and so they keep putting off the trip. But elsewhere we are told that Levin quarrels with Kitty about her desire to accompany him to the provincial town where his brother Nikolai was stranded with an illness. There is ultimately neither harmony nor complete disagreement between them on the subject, and yet they both go, and Kitty proves to be very helpful (489). Again, it is difficult not to yield to a suspicion that wise generalizations are being produced and purveyed here *ad hoc*.

The narrator's maxims in *Anna Karenina* emerge as something of an atavistic twitch, precipitated perhaps by Tolstoy's archaist resistance to the veridictory mutation, but no longer capable of fulfilling their original function. And in fact the novel contains very few instances of such timeless truths aspiring to illuminate a series of episodes. Here, the episodes themselves are not given to us as such, but as already bound into provisional wholes by the meaning-making consciousness of the hero, and it is on the manner of the hero's understanding and emplotment of events that the narrator is most often provoked to comment. We recall that Stendhal's narrator again and again indulgently mocks Julien for his insistence on the relevance of social class in his affair with Mme de Rênal. The narrator in Tolstoy undermines, among other things, Vronsky's attempts to conceive of his relationship with Anna in chivalric terms: "His relations with society were also clear. Everyone might know or suspect [his affair with Anna], but no one should dare to talk. Otherwise, he was prepared to silence the talkers and make them respect the *nonexistent* honor of the woman he loved" (305, emphasis added). Truth breaks out suddenly through the veil of Vronsky's self-delusion, truth in the guise of narratorial judgment. The word "nonexistent" here could not possibly have been part of Vronsky's interior monologue. It is smuggled in by the narrator with the obvious intention of undermining the hero's understanding of events.

What is activated in the site of the narrator, then, is a tireless critique of veridiction by emplotment, a dismantling of the alliance between truth and time, the work of the negative, of dissolution and dispersal. The narrator is no longer—as he is in the eighteenth century—the guarantor of significance for the episodic narrative. Nor is he—as in Dostoevsky and Balzac—the plot's servant and dupe, demeaned and ultimately obviated by the effects of the veridictory mutation. Rather, he is the agent of disemplotment, the place from which the consequences of this mutation are resisted.[29]

Occasionally, this narrator withdraws and falls silent. Stendhal's retreats and takes with him the ironizing epigraphs after Julien is condemned to execution. On the verge of death, Julien comes closest to living day-to-day. There are no more schemes to hatch, no more promises to fulfill, no more ideals to realize. As far as Julien is concerned, he occupies the space and time of disemplotment as such. At least subjectively, at least for the most part, he already lives in the truth of a perpetual present, and there is nothing for the narrator to negate. Tolstoy's narrator, meanwhile, quite intrusive vis-à-vis Anna, Vronsky, and Karenin, has almost nothing to say about Levin. Levin's schemes are decomposed without his help, in the *fabulaic* time of his plotline, and so the narrator has nothing, or little, to debunk.

In fact, rather than rise above Levin's point of view, the narrator often aligns himself with it, especially when a certain self-important falsehood is in need of exposure and deflation. Thus, during the scene of the provincial elections, where Levin understands nothing or nearly nothing of what is happening around him, narration is heavily filtered through his consciousness and is thus extremely confusing. The scene culminates with an uproar among the members of the council: "To the vote! To the vote! Every nobleman will understand. We shed our blood . . . The monarch's trust . . . Don't count the marshal, he's no one to give orders . . . That's not the point . . . The vote, if you please! Disgusting! . . . Angry, furious cries came from all sides. The looks and faces were still more angry and furious than the talk. They expressed irreconcilable hatred. Levin had no idea what it was all about" (651).[30] Here and throughout the elections, Levin is unable to go beyond the surface of events. Actions and words fall apart for him into discrete segments; he fails to grasp their "togetherness," their meaning. They are estranged. But what this incident makes vivid once again is that in order for the estrangement effect to emerge, it is necessary for the character whose perspective is being employed to enter the situation without a set of appropriate expectations. Levin, whose progress, as we have seen, is marked precisely by a kind of temporal nearsightedness, is of course a perfect candidate for estranged narration. His is the story of permanent or compulsive estrangement, the estrangement of critique.

And yet, on closer examination, something about all this should give us pause. After all, we know that by the beginning of the novel, Levin has already *stopped* attending provincial council meetings. How is it, then, that he is so confused? Shouldn't he be better prepared to understand the procedural subtleties of provincial elections? We seem to be confronted here with a situation in which the zone of the narrator not only aligns itself with the zone of the estranging hero but moreover appears to warp that zone for the sake of its own veridictory purposes.[31]

A similar warping, though one that goes in the reverse direction, occurs when the narrator's zone intersects with Anna's. In one particularly striking instance of such free indirect discourse in the novel, we have Anna on the verge of suicide, distraught, riding around in a carriage, casting a "bright," "piercing," "truthful" light on her surroundings and her relationship with Vronsky. In that light, everything appears meaningless, ugly, cruel:

> "Yes, I no longer have the same savour for him. If I leave him, at the bottom of his heart, he'll be glad."
>
> This was not a supposition. She saw it clearly in that piercing light which now revealed to her the meaning of life and of people's relations. (763)

If, in the earlier example, the narrator's alignment with Levin usurps his characterological specificity, neglects to take into account what the hero could or should know, then, here, the exact opposite is the case. The heroine pulls the zone of the narrator into her axiological sphere, emptying it out of the accumulated information (what the narrator might have "witnessed" elsewhere in the novel, say, within the Levin-Kitty plotline), and producing within it generalization about the meaning of life as a whole on the basis of a single experience of a character on the brink of violent death. Such is the centripetal pull of her tightly emplotted storyline that even the narrator has a difficult time keeping his distance. With Levin's help, the narrator's zone can register the loosely temporalized world through the prism of a perpetually unprepared, estranging consciousness. In tandem with Anna, it inevitably finds itself drawn into the dense temporality of the world proleptically made whole. And so while it can align itself with Levin without reneging on its function as an agent of disemplotment, it must stay away from Anna, must pronounce upon her from a distance, if it is to avoid lending its authority to the tightly wound truth discourse of which she is both subject and object.

What we have in Tolstoy and in Stendhal, then, are narrators who in one way or another buttress a veridictory discourse that is neither temporal (as in Balzac or Dostoevsky), nor pretemporal (as in earlier novelistic texts), but properly *posttemporal,* repeatedly undermining attempts to reach the truth through emplotment.

The Jurisdiction of the Epigraph

The magic skin, the chronicles of de La Mole, the resurrection of Lazarus and, finally, now, the epigraph "vengeance is mine, I shall repay"—these are the archaic sediments of romance narratology that weave shapes of timelessness into the modern novel. Throughout the history of *Anna Karenina*'s reception, the question of its biblical epigraph has been perhaps the most troubling of all. How exactly is it supposed to relate to the novel? What is meant by vengeance? Who deserves it? Who doesn't? And why? After all, doesn't the novel contain quite a number of cheerful sinners on whom no revenge whatsoever is wreaked in the end? If we consider the epigraph as a statement of condemnation and a promise of punishment, then how is one to explain that Anna and Vronsky, the most reluctant offenders of all, are condemned and punished, while such habitual profligates as Stiva, Betsy, and Yashvin are not only spared retribution but even, as in the case of Stiva, depicted with a great deal of sympathy? Can the universal law have limited application? Can it be inconsistent?

Some of these questions can perhaps be readily dismissed. Just as the story of Lazarus heightens Raskolnikov's plight, elevating him into the realms of (profane) Christology, so the epigraph—with its authoritative sources in the Old and New Testaments as well as in Arthur Schopenhauer's *World as Will and Representation* (1819)—lifts Anna's story of high passion out of the sphere of merely frivolous dissipation. Her fate and Vronsky's are genuinely "romantic." Stiva's, Betsy's, Yashvin's are so trifling that the universal law refuses even to condescend.

Thus, considered from the point of view of genre, the epigraph's limited applicability makes sense. And this is only confirmed when the question is taken up from the narratological perspective. After all, the Betsys and the Yashvins are secondary characters, fit for constituting "semantic fields" across which protagonists operate, but not for representing "free moral agents," capable of crossing significant moral boundaries.[32] Still, the question might be posed again: what do we make of the fact that the epigraph does not appear to apply to Levin and Kitty, who are at least as full fledged as their counterparts from the more romantic parallel plot? It appears then that the generic boundaries of the epigraph's applicability must be narrowed still further.

Indeed, prominent though Levin and Kitty are, they are not properly "romantic," not heightened heroes; accordingly, they are not subject to transcendent emplotment. The constructive principle underlying their narrative eschews *sjuzhet*-dependent veridiction and generates its truths otherwise, through a perpetual struggle, in time, between the centripetal, synthetic aspirations of thought and the centrifugal, decomposing effects of reality. Thus, no predictive epigraph could apply to them, let alone one as authoritative and fatidic as "Vengeance is mine . . ."

The position of the epigraph outside and above the novel, its veridical weight, its authoritative sources—all thus acquire a somewhat paradoxical aspect. Either the universal law it presumes to pronounce is in fact quite particular (applying only to Anna), or it is there simply by mistake. These have indeed been the most common solutions to the enigma that confronts us. But we seem to have prepared the ground for another, and perhaps a trickier, resolution. It has by now become sufficiently clear that unity and duality in this novel are mediated by something like the principle of inflection; one and the same element acquires a different shape and significance depending on the plotline in which it appears. The epigraph, then, is not an exception: looming over the novel as a whole, it throws an ominous shadow over one of its plotlines while appearing to be mute and indifferent with respect to the other. Universality itself, and especially the binding, *sjuzhet*-centered universality of temporal veridiction, does not cease to be "universal" (insofar as it presents us with the dominant shape of the modern narrative), and yet it is revealed as in fact not universally applicable (insofar as there are narratives that manage to escape the very logic of this modernity).

The magic skin and the raising of Lazarus in the Gospel of John—these transcendent plots and sediments of romance idealism—provide the veridictory framework for the entire narratives of *Crime and Punishment* and *La Peau de chagrin*. The chronicles of de La Mole and the biblical epigraph function similarly, but in relation only to limited fields within *Anna Karenina* and *Le Rouge et le noir*. The latter two novels thus incorporate and at the same time—

insofar as some narrative trajectories within them manage to evade transcendent emplotment—resist the hypostatization of modernity in the guise of "the world as a whole."

Comparative Interlude II: The Double Plot (Stendhal)

The formal corollaries of this simultaneous incorporation and resistance are far reaching and have to do with the ways in which these authors extend the analytical method far beyond the mere presentation of minute psychological detail to produce visible rifts within the overall plots of their novels. In Stendhal, the plot of *the whole* and the (anti)plot of *the true* still make up one and the same, complicated, narrative shape. Tolstoy goes further on the path of analysis, breaking this shape down into its constitutive parts. Thus, Julien Sorel shares some central features of his narrative trajectory with Anna and others with Levin.

Like Anna's, his end is enciphered in his beginning; like her, he is caught within a totalizing modernity, a modernity that paradoxically comes to rely on the veridictory structures of its past; like her, he is trapped in the falsehood of the whole and perishes in this trap. Like Anna between two railway stations, he finds himself densely (epanaleptically) emplotted between two churches, which are, moreover, actually one and the same church. Anna's death on the rails is his overdetermined decapitation by guillotine; her romance idealism is his romantic historiography; even his name, like hers, gives rise to emplotting anagrams (Louis Jenrel—Julien Sorel). Both of their stories instantiate an open conflict and a disturbing behind-the-scenes alliance between societal conventions and poetic formulas.

And yet Julien's story also resembles Levin's. Adventure, the unexpected, the temptation of the idyll, the truth effect of sudden disemplotment, *frondeur* subjectivism—all characterize them both. Both novels then can be said to be double-plotted and to contain two distinct conceptions of truth. In both novels, one of them, the one staging an affinity between truth and time, is revealed as fraudulent. In Stendhal's case, the plots are woven together: the true, without ceasing to be true, turns out to be a moment of the false. Tolstoy disentangles them and presents the two plotlines and two veridictory shapes independently. The world of *Anna Karenina* as a whole is less hermetic than that of *Rouge*, the power of romantic containment within it is weaker, or, perhaps more precisely, its domain is more limited.

What accounts for this limitation and for the robust sense, in Tolstoy's novel, that alternative narrative possibilities are open? What are the social conditions for the possibility of this openness? Here perhaps a glance back at Tolstoy's compatriot counterpart can be illuminating. Beyond the dense, stifling narrative of *Crime and Punishment* lie vast spaces of what Porfiry Petrovich calls "air," the open spaces of exile in the midst of which the Siberian ordeal by patience can unfold. Dostoevsky's novel can only gesture beyond itself toward the kind of narrative that would not be infected by the modern tempos of the modern city. Tolstoy gives us a whole plotline (Levin's) that, though it passes through Moscow, is not deformed by its force field. The point, of course, is not the city itself, but the kind of modernity it instantiates and exudes. Much of Julien's story takes place outside Paris, but Parisian Restoration modernity weighs heavily and, in the final analysis, decisively over the trajectory of his life. As for Tolstoy, he displays precisely the disposability of this sort of modernity, tracing the shape of a life that would largely bypass it.

Lukács notes that Tolstoy never identifies modern reality with reality as such, always opposing to its distortions a reality that would be natural and truly humane.[33] In this sense, he can be seen as both crowning and transcending the tradition of eighteenth-century Enlightenment narrative, where social evils are represented as falling short of the ideals of natural existence.[34] He does not merely rely on the notorious distinction between the city and the country, describing, as so many eighteenth- and nineteenth-century novelists do, the disappointments and corruptions that overtake the hero as he crosses the border to capital-city modernity. Rather, for him, crossing that border does not appear to be a necessity. He manages to envision another trajectory and endow it with a shape of its own: neither a *Bildungsroman* educating the hero and the reader in the ways of the modern world, nor an idyll isolating and belaboring nature, but an adventure in an alternative—and an "earlier"—modernity, the modernity of dissatisfaction and critique.

Chronotopes of Modernity: The Railway and the Road

To each of the two modernities whose figure Tolstoy traces out in *Anna Karenina*, to each of the two truth shapes implicit in them, corresponds something like a distinct image of time, in which, as in the Bakhtinian chronotope, "time thickens, takes on flesh, becomes artistically visible."[35] In this respect, when it comes to the intensity and vividness with which it links distinct time shapes and truth shapes with specific locales, Tolstoy's novel differs somewhat from the others we have considered. The suffocating temporality of the magic skin, for example, operates across various locales, confined only to Raphael's biography. Julien Sorel's dutiful haste is with him regardless of where he is, and one might even say that its force weakens as the hero moves closer to Paris, the center with which this impetuous temporality is initially associated. The various veridictory emplotments in *Crime and Punishment* converge on the figure of the enigmatic protagonist and can only loosely, if at all, be associated with specific spaces or locales. The sharp separation of *Anna Karenina* into distinct plotlines, its ability and willingness to disentangle the interdependent but conflicting temporalities of modernity and set them flowing side-by-side, seems to solicit a chronotopic complement to the veridictory analysis already provided. Thus, the dominant chronotope for Anna's *sjuzhet*-heavy veridiction is, unmistakably, the railway; for Levin's looser, meandering shape of truth, it is, more properly, the road.[36]

The railway is most often invoked, with a more or less explicitly negative tinge, in connection with Anna's brother, Stiva Oblonsky.[37] Thus, early on in the novel, the Oblonsky children quarrel over a toy train, compounding the atmosphere of confusion and disorder in the family. Toward the end of the novel, now "motherless" Seryozha Karenin mentions to his uncle a popular game at school, involving an imaginary railroad. Stiva's poor financial situation compels him to seek a position as a member of the convoluted Committee of the Joint Agency of the Mutual Credit Balance of Southern Railways and Banking Houses—a process involving a humiliating encounter with a Jew and compromising to his aristocratic honor. The railway also appears as an object of Levin's criticism in his work on the contemporary economic situation in Russia. Here it is prominent among those agents of rapid modernization that contribute to the poverty of the peasant, the desperate state of agriculture in Russia, and more generally to the unnatural consequences of uneven development. Occasionally, the railroad is invoked in the capacity of a metaphor for habitual, conventional social existence. Thus, "though the whole of Vronsky's inner life was filled with his passion, his external life rolled inalterably and irresistibly along the former, habitual rails of social and regimental connections" (173).[38] Though used here in relation to Vronsky, the metaphor sheds light on the consistent connection between the railway motif and Stiva, the most thoroughly socialized character in the novel.[39]

It is thus shadowed by these negative connotations—confusion, immorality, neglect of family and children, poverty, humiliation, social convention—

that the railroad emerges as the key "chronotope" of the Anna-Vronsky narrative line. It is at a railway station that the future lovers meet at the beginning of the novel. It is also there and then that the two of them hear of the fatal accident on the tracks, which Anna takes to be a bad omen. Later on, the snowstorm on the tracks serves as a setting for Vronsky's declaration of love for Anna, and the train itself for the memorable scene of reading by the light of the candle lantern, to which the final moments of Anna's life will refer us again. It is also here that a railway worker appears, invoking the man killed earlier, the one who appears in Anna's (and Vronsky's) dreams and the one who will reappear at the moment of her death under a passing train.

The train's extraordinary capacity for narrative binding is not uniquely a feature of this novel's imagery. A telling instance can be found in Tolstoy's late novella, *The Kreutzer Sonata* (1890), where the train is revealed not only as the site of narration (after all, this is where the protagonist, Pozdnyshev, tells his story) but also as a powerful engine behind passion, obsession, and emplotment. In the culminating moments of the story, Pozdnyshev, who has gone away on business, is overcome with jealousy of his wife and decides to return immediately. His trip involves some travel by road and then by train. While in the carriage, he feels relatively calm, even enjoys the ride; and when thoughts about his wife's possible affair with the musician Trukhachevsky come, he manages to ward them off: "We shall see when the time comes: I must not think about it."[40] But as soon as he gets on the train, everything radically changes: "Whether it was that having taken my seat in the carriage I vividly imagined myself as having already arrived, or that railway traveling has such an exciting effect on people, at any rate from the moment I sat down in the train I could no longer control my imagination.... The more I gazed at those imaginary pictures the stronger grew my belief in their reality" (415–16). He tries to think of something else, but is again and again pulled back to his preoccupation. He thinks of the innkeeper where he had his tea, remembers the innkeeper's grandson and then, by association, his own son, who might have witnessed his mother kissing the musician. He thinks of a doctor at the district hospital, and the doctor's mustache reminds him of Trukhachevsky's. Pozdnyshev's imagination, put to frenetic work by the movement of the train, yields to the formidable centripetal force of his central concern. Much like Anna's plotline, it is unable to digress, to wander aimlessly, or to be distracted by extrinsic concerns.[41]

Moving so much faster than any other contemporary means of transportation, the train binds time.[42] While traveling in the carriage, Pozdnyshev is able to distinguish between the present and the future; he can put off thinking about what will happen when he arrives. But once he has boarded the train, he is, in his mind, instantly at the point of destination.[43] The train, Tolstoy's own onager, facilitates the anchoring of random events to the core of more or less conscious preoccupation, the becoming *sjuzhet* of *fabula*. As an agent of radical modernization, it both figures and promotes tight and tightly conventional emplotment, connecting points in space, events in time, people in social networks, and fragments of reality in emotionally charged "literary" patterns.

Late in the novel, Stiva meets with his brother-in-law Karenin to ask him for help in procuring a position with the railroad. In the course of the conversation, Karenin outlines his understanding of the reasons for the bad state of Russian finances. Stiva interjects that after all, "the principle of our time is freedom." Karenin replies: "Yes, but I put forward another principle that embraces [*obnimaiushchii*] the principle of freedom" (720). This embracing (or rather, containing) principle, as it turns out, is free trade, an opposition to protectionism. Karenin is here defending precisely that which Levin attacks in his book: the rapid development of industrial and financial capitalism in Russia, enabled largely by the construction of railroads. As a mechanism and symbol of modernization, the railroad itself is this principle embracing [*obnimaiushchii*] the principle of freedom, contributing to the congealment of the modern world into "the world as a whole."

Anna's densely emplotted storyline, figured by the railway, instantiates the vision of truth as coherent and continuous. But we have seen that for Tolstoy this is imposter veridiction, seducing us away from the recognition that real truth, or, in the terms of the novel's conclusion, "a truthful life," is essentially disjointed and confused, relying on and repeatedly reaffirming the disjunction between consciousness and the world and the hero's dissatisfaction with life. Hence, Levin's endless meanderings, his inability to stay in one place or to move in a single direction or to become a determinate thing. His is the story infused by the more familiar image of the road of life, with what Bakhtin has called the "adventure-everydayness" (*avantiurno-bytovoi*) chronotope.[44] The adventure-everydayness chronotope, as it is elaborated by Bakhtin, differs from the older chronotope of adventure proper insofar as it no longer conceives of time as merely external. Here we have the kind of time that—though it is still episodic—allows for radical transformation of the hero himself. The hero then does not experience mere adventures, essentially remaining unchanged; he undergoes genuine change, even metamorphosis, and, at least potentially, with each episode he can become a different person, be reborn. Crucially, however, this is not yet the chronotope of development, teleologically foreclosing the potentially endless series of crises and transformations: "Metamorphosis or transformation is a mythological sheath for the idea of development—but one that unfolds not so much in a straight line as spasmodically [*skachkoobrazno*], a line with 'knots' in it, one that therefore constitutes a distinctive type of *temporal sequence*."[45]

According to Bakhtin, the hero whose story is guided by this chronotope is not a part of the world he traverses, and it is this nonbelonging to the world that allows him, in passing through it, to expose its darker sides, to gain insight into what is for the most part invisible.[46] In Levin's case, this externality is both sociohistorically and psychologically conceived. He is an avowed and incorrigible landowner in the midst of a world increasingly "embraced" by railroads and urban life. But he is also, unlike the earlier heroes of this chronotope, in possession of a rich inner life and a thoroughly philosophical mindset—two inexhaustible sources of disgruntled eccentricity. Early on in the novel, Levin, a perpetual misfit, is juxtaposed to Stiva, who is comfortable everywhere and with everyone. Each has a certain contempt for the other's lifestyle, each secretly laughs at the other, but "Oblonsky, while doing as everyone else did, laughed confidently and good naturedly, whereas Levin laughed unconfidently and sometime crossly" (17). This lack of confidence is the psychic corollary of Levin's epistemological "estrangement," of what allows him to perceive the profound imperfections of the world he inhabits. It is a characteristic of an updated and specifically Tolstoian *picaro*—the *philosophe-cum*-aristocratic *frondeur*, refusing to accept a modernity foreclosing upon itself.[47]

His crises, too, are updated or internalized. No longer actual metamorphoses into animals and plants, they are significant nevertheless, repeatedly producing before us Levin reborn. The endless "turns of fate" experienced by the *picaro* are here also *inner* turns, changes in worldview and in the hero's comportment in the world. And *pace* Bakhtin himself, who takes Levin for a hero of a modern *Bildungsroman*,[48] nothing like a narrative of development results. Rather than pass through stages on life's way, progressively becoming who he is, Levin is who he is from the beginning; but being true to himself means that he must constantly change.

There are in fact many moments in the novel when Levin appears to have arrived. In chronotopic terms, the most convincing of them appear in the shade of the idyll. According to Bakhtin, the cyclical time and static location of the idyll, when reconfigured (primarily by Jean-Jacques Rousseau) in the context of modernity, acquire the dimensions of the philosophical category of the natural—everything that is wise, good, and true. At the same time, the modern idyll is no longer given objectively, as the essential condition of the fictional world, but comes to us from the perspective of the lonely, suffering individual who returns to nature briefly in order to be healed, purified, and calmed.[49]

The most strikingly idyllic scene in the novel is surely the scene of mowing with the peasants. Here, Levin loses track of time, enters a state of blissful self-presence, and works effortlessly, "the scythe [cutting] by itself" (252). Throughout the scene, mowing between an old peasant and a youth, Levin occupies the proper place in the natural order of life. The idyll is tempting. Levin spends the night in the field and dreams of changing "that so burdensome, idle, artificial life he lived into [the] laborious, pure and common, lovely life" of the peasant. He imagines selling his land, buying a smaller plot for himself, marrying a peasant girl, forgetting his past. But as soon as he walks off the field and onto the main road leading to the village, he glimpses Kitty in a passing coach (presumably coming from the train station) and instantly renounces his dreams, recalling them now with disgust.

If the field of peaceful peasant labor where Levin experiences his momentary bliss is an instantiation of the idyll, the road serves as a common image precisely within the "adventure-everydayness" chronotope. Within the chronotopography of the scene, it lies between the field and the railway. Off the field and back on the road (but not on the railroad), Levin is once again in the grips of his adventure, on the path of chance encounters and sudden conversions. The ideal is always there in the form of the idyll, but Levin does not move closer and closer to it or understand it better and better. Rather, he is at times allowed to glimpse it only to be nudged along his adventurous path past it. And so if Anna's railway chronotope, the chronotope of the modern "world as a whole," collapses distinctions between beginnings and ends, Levin's crisis-ridden adventure does away with beginnings and ends altogether and thus persists in another modernity, one that posits a decisive rift between the self and the world and celebrates the life of dissatisfaction and estrangement.

Comparative Interlude III: The *Bildungsroman* (Dostoevsky)

If there is a narrative form that best internalizes the historical alliance between truth and time, it is the Hegelian *Bildungsroman*, with its logic of progressive development and perfectibility. *Crime and Punishment* can be understood as a telling and formally fruitful attempt to come to terms with its historical unattainability. The novel proceeds in the shadow of a (hagiographically inflected) *Bildungsroman*. Raskolnikov's future, postexile deed distended in time is the ideal narrative shape the novel could only strain for but could never achieve. Its quest for the story in which the truth about Raskolnikov (and Russia) could be told ends with a gesture of both resignation and hope: perhaps such a story can be found, but it is certainly not the one that has been told.

By contrast, *Anna Karenina* can be said to be deliberately engaged in a creative disassembly of the generic shape of the *Bildungsroman* into its constitutive parts, laying bare the conflicting historical and ideological trends underlying its veridictory makeup. Had the two plotlines of the novel been woven together—Levin's meandering, *fabulaic* trajectory eventually molded into the shape of Anna's *sjuzhet*-heavy Absolute—then we would indeed have something like the *Lehrjahre*, with its early looseness and late tying up of loose ends. Instead, we have a novel that denies the satisfaction (and critiques the expectation) of witnessing how subjective estrangement and discontent acquire the shape of an objective destiny.

In short, then, for Dostoevsky the *Bildungsroman* is impossible, while for Tolstoy it is undesirable. But on one level, this amounts to the same thing. After all, Goethe locates the standard of truth and the aim of temporal succession in the structure of the world as it is. Neither Dostoevsky nor Tolstoy is willing to do the same. For neither does contemporary modernity offer anything like an attractive condition of veridictory emplotment. And so the difference between impossibility and undesirability lies in the authors' divergent conceptualizations of what it means to tell the truth in narrative. Dostoevsky's acceptance of the alliance between truth and time (recall, "time brings truth to light"), his obsession with emplotment as the key to the enigma of the hero, symptomatically produces a yearning for a *Bildungsroman*-like narrative shape even as he recognizes the illegitimacy of the *Bildungsroman*'s (Western, bourgeois) ideological pretensions. This yearning, in other words, is detectable not only at the end, in the formula of the distended deed, but everywhere in the novel, and its final beckoning to a gradualist narrative on the horizon is thus largely overdetermined.

As for Tolstoy, his dissolution of the form represents an economical act dismissing in one gesture both the claims of "the world as a whole" and the corresponding rapprochement between truth and time. In the process, it makes vivid an elective affinity between conventional socialization and temporal veridiction. But at the same time, in narrating Levin's alternative story against the grain of both of these historical exigencies, it forecloses the possibility—one that so vividly strains the narrative fabric of *Crime and Punishment*—that the truth-time alliance and the triumphalism of socialization might be told apart from each other.

Conclusion:
Enduring the *Schema* in Modernist Time

Tracing Goethe's inaugural transition from the episodic structure of *Wilhelm Meister's Theatrical Mission* to the more holistic *Lehrjahre*, we witnessed the site of novelistic truth migrate from authoritative narratorial discourse, pronouncing eternal verities over a mistake-ridden temporal succession, to that succession itself, now capable of yielding truth immanently. The new narrative appeared to transcend the opposition between truthless time and timeless truth, and instead to align them, warping the episodic trajectory into a truth-giving loop. This is the structure of *Lehrjahre*: a series of erroneous episodes culminating in truth-bestowing emplotment.

In the middle chapters of the book we saw the alliance of time and truth realized in a number of varied configurations, some (those of Balzac and Dostoevsky) privileging emplotment as a fundamental principle of truth telling in time, others (those of Stendhal and Tolstoy) mounting formal resistances to this principle, promoting the opposing operation of disemplotment as the narrative instantiation of authenticity and vitality. Throughout, however, the two tendencies were shown to be mutually implicated, each acknowledging and struggling to disentangle itself from the other. The homogenous empty time of the disemplotted episode could yield truth only insofar as it was mobilized against the stifling holism of conventionality, habit, industrialization. Meanwhile, the veridictory powers of the enigma-driven "full" time of emplotment came from the promise that time, episodic and fragmentary though it may seem, is capable of engendering truth.

Anna Karenina emerged as an exception in this sense. Here, we have two discourses of truth operating not against each other but, for the most part, side by side. Reading it against the model of the Goethean *Bildungsroman*, we can understand this parallel structure as a result of the dissolution of this exemplary veridictory subgenre into its basic elements—serial temporal unfolding on the one hand and meaningful shaping of events on the other—and consequently as a failure of immanently temporal veridiction. From Tolstoy's point of view this failure is in fact a rejection of such immanence and a retreat (within the Levin plotline) to the earlier, pre-Goethean models of the eighteenth-century picaresque. But, in a more forward-looking mode, the very same dissolution can be read as an intimation of the impending modernist breakdown of the veridictory alliance, the ultimate acknowledgment that time, taken seriously as homogeneous and atomistic, is incapable of immanently producing truth, and that truth does not unfold in, but transfixes time.

In what follows I would like to effect precisely the shift in perspective that would allow us to see the formal dualism of Tolstoy's novel as participating in a modernist crisis of veridiction. It will of course be impossible to speak of modernism (both philosophical and literary) exhaustively; a few exemplary figures will have to suffice. Thus, I will begin with a discussion of what is perhaps the most strikingly original and influential "modernist" philosophy of time, that of Henri Bergson. Walter Benjamin's late methodological work will then help situate Bergson's key categories in a broader historical context of the changing experience of modernity and provide them with historico-philosophical correlates. Bergson and Benjamin, then, with their focus on individual and historical configurations of time and truth, respectively, will serve as "modernist" counterparts to the Kant and Hegel of the introduction.

This representative cluster of texts will of course exclude many others no less important for an overall understanding of the rich and varied veridictory terrain in turn-of-the-century Europe. Like the period constituting the subject of the central part of this book, it cannot be understood as univocal, but it might best be seen as containing competing residual and emergent as well as, perhaps, dominant tendencies. To my mind, while such philosophers as Husserl, Heidegger, and, somewhat later, Sartre modify and build on the conceptions of time elaborated in Kant and Hegel,[1] Bergson and Benjamin, with their emphasis on the veridictory power of a certain "thick present" torn out of succession and launched onto an incalculable future, voice the most forceful rejection of the temporal shape of truth articulated by the philosophical forebears of nineteenth-century veridiction.

Moreover, in elaborating a positive reconceptualization of the relation between truth and time, they develop categories that bear an unmistakable affinity to the veridictory structures that animate some of the most striking formal innovations in modernist narrative. It is thus with a discussion of two exemplary modernist novels—Marcel Proust's *Remembrance of Things Past* (*À la recherche du temps perdu,* 1913–1927) and Andrei Bely's *Petersburg* (1913; revised 1922)—that I conclude. Two novels could hardly appear more different from each other, and yet, as I will argue, both display a profound (Bergsonian and Benjaminian) skepticism concerning the ability of successive time to serve as the medium for truth and develop veridictory alternatives that render the nineteenth-century novelistic dichotomy between emplotment and disemplotment inconsequential.

Bergson: Memory as *Schema*

Toward the end of his last great metaphysical work, *Creative Evolution* (*L'Évolution créatrice*, 1907), Bergson outlines a distinction between ancient and modern conceptions of time. For the ancients, he argues, time as a medium of change is philosophically negligible; a thing in time is a thing degraded, unworthy of the attention of those who seek the truth. Where ancient metaphysics and science are concerned, only certain special, privileged moments in time count. Knowledge of a thing is achieved by observing it at the crucial moment when the changing object "just touches its intelligible form."[2] Only at such a moment does the thing yield its truth. Change as such, constant change, is the privative medium of blindness and error.

A very different conception of time, Bergson argues, can be found in modern science. Here, there is no such thing as a privileged, emblematic moment in which an object reveals its essence. Here, to understand anything at all is to understand the behavior of changing objects, of objects inextricable from the temporal continuum. For the moderns, in other words, "the flux of time is the reality itself, and the things which [they] study are the things that flow" (*CE,* 344). With this in mind, modern science strives to divide time into ever smaller units so as to be ever more precise in identifying the manner in which change happens. The proper vehicles of truth, then, are no longer essences and concepts, which deny or transfix time, but laws governing change; what we need is to determine constant relations between quantitative variations in movement (*CE,* 333).

Thus, *"modern science must be defined pre-eminently by its aspiration to take time as an independent variable"* (*CE,* 336). Yet, paradoxically, this doesn't mean that the moderns have made a lot of progress in coming to terms with change as the ceaseless appearance of the new. The trouble is that science, far from being an independently equipped inquiry into the hidden nature of things, takes its cue from ordinary knowledge. "It perfects this knowledge, increases its precision and its scope, but it works in the same direction and puts the same mechanism into play" (*CE,* 336). This mechanism is one whereby time is spatialized, reduced to the dimensions of space.[3] Constantly predicting the outcomes of our actions, relying on the calculability of the future, we learn to conceive of events as spread out on an imaginary timeline and thus come to think of them as given simultaneously, as if in two-dimensional space. Our ordinary, everyday reliance on the predictable future is the very impetus behind the development of the modern scientific attitude toward time. In the process of perfecting our ability to organize our actions with a view to their ends, modern science produces a "motionless design" of real change, a spatialized map of all possible happening, with the help of which humanity can rid itself of the threat of the absolutely new. Consequently, "real time, regarded as a flux, or, in other words, as the very mobility of being, escapes the hold of scientific knowledge" (*CE,* 337). Modern science, in other words, comes no closer than ancient metaphysics to grasping the true character of time as the ceaseless creation of the qualitatively new. Or, put another way, the scientific valorization of time relies on the occlusion of the true nature of change.

We should observe that the narrative traced out in the concluding sections of *Creative Evolution* is readable in terms of the overall trajectory of veridiction in modernity as it has been outlined in the preceding chapters.[4] Indeed, Bergson understands the work of modern thought as defined by a paradox in which openness to the experience of temporality as change coincides with an anxious need to foreclose it. Such an account of modern temporality would seem to open up the space for an inquiry into the tensions, organizing exemplary nineteenth-century narratives, between two visions of time-bound truth, visions that have been treated here as emplotment and disemplotment veridiction. In this account, the former, organizing the narratives and thought of Balzac and Dostoevsky, display a fascination with the possibility of shaping time into a spatialized whole, while the latter, articulated and enacted by Stendhal and Tolstoy, would insist precisely on time as the medium for the emergence of truth as the new. As we shall see momentarily, this is not quite right; or rather, this description of how things stand with our two veridictory trajectories is already skewed by an implicit anachronism. For while it is possible to say that Bergson produces something like a genealogy of modern veridiction, he must also be seen as elaborating a more general philosophy of time that transcends the nineteenth-century veridictory problematic altogether.

Starting with his first major work, *Time and Free Will* (*Essai sur les données immédiates de la conscience,* 1889), Bergson elaborates a dual temporality, which can be articulated with reference to the subject-object distinction. Inner time, the time experienced in the locus of our innermost, deep-seated self, is pure duration (*la durée pure*), defined as "a succession of qualitative changes, which melt into and permeate one another, without precise outlines, without any tendency to externalize themselves in relation to one another, without any affiliation with number."[5] Outer time, on the other hand, is the temporality that organizes the experience of our practically oriented "external self" and operates according to homogeneous clock time: discrete rather than continuous, spatialized rather than durational, quantitative rather than qualitative. Here, an hour is invariably equivalent to an hour and a year to a year, no matter how these hours and years are experientially "filled." Without such standardization, Bergson argues, neither practical activity nor social life would be possible. And it is this quantified, spatialized temporality that is accentuated in modern scientific inquiry. Moreover, "in proportion as the conditions of social life are more completely realized, the current which carries our conscious states from within outwards is strengthened; little by little these states are made into objects or things; they break off not only from one another but from ourselves" (*TFW*, 138). A certain reification of consciousness inevitably compels the subject to represent its own consciousness to itself in a spatialized manner, modeling inner states on outer objects and relations of mutual externality between them.

In *Time and Free Will*, accessing authentic, qualitative temporality, the temporality of *durée*, involves retreating into "the deep-seated self," abstracting from practical and social life, from language and from space itself and, in a feat of inner-directed intuition, abandoning ourselves to the rhythms of ceaseless qualitative change that constitutes the true life of the self. In this early work, the default condition is one of reified consciousness and spatialized time, since the objective world, the world of praxis and social relations, imposes its exigencies on the inner life of the subject. But already in *Matter and Memory* (*Matière et mémoire*, 1896), we find a differently accentuated account of the subject-object relation, introducing an idiosyncratic concept of memory to mediate between inner and outer time.

Bergson's account of experience in *Matter and Memory* begins with the premise that living organisms react to their environments with varying degrees of complexity and freedom. The most primitive among them respond in a purely reflexive manner, rendering them nearly indistinguishable from material objects that cannot but follow physical laws.[6] Thus, when it comes to the simplest living organisms, a rigid causality obtains: everything is determined with the view to survival. The more developed organisms, on the other hand, are capable of responding to their environments with a greater degree of variability. To be sure, we, too, are largely in the grips of reflexes. These reflexes may be more complex, but still "our representation of matter is the measure of our possible action upon bodies" (*MM,* 38). Our perception of the world is delimited by the principle of utility. Only those elements of reality that can be of use to us come into our field of perception. The rest is left in darkness.

What we call reflex when it comes to lower animals, then, we can call spatialization when we speak of humans. And yet, according to Bergson, the degree of variability and freedom of human action is significantly higher than that of lower organisms. For this to be the case, something of our "inner self" must be affecting our outer actions; spatialized time must be intersected by the temporality of *durée*. And indeed, by arguing that we can distinguish between lower and higher organisms in terms of the length of the temporal dilation between stimulus and response, Bergson delineates precisely such a point of intersection. It is into the space opened up by this dilation—negligible in single-cell organisms and prominent in humans—that *durée* intrudes as memory.

Memory, in Bergson's special use of the word, ensures the preservation of that which evades conscious perception due to its presumed practical uselessness. Bergsonian memory records "all the events of our daily life as they occur in time; it neglects no detail; it leaves to each fact, to each gesture, its place and date. Regardless of utility or of practical application, it stores up the past by the mere necessity of its own nature" (*MM,* 81). Side by side with conscious perception, which is always directed toward a purposeful horizon, another, unconscious recording mechanism is at work, storing those perceptions along with everything that they leave out. Or, in the words of one commentator: "Beyond the teleology and intentionality of conscious perception, this memory is the faithful preservation of a life I never consciously experienced."[7] As recorded in memory, the past can preserve all of its durational qualitative richness because (and insofar as) it is useless and can thus evade (in fact, has at some point evaded) the spatializing procedure of conscious perception. Moreover, because most of what is stored in memory was never consciously perceived, something altogether unpredictable, some genuine future, can arise if a recollection is invoked by an element in our experience of the present. Thus, memory in Bergson is a depository of experience unactualized but preserved—preserved in its durational rather than spatialized form precisely because unactualized—and constantly interpolating our present, teleologically organized experience with traces of the useless.[8] It is because these memories can find their way back into our perceptions that our response to the world is more than just reflexive. Thanks to the intrusion of memory, understood as virtual (that is, nonactualized) perception, newness finds its way into the world and a non-spatialized, unpredictable future comes to pass.

In *Matter and Memory,* Bergson demands that "questions relating to subject and object, to their distinction and their union . . . be put in terms of time rather than space" (*MM,* 71). In accordance with this demand, we can now see subject and object mediated by two temporalities constantly weaving into each other: the spatialized time of practical utility, or matter, and the durational, "useless," or better, "use-free" time of memory. Insofar as memory is always called upon to illuminate the instant of perception and activity, these two temporalities are operative, to different degrees, at every moment of a person's life. Acting on pure impulse, one might invoke no more than a certain section of what Bergson calls habit memory; delaying and hesitating, one will find oneself in the midst of recollections "without any advantage for the present situation" (*MM,* 153).

It appears, then, that as a veridictory procedure of temporal mediation between subject and object, Bergson's *mémoire* can be seen as an "updated" version of the Kantian *Schema.* To be sure, it is a radically heterodox version, first because it presupposes a monist, merely polar understanding of the distinction between subject and object: the further one finds oneself in the realms of recollection, the closer one is to the limit of subjectivity; while the more one is engrossed in practical activity, the more one is indistinguishable from matter. But it is also an odd sort of *Schema* because it depends on the assumption of unconscious experience. Replacing the Kantian transcendental realm with that of the unconscious is itself enabled and encouraged by the conception of experience as wholly embodied. Thus, experience itself, albeit the unconscious experience stored up in memory—"the past that has never been present"[9]—becomes the condition for the possibility of conscious experience, depriving the subject of its transcendental haven but at the same time endowing it with the capacity to introduce the radically new into the world. Memory can be read as the sort of schematism that enables not the knowledge of nature, the ability to predict how it will behave, but its constant, unpredictable transformation.

In the next section, more will be done to explore and to historicize the parallels between veridiction as conceived by Kant (and Hegel) and as it appears in Bergson. For now, it is important to emphasize that, with the latter, we have transcended the modern scientific problematic of veridictory spatialization. In having transcended it, however, we did not end up back with the ancient (or pre-Kantian) disdain for the passage of time, but have instead opened up another veridictory region with significant ramifications for historiography and narrative more broadly.

Benjamin: The Veridiction of the Now-Time

One way to situate Bergson's theory of time in its historical context, a way that is particularly germane for the questions we are asking, was suggested in Walter Benjamin's 1939 essay "On Some Motifs in Baudelaire." There, Benjamin hazards that, though Bergson steers clear of historicizing his own theory of memory, this theory does nevertheless register contemporary experience as a reaction to "the inhospitable, blinding age of big-scale industrialism."[10] In a well-known argument, the essay suggests that the experience of modernity, especially in its urban and industrial avatar, is most paradigmatically the experience of shock. Concretely instantiated in the experience of being jostled in the crowd, in having to adjust one's movements to the jolting motions of the assembly line, in being bombarded by images in film, shock can be understood as a stimulus, more or less powerful, for which consciousness finds itself to be inadequately prepared. Closely related to Freudian trauma, shock names the experience of an event that, due to the lack of sufficient preparation on the part of consciousness, cannot be made sense of at the time it happens. It is that which comes to pass without having been properly present (to consciousness) in the first place. In Bergsonian terms, then, shock can be understood as a disturbance in the spatializing procedure. It is what slips through the anticipatory net cast by consciousness and becomes memory without having been properly perceived.

So much is true on the level of individual experience. But in Benjamin's account of the broader historical perspective, the relation between shock and spatialization appears to be reversed. Here, it is the shock structure of modern experience itself that produces spatialization to begin with. "The greater the share of the shock factor in particular impressions," Benjamin writes, "the more constantly consciousness has to be alert as a screen against stimuli; the more efficiently it is so, the less do the impressions enter experience (*Erfahrung*), tending to remain in the sphere of a certain hour in one's life (*Erlebnis*)."[11] In anticipation of shock, consciousness as it were recoils, tenses up, shutting out a great number of stimuli, failing to synthesize them into coherent experience (*Erfahrung*) and leaving them on the level of mere sense data (*Erlebnis*). Thus, in Benjamin's speculative psychology of modern experience, modernity can be said to be particularly generative of the sort of past that has never been present in experience.

Susan Buck-Morss helpfully glosses Benjamin's use of the term *Erfahrung* here as "active, reflective experience [related to] the Kantian sense of the unity of perception."[12] A failure of *Erfahrung*, then, is a failure in the procedure of combining the multiple and varied stimuli we receive from the world into a coherent whole, a failure of synthesis. In Kantian terms, we might formulate the following possibility: what if the transcendental subject, with its schematized categories, were no longer capable of keeping up with the pace of bombardment by intuitions, and as a result some of these intuitions were to fail to be properly subsumed by temporalized concepts, either vanishing into oblivion or getting stored up in unconscious memory? To be sure, this attempt to historicize the transcendental structures of experience would have been deeply inimical to Kant. But posing the question in this way brings to light the fact that, when contrasted with Bergson's dichotomy of spatialization and *durée*, Kant's vision of the schematism presupposes time as a highly felicitous medium for the harmonious coming together of mind and world, subject and object. As an "art concealed in the depths of the human soul," the schematism ensures a perfect fit between what is present to consciousness and consciousness itself, such that nothing of the phenomena is lost.[13] Here, time is the perfect vehicle of truth.

What happens in Bergson, on the other hand, can be understood as a response to the condition of modernity in which the experience of time, having reached a certain degree of homogeneity and swiftness, is rendered incapable of serving as a support for Kantian experiential synthesis. In the era of industrial capitalism the schematism emerges not as a mysterious art of the soul but as an art that, like the art of craftsmanship in Benjamin, has been lost. It is here that rigid Bergsonian spatialization, as the tightening of the defense against stimuli, begins to replace the more organic, artful ordering of the schematism. It is also here that the concepts of *durée* and memory emerge to account for the past that has never been present. Thus, in Bergson, the Kantian schematism (as truth's skillful midwife) splits into spatialization (as the occlusion of the truth of experience by concepts in the service of utility) on the one hand and *durée* (as the stream of ceaseless qualitative change given to us in intuition) on the other.[14] And the new mystery, the mystery in Bergson, is that the latter somehow, "by the mere necessity of its own nature," weaves itself into the former, so that what is stored up in memory can and must find its way back into experience.

Just as Kant's contemporaries took issue with the schematism largely or in part because of its enigmatic, almost mystical status, so Benjamin appears to find fault with the Bergsonian *durée* for its metaphysical pretensions. The *durée*, he writes, "is the quintessence of the passing moment [*Erlebnis*] that struts about in the borrowed garb of experience."[15] As such it is the bad-faith double of Baudelaire's homogeneous empty temporality of *spleen*, which "exposes the passing moment in all its nakedness." The latter is, in a sense, preferable as the figure of time in modernity because it allows Baudelaire to get hold of "the scattered fragments of genuine historical experience," while Bergson's *durée* serves as a cheap metaphysical comfort for the loss of genuine experience in modernity and thus testifies to a still more profound estrangement from collective history.[16]

Benjamin's argument here appears to follow that of Max Horkheimer in his earlier essay "On Bergson's Metaphysics of Time" (1934). In that essay, which Benjamin cites with approval, Horkheimer objects to Bergson's relegation of spatialization to the realm of untruth by claiming that the concepts produced by "the spatial-ordering understanding" do in fact truthfully reflect the social divisions characterizing the historical condition of the present. Bergson's postulation of absolute durational unity, on the other hand, is, according to Horkheimer, untrue because it reflects nothing that is historically given and is thus merely mythic, diversionary, a product of false consciousness.[17]

What is curious about this argument is that Horkheimer appears determined to historicize only one side of the Bergsonian dichotomy, banishing the other, *durée,* to the realms of mere fantasy and wish fulfillment. But the question remains: why just such a fantasy and not some other? For a thoroughgoing historicization of a philosophical system, would we not have to account even for those elements of the system that appear to deny history itself? For that to happen, we would admittedly have to conceive of the historical truth content of cultural production in terms not merely of *reflection* but also of reaction, recoil, diversion, compensation, and other forms of relatively autonomous *response.* And I would argue that despite his reliance on Horkheimer, Benjamin develops the means (though he does not utilize them) for a more flexible engagement with Bergsonian categories. In fact, by characterizing the structure of modern experience as marked by a breakdown in the synthetic work of conscious perception, Benjamin allows us to understand Bergson's *mémoire* as a category that endows the pure negativity of experiential loss with continued efficacy. By doing so, he twists out of Horkheimer's (here, still Hegelian) presumption that thought must be absolutely adequate to its age and that whatever is untimely lacks genuine actuality. He twists out of it most explicitly in his "Theses on the Philosophy of History" (1940) and in certain methodological sections of *The Arcades Project*. It is here, in his reflections on time, truth, and historiography, that Benjamin's philosophical convergence with Bergson is in fact most striking.

One of the fragments assembled in *Convolute* N (*On the Theory of Knowledge, Theory of Progress*) of *The Arcades Project* states: "'The truth will not escape us,' reads one of Keller's epigrams. He thus formulates the concept of truth with which these presentations take issue."[18] Though the statement was not discovered among Gottfried Keller's epigrams, it should probably not come as a surprise, at least after what has been said in the preceding chapters, that the vision of truth as allied to (rather than opposed to or threatened by) time would be associated with the author of a classic nineteenth-century *Bildungsroman*, *Green Henry* (*Der grüne Heinrich*, 1855). It is just this alliance, however, that Benjamin unambiguously rejects, at least in *Convolute* N. Benjamin returns to Keller's formulation with more nuanced commentary in the "Theses on the Philosophy of History": "'The truth will not run away from us': in the historical outlook of historicism these words of Gottfried Keller mark the exact point where historical materialism cuts through historicism. For every image of the past that is not recognized by the present as one of its own concerns threatens to disappear irretrievably."[19]

It appears, then, that there may be two ways to read Keller's statement: a historicist way, which must be rejected, and the historical materialist way, which should be endorsed. In the former, historicist inflection, the claim converges with a certain Hegelianism (and "*Bildungsroman*-ism") according to which the past is seen as having contributed all that was worthwhile in it to the present historical moment. The historicist's truth will not escape one because whatever is true is preserved and purified in time. That which is annihilated in time, on the other hand, is the false. This, according to Benjamin, is the formulation of the veridictory stance of historical triumphalism: the victors won because they were right, the losers lost because they were on the wrong side of the truth, and "whoever has emerged victorious participates to this day in the triumphal procession in which the present rulers step over those who are lying prostrate."[20] This is the vision of nineteenth-century historicism, and it is this stance that the historical materialist resists by brushing history against the grain.

Deprived of historicist optimism, the historical materialist is not left to despair. For him, too, there is hope because "the past carries with it a temporal index by which it is referred to redemption. Our coming was expected on earth.... Nothing that has ever happened should be regarded as lost for history."[21] Thus, while there is in fact a very good chance that the truth *will* run away from us—moreover, in human history up to now, it always has—this running away is not decisive, and the fleeting truth is not irretrievable. The past persists, waiting for us (historical materialists) to redeem it through our recollection and action. In other words, rather than a statement of fact independent of us, the notion that truth will not escape us becomes a ceaseless solicitation, a demand: the oppressed truth of the past is still there, waiting for us to testify to it and redeem it. The activist reading of Keller's aphorism, then, cuts through its contemplative, historicist double, presupposing a different relation between the present and the past and, in fact, relying on a different conception of time altogether.

In order to understand the nature and the extent of the difference, in Benjamin, between historicist and historical materialist views of time, it is worth turning to *Convolute* N once again and considering a passage in which Benjamin contemplates a reply to a letter he received from Horkheimer. Appearing once again on the side of historical pessimism, Horkheimer accuses Benjamin of the very mystification he attributes to Bergson. Just as Bergson was to be rebuked for positing the reality of organic *durée* in the world of mechanized divisions, so here Benjamin is taken to task for smuggling into his philosophy of history messianic categories in order to hold on to the promise of redemption in the world where suffering is irremediable, where the wrongs endured in the past will forever remain in the past. A promise of redemption by means of historiography involves a metaphysical sleight of hand no less invidious than the positing of an intuitively accessible, qualitative flow in industrialized society. "Past injustice has occurred and is completed," Horkheimer asserts. "The slain are really slain."[22]

To this Benjamin forms the following hypothetical reply: "The corrective to this line of thinking may be found in the consideration that history is not simply a science but not least a form of remembrance. What science has determined, remembrance can modify. Such mindfulness can make the incomplete (happiness) into something complete, and the complete (suffering) into something incomplete."[23] The work of history involves here much more than simply fixing what happened on a timeline. It involves memory, and memory is understood, in a thoroughly Bergsonian fashion, as capable of reanimating the past, of interpolating it into the present and in the process transforming the present itself. Time is here conceived in a durational mode, not on the model of mutually external points on a line but as something like a melody, its sounds permeating one another, soliciting one another's response and transforming one another's valence and meaning.[24]

In short, both Horkheimer and Benjamin oppose the Hegelian formula that the false is but a moment of the true, that past wrongs are made right by the mere fact of their contributing to a better future. But while Horkheimer appears to retreat to the positions of a kind of Enlightenment philosophy of history, condemning the past as a series of unredeemable stupidities, injustices, and disasters, Benjamin sides with a certain messianism, preserving the hope that the dead will rise and past injustices will spur us on to justice. To be sure, this will not happen on its own, in the course of the unfolding of the Spirit, which in any case only guarantees the moral and conceptual vindication of the victors, but through something like revolutionary remembrance or commemorative action. If, in other words, Horkheimer appears to affirm, against Hegelian time as the empirical unfolding of the Concept, the vision of homogeneous empty time in which truth can have no place, then Benjamin moves in the opposite direction. For him, as much as for Bergson, time is neither homogeneously successive and truthless nor teleologically additive and truth-bound; it is rather, in its authentic instantiation, truth itself, the now-time (*die Jetztzeit*) as the gate through which what has been lost ceaselessly reenters experience and forces an unforeseeable future.

"At any given time," Benjamin writes in *Convolute* N, "the living see themselves in the midday of history. They are obliged to prepare a banquet for the past. The historian is the herald who invites the dead to the table."[25] The implication is that the dead have, more often than not, been wronged. They need have no manners and are likely to speak their minds. The banquet then is the now-time of truth itself. This now-time is Benjamin's historical double of Bergson's "dilation" into which memory ushers the past (that has never been present and that is therefore also "oppressed" by the principle of utility) so that it can have its say on what the future will be like.

Benjamin's methodological fragments, then, help us appreciate the pathos of Bergsonian *mémoire* as a depository of experiences repressed by the "industrialization" of existence but, because what is repressed is also preserved, capable of being redeemed in the liberating *Jetztzeit* for the sake of an unpredictable, incalculable future. They also help us understand the insufficiency of analyses, such as those by Lukács, of modernist literary and philosophical works (among them those of Bergson) as predicated on a rigid distinction between subjective and objective time.[26] Though such a distinction is indeed important for Bergson and his contemporaries (Husserl, Heidegger), the fruitfulness of his theories of temporality for thinking about history seems to indicate that something other than the subjectivization of time is ultimately at stake. It appears, rather, that at stake is the splitting apart of conceptual from experiential time; of the spatialized, calculable time of thought in the service of practical utility and industrial production from the durational, qualitative time of memory, the time of the past that has never been present, the past of uselessness or oppression.[27] What we thus arrive at with both Bergson and Benjamin can be understood as an elaboration of a historically determined malfunction in the mysterious procedure of the transcendental schematism. This malfunction accounts for the possibility of experiencing, in time, something that is not however present to consciousness. And it entails a compensatory procedure whereby what is not present to consciousness is nevertheless stored up in memory and virtually co-present with experience in such a way as to be available for actualization.

A parallel malfunction is detectable on the level of history, which can no longer be conceived as a dialectical unfolding in which the truth (the actuality, *die Wirklichkeit*) of the past is preserved in the present. Here, the official spatialized face of history is understood as a continued oppression rather than a preservation or a development of the past. Liberal or Social Democratic historical optimism must give way to (Marxist) messianic hope, based on the belief/demand that nothing that has ever happened is/be irretrievably lost to history and that an act of remembrance of the oppressed past can help rescue the present from the deterministic march of the victors. It can thus also deliver an authentic (that is, incalculable) historical future, the possibility of which now depends not on what has been *aufgehoben* up to now but on what has been lost in the *Aufhebung*. This act of remembrance is then a veridictory act, a "truth charged to the bursting point with time,"[28] capable of blasting a moment of the past out of the darkness of historical uselessness and oppression while at the same time opening up a possible future within which the earlier moment will find a place of honor.

In short we can see that, with Bergson and Benjamin, the veridictory alliance articulated in Kant and Hegel is dissolved. It is dissolved insofar as, here, we no longer find a temporal medium hospitable to truth as correspondence between experience and meaning. Kantian *Schema* and Hegelian Spirit were once understood as naming the temporal conditions of coherent human experience; now they emerge as industrialized spatialization and oppressive historicism. Bergson's critique of Kant, and Benjamin's polemic with Hegel, can thus be said to testify to the transformation of the experience of time, rendering it incapable of grounding the veridictory alliance. From now on truth is no longer a function of the meaningful shaping of homogenous succession but rather a mechanism of temporal suspension or dilation, precipitating a recovery of what has been lost, of what is constantly escaping the senile grasp of spatialization.

Proust, Bely, and the Sonority of Truth

To the philosophical suspicion concerning the ability of temporal succession to serve as the proper medium of truth corresponds a parallel veridictory disempowerment of time in narrative. It is poignantly detectable already in Flaubert's *Sentimental Education* (*L'Éducation sentimentale*, 1869). Here time is revealed as truly homogeneous and empty, as mere succession of situations and events incapable of adding up to anything significant (as in Balzac and Dostoevsky) or, for that matter, of undermining anything false (as in Stendhal and Tolstoy). As if in a kind of proto-Bergsonian compensation for the homogeneity of temporal succession, the novel is haunted by its own memory, its own unrealized past, until it becomes clear, in the course of the final scene between the protagonist Frédéric and his friend Deslauriers, that the height of happiness and fulfillment was to be located somewhere outside the bounds of the preceding narrative altogether: an attempted youthful visit to a brothel.[29] In a similarly proto-Benjaminian fashion, we might say that various moments of the past call out for redemption or completion. The unconsummated love between Frédéric and Madame Arnoux, for example, gets one last chance in the penultimate chapter of the novel. But Madame Arnoux's hair is gray and Frédéric feels a repugnance "akin to a dread of committing incest,"[30] and so all that can happen is mere impotent (Benjamin might have said, "historicist") recollection of their past love: "She rapturously accepted this adoration of the woman she ceased to be."[31] In short, the novel is heavy with the melancholy weight of irredeemably lost experience, of the past that has never been properly present, and will never be present again.

What is thus not quite Bergsonian here is the lack of anything like a vision of what an actualization of the virtual past might look like. What is, concomitantly, not quite Benjaminian is the sense that the past will not be redeemed. Both the form of a grand narrative redemption of time and its theorization will of course appear—converging, in many important respects, with the conceptions of time that can be found in Bergson and Benjamin—in Proust, whose immense novelistic effort at gathering together the shards of lost experience ceaselessly foregrounds the enemy against which it is fighting: the passage of homogeneous empty time itself. Thus, the vertiginous fleeing of experience organizing Flaubert's novel reappears at the end of *Time Regained* (*Le Temps retrouvé*, 1927) in a metaphor that both thematizes that experience and sublates it. "A feeling of vertigo seized me," says the narrator, "as I looked down beneath me, yet within me, as though from a height, which was my own height, of many leagues, at the long series of the years."[32]

Time Regained as a whole, a site for the consummation and theorization of the form of the Proustian novel as a mechanism of reclaiming experiential loss—"our inherent powerlessness to realize ourselves in material enjoyment or in effective action" (3:911)—is structured around one scene that brings together in condensed form the fundamental anxiety that the novel struggles to quell. Having arrived in Paris after a long absence, Marcel receives an invitation to an afternoon tea party at his friends the Guermantes. Arriving at the party, he initially gets the impression that he is at a masquerade at which the guests are wearing masks of their older selves (963). The confrontation with the aging of others is then rendered still more traumatic by several encounters that make it clear to Marcel that he, too, is now, quite suddenly, of a respectable age. The events of the afternoon, baring as they do time's destructiveness, are nevertheless made bearable to Marcel by the fact that only minutes before entering the Guermantes' house, he discovers the method with the help of which lost time can be regained. Thus, the party is framed by lengthy disquisitions on the redeeming power of art, practiced in a particular way, the kind of art that shares its form and pathos with the novel Proust has just written (or, within its own fictional world, is about to write), a novel especially suited for confronting and overcoming the veridictory embarrassment that the ascendance of homogeneous empty time poses for experience and truth. Thus, in one formulation:

> Truth will be attained by [the writer] only when he takes two different objects, states the connection between them—a connection analogous in the world of art to the unique connection which in the world of science is provided by the law of causality—and encloses them in the necessary links of a well-wrought style; truth—and life too—can be attained by us only when, by comparing a quality common to two sensations, we succeed in extracting their common essence and in re-uniting them to each other, liberated from the contingencies of time, within a metaphor. (3:924–25)

What is noteworthy here for our purposes is the reappearance of a radical disjunction between truth and time. We are suddenly very far from being able to affirm, as Dostoevsky did in the letter to his brother Mikhail, that *"Time and Truth* are one and the same." In fact, one appears to exclude the other, and we seem to be back with the pre-veridictory model that affirms the rationalist disjunction between the clarity of timeless ideas in the mind and the confusion of events in time, along with the corresponding novelistic subordination of the error-ridden narrative of adventure to the truth-purveying discourse of moral instruction. And indeed, as has often been remarked, we do find in Proust a veritable inflation of discourse, a swelling perhaps most flagrant precisely around those moments in the narrative where the fleeting nature of time, its inability to anchor experience and thus to serve as the medium for truth, is most evident.

Yet the convergence between Proust and the eighteenth-century veridictory tradition encounters its limit in the fact that for him it is the novelist and not the philosopher who has privileged access to the truth. Rather than being independent of time, in other words, the truth in Proust is both enabled by and must be wrested from temporal existence. Time is already too worthy an opponent here to refuse to acknowledge. It must be reckoned with, and so the novelist's advantageous position vis-à-vis the truth has to do precisely with his positioning in time, with the intimate relation that narrative inevitably has with temporality.

Similar considerations allow us to differentiate on the formal level between the alliance of discourse with truth in Proust and an apparently similar convergence between them in the eighteenth-century novel. In a novel like *Tom Jones,* discursive interpolations reassure the reader of the authorial position outside temporal succession and hence of this position's stability as the site in which the (moral and factual) truth of the narrative is lodged. In Proust, on the other hand, rather than asserting the fact of the matter and delivering narrative over to error, discourse penetrates to the deepest, as it were, subatomic level of narrative itself, the omnipresent "well-wrought style" shadowing the narrative of the novel so closely that it becomes indistinguishable from the incidents it narrates and the situations it describes. In other words, in Proust, discourse does not simply speak the truth of the narrative, does not pronounce the moral of the story; it occupies the very site of truth itself, so that the reader is "in truth" as soon as s/he begins reading.

This truth is not properly atemporal, then, at least not in the sense in which it can stay clear of time in eighteenth-century novels; nor is it parasitic on temporal succession, as it appears to be in the nineteenth-century novels we have discussed. Rather, the site of truth is the locus of a certain temporal dilation, a thick *Jetztzeit,* in which the past, the present, and the future, along with multiple modulations of each, can coexist in simultaneity. It is the function of Proustian discourse to create the space of what Gérard Genette has called "temporal autonomy,"[33] from within which any moment can be accessed at will and brought together with any other moment in what can now hardly be reconstructed as a narrative unfolding in successive time.[34] For example, here is a representative sentence from the end of *Combray*:

> Thus would I often lie until morning, dreaming of the old days in Combray, of my melancholy and wakeful evenings there, of other days besides, the memory of which had been more recently restored to me by the taste—by what would have been called at Combray the "perfume"—of a cup of tea, and, by an association of memories, of a story which, many years after I had left the little place, had been told me of a love affair in which Swann had been involved before I was born, with a precision of detail which it is often easier to obtain for the lives of people who have been dead for centuries than for those of our own most intimate friends, an accuracy which it seems as impossible to attain as it seemed impossible to speak from one town to another, before we knew of the contrivance by which that impossibility has been overcome. (1:203)

The number of temporal indicators alone is difficult to enumerate. We have, to begin with, the "now" of discourse (one) in relation to which the later point in which the narrator is recalling (two) his earlier, childhood days at Combray (three) is located. Not long before the "now" (four) we have the revelatory moment of the tasting of the madeleine, which adds to the memories of Combray and is linked to the memory of someone else about Swann, whose love affair, taking place before the narrator's birth (five), is to become the subject for the next section of the book, forming a new present of discourse (six). Here, we switch from first-person experiences to generalizing judgments comparing deep-historical (seven) knowledge to knowledge of one's friends' lives and indicating that what seems impossible turns out to be possible just as the recent discovery of the telephone in the recent past (eight) eliminated people's inability, in the less recent past, to speak to one another while living in different towns (nine).

The work that discourse performs in Proust, then, is very different from the authoritative didacticism of the eighteenth-century novel. But it is no less distinct from the formidable monotone of Flaubert's style, with its perpetual "no" to both characters and events, telling us not to expect anything veridical from time (not even the rewards of enlightened exemplarity). Instead, the supreme control that Proustian discourse exercises over narrative is the very condition for the possibility of the metaphoric veridictory procedure that posits connections between objects separated by vast temporal and narrative distances. Linear succession itself is here the domain of lies and, still worse, of aging and death; truth and life thrive on its subversion, and the unexpected, constantly propelled by the intrusion of associative memory, is always around the syntactic corner. In short, to eighteenth-century discursive sublation of narrative as well as to Flaubert's stylistic disdain for it, Proust can oppose a more Bergsonian[35] and Benjaminian[36] vision of time as multilayered and multidirectional, each temporally anarchic moment filled to the brim with the possibility of meaningful connections and discoveries, each a dilated moment of truth.

It is perhaps not surprising, from the point of view of the shared history of narrative form, that Proust's critique of the Naturalist school in literature converges with Benjamin's critique of historicism. Thus: "The kind of literature which contents itself with 'describing things,' with giving of them merely a miserable abstract of lines and surfaces . . . has more than any other the effect of saddening and impoverishing us, since it abruptly severs all communication of our present self both with the past, the essence of which is preserved in things, and with the future, in which things incite us to enjoy the essence of the past a second time" (3:921). The post-Flaubertian realist appears here as a kind of historicist, who tries his best to provide a disinterested, detached account of the past and as a result finds himself haunted by a certain sadness, an *acedia* accompanying the sense that what happened, happened, and nothing more can be said or done.[37] The Proustian narrator, meanwhile, is closer to the historical materialist, who "grasps the constellation which his own era has formed with a definite earlier one" and can therefore establish a conception of the present as "shot through with chips of Messianic time."[38] The explicit pathos of Proust's discourse is messianic indeed, holding on to the hope of redemption for what Flaubert consigns to the realm of the irredeemable: "the past that has never been present," his own past and the past of those others he knew and loved (3:941).

À la recherche finds an unlikely companion in Russia's most prominent modernist novel, *Petersburg* (1913, revised 1922) by Andrei Bely. It is a companion because it reveals a strikingly similar set of concerns, especially when it comes to confronting the modern experience of time. It is unlikely, however, because when it comes to form, it is in so many respects a very different kind of novel. Unlike Proust's vast, sociohistorically embedded "auto-biography," *Petersburg* stages a time span of little more than a day at the very edge of history. Most of the action of the novel takes place against the background of a ticking time bomb, set to work by the neo-Kantian philosopher and reluctant revolutionary Nikolai Apollonovich Ableukhov in a dazed attempt to assassinate (at the instigation of a radical organization practicing political terror) his own father, the reactionary government minister Apollon Apollonovich. Patricide, Revolution, the Apocalypse—the thematic crux of the novel is formed by the problem of the abolition of successive time. Overcome by sleep immediately after he has wound up the bomb, his head resting on the ticking "sardine can," Nikolai sees his father's face, which is at the same time the face of Chronos, and realizes that he has dared to blow up "fast-flowing time itself."[39]

Moving from the mythopoetic level to that of the social, we find the statesman Apollon Apollonovich driving to work in his carriage, daydreaming of "a network of parallel prospects, intersected by a network of prospects, [expanding] into the abysses of the universe in planes of squares and cubes: one square per 'solid citizen.'"[40] Apollon Apollonovich, as his name and patronymic insist, has a particular penchant for symmetries and harmonies, clear lines and geometrical shapes. Most of all, we are told, he loves the linear prospect, which reminds him of "the flow of time between two points in life" (10).

Apollon Apollonovich's bureaucratic instrumentalization of space and spatialization of time finds its historico-philosophical correlate in the aforementioned scene of Nikolai's dream. Here, his father, a convinced positivist and admirer of Auguste Comte, gets hold of and corrects the outline of his projected neo-Kantian treatise. In the process of correction, the elder Ableukhov makes several substitutions. For "Kant" he substitutes "the Prospect." He replaces "value" with "numeration: by houses, floors, and rooms for time everlasting." Instead of the vision of the new social order based on genuine values, he writes "the record of the circulation of the citizens of the Prospect." And for the destruction of old regime Europe, he substitutes Europe's establishment as immutable. Only now, says the paternal apparition, can "the task" (of philosophy? of progress?) be properly understood (166).

This vision of the degraded Kantianism of turn-of-the-century modernity, Kantianism turned Comtianism, resonates with Bergson's critique of Kant's instrumental spatialization of temporal experience. Both in Ableukhov's correction of his son's work and in Bergson's critique of Kant we are dealing with instances of "reception"; Kant speaks no longer to his contemporaries but to descendants facing a different, historically specific experiential horizon. This horizon is delineated with a great deal of clarity in the course of an early scene. Riding in his ministerial carriage through a crowd, Apollon Apollonovich encounters the insolent, "inadmissible," threatening gaze of a certain "upstart intellectual," the revolutionary Dudkin with "a not exactly small and yet not very large bundle" in his hand:

Suddenly—
—[Apollon Apollonovich's] face grimaced and began to twitch. His blue-rimmed eyes rolled back convulsively. His hands flew up to his chest. And his torso reeled back, while the top hat struck the wall and fell on his lap.
The involuntary nature of his movement was not subject to explanation. The senator's code of rules had not foreseen . . . (14)

At stake in this attachment to linear shapes and to the even, predictable flow of time is a kind of anticipatory recoiling, a defense against sudden, mysterious events, against something like the Benjaminian shock, instantiated here by political terror. The senator's code of rules cannot foresee the stranger's insolence, nor is it capable of establishing the contents of the medium-sized bundle. The sudden "sneaks up behind your back," says the narrator, addressing the reader. "'Suddenlys' are familiar to you. Why, then, do you bury your head like an ostrich at the approach of the inexorable 'suddenly'?" (23). The narrator's self-conscious attention to the pronoun *suddenly* possesses an intertextual dimension, invoking Dostoevsky's Petersburg narratology in *Crime and Punishment*. There, too, the accidental, the unexpected are construed as interruptions in the predictable, manageable flow of time. But whereas for Dostoevsky such interruptions serve as miraculous, ultimately welcome openings soliciting veridictory reemplotment of the hero, for Bely the logic of the sudden emerges as significantly more hermetic. The still relatively Hegelian veridictory narratology of *Crime and Punishment*, still nostalgic for *Bildung*, allows for the truth to emerge immanently from temporal unfolding, answering questions, filling in silences, solving mysteries. In Bely, this is no longer the case. Rather, the potentially explosive, revolutionary or apocalyptic opening of the sudden event, the opening that comes to the bureaucrat or "solid citizen" in the form of sensory shock, is transfixed as the very constructive principle of the novel.

Returning to the passage that registers the statesman's fright, we find in it something like the formal microcosm of the novel as a whole. Unexpected paragraph breaks, indentations of variable depth, dashes, ellipses, exceptionally short chapters—all instantiate the principle of interruption, if not indeed of actual sensory shock, disrupting the smooth narrative progression of the novel. In other words, the novel takes the clash of the opposing and increasingly entrenched forces of contemporary modernity—the forces of spatialization and disruption, of the tensing up of consciousness and sensory shock—seriously enough to register it on the level of form as a radical fragmentation of the narrative. The payoff of such fragmentation of temporal continuity consists in the novel's exceptional ability to present in simultaneity and proximity characters, situations, and events that are presumed to be spatially, temporally, and even ontologically distant from one another. Thus, the elder Ableukhov's trip to the office is interrupted by a meditation on St. Petersburg, a description of a certain stranger, an address to the Russian people, Ableukhov's encounter with the stranger, a description of a caryatid of a satyr, barely comprehensible scraps of conversations in the street and in a tavern, and the narrator's promise of a disquisition on the sudden (11–18).

The impression one gets is that of simultaneity, not only among the various situations and events that are meant to be happening in the diegetic present, but also in the more or less distant historical and mythological past. The famous equestrian monument to Peter the Great comes alive and gallops through the city chasing carriages or pays death-dealing visits to the city's inhabitants, at one crucial point melting and pouring its metals into Dudkin's veins. This central symbolic transfusion is in fact only the most explicit and vivid instantiation of the more general constructive principle of the novel, according to which every main character is identified with two or more literary or mythological figures. Dudkin is both the pursued Evgeny and, toward the end, the pursuing statue from Pushkin's foundational Petersburg poem, *The Bronze Horseman*. Apollon Apollonovich combines Gogol's lowly copy clerk Akaky Akakievich Bashmachkin with Tolstoy's Alexei Alexandrovich Karenin, with mythological Chronos and anthroposophic Saturn. Nikolai is Pushkin's (and Tchaikovsky's) Hermann from *The Queen of Spades,* but also suffering Dionysus. In the end, all individuation is in question; nothing is either spatially or temporally itself. In fact, it is precisely this work of deindividuation, accomplished by means of the fragmentary form, that can ultimately be seen as the veridictory work of the novel itself. By internalizing the breakup of temporal *Erfahrung* into a spatializing tensing up of consciousness and the suddenness of shock, the novel aspires to represent a deeper veridical level of existence, on which nothing can be grasped in succession or in isolation.[41]

In the influential 1945 essay "Spatial Form in Modern Literature," Joseph Frank argues that Proust's quest for "pure time," that is, for the simultaneous grasp of the past and the present, results in an assimilation of time to space. This claim fits neatly into Frank's vision of the modernist novel as essentially a form of temporal occlusion. Here, the work of Proust, Joyce, Flaubert, and Djuna Barnes serve as examples of ingenious novelistic attempts "to overcome the time elements involved in their structures."[42] In connection with Proust in particular, Frank observes, following Ramon Fernandez, that ultimately the method of *À la recherche* has much in common with what Bergson has identified as spatialization. At first glance at least, Bely's novel, with its fragmentary form juxtaposing discrete moments in time and loci in space, would have served him just as well.[43] But the above brief readings of the two novels militate against this conclusion.

Perhaps the confusion that leads Frank to see these modernist texts as instantiating Bergsonian spatialization has to do with Bergson's initial framing of the duration-spatialization dichotomy in terms of an ambiguous conception of the present. Spatialization takes distinct moments in time and makes them present simultaneously, reducing motion to stasis and change to a re-shuffling of already given elements. This is Apollon Apollonovich's rectilinear Prospect, comfortably reminiscent of the flow of time between two points in life. This is also, in our terms, a degraded version of the veridictory alliance, the "Bacchanalian revel" of Hegel's *Phenomenology* forestalled and obviated by "simple repose."[44] The present of *durée*, on the other hand—and this, I would argue, is the temporality underlying the novelistic form in Bely and Proust—is the present bursting at the seams with the untapped depths of the past and the unseen horizons of the future. The present of Proustian discourse or of Bely's fragmentation is dilatory and messianic, charged with the anarchic energy that is determined precisely to subvert spatialization as coherent successive movement, step by predictable step, from a stable beginning to a predetermined end.

I would like to suggest that a more appropriate figure for the description of the veridictory dynamics of the modernist novels here at issue can be found in a nearly contemporary text by Theodor Adorno on yet another iconic modernist practitioner of yet another "temporal art." Adorno's book *In Search of Wagner* (*Versuch über Wagner*), written in 1937/1938 but published only in 1952, is in large part dedicated to exploring those features of Richard Wagner's work that register and attempt to transcend a historically determined crisis in musical development. Adorno is thus trying to work through a set of issues similar to those preoccupying Frank, but his categories are more nuanced, allowing us to distinguish between two temporal modes of the present relevant to our understanding of the modernist novel—the present of design and the present of dilation.

Wagner's importance for Adorno consists in his exemplary confrontation with the languishing of the properly temporal dimension of music. If a Beethoven sonata or symphony thrives precisely on the passage of time, filling it with meaning and truth, in Wagner repetition comes to replace development as the dominant purveyor of order. Between Beethoven and Wagner, much like between Kant and Bergson or between Goethe and Proust, time seems to have "become" homogeneous and empty, resistant as much to the schematizing procedure of consciousness as to the unfolding of historical spirit. Instead of complex but coherent temporal *Erfahrung*, we now have repetition (of musical gesture, leitmotif, the beat) posing as development, and instead of universal history we have static myth. "The eternity of Wagnerian music," Adorno writes, "like that of the poem of the *Ring*, is one which proclaims that nothing has happened; it is a state of immutability that refutes all history by confronting it with the silence of nature."[45]

Frank diagnoses the modernist novel with a parallel ailment: "What has occurred, at least so far as literature is concerned, may be described as the transformation of the historical imagination into myth—an imagination for which historical time does not exist, and which sees the actions and events of a particular time only as the bodying forth of eternal prototypes."[46] Whatever one might want to conclude about the dominance of myth proper in the novels here discussed—and at least in the case of Bely, its shadow is unmistakable—a certain "state of immutability" does appear to enclose the dynamism of the works. The bomb explodes, but nobody is hurt and the status quo still reigns in a culture that will one day simply "crash into ruins" (292); Marcel precipitously ages but at the last moment escapes from time. No longer possible or at stake, development breaks down into myriad incidents and details on the one hand and an unshakable totalizing structure of the spatialized whole on the other.

Like Adorno's Wagner, then, Proust and Bely compensate for the languishing of developmental time with strategies of spatialization on the level of the plotted whole. As such they contain within them remnants of a degraded veridiction, which, having lost its foundation in a certain experience of time, finds itself dependant on rather rudimentary and hackneyed techniques of finalization.

But like Wagner, too, they invent techniques that evade the dialectic of acceleration and spatialization and serve as anchors for a different sort of truth-time configuration.

For Adorno, the feature of Wagner's music that allows him to transcend the impasse in which "eternal sameness presents itself as the eternally new" can be found in his particular use of sonority "with its two dimensions of harmony and color."[47] Sonority, as it appears in Adorno's discussion of Wagner, possesses two functions. On the one had it can be seen as a technique for the "emancipation of the dissonance from its various resolutions."[48] This is its negative dimension, subverting the tendency to resolve change in sameness; it is a kind of resistance to plot, a refusal to understand an event as always already made sense of within a larger harmonious whole. Sonority, then, is a category of disemplotment. But as such, it possesses a positive, constructive dimension as well: renouncing the "now unattainable claim to give meaningful shape to the passage of time," it transfixes time in simultaneity. Put another way, the space produced by the suspension of harmonious resolution, the moment of disemplotment, is not instantly closed down (as it tends to be in nineteenth-century narratives); rather it persists and infinitely dilates, fills up with unrealized past possibilities and potential future directions. The tension that such sonority manages to sustain ensures that "as in a giant credit system, the negation of the negation, the full settlement of debt, is indefinitely postponed."[49] The sonorous present lasts because its proper future, what might have consummated it, never comes; it lasts as well because it does not do away with, but holds on to its past.

It is thus "sonority" in Adorno's use of the word, rather than Frank's "spatial form," that captures the veridictory dynamics of the narratives here in question. In producing veridictory effects, Proust and Bely manage to eschew the nineteenth-century reliance on plot by cultivating a present quite different from Bergsonian spatialization. Such spatialization names instead precisely the degraded condition to which plot, as a temporally unfolding whole, has been reduced under the conditions of the industrial instrumentalization of time. Sonority, on the other hand, in its double guise of subversion of harmony/plot and dilation of time, describes a formal veridictory procedure for the elaboration of an authentic temporal experience, an experience in which the past, the present, and the future are given at once in mutually penetrating coexistence. In Proust this is the temporally sonorous sentence as the device for the disruption of the successive course of time and the constitution of the thick present of discursive *durée*, an anarchic present from within which any point on the spatialized timeline is accessible by association or at will. In Bely, veridictory sonority is constituted in the very place where coherent temporal experience is lost, in the locus of the sudden, which is no longer teleologically sublated but is rather embraced as a kind of *Jetztzeit* or Bergsonian dilation, a boundary on which the past and the future forcefully converge to affirm a rich, differentiated present of truth.

Earlier, I suggested that *Anna Karenina* is in some important respects already a modernist text. It is now easier perhaps to capture the "precocious" modernism of Tolstoy's novel by recognizing the conceptual and figural convergence between one of its central chronotopes, the railroad, and Bergson's category of spatialization. We have seen that Tolstoy consistently casts the railroad as a figure of spatiotemporal condensation characteristic of the experience of modernity. Though not the only person to make this connection in his own day,[50] he is certainly one of the first to construct a novelistic plot on its basis. What is made vivid as a result is an accelerated trajectory along which Goethe's anxiety about having to keep up with the relentless progress of human knowledge becomes, in Tolstoy, dread of death-dealing simultaneity. And while Goethe works to endow the episodic form of the travel novel with the veridictory shape of a meaningful whole, Tolstoy, to whom this whole already appears as suffocating, struggles to reconstitute the slower and still genuinely dynamic "road" under the conditions of increasingly exigent modernity and, in the same gesture, to free the "true life" from the grasp of spatializing *sjuzhet*. The latter, together with its figurative embodiment in the railway, is then expunged into the realm of foregone conclusions, inauthenticity, and death.

But as we survey the literary-historical ground covered in this book from the position at which we have just arrived, we see that, though Tolstoy's imagery is perhaps the most "technologically advanced," he is certainly not alone in confronting the dilemma of spatialization. Already Balzac's *La Peau de chagrin* contains a figure similar to that of the railroad, though more fantastically cast. It is of course the magic skin itself, which literally projects the time of Raphael's life onto a spatial plane and thus allows him to see it, precipitously, all at once. As a figure of speed, the onager from which the skin is taken is shown to "outrun" the modern sciences called upon to reckon with it. The skin does not yield to chemistry or to mechanics, and with the benefit of a Bergsonian hindsight, we might venture to guess that the reason it does not yield is that the methods of confronting it are too much like itself. The skin, like the railroad, is death-dealing, but rather than falsifying, it is veridical, it is the truth.

And here, Balzac's position near the origins of the veridictory mutation makes itself felt as an obsessive quest for the means of weaving together *fabula* and *sjuzhet,* of making a whole out of a series of incidents. Thus, what appears to the retrospective early twentieth-century glance as spatialization was once perhaps a vision, only with difficulty achieved, of time producing out of itself a meaningful whole.

A similarly spatialized vision of truth can be found in *Crime and Punishment*; its frenetic quest for the hero's identity begins with the instrumental crime itself and ends with the ambiguous emplotment of the hero as about to embark on a saint's life in *Bildung* time. And again, spatialization here is an anachronism, since the novel appears to operate with a conception of time as less homogenous and empty than qualitative and diverse. All the same, as readers have noted again and again, its ultimate solutions are, much like in Balzac, too close to its original problems: the redemptive ending—with all of its archaic overtones—is insufficiently distinct from the "modern," utilitarian arithmetic on which the hero relies to justify his crime. Thus, beyond the qualitative diversity of temporal shapes competing for the status of the "true story" lies a fundamentally unalterable assumption that truth is a function of a proper emplotment.[51]

Read as forming a Benjaminian constellation with the modernist veridictory moment, Balzac's vision of the truth as granting the hero the deadly means for comprehending the whole of his life, as much as the ceaseless solicitation of emplotment underlying the structure of Dostoevsky's hero, is revealed to resonate with another strain of modernist thinking about time, one that emerges within the philosophical movements of phenomenology and existentialism. And it is perhaps clearer now, when these philosophies of time are seen in constellation with the dominant nineteenth-century veridictory line, why they were not foregrounded here. Whether in Husserl's intentional consciousness or, in a still more strikingly Balzacian mode, in Heidegger's *being-toward-death*, we have subjectively inflected rearticulations of nineteenth-century veridictory narratology with its underlying assumption that what grants time truth-bestowing potential is its capacity for totalization or emplotment.[52]

Conversely, it is with disemplotment—that is, with the "second novelistic line" linking Stendhal to Tolstoy—that Bergson and Benjamin, in their struggle to envision time that would be free from instrumental spatialization, align their conceptions of veridiction. Thus, the estrangement and persistent disenchantment experienced by Levin opens up gaps within his own instrumental thinking, gaps that can be filled with the blissful experience of *durée pure*, like that of working in the field. Still more noteworthy in this respect is the manner in which veridictory disemplotment comes about in Stendhal through the intrusion into the spatialized present of the memory of the historical lost cause. It is precisely this memory that, in paradigmatically Bergsonian and Benjaminian fashion, can bring about the experience of the genuine future, what is called in Stendhal the *imprévue.*

Of course, in Stendhal, the moment of breakdown in the spatialized order of things is all-too-quickly co-opted by that order itself, while a stubborn resistance to the status quo (recall Mathilde) results in little more than predictable Romantic histrionics. The moment of truth as disemplotment must thus be forever parasitic on emplotment falsehood; the novel does not yet possess the formal means for sustaining plotless veridiction. All it can do is formulate, as is done at the end of the Levin plotline in *Anna Karenina,* the anti-Hegelian principle of truth's noncoincidence with time. Still, it is on the formal grounds broken by these—at the time backward-looking, but, in retrospect, prescient—narratives that the modernist rearticulation of the relationship between truth and time takes place.

What takes place in our modernist novels, then, can be understood as the decisive emancipation of the dissonance that weathered the nineteenth-century veridictory dogma in the formal interstices and alternatives staged by such latecomers as Stendhal and Tolstoy. Now, the positive face of sonority—discursive in Proust, palpably producing narrative out of itself, and fragmentary in Bely, staging the permeability of each moment torn out of succession by any other such moment—renders the formerly crucial veridictory dynamic of emplotment and disemplotment no more than epiphenomenal. Discourse and fragment—the sites of truth that languished with the ascendance of plot-centered veridiction—these sites now experience a resurgence, testifying indirectly to the Russian Formalist (Bergsonian) insight that the new comes about in literary form when, in struggling against the conventions of its "fathers," a generation begins to resemble its "grandfathers."[53]

This of course is not to say that we have somehow come full circle. Both Proust and Bely find themselves having to reckon with the form of the novel as they inherit it. The *Künstlerroman* in the case of Proust and the "Petersburg text" in the case of Bely possess formidable generic momenta that carry with them assumptions about the alliance of truth and time. Thus, unlike the fragmentary Romantic novel, *Petersburg* is packed with action; and unlike the eighteenth-century adventure novel, *À la recherche* is unable to condescend to what happens in time but finds itself confronted with the urgent need to redeem it. It is action in the world, and not a dream, a fantasy, or a lyrical meditation, that is broken up into fragments in Bely. It is the fear of old age—a fear practically unfamiliar to the eighteenth-century novel—that discourse is called upon to neutralize in Proust.

In short, time and its constitutive role as a determination of experience has not been forgotten. But a certain kind of time, time as succession, once so crucial to the constitution of the truth, is now discredited. Such time appears to flow too fast, to deliver too many shocks; and too much is lost when anticipatory and instrumental spatialization replaces the more organic "inner sense," the more properly human *Schema*. It is in order to account for what is lost that the relationship between truth and time receives a fundamental rearticulation in Bergson and Benjamin, a rearticulation that, as it were, turns the tables on succession by positing a dilatory present, a moment within succession and not succession itself, as capable of anchoring the truth in its capacity to illuminate a genuine past (the past that was never present) and an authentic future (the future that cannot be foreseen).

The modernist novels we discussed, then, supply two possible formal instantiations of the manner in which the bad dialectic of speed and spatialization can be eluded in narrative. Instead of this dialectic they offer a vision of truth divorced from eternity as much as from accelerating or spatialized time, and thriving in the rich sonority of the discursive or fragmentary present shot through with traces of the past and glimpses of the future. Thus, they provide instances of the formal rearticulation of the veridictory alliance. From the perspective of the period in the history of narrative form central to this book, this rearticulation can hardly be seen as anything but a dissolution.

Notes

Introduction

1. These are characterizations central to the way the novel is conceived by Georg Lukács, Goethe, Ian Watt, Erich Auerbach, Mikhail Bakhtin, and Franco Moretti, respectively.
2. Georg Lukács, *Theory of the Novel*, trans. Anna Bostock (Cambridge: MIT Press, 1971), 29.
3. Franco Moretti, "The Moment of Truth," *New Left Review* 159 (September–October 1986): 39–48, at 43.
4. Ian Watt, *The Rise of the Novel: Studies in Defoe, Richardson, and Fielding* (London: Chatto and Windus, 1957), 32.
5. Michael McKeon, *The Origins of the English Novel: 1600–1740* (Baltimore: Johns Hopkins University Press, 2002), 25–28.
6. Northrop Frye, *Anatomy of Criticism: Four Essays* (Princeton: Princeton University Press, 1957), 187.
7. Gottfried Wilhelm Leibniz, *Theodicy: Essays on the Goodness of God, the Freedom of Man, and the Origin of Evil*, trans. E. M. Huggard (La Salle, Ill.: Open Court, 1985), 217.
8. The *locus classicus* of such a narrative critique of romance presuppositions, and a no less ambiguous one, can be found of course in *Don Quixote*. For a brief and subtle analysis of that novel's relation to romance see Ioan Williams, *The Idea of the Novel in Europe: 1600–1800* (New York: New York University Press, 1979), 1–7.
9. Indeed, the novel's antiromance empiricism, its rhetoric of historicity, of the fact, the actual, or the probable can be said to correspond to the emergence, in philosophical discourse, of a new conception of truth as correspondence. The influence of philosophical empiricism, and specifically of Locke, on the rise of the novel is thus not limited to his valorization of the particular or his conception of personal identity, but more centrally perhaps involves his modern reformulation of the correspondence theory of truth. See Richard Campbell, *Truth and Historicity* (Oxford: Clarendon Press, 1992), 212–16.
10. Francis Bacon, *The New Organon*, ed. Lisa Jardine and Michael Silverthorne (Cambridge: Cambridge University Press, 2000), 69.
11. Cited in Reinhart Koselleck, *The Practice of Conceptual History: Timing History, Spacing Concepts*, trans. Todd Samuel Presner and others (Stanford: Stanford University Press, 2002), 113.
12. Ibid.
13. Hayden White, *Metahistory: The Historical Imagination in Nineteenth-Century Europe* (Baltimore: Johns Hopkins University Press, 1973), 63–64.
14. Watt, *The Rise of the Novel*, 22. In support of this claim, Watt cites the opinions of E. M. Forster, Oswald Spengler, and Northrop Frye. We could add Georg Lukács, Walter Benjamin, Fredric Jameson, J. M. Bernstein, Joseph Frank, and Frank Kermode, among others.
15. Pierre-Daniel Huet, *The History of Romances: An Enquiry into Their Original; Instructions for Composing Them; An Account of the Most Eminent Authors*, trans. Stephen Lewis (London, 1715), 4–5.
16. Stephen Lewis, "Preface," in Huet, *History of Romances*, ii–vi.
17. Huet, *History of Romances*, 17–34.
18. The view of the novel as deriving from and essentially related to moral teachings is preserved by a

certain aesthetics well into the nineteenth century. Thus Nietzsche writes in *The Birth of Tragedy*: "Indeed, Plato has given to all posterity the model of a new art form, the model of *the novel*—which may be described as an infinitely enhanced Aesopian fable, in which poetry holds the same rank in relation to dialectical philosophy as this same philosophy held for many centuries in relation to theology: namely, the rank of *ancilla*." Friedrich Nietzsche, *The Birth of Tragedy and The Case of Wagner*, trans. Walter Kaufmann (New York: Vintage, 1967), 91.

19. Antoine François Prévost, *The Story of the Chevalier Des Grieux and Manon Lescaut*, trans. Angela Scholar (Oxford: Oxford University Press, 2004), 4–5.

20. Jean-Jacques Rousseau, *Julie or the New Heloise: Letters of Two Lovers Who Live in a Small Town at the Foot of the Alps*, trans. and annotated by Philip Stewart and Jean Vaché (Hanover: Dartmouth College Press, 1997), 19.

21. Henry Fielding, *The History of Tom Jones*, ed. R. P. C. Mutter (London: Penguin, 1966), 5.

22. Northrop Frye writes that "as soon as the novel established itself as a respectable literary medium, critics promptly assimilated it to the old Platonic-Christian [discursive hierarchy]." Northrop Frye, *The Secular Scripture: A Study of the Structure of Romance* (Cambridge: Harvard University Press, 1976), 41. It appears in fact that the sequence can with equal justice be reversed, allowing us to say that the work of assimilating the novel to nobler discourses predated and made way for its eventual acceptance as respectable.

23. Yuri Lotman, "Puti razvitiia russkoi prosvetitel'skoi prozy XVIII veka," in *Problemy russkogo prosveshcheniia v literature XVIII veka*, ed. Pavel Berkov (Moscow: Akademiia nauk, 1961), 89; my translation.

24. Mikhail Kheraskov, *Numa Pompilius, ili protsvetaiushchii Rim* (Moscow: Universitetskaia tipografiia, 1803), 70; my translation.

25. The disposition here is not so different from the one we find in Milton's poem "On Time" (1633):

> Fly envious Time, till thou run out thy race
> Call on the lazy leaden-stepping hours,
> Whose speed is but the heavy Plummets pace;
> And glut thy self with what thy womb devours,
> Which is no more then what is false and vain,
> And merely mortal dross
> So little is our loss,
> So little is thy gain.
> For when as each thing bad thou hast entomb'd,
> And last of all, thy greedy self consum'd,
> Then long Eternity shall greet our bliss
> With an individual kiss
> And Joy shall overtake us as a flood,
> When every thing that is sincerely good
> And perfectly divine,
> With Truth, and Peace, and Love shall ever shine
> About the supreme Throne
> Of him, t' whose happy-making sight alone,
> When once our heav'nly-guided soul shall clime,
> Then all this Earthy grossness quit,
> Attir'd with Stars we shall for ever sit,
> Triumphing over Death, and Chance, and thee O Time.

Thus, on the one hand, "envious time" devouring "mortal dross," on the other Truth, Peace, and Love reigning around God's throne. When time runs its course, draining error of its strength, Truth comes to reign. When Tom's "erring" adventure is over, then we find out who he is. See John Milton, *Complete Poems and Major Prose*, ed. Merritt Y. Hughes (Upper Saddle River: Prentice Hall, 1957), 80.

26. Fielding, *Tom Jones*, 750.

27. At one point, toward the end of the novel, Tom's story threatens to take a distinctly tragic turn.

While in prison, he comes to believe that he has "gone to bed" with his own mother. Tom is struck with horror, and a scene of tragic *pathos* ensues, in which Tom first blames Fortune, then himself, and then falls into "the most violent and frantic agonies of grief and despair" (765). Soon enough this discovery is cancelled out by the friendlier (and more properly comic) truth of his actual parentage, but what is in the process illuminated is the perhaps unexpected similarity between the veridictory shape of tragedy and that of a novel like *Tom Jones*. Indeed, despite its obsession with the ability of "all-seeing time" to deliver the truth, tragedy presents us with what is probably only a slightly less disjunctive view of the two.

As the tragic plot unfolds, truth is unavailable to the hero, who, according to the logic of *peripeteia*, needs to experience catastrophic change ("when time is broke and no proportion kept," *Richard II*) in order to ascend to knowledge. But the hero's ignorance is complemented by full knowledge in the audience, reanimated by prophetic characters in whom, as in Tiresias, truth is "inborn," or, as in the case with Shakespeare's John of Gaunt, intuited in the shadow of approaching death ("for they breathe truth that breathe their words in pain," *Richard II*). The decree of the gods, the family curse, the fatefulness of passion—or, more generally, the "grim Necessity" of truth—altogether transcends the horizon of the hero until, in a kairotic moment, it radically impinges on it, crushing (or at least transforming) the hero once and for all. Thus, while the comic plot of *Tom Jones* ultimately stages the intrusion of a benevolent truth into the world of erring time, tragedy casts the same intersection between the timeless order of the oracles (prophesy, curse, etc.) and the time-bound, successive shape of human life as violent and destructive. In both cases, however, the two orders remain separate, and had the horrific revelation of incest proved—contrary to all generic expectations—to be more than a mere imposter of truth, the fundamental veridictory shape of the novel would have remained much the same.

28. Tzvetan Todorov, "The Secret of Narrative," in *The Poetics of Prose*, trans. Richard Howard (Ithaca: Cornell University Press, 1977), 147.

29. In "Anamorphic Realism: Veridictory Plots in Balzac, Dostoevsky, and Henry James," I argue against Todorov's disjunctive reading of the poetics of truth in James. See *Comparative Literature* (Fall 2007): 294–314.

30. See also Roland Barthes' similar characterization of the relation between truth and narrative in *S/Z*. Here Barthes defines truth as "what completes, what closes." Roland Barthes, *S/Z*, trans. Richard Miller (New York: Farrar, Straus and Giroux, 1974), 76. This raises the more general questions of the relation between veridiction and closure and between truth and knowledge. As we shall see in the chapters that follow, in both cases, the terms of the relations should not be conflated. Only in some cases is truth delivered by narrative closure; and only in some cases does it coincide with knowledge. Often, the opposite is the case: closure has the function of falsification, and knowledge is a matter of prejudice and conventional thinking. Barthes' attention to Balzac rather than, for example, Stendhal, and, moreover, his attention to certain elements in Balzac over others, reveals the critic's "modernist" predilection for neglecting skeptical, dissident, and outright subversive tendencies within realist veridiction.

31. Epistolary novels of the time and novels narrated in the first person, even though they lack an objective narrator as the purveyor of truth, do not begin to rely on immanent temporal veridiction, but rather depend on prefaces, postscripts, and oddly authoritative, often obsessive acts of self-evaluation and accusation staged by the characters themselves.

32. Fielding, *Tom Jones*, 219.

33. The superfluousness and even undesirability of immanent (temporal) guarantees is perhaps even more evident in Samuel Richardson's epistolarity. In the postscript to *Clarissa* retrospection emerges as a characteristic of discredited romance: "Romances in general, and Marivaux's amongst others, are wholly improbable, because they suppose the history to be written after the series of events is closed by the catastrophe; a circumstance which implies a strength of memory beyond all example and probability." Quoted in Watt, *The Rise of the Novel*, 192. Rather than tell the story from the end, the letters record mental states moment-by-moment, in the dark with regard to the future, near as much as distant. In identifying retrospection as a technique of romance, and in focusing his critique not on the unlikelihood of events but on the unrealism of perfect recollection, Richardson reminds us here precisely of the *romantic* tendency to abolish time, of the alliance of romance with the logic of Platonic *anamnesis*. There is of course nothing intrinsically less plausible about the memory of "romancers" than about the obsessive amanuentic letter

writing of Richardson's own characters. What emerges, however, is the logic of specifically temporal plausibility, what can and cannot be done with time: inhabiting its flow and registering the minutiae of experience is possible, while perfect recollection, binding events into a coherent whole, is not. And yet paradoxically this does not obviate, but rather only reinforces, the authority of external and timeless Truth, the authority that, in Richardson's case, does not rely on a vocal narrator (though it certainly relies for veridictory generalizations and sundry wisdoms on the virtuous letter writer) and, at least in *Clarissa*, refuses even the poetic justice of a benevolent plot. This authority is supposed to be otherworldly; punishments for sins committed against eternal norms and rewards for having been faithful to them are meted out all the more surely beyond the boundary of the novel. See Samuel Richardson, *Clarissa Harlowe* (London: Chapman and Hall, 1902), 9:309. But of course this boundary itself is marked by lengthy prefaces and postscripts, in case readers have missed the point, misconstrued the intention, or find it difficult to locate the moral.

34. Patricia Tobin, *Time and the Novel: The Genealogical Imperative* (Princeton: Princeton University Press, 1978), 31.

35. In book eleven of the *Confessions*: "When from changing creatures we learn anything, we are led to Truth which does not change." See Augustine, *Confessions,* trans. R. S. Pine-Coffin (New York: Penguin, 1961), 260.

36. As Georges Poulet points out, the very first step in Descartes' project in the *Meditations* is radical detemporalization, the production of the *cogito* as "the power capable of raising itself up to the world of law and harmony in which time has no part at all; where one is completely cut off from the past and from temporality." See Poulet, *Studies in Human Time,* trans. Elliott Coleman (New York: Harper Torchbooks, 1956), 54.

37. See his poem "On Time," quoted above.

38. Fielding, *Tom Jones,* 59.

39. Jürgen Habermas, *The Philosophical Discourse of Modernity,* trans. Frederick G. Lawrence (Cambridge: MIT Press, 1990), 12.

40. In a similar vein, Erich Auerbach speaks of the "temporal concentration" that the French Revolution and subsequent events made possible, a concentration that would, according to him, eventually lead to the "unification of human life throughout the world." See Erich Auerbach, *Mimesis: The Representation of Reality in Western Literature,* trans. Willard R. Trask (Princeton: Princeton University Press, 1953), 457.

41. Immanuel Kant, "Idea for a Universal History," in *On History,* trans. Lewis White Beck, Robert E. Anchor, and Emil L. Fackenheim (New York: Macmillan, 1963), 24.

42. Kant, *On History,* 39.

43. White, *Metahistory,* 75.

44. To be sure, there is continuity as well. The affiliation between history and prose fiction was widespread throughout the seventeenth, eighteenth, and even early nineteenth centuries, and it is not surprising that both Leibniz and Kant resort to the analogy. What is noteworthy is the fact that both invoke romance (*roman*) to suggest precisely design, plan, coherence. This association is far from self-evident. Hegel, in his *Lectures on the History of Philosophy,* calls Leibniz's exposition of his system a "metaphysical romance," implying precisely the opposite: an episodic, arbitrary arrangement: "Leibniz's philosophy therefore appears like a string of arbitrary assertions, which follow one on another like a metaphysical romance (*roman*)." See Georg Wilhelm Friedrich Hegel, *Lectures on the History of Philosophy,* vol. 3, *Medieval and Modern Philosophy,* trans. E. S. Haldane and Frances H. Simson (Lincoln: University of Nebraska Press, 1995), 3:330. For Hegel here, and for the later Hegel of the *Lectures on Aesthetics,* the *roman* is first and foremost a string of adventures, without a plan or a clear pattern, though perhaps with a predetermined result. The alliance between history and romance, then, did not have to—and in fact, in much of seventeenth- and eighteenth-century discourse, did not—cast history as patterned. See Vivienne Mylne, *The Eighteenth-Century French Novel: Techniques of Illusion* (Cambridge: Cambridge University Press, 1981), 20–31. In this respect there is a great deal of continuity in the use of the analogy from Leibniz to Kant.

45. Leibniz, *Theodicy,* 129.

46. Ibid., 33.

47. This is Foucault's characterization of the epistemic shift at the turn of the nineteenth century. See

Michel Foucault, *The Order of Things: An Archaeology of the Human Sciences* (New York: Random House, 1970), 220.

48. Ibid., 219–20.

49. Plato, *Timaeus*, in *The Dialogues of Plato*, vol. 2, trans. B. Jowett (New York: Random House, 1892).

50. Immanuel Kant, *The Critique of Pure Reason*, trans. Norman Kemp Smith (New York: St. Martin's Press, 1965), 186.

51. Henry E. Allison, *Kant's Transcendental Idealism: An Interpretation and Defense* (New Haven: Yale University Press, 1983), 173.

52. Kant, *Critique*, 181.

53. Precisely how schematism happens remains, in Kant, a mystery ("an art concealed in the depths of the human soul"). See Kant, *Critique*, 183. His examples are spare: the category of substance, when schematized becomes duration in time; the category of causality becomes necessary succession in time, etc. But that schematism *must* happen is assured to us by the logic of the transcendental deduction: for experience to be coherent, categories must be rendered applicable to experience, and vice versa, and the only medium that the two share is time.

54. Alexandre Kojève, *Introduction to the Reading of Hegel: Lectures on the "Phenomenology of Spirit,"* trans. James H. Nichols Jr. (Ithaca: Cornell University Press, 1969), 127.

55. Kant, *Critique*, 232.

56. Ibid., 93.

57. Kojève, *Lectures on the "Phenomenology of Spirit,"* 142.

58. This is also Lukács' gloss on Hegel in "Reification and the Consciousness of the Proletariat": "It is true that reality is the criterion for the correctness of thought. But reality is not, it becomes—and to become the participation of thought is needed." See Georg Lukács, *History and Class Consciousness: Studies in Marxist Dialectics,* trans. Rodney Livingstone (Cambridge: MIT Press, 1971), 204.

59. Georg Wilhelm Friedrich Hegel, *Phenomenology of Spirit*, trans. A. V. Miller (Oxford: Oxford University Press, 1977), 52.

60. Ibid., 53.

61. Jean Hyppolite, *Genesis and Structure of Hegel's "Phenomenology of Spirit,"* trans. Samuel Cherniak and John Heckman (Evanston: Northwestern University Press, 1974), 24.

62. Hegel, *Phenomenology*, 2.

63. Hyppolite, *Genesis and Structure*, 25.

64. Hegel, *Phenomenology*, 56.

65. Ibid., 11.

66. Interpretations of this third dialectical moment abound and vary considerably with regard to its ontological status. Hegel himself frequently appears to believe it to refer to a real moment in human history, a moment that has essentially arrived. A series of nineteenth- and twentieth-century rereadings of Hegel insist on understanding totality or absolute knowledge in a Kantian mode, that is, as merely regulative, an ideal not yet—or never to be—achieved but immanent to any genuine inquiry. For one of the latest examples of such a reading, see Jean-Luc Nancy's recent book *Hegel: The Restlessness of the Negative*, trans. Jason Smith and Steven Miller (Minneapolis: University of Minnesota Press, 2002). More recently still, see Fredric Jameson, *The Hegel Variations on the Phenomenology of Spirit* (New York: Verso, 2010), 1–5. Regardless of whether we adopt a teleological or a nonteleological reading of *Phenomenology* as a history of spirit, the *logical* moment of the "for-us" is an unavoidable operation within the dialectic. Thus the point of view of "the whole," whether robustly or provisionally conceived, is an inevitable element in Hegel's "narratology of truth."

67. Hegel, *Phenomenology*, 27.

68. Ibid. And of course in this consists the essential ambiguity at the heart of Hegel's most central category, *Aufhebung*, implying the process of simultaneous negation and preservation of past content in the present.

69. Hyppolite, *Genesis and Structure*, 12.

70. Fielding, *Tom Jones*, 425. Witness also the obsessive indications of the amount of time covered in

each book of *Tom Jones*, as if the events themselves could not be counted on to make vivid their duration, as if duration itself were not imminent to those events.

71. Johann Wolfgang von Goethe, *Wilhelm Meister's Apprenticeship*, trans. and ed. Eric A. Blackall (Princeton: Princeton University Press, 1995), 68.

72. Ibid., 55.

73. I am intentionally leaving out of the account the inserted narrative in book six since it would take us too far afield, necessitating a discussion of the representation of immediacy in the novel. Immediacy, and especially subjective immediacy, is here rather an exception than the rule, which stipulates that the way to the self lies through external reality. Mignon and the Harpist are two other figures in the novel who appear to lack the ability for such a detour. We could say that it is the Romantic novel that will shortly take up images such as these and develop them into particular narrative configurations that turn the structure of Goethe's novel inside out. But more on this later.

74. Goethe, *Wilhelm Meister's Apprenticeship*, 306.

75. Ibid., 337.

76. Notwithstanding the fact that *Tom Jones* is actually mentioned in *Lehrjahre* as an exemplary novel, the two narratives present us with very different visions of the individual, of experience, and ultimately with two widely diverging veridictory shapes.

77. In "The Concept of Criticism in German Romanticism," Walter Benjamin writes: "As soon as the history of philosophy, in Kant (although not for the first time), still explicitly and emphatically affirmed both the possibility of thinking an intellectual intuition and its impossibility in the realm of experience, a manifold and almost feverish endeavor emerged to recover this concept for philosophy as the guarantee of its highest claims." See "The Concept of Criticism in German Romanticism," in *Walter Benjamin: Selected Writings*, vol. 1, *1913–1926*, ed. Marcus Bullock and Michael W. Jennings (Cambridge: Belknap Press of Harvard University Press, 1996), 1:121. Fichte, Schelling, Novalis, Friedrich Schlegel—all seek a method that would effect such a recovery. Rodolphe Gasché in his foreword to the English edition of Friedrich Schlegel's *Philosophical Fragments* also focuses on Kant as the crisis-ridden point of departure for the Jena Romantics. For Gasché the central category is "completion" or the absolute, both of which point to the possibility of overcoming the partition and division introduced precisely in Kant's first *Critique* and never overcome by Kant himself in the two subsequent ones. See Rodolphe Gasché, "Foreword: Ideality in Fragmentation," in *Friedrich Schlegel, Philosophical Fragments*, trans. Peter Firchow (Minneapolis: University of Minnesota Press, 1991), xi.

Finally, Philippe Lacoue-Labarthe and Jean-Luc Nancy in their study of the *Athenaeum* period of Jena Romanticism point to Kant once again, this time to the split within the subject, depriving philosophy of what had from the time of Descartes been its point of departure, the self's intuition of itself (or, in the empiricist camp, the immediacy of pure empirical sensibility). See Philippe Lacoue-Labarthe and Jean-Luc Nancy, *The Literary Absolute: The Theory of Literature in German Romanticism*, trans. Philip Barnard and Cheryl Lester (Albany: State University of New York Press, 1988), 30. The concept that Lacoue-Labarthe and Nancy coin in order to nominate the specifically Romantic solution to the problem serves as the title of their study, *The Literary Absolute*. There is something like consensus, therefore, among three of the most prominent scholars of Jena Romanticism, in placing "the blame" for the philosophical problems encountered by the group on Kant. The loss of intellectual intuition (i.e., of the ability to intuit essences immediately), the disappearance of the whole, and perhaps most painfully of all, the split within the self—all of these are indeed consequences of Kant's radical transcendental reinterpretation of the concept of truth in *The Critique of Pure Reason*.

78. Schlegel, *Philosophical Fragments*, 46.

79. Frederick C. Beiser, *The Romantic Imperative: The Concept of Early German Romanticism* (Cambridge: Harvard University Press, 2003), 116.

80. Kant, *Critique*, 182.

81. Johann Gottlieb Fichte, *Science of Knowledge (Wissenschaftslehre)*, trans. and ed. Peter Heath and John Lachs (New York: Meredith, 1970), 195–96.

82. Ibid., 200.

83. Ibid., 201.

84. Ibid., 202.

85. Schlegel, *Philosophical Fragments*, 24.

86. An almost comic confirmation of Fichte's contempt for time can be found in a parenthetical remark in his "Lectures Concerning the Scholar's Vocation": "Still, just as it is certain that we share a common calling—to be good and to become better and better—it is equally certain that there will come a time (*it may take millions or trillions of years—what is time!*) when I will draw you into my sphere of influence." See Johann Gottlieb Fichte, *Fichte: Early Philosophical Writings*, trans. and ed. Daniel Breazeale (Ithaca: Cornell University Press, 1988), 160; emphasis added. Fichte is also reported to have told Schlegel himself that he would rather count peas than study history. See Beiser, *Romantic Imperative*, 121.

87. Fichte, *Science*, 203.

88. Ibid.

89. Schlegel, *Philosophical Fragments*, 32.

90. Fichte's *Schweben* thus understood fulfills a function similar to that of Friedrich Schiller's *Spieltrieb*, though the latter, more closely in line with Kant's own solution to the problem of experience in the *Schema*, is "directed towards annulling time within time, reconciling becoming with absolute being and change with identity." See Friedrich Schiller, "Letters on the Aesthetic Education of Man," trans. Elizabeth Wilkinson and L. A. Willoughby, in *Friedrich Schiller, Essays*, ed. Walter Hinderer and Daniel O. Dahlstrom (New York: Continuum, 1993), 126.

91. Schlegel, *Philosophical Fragments*, 123.

92. Ibid., 102.

93. There is much to be said, then, for the hypothesis that Goethe's novel, far from serving as a model Romantic novel, actually represents its very antithesis. This is indeed quite explicitly the central presupposition of another novel coming out of the Jena Romantic circle, Novalis's anti-*Meister*, *Heinrich von Ofterdingen* (1802). Tzvetan Todorov's analysis of the novel shows that it, too, resolutely avoids linear narrative. Just as in *Lucinde*, here "the reign of logico-temporal relations among phenomena [is] abolished, replaced by an order of 'correspondences.'" Temporal progression is neutralized through endless digressions, a-causal links, allegorical language and presentiments, such that, "whatever happens, the characters feel they have already experienced it." Once again, it is as if, bypassing the mediation of content and temporal development, we are allowed to witness the identity-producing action of timeless form. See Todorov, *Genres in Discourse*, trans. Catherine Porter (Cambridge: Cambridge University Press, 1990), 58–59.

94. Frye, *Anatomy of Criticism*, 35.

95. Georg Wilhelm Friedrich Hegel, *Hegel's Aesthetics: Lectures on Fine Art*, trans. T. M. Knox (Oxford: Clarendon Press, 1975), 1:66.

96. Ibid., 593.

97. The conception of *Lehrjahre* as a sort of literary-historical synthesis is perhaps something of a trope in its own right, starting probably with Georg Lukács' *Theory of the Novel*, in which Goethe's *Bildungsroman* appears as an attempt to reconcile the two lines dominating the European novel, "abstract idealism" and "the romanticism of disillusionment." Thus Lukács sees *Lehrjahre* as exemplary of the kind of novel in which "the type of personality and the structure of the plot are determined by the necessary condition that a reconciliation between interiority and reality, although problematic, is nevertheless possible." Lukács, *Theory of the Novel*, 132. This conception of the novel is echoed more recently in Ioan Williams's *The Idea of the Novel in Europe*, which hazards that "the balance of internal action and external event that Goethe struck out [in this novel] is basically that which dominates the fiction of the following century" (237). In light of the problematic at hand, I would suggest that one of the conditions for the possibility of this reconciliation is a new, developmental conception of the relation between truth and time.

98. And so it is only partially correct to define realism, with Fredric Jameson, as "*par excellence* the moment of the discovery of changing time." See Frederic Jameson, *The Ideologies of Theory: Essays (1971–1986)*, vol. 2, *The Syntax of History* (Minneapolis: University of Minnesota Press, 1988), 2:129. To this must be added the principle of coherence: that realism is *par excellence* the discovery of coherently changing time.

99. J. M. Bernstein, *The Philosophy of the Novel: Lukács, Marxism, and the Dialectics of Form* (Minneapolis: University of Minnesota Press, 1984), 34.

100. Michael McKeon, *Origins of the English Novel, 1600–1740* (Baltimore: Johns Hopkins University Press, 2002), 93–94.

101. Ibid., 419.

102. Here, my analysis converges with Hayden White's in *Metahistory*, where he famously inquires into the implicit assumptions within "realist" historical narratives about what they must look like in order to count as adequate explanations. White conducts his analysis in terms of motifs, tropes, and genres, however, and does not tend to focus on the specifically temporal conditions for the possibility of truth.

103. In what sense, for example, could one say, as Hegel seems to suggest, that the French Revolution is followed by Kantian moral philosophy? Why not—given that both his *Groundwork of the Metaphysics of Morals* and *Critique of Practical Reason* came out before 1789—the other way around?

104. Hans Robert Jauss, for example, speaks of "the discrepancies of the various 'histories' of the arts, law, economics, politics, and so forth." See Hans Robert Jauss, *Toward an Aesthetic of Reception*, trans. Timothy Bahti (Minneapolis: University of Minnesota Press, 1982), 36. We might add, together with Koselleck, "various countries, social strata, classes, or areas" (Koselleck, *Practice of Conceptual History*, 166), and with Siegfried Kracauer, "political affairs, social movements, philosophical doctrines, etc." See Siegfried Kracauer, *History: The Last Things Before the Last* (New York: Oxford University Press, 1969), 145. See also Ernst Bloch's original elucidation of the concept in *The Heritage of Our Times*, trans. Neville Plaice and Stephen Plaice (Berkeley and Los Angeles: University of California Press, 1990), 97–103, as well as a later account in Louis Althusser and Étienne Balibar, *Reading Capital*, trans. Ben Brewster (London: Verso, 1979), 99–101.

105. J. G. Herder, *On Social and Political Culture*, trans. and ed. F. M. Barnard (Cambridge: Cambridge University Press, 1969), 188.

106. Ibid., 214.

107. According to the same logic, universal history comes to be replaced by national histories—a plural conception of relatively autonomous development. For a brief account of the way this tendency reflects on literary history, see Jauss, *Toward an Aesthetic of Reception*, 6–7.

108. It is certainly to Mikhail Bakhtin that we owe the most thoroughgoing theorization of the novel as the genre of heterogeneity *par excellence*. And although for the most part he conceives of this heterogeneity in discursive terms, as a multiplicity of worldviews expressed in speech, there are indications in his work that a similar multiplicity might be found on the level of temporal organization. Thus, in the concluding remarks to his essay "Forms of Time and Chronotope in the Novel," he writes: "Chronotopes are mutually inclusive, they co-exist, they may be interwoven with, replace or oppose one another, contradict one another or find themselves in ever more complex interrelationships." See Bakhtin, *The Dialogic Imagination: Four Essays*, trans. Caryl Emerson and Michael Holquist (Austin: University of Texas Press, 1981), 252. See also a discussion of "heterochrony" in Gary Saul Morson and Caryl Emerson, *Mikhail Bakhtin: Creation of a Prosaics* (Stanford: Stanford University Press, 1990), 425–29.

109. Thus, in politico-economic terms, Bakhtin identifies the "objective preconditions" for the emergence of the polyphonic novel in the abrupt, "catastrophic" onslaught of capitalism in Russia. See Mikhail Bakhtin, *Problems of Dostoevsky's Poetics*, trans. and ed. Caryl Emerson (Minneapolis: University of Minnesota Press, 1984), 19–20.

110. The authors, as we find them in letters, diaries, drafts, and journalistic writings, will not be treated as authorities on their own fictional work. Far from it, for it will soon become clear that the veridictory shapes dominating their narratives are often inconsistent with their explicit attitudes to contemporary modernity. And even when explicit attitudes and veridictory shapes emerge as consonant—given that the latter are necessarily more specific ("schematized") than the former—no one-to-one relation can be established between them.

111. Here, in the chapter on Tolstoy, more than elsewhere in the book, Bakhtin's category of the chronotope suggests itself as appropriate for the discussion of veridictory temporal shape. For Bakhtin, however, the chronotope, "functioning as the primary means of materializing time in space, emerges as a center for concretizing representation." See Bakhtin, *The Dialogic Imagination*, 250. A veridictory temporal shape, on the other hand, does not possess an *essential* relation to space (hence, "time of dutiful action," "magic

time," "time of the accident"). Rather, it can be said to concretize time in plot and thus to *schematize,* in the technical Kantian sense, representation according to a particular vision of truth.

Chapter 1

1. Honoré de Balzac, *Écrits sur le roman: Anthologie* (Paris: Librairie générale française, 2000), 196.
2. Ibid., 197.
3. M. Victor Cousin, *Course of the History of Modern Philosophy,* trans. O. W. Wright (New York: D. Appleton, 1857), 1:257.
4. Ibid., 251–73.
5. Balzac, *Écrits sur le roman,* 202.
6. Toby A. Appel, *Cuvier-Geoffroy Debate: French Biology in the Decades Before Darwin* (New York: Oxford University Press, 1987), 193.
7. Balzac, *"La Comédie Humaine" of Honoré de Balzac* (New York: The Century, 1906), 1: xlii.
8. Graham Robb, *Balzac: A Biography* (New York: W. W. Norton, 1994), 242.
9. Georg Lukács, *Studies in European Realism,* trans. Edith Bone (New York: Grosset and Dunlap, 1964), 72.
10. Hippolyte Adolphe Taine, *Balzac: A Critical Study,* trans. Lorenzo O'Rourke (New York: Funk and Wagnalls, 1906), 123.
11. Gérard Genette, *Figures, essais* (Paris: Éditions du seuil, 1966), 2:81. My translation.
12. Franco Moretti, *The Way of the World: The Bildungsroman in European Culture,* trans. Albert Sbragia (London: Verso, 1987), 146.
13. Ibid., 143.
14. Roland Barthes, *S/Z,* 209–10.
15. Moretti, *The Way of the World,* 262.
16. Balzac, *La Cousin Bette,* trans. Kathleen Raine (New York: Modern Library, 2002), 139.
17. Ibid., 156.
18. Ibid., 152.
19. Balzac, *Eugénie Grandet,* trans. Sylvia Raphael (Oxford: Oxford University Press, 1990), 6.
20. Balzac, *Le Père Goriot,* trans. Burton Raffel (New York: W. W. Norton, 1998), 11.
21. Balzac, *The Quest of the Absolute and Other Stories* (Philadelphia: Gebbie Publishing, 1899), 221.
22. Balzac, *Cousine Bette,* 74.
23. This is Christopher Prendergast's astute formulation in *Balzac: Fiction and Melodrama* (London: Arnold Press, 1978), 72.
24. Similarly, as D. A. Miller points out, Rastignac's notorious taking possession of Paris at the end of *Père Goriot,* a moment of truth if there ever is one in Balzac, points to continued, rather than satisfied or arrested, desire. Thus: "the truth about the world is revealed to be only the truth of one's desire for the world." See D. A. Miller, "Balzac's Illusions Lost and Found," *Yale French Studies* 67 (1984): 168.
25. *The Works of Honoré de Balzac,* vol. 2, *Louis Lambert* (Boston: Dana Estes, 1901), 2:147. Subsequently references to this edition of *Louis Lambert* will be given parenthetically in the text.
26. Here it might be possible to detect the influence of one of Balzac's and Louis's intellectual heroes, Emanuel Swedenborg, and his *A Hieroglyphic Key to Natural and Spiritual Arcana by way of Representations and Correspondences* (1744).
27. On the importance of metaphor for the *Comédie humaine* as a whole, see Peter Brooks's discussion in *The Melodramatic Imagination: Balzac, Henry James, Melodrama, and the Mode of Excess* (New Haven: Yale University Press, 1995), 110–52.
28. Ibid., 118.
29. Balzac, *Oeuvres complètes de Honoré de Balzac,* rev. and annotated by Marcel Bouteron and Henri Longon, vol. 38, *Oeuvres diverses, vol. I (1824–1830)* (Paris: L. Conard, 1912–1940), 38:404.
30. The category of a "character zone" is drawn here from Mikhail Bakhtin: "A character in a novel

always has . . . a zone of his own, his own sphere of influence on the authorial context surrounding him, a sphere that extends—and often quite far—beyond the boundaries of the direct discourse allotted to him. See Bakhtin, *The Dialogic Imagination*, 320.

31. Balzac, *Oeuvres complètes*, 38:449.

32. Ibid., 448.

33. Ibid., 404–5.

34. Balzac, *The Girl with the Golden Eyes*, trans. Carol Cosman (New York: Carroll and Graf, 1998), 11.

35. Ibid., 14.

36. Balzac, *Eugénie Grandet*, 179.

37. See Roman Jakobson, "Two Aspects of Language and Two Types of Aphasic Disturbances" and "Linguistics and Poetics" in *Language in Literature* (Cambridge: Harvard University Press, 1987), 62–114.

38. Friedrich Schlegel, *Lucinde and the Fragments*, trans. Peter Firchow (Minneapolis: University of Minnesota Press, 1971), 43.

39. Balzac, *Lost Illusions*, trans. Herbert J. Hunt (New York: Penguin Classics, 1971), 221.

40. Brooks, *The Melodramatic Imagination*, 110.

41. Ibid., 1–2.

42. Balzac, *The Magic Skin*, trans. Ellen Marriage (Gainesville: Blue Unicorn Editions, 2005), 6.

43. Schlegel, *Philosophical Fragments*, 21; emphasis added. It is of course improbable that Balzac would have been intimately familiar with the work of the Jena Romantics and especially with their theories of the novel and of the fragment. He is likely to have gleaned the names of the brothers Schlegel and received a sense of the general philosophical ("Romantic") developments in turn-of-the-century Germany from the pages of Madame de Staël's book *De l'Allemagne* (1810). Madame de Staël, a friend and patron of the Schlegels, plays an important role in Louis Lambert's life (precisely that of a patron) and her book, published immediately after the fall of Napoleon, is mentioned in the novel. By the 1830s, the debates over Romanticism and Classicism, inspired in part by *De l'Allemange*, were still raging, and Balzac himself bore witness to their prominence on the French cultural scene as late as 1843 in *Illusions perdues*. See René Wellek, *A History of Modern Criticism 1750–1950*, vol. 2, *The Romantic Age* (New Haven: Yale University Press, 1992), 216–40. Yet another echo of Romantic theory is heard as the narrator comments on Raphael's impressions of the shop: "This sea of inventions, fashions, furniture, works of art and fiascos, made for him a poem without end" (18). As we have seen, according to Schlegel, Romantic poetry is indeed endless, always in becoming, as long as this becoming is not temporally conceived.

44. Schlegel, *Philosophical Fragments*, 45.

45. Lacoue-Labarthe and Nancy, *The Literary Absolute*, 44.

46. Recall that in the *Lehrjahre*, too, the rather artificial device of the mysterious Society of the Tower was needed to link up temporal progression to its meaning.

47. Thus, in *The Formal Method in Literary Scholarship* (1928), a book that is most likely authored collaboratively by Pavel Medvedev and Mikhail Bakhtin, the authors object to a strict distinction between *fabula* and *sjuzhet*. Such a distinction, they argue, is merely abstract. Concretely, not only do we never meet with *fabula* in a literary work, we never see it in "real life": "Even in life we see the story [*fabula*] with the eye of the plot [*sjuzhet*]." Moreover, the correct way of conceiving the two would be as follows: "Thus story and plot are essentially the same constructive element of the work. As story, this element defines the reality being finalized in terms of thematic unity, while, as plot, it determines the finalization of the actual reality of the work." See Pavel Medvedev, *The Formal Method in Literary Scholarship*, trans. Albert J. Wehrle (Baltimore: Johns Hopkins University Press, 1978), 139. See also a more extended discussion of the possibility of treating the two categories as poles of narrative organization in Ilya Kliger and Nasser Zakariya, "Organic and Mechanistic Time and the Limits of Narrative," *Configurations* 15, no. 3 (2007): 341–44.

48. Other narratologists have conceived of the distinction differently, presenting a much wider conception of discourse that, for our purposes, would cast an overly wide net.

49. In the spirit of tragic equivocation, the French reads: "'Vous épouserez une femme riche!,' dit-elle, 'mais elle vous donnera bien du chagrin. Ah! Dieu! elle vous tuera.'" See Balzac, *La Peau de chagrin* (Paris: G. F. Flammarion, 1971), 188. All subsequent references to this edition will be given parenthetically in the text.

50. Balzac, "Du droit d'ainesse," in *Oeuvres complètes*, 23:7.

51. See Frye, *Anatomy of Criticism*: "If superior in degree to other men and to his environment, the hero is the typical hero of romance, whose actions are marvelous but who is himself identified as a human being" (33). Samuel Weber emphasizes the parallel between Raphael and the fabulous creature from which his talisman is made: "Raphael's destiny seems to repeat that of the *onagre*: he is compelled to flee the society of his fellows." See Weber, *Unwrapping Balzac: A Reading of "La Peau de chagrin"* (Toronto: University of Toronto Press, 1979), 138.

52. Another case in point: while Raphael is hiding from the world, what happens to Pauline? She becomes a rich heiress. How? Her father returns belatedly and miraculously from a Napoleonic campaign, fabulously rich. Once again: romance is parasitic on energy, modernity, movement.

53. Moretti, *The Way of the World*, 154.

Chapter 2

1. Stendhal, *Red and Black*, trans. and ed. Robert M. Adams (New York: W. W. Norton, 1969), 47. Subsequent references to this translation will be given parenthetically in the text.

2. Balzac, "Du Droit d'ainesse," in *Oeuvres complètes*, 23:5.

3. Stendhal, *Racine and Shakespeare*, trans. Guy Daniels (New York: Crowell-Collier Press, 1962), 15.

4. See Sheryl Kroen, *Politics and Theatre: The Crisis of Legitimacy in Restoration France, 1815–1830* (Berkeley and Los Angeles: University of California Press, 2000), 39–75.

5. The English version of the charter is in *Constitutions and Documents Illustrative of the History of France, 1789–1901*, ed. Frank Maloy Anderson (Minneapolis: H. W. Wilson, 1904), 464. The translation reads: "Given at Paris, in the year of grace, 1814, and of our reign the nineteenth."

6. Guillaume de Bertier de Sauvigny, *The Bourbon Restoration* (Philadelphia: University of Pennsylvania Press, 1966), 71.

7. Louis de Bonald, *On Divorce*, trans. and ed. Nicholas Davidson (New Brunswick: Transaction, 1992), 26.

8. In other respects of course, such as in his valorization of movement, Lambert is a veritable philosopher of modernity. In him, a conservative and an insightful diagnostician of contemporary life coexist as productively as they do in his creator.

9. Stendhal, *Racine and Shakespeare*, 144.

10. Hans Robert Jauss, "Modernity and Literary Tradition," in *Critical Inquiry* 31 (2005): 21.

11. Stendhal, *Racine and Shakespeare*, 38

12. Stendhal, *Memoirs of an Egotist*, trans. Andrew Brown (London: Hesperus Press, 2003), 95; emphasis added.

13. White, *Metahistory*, 62.

14. Stendhal, *On Love*, trans. H. B. V. under the direction of C. K. Scott Moncrieff (Garden City: Doubleday, 1957), 62–63.

15. Stendhal, *Memoirs of an Egotist*, 7.

16. Stendhal, *Racine and Shakespeare*, 97.

17. Stendhal, *Correspondance (1830–1832)* (Paris: Le Divan, 1968), 7:56.

18. In a brilliant juxtaposition between Chateaubriand's *Mémoirs d'outre-tombe* and Stendhal's *Vie de Henry Brulard*—two autobiographies that rely on opposing conceptions of history and time—Yves Ansel analyzes the mechanism whereby, within the logic of the "temps de vicomte," a historical or biographical event is immobilized through an accumulation of more-or-less *longue-durée* patterns and precedents, while in Stendhal, on the contrary, the emphasis is entirely on the particularity of what happens, on the "perspective humble, bornée par le seul horizon présent." See Yves Ansel, *Stendhal: Le Temps et l'histoire* (Toulouse: Presses universitaires du Mirail, 2000), 153–64.

19. According to Fernand Rudé, Stendhal went further in his liberalism than Constant; he was, more

properly, "plus qu'un liberal et pas encore un socialiste." See Fernand Rudé, *Stendhal et la pensée sociale de son temps* (Brionne: G. Monfort, 1983), 362–64.

20. See Benjamin Constant, *De la Liberté chez les modernes* (Paris: Le Livre de Poche, 1980), 491–515.

21. Tzvetan Todorov, *Passion for Democracy: Benjamin Constant*, trans. Alice Seberry (New York: Algora, 1999), 42.

22. George Poulet, "Stendhal and Time," in Stendhal, *Red and Black*, 475.

23. Stendhal, *Memoirs of an Egoist*, 29.

24. Stendhal, *On Love*, xix.

25. Stendhal, *Memoirs of an Egoist*, 7.

26. Stendhal, *Short Novels of Stendhal*, trans. C. K. Scott Moncrieff (New York: Liveright, 1946), 44.

27. Stendhal, *Racine and Shakespeare*, 88.

28. Joseph de Maistre, "The Saint Petersburg Dialogues," in *The Works of Joseph de Maistre*, trans. Jack Lively (New York: Macmillan, 1965), 214

29. Ibid., 216.

30. Stendhal, *Memoirs of an Egoist*, 7.

31. Cited in Todorov, *Passion for Democracy*, 133.

32. Benjamin Constant, *Adolphe*, trans. Margaret Mauldon (Oxford: Oxford University Press, 2001), 11. Subsequent references will be given parenthetically in the text.

33. De Maistre, *Works*, 214.

34. Fredric Jameson, "*La Cousine Bette* and Allegorical Realism," *PMLA* 86, no. 2 (1971): 253.

35. See Georg Lukács' discussion of the two authors' different conceptions of totality in *Studies in European Realism*, 72.

36. Stendhal, *Correspondance (1830–1832)*, 1:251.

37. For an in-depth account of the question of paternity in *Rouge*, see Peter Brooks, *Reading for the Plot: Design and Intention in Narrative* (Cambridge: Harvard University Press, 2000), 62–89.

38. Stendhal, *Short Novels*, 83. It is difficult at this point not to hear echoes of the neoclassical tragic tradition, and in particular Pierre Corneille's *Le Cid*, in which Rodrigue castigates himself for having tarried too long with the decision: "Je m'accuse déjà de trop de négligence; / Courons à la vengeance; / Et tout honteux d'avoir tant balancé, / Ne soyons plus en peine." See Pierre Corneille, *Théâtre 2* (Paris: GF Flammarion, 1980), 227. Just as it is true, then, that Stendhal's conception of duty radically diverges from its neoclassical predecessor with regard to its object, so also it must be admitted that, at least as far as duty's proper temporality is concerned, Stendhal appears to follow the neoclassical tradition.

39. Stendhal, *Le Rouge et le noir* (Paris: Gallimard, 1951), 105.

40. It is in this sense that Auerbach's apposite characterization of Stendhalian realism as "the realism of resistance" should be understood: reality is given in the mode of being exposed for what it is by the hero who resists and rejects it. See Auerbach, *Mimesis*, 465.

41. See Guy Debord, *The Society of the Spectacle*, trans. Donald Nicholson-Smith (New York: Zone Books, 1995), 14.

42. Stendhal, *Short Novels*, 205.

43. See Margaret Cohen, *The Sentimental Education of the Novel* (Princeton: Princeton University Press, 1999), 94.

44. Stendhal, *Short Novels*, 217.

45. See Louise K. Horowitz's essay on "Pastoral Fiction" in *A New History of French Literature*, ed. Denis Hollier (Cambridge: Harvard University Press, 1989), 258–62.

46. Auerbach, *Mimesis*, 459.

47. "Instant" is almost an understatement here. It is a bitter irony thoroughly characteristic of the novel's plotting that Julien's heroic, dutiful conquest of Mme de Rênal can be foreseen (that is, intuited *ahead of time* and cast in an utterly vulgar register) by the meanest mind of a shrewd peasant, that of his father to boot (14).

48. This is what D. A. Miller calls "the revolutionary verb" that is not the transitive verb of history as uninterrupted process but the copulative verb of immediacy. See D. A. Miller, "Narrative 'Uncontrol' in

Stendhal," in *Modern Critical Interpretations: Stendhal's "The Red and the Black,"* ed. Harold Bloom (New York: Chelsea House Publishers, 1988), 39. Miller associated this temporality with daydream in the novel, but it seems more pervasive and more precisely copulative when applied to the demand of immediacy that duty imposes on the self. By contrast, daydreams in the novel tend to have few effects on the overall shape of the narrative.

49. Moreover, their historical alliances lie with the dynamic periods of French history, with those periods that are celebrated as the most adventurous: the Wars of the League, the Revolution, the early military exploits of the Empire. From their point of view, *le grand siècle,* so valorized in the official culture of the Restoration, is no more than, in the words of Sainte-Beuve, "un pont élégant et fragile jeté sur l'abyme." See Charles Augustin Sainte-Beuve, *Tableau historique et critique de la poésie français au XVIe siècle* (Coeuvres-et-Valsery: Ressouvenances, 1999), 285. For the Romantics of the 1820s and 1830s, the classical, mannered seventeenth century, and by extension the Restoration, is only an interlude in the true history of France, the dynamic, heroic, history of the Wars of the League and the Revolution.

50. Thus, in his discussion of *Rouge,* Franco Moretti arrives at the following conclusion: "It may be an unpleasant thought, but in an appeased world that invites everybody to enjoy the pleasures of the reality principle, running the risk of being a parody is one of the highest examples of courage." See Moretti, *The Way of the World,* 109.

51. François-René Chateaubriand, *Political Reflections on the True Interests of the French Nation* (London: Schulze and Dean, 1814), 28.

52. See Steven Kale, *French Salons: High Society and Political Sociability from the Old Regime to the Revolution of 1848* (Baltimore: Johns Hopkins University Press, 2004), 141–43.

53. Just as Raphael is unable to keep up with Foedora, and as, in a lighter key, the men in the *Lehrjahre* find it difficult to keep up with the fickle Philine, Julien is confronted, in Mathilde, with modern time itself, the time that is constant annihilation.

54. Needless to say, the link between temporal acceleration and Paris is here just as strong as (though less insistently thematized than) in Balzac.

55. Listed as 30 percent in D. G. Charlton, "Prose Fiction," in *The French Romantics,* ed. D. G. Charlton (Cambridge: Cambridge University Press, 1984), 1:190.

56. In fact Dominick LaCapra suggests that it is precisely because the letter approximates the truth so closely that, in an attempt to prove it wrong, Julien reacts to it with such vehemence. See LaCapra, *History, Politics, and the Novel* (Ithaca: Cornell University Press, 1987), 25.

57. It is for this reason that René Girard's analysis of the novel, focusing on the opposition between the passionate person and the *vaniteux* and casting the former as "the arrow which points the direction of a topsy-turvy world," seems to fall short of accounting for the complexity of the novel's veridictory structure. For Girard, the model of such a passionate person is Mme de Rênal, but in fact a number of characters rise to the status of "right-side-up hero in an upside-down-world"—Julien more often than others, sometimes Mathilde, and, toward the end of the novel, Mme de Rênal—but none of them ever manages to occupy that position for long. Insofar as Mme de Rênal's actions do indeed seem more direct, less mediated by preexisting models than those of Julien and Mathilde, she is also for the most part isolated from the social world of the novel, inhabiting a space more common to the sentimental *Armance* than to *Rouge* itself. As for the more "realistically" deployed agents of truth, each of them appears capable of "pointing the direction in a topsy-turvy world" only with the help of historically transcendent models (and then not so much through passion as through duty). See René Girard, *Deceit, Desire, and the Novel: Self and Other in Literary Structure,* trans. Yvonne Freccero (Baltimore: Johns Hopkins University Press, 1990), 140–41.

58. See, for example, Victor Brombert's discussion of the Stendhalian prison in *Stendhal: Fiction and the Themes of Freedom* (New York: Random House, 1968), 92–94. See also Christopher Prendergast, *The Order of Mimesis: Balzac, Stendhal, Nerval, Flaubert* (Cambridge: Cambridge University Press, 1986), 138.

59. The most noticeable mark of a break between the post-trial chapters and the rest of the novel is the abrupt disappearance of chapter headings, epigraphs, and narratorial intrusions. The whimsical epigraphs and usually deflating chapter headings are withdrawn, freeing the hero from their ironic, distancing shadow. The narrator—insofar as he appears as a generally sympathetic but consistently patronizing figure,

whose function is to explain, justify, or mildly chastise Julien before an imaginary public—vanishes. Normative, socializing omniscience is lost. The narrator is reduced either to an objective chronicler of events, or is aligned so closely with Julien's point of view that the two become inextricable in free indirect discourse. Julien does not need any mediators between himself and the public, presumably because the public no longer exists. For a discussion of the narrator's withdrawal in the concluding chapters of the book in the context of the paternal metaphor, see Peter Brooks, *Reading for the Plot*, 86.

60. Gérard Genette, *Figures of Literary Discourse,* trans. Alan Sheridan (New York: Columbia University Press, 1982), 169.

61. It is here that the noncoincidence of truth with knowledge is perhaps most vivid in Stendhal. What is known, what we can know—predict, intuit, foretell—is precisely in the order of the lie. Conventional falsehoods are the easiest, most readily available objects of knowledge. The truth, on the other hand, is what falls out of this kind of knowledge; the truth is the unpredictable and the unexpected. It is tempting to say that, unlike in Balzac, veridiction works here not *with* but *against* epistemophilia.

62. Yet another reversal of the classic Hegelian formula: see Theodor Adorno, *Minima Moralia: Reflections on a Damaged Life,* trans. E. F. N. Jephcott (London: Verso, 2005), 50.

63. Franco Moretti, *The Way of the World,* 102.

Chapter 3

1. "Время требует правды . . . вызывает на свет правду" и т.д., так чтоб ясно было, что это намек, что "Время" и "Правда"—одно и то же." In a letter of November 1863 to his brother Mikhail, after their journal *Time* (*Vremia*) was closed down by the authorities and in the hopes of starting a new journal named, provisionally, *Truth* (*Pravda*), Dostoevsky suggests ways of connecting the two journals in the readers' minds. See F. M. Dostoevsky, *Polnoe sobranie sochinenii v tridtsati tomakh.* ed. and annotated by G. M. Fridlender et al. (Leningrad: Nauka, 1982), vol. 28, book 2: 56. Here and below, the translations of passages from *PSS* are mine.

2. Fyodor Dostoevsky, *The Eternal Husband and Other Stories,* trans. Richard Pevear and Larissa Volokhonsky (New York: Bantam, 1997), 248–49. Subsequent references to this edition will be given parenthetically in the text.

3. In this respect, the narrator of "The Meek One" partakes of the mock-Christological dynamic so fundamental to a certain kind of Dostoevskian hero. A mean, all-too-earthly appearance hides a divine essence, and the others must exercise the free activity of their faith in order to recognize "a god" in the body of a carpenter's son or, what's worse, a pawnbroker. Thus, the narrator exclaims: "No, take a deed of magnanimity that's difficult, quiet, inaudible, unglamorous, with calumny, where there's much sacrifice and not a drop of glory—where you, a shining man, are presented as a scoundrel before everyone, whereas you're more honest than anyone else on earth. . . . And I—all I've done all my life is bear that deed" (263).

4. The importance of knowing everything about a person, the sense that one knows nothing at all unless one knows everything, is a genuine preoccupation of Dostoevsky's fiction. Prince Myshkin's half-mad tirade toward the end of *The Idiot* clarifies the stakes: "Oh, if Aglaya knew everything [*vsio*] . . . that is, absolutely everything. Because here you have to know everything, that's the first thing! Why can we never know *everything* about another person when it's necessary, when the person is to blame!" See Fyodor Dostoevsky, *The Idiot,* trans. Richard Pevear and Larissa Volokhonsky (New York: Vintage Classics, 2001), 583. Dostoevsky's insistence on the impossibility of truthfulness outside "the whole story" is of course analogous to Balzac's emphasis on the veridictory function of totality. In both cases, emplotment, preferably total emplotment, is the condition for the possibility of truth.

5. Fyodor Dostoevsky, *The Brothers Karamazov,* trans. Richard Pevear and Larissa Volokhonsky (New York: Vintage Classics, 1990), 235.

6. To be sure, some of the most prominent representatives of the detective camp can at times also seem mysterious, just as the enigmatic types frequently have a good deal of insight into others. The distinction must be drawn in terms of tendencies and functions and not in terms of absolute, static characteristics.

7. For a more detailed, though differently framed, elaboration of the manner in which the problematic of the self changes from Dostoevsky's "early" to "late" novels, see Michael Holquist, *Dostoevsky and the Novel* (Princeton: Princeton University Press, 1977), 35–37.

8. Geoffrey Kabat and others have pointed out that "the central problems which preoccupy Dostoevsky in the nonfiction are the same as those that preoccupy his characters in the fiction." See Kabat, *Ideology and Imagination: The Image of Society in Dostoevsky* (New York: Columbia University Press, 1978), 113. The approach I am offering here largely bypasses inquiry into the unquestionable thematic overlap between Dostoevsky's journalism and his novels. Instead it focuses on the fundamental *isomorphism* between his political and novelistic "temporal imaginations." With this in mind, I am less interested in what characters, and in particular the protagonists, think or say and more interested in what function they serve in grounding multiple and variously shaped narrative possibilities. Indirectly, this focus on emplotment makes problematic the very distinction between "ideology" and "imagination" that ground thematic inquiries into Dostoevsky's "art and thought."

9. See M. D. Karpachev, "Obshchestvenno-politicheskaia mysl' poreformennoi epokhi," in *Ocherki russkoi kul'tury XIX veka*, ed. L. D. Dergacheva et al. (Moscow: Moscow State University Press, 2003), 4:197–398.

10. "Sovremennoe obozrenie," in *Vremia* (1863), 3:123. Here and below, translations from the journals *Vremia* and *Epokha* are mine.

11. *PSS*, 20:217.

12. *PSS*, 18:57.

13. Ibid., 66.

14. Ibid., 69.

15. Whenever Dostoevsky explicitly addresses the goals of *Time* and, later, of *Epoch*, one gets the sense that he imagines the journals to occupy a space of externality in relation to contemporary debates about the fate of Russia. He conceives of their work as monitoring other journalistic activity, as surveying a wide range of existing opinions and determining their relative merits. Of course, both *Time* and *Epoch* have clear and relatively consistent views of their own. But what distinguishes those views from competing contemporary conceptions of Russia's future is precisely the insistence on mystery, on the fact that we do not yet know and have no way, as yet, of knowing what Russia will or should become. It is perhaps this insistence that opens these journals to the multiplicity of available emplotment options, turning them into something like *metajournals* and thus rendering them isomorphic with the post-Reform Dostoevskian novel, structured by an awareness of multiple possibilities for the emplotment of that which persists in its enigmatic status.

16. Put this way, both questions, the question of history and the question of fictional biography, recapitulate the Kantian schematism: how to bring the universal (Country, Person) and the particular (this specific hero, Russia) together in time.

17. Michael Holquist has argued that *Notes from the Underground*, first published in *Epoch* in 1864, stages an attempt on Dostoevsky's part to eschew the limitations of preexisting historical plots by telling the story of a life that is in crucial respects plotless, thus undermining, on the level of fiction, the widespread belief in Russia's adaptability to universal-historical stages of development (Holquist, *Dostoevsky and the Novel*, 48). Russia, then, is synecdochically represented by the hero-narrator, and the plotlessness of his life, its inability to fit into preexisting literary models, recapitulates arguments about Russia's self-historicity. But this plotlessness itself, this apparently *fabulaic* narrative of *Notes from the Underground*, turns out to consist in fact of multiple emplotments (the most prominent of which partake of scientific and literary-Romantic discourses), all vying for veridictory authority over the identity of the hero. After all, the possibility of self-historicity, of unique plot, is necessarily complemented by the condition of multihistoricity. For if history is single and unilinear, then Russia must either stand still and be, in the classical Hegelian sense, nonhistorical, or it must move along the wide road paved by Western civilization. Thus the dichotomy placing universal history, "Romantic" plot, and the West on one side, and the self, plotlessness, and Russia on the other emerges as complicated by the ineluctable multiplicity characterizing all of these categories as they appear in Dostoevsky's post-Reform art and journalism. For other attempts to cast the relationship

between Dostoevsky's journalistic discourse on Russia and novelistic representations of character in allegorical terms, see Susan McReynolds, *Redemption and the Merchant God: Dostoevsky's Economy of Salvation and Antisemitism* (Evanston: Northwestern University Press, 2008); and Andrew Wachtel, *An Obsession with History: Russian Writers Confront the Past* (Stanford: Stanford University Press, 1994).

18. Philip Rahv, "Dostoevsky in *Crime and Punishment*," in *Dostoevsky: A Collection of Critical Essays*, ed. René Wellek (Englewood Cliffs: Prentice Hall, 1962), 20. Joseph Frank makes a similar point in *Dostoevsky: The Miraculous Years, 1865–1871* (Princeton: Princeton University Press, 1995), 201–2.

19. Fyodor Dostoevsky, *Crime and Punishment*, trans. Richard Pevear and Larissa Volokhonsky (New York: Vintage Classics, 1992), 65. Subsequent references to this edition will be given parenthetically in the text. Russian excerpts are from *Polnoe sobranie sochinenii v tridtsati tomakh*, ed. G. M. Fridlender et al., vol. 6 (Leningrad: Nauka, 1973).

20. See Mikhail Bakhtin, *Speech Genres and Other Essays*, trans. Vern W. McGee, ed. Caryl Emerson and Michael Holquist (Austin: University of Texas Press, 1996), 14–16.

21. *PSS*, 18:68.

22. "Sovremennoe obozrenie," 333.

23. *PSS*, 5:77.

24. Ibid., 74–75.

25. Much has been said about the prominence in *Crime and Punishment* of the subtext of Alexander Pushkin's story "The Queen of Spades" (1833). It has been noticed that certain moments in the novel invoke a comparison between Raskolnikov and Pushkin's reckless hero Hermann, who risks everything to acquire the secret that would instantaneously make him rich and instead ends up in an insane asylum. But if it is true that Hermann carries with him the impetuous narratological prototype of Raskolnikov, it is important to note that the story also contains a character whose updated, bourgeois counterpart we find in Luzhin. This is Tomsky, who risks nothing and is at the end of the story married and promoted, providing the narratological model for step-by-step advancement, patient careerism, and thus sharply contrasting with the trajectory of the hero.

26. See, for instance, Dostoevsky's announcement of the publication of *Epokha* for 1865 in *PSS*, 20:216–21.

27. For an alternative reading of the issue of translation in *Crime and Punishment*, one focusing on the question of Dostoevsky's views of national originality, see Brian Baer, "Translating the Transition: The Translator Detective in Post-Soviet Fiction," in *Linguistica Antverpiensia* 4 (2005): 243–54. Baer's views resonate with the analysis presented here. The latter understands translation as signaling the gradualist and mediating temporality of the Western European *Bildungsroman*, while Baer sees it as a technique of engaging (either imitatively or creatively) with the cultural heritage (one might say *Bildungsgut*) of the West.

28. Goethe, *Wilhelm Meister's Apprenticeship*, 306.

29. On character zones, see Bakhtin, *The Dialogic Imagination*, 316–20. Bakhtin's hostility toward the literary-theoretical category of plot (as distinct from the broader philosophical conception of temporality) due to its finalizing pretensions is, however, well documented. It is here, that is, in affirming the epistemological centrality of emplotment zones as *end-directed, finalizing* temporal discourses that this essay sharply departs from Bakhtin's understanding of multiplicity in the novel. For an account of Bakhtin's polemic against the prominence of plot as a literary-theoretical category in the 1960s and 1970s, see Bakhtin, *Sobranie sochinenii*, ed. S. Bocharev and V. Kozhinov (Moscow: Iazyki slavianskoi kul'tury, 2002), 6:388, 585–88.

See also Leslie Johnson's analysis of subjective time in *Crime and Punishment*, which presupposes a loosely existentialist framework and is largely incompatible with a zones-of-emplotment approach adopted here. The latter, by analogy with the conception of character zones offered in Bakhtin, focuses less on characters' *personal experiences* of time than on objective, that is, historically operative, specific, and therefore *generic*, "auras" of temporality accompanying them through the novel. Leslie Johnson, *The Experience of Time in "Crime and Punishment"* (Columbus: Slavica, 1984).

30. See Leonid Grossman, *Dostoevskii: Put', poetika, tvorchestvo* (Moscow: Sovremennye problemy, 1928), 94.

31. Dmitry Likhachev, in his essay "Dostoevsky in Search of the Real and the Authentic" (*Dostoevskii v poiskakh real'nogo i dostovernogo*), argues that the centrality of the accidental in Dostoevsky's poetics is related to his conception of verisimilitude. According to Dostoevsky, argues Likhachev, the general and the typical never properly happen; they are thought up, abstracted from reality. Reality itself consists of particulars, of accidents, of strange circumstances and events. Thus, it is Dostoevsky's conception of realism itself that justifies his preoccupation with the unsystematic and the peculiar. See Dmitry Likhachev, *Izbrannye raboty v trekh tomakh* (Leningrad: *Khudozhestvennaia literatura*, 1987), 3:262. In an apparent contradiction to this account stands Yuri Lotman's theory of the specifically literary accident. According to Lotman, while in "life" one may encounter events that are properly accidental, that are unaccountable, unsystemic, in art the accident is always only an effect. And as an effect, it is produced not in the process of desystematization, but precisely the opposite, through multiple encoding. In other words, the "literary" accident always belongs to at least two systems or "semantic fields" and stands at the point of their intersection. See Yuri Lotman, *Struktura khudozhestvennogo teksta* (Providence: Brown University Press, 1971), 78–79. The contradiction between these two views emerges as apparent only once we take into account the temporal dimension of plot, something neither theorist does. What then becomes clear is that the "literary" or plotted accident, and the Dostoevskian accident in particular, possesses an essentially perspectival character. Seen from the point of view of the hero, whatever falls out of his forward-looking plot is an accident, something unsystemic and uncanny. But perceived from the place of retrospection, the accident turns out to have been necessary, to have contributed something to the pattern of the hero's life. The accident, then, is, minimally, a meeting point between a prospective plot and a retrospective one.

32. And toward the end of the novel, he is still struggling with the uncanny absence at the place of the agent of the crime: "It was the devil killed the old crone, not me" (420).

33. Hence, there is yet another way to understand the significance of his name. *Raskol*—a split, a crack; here, between the one who acts and the one who tries to understand the act.

34. In this regard, see the paradigmatic and explicit instance in *The Idiot* where Aglaya "sets riddles" for her sisters. Dostoevsky, *The Idiot*, 345.

35. In fact, Porfiry Petrovich also shows himself to be a master at provoking such accidents. In describing his investigative method, Mikhail Bakhtin remarks: "Porfiry speaks in innuendos, addressing himself to Raskolnikov's covert voice. . . . Porfiry's goal is to force Raskolnikov's inner voice to break out into the open and to create interferences in his calculatingly and skillfully acted-out speeches. That is why real words and intonations from Raskolnikov's actual voice are constantly breaking into the words and intonations of his role." See Bakhtin, *Problems of Dostoevsky's Poetics*, 222.

36. Relevant to this account of the function of the accident in the novel are Gary Saul Morson's remarks on Dostoevsky's practice of depicting "the present moment in all its openness and 'incompleteness.'" Morson suggestively calls this practice *sideshadowing*. See Morson, "Introductory Study," in *Fyodor Dostoevsky, A Writer's Diary*, vol. 1, *1873–1876*, trans. Kenneth Lanz, ed. Gary Saul Morson (Evanston: Northwestern University Press, 1994), 82. Morson points to passages in which a limited third-person narrator suggests several possible accounts of an enigmatic event. "The real point," he concludes, "is that whatever happened, *any* of these incidents could have happened. What is important is the field of possibilities, not the one possibility actualized" (86).

Though it is easy to agree with Morson when it comes to the open-ended and as it were multiple nature of Dostoevsky's representation of the temporal present, his conception of the specific character of this multiplicity seems to me to fall short of what is actually at stake, at least in *Crime and Punishment*. First, the temporal plurality at issue here pertains to the representation of many *shapes* of time rather than many possibilities within a time that is itself uniformly conceived. Second, in connection with this emphasis on the plurality of possible *shapes* rather than *actualizations* of time and contrary to Morson's reading of sideshadowing in Dostoevsky, multiplicity is here not understood as in the service of an antitotalizing and antiutopian worldview, rejecting rigid causality and celebrating indeterminacy, freedom, and personal responsibility. This would indeed presuppose multiple possibilities within a singular time. Rather, here, multitemporality is seen as allowing for narrative experimentation with specific, historically determinate and socially grounded temporal trajectories, specific life shapes available to the protagonist at a particular historical moment. Here, freedom is more than the freedom to choose between several options and possibility is more than the possibility for things to have turned out otherwise. Instead, freedom involves choice that is radical, the choice of occupying an altogether different life, say, of switching from the biography of a great man to the life of a saint or, more miraculously still, to the life of a petit bourgeois. And historical possibility is understood as the possibility of belonging to an altogether differently shaped history, moving, for example, from the universal clock according to which Russia is far behind and in need of catching up, to a national one, showing it to be right on time; or from a liberal future-centric gradualist time to a conservative past-heavy but similarly gradualist one, or even to a radically presentist, apocalyptic "now."

37. Moretti, *The Way of the World*, 46.
38. See *PSS*, 20:218.
39. Balzac, *Oeuvres*, 20:461.
40. There are also, of course, "extrinsic" reasons for reading the relationship between the story of Lazarus and the rest of the novel in this way. The authority that the Gospels preserved through the nineteenth century, even among the nonreligious members of the educated class, is as well documented as the fascination that the New Testament (and especially, the fourth Gospel) held for Dostoevsky in particular.
41. Susan McReynolds addresses the disturbing analogy between the sacrificial logic of "Western utilitarianism" and Christian narrative as the two are presented in the novel. See *Redemption and the Merchant God*, 117–32.
42. There is also perhaps a possibility of reading Raskolnikov as a Caiaphas, the high priest who, having learned about Jesus's most recent and glorious miracle, decides that it is better for one man, Jesus, to die than for the whole of the Jewish people to be destroyed. Here, the narrator of the Gospel of John comments that, in plotting Jesus's murder, Caiaphas is not acting freely, "of his own accord," but merely fulfilling a preexisting providential plan. As a Caiaphas figure, Raskolnikov emerges as a character who acts out a sacrificial logic while relying on an unfounded presumption of mastery. This is indeed how Raskolnikov sees himself at moments of despair. See also Peeter Torop's reading of *Crime and Punishment* for signs of similarity between the characters of the story of Lazarus and those of the novel: *Dostoevskii—Istoriia i ideologiia* (Tartu: Tartu University Press, 1997), 110–12.
43. On the frequency and function of the word "suddenly" in *Crime and Punishment*, see Viktor Toporov, "O strukture romana Dostoevskogo v sviazi s arkhaichnymi skhemami mifologicheskogo myshleniia (*Prestuplenie i nakazanie*)," in *Mif, ritual, simvol, obraz: Issledovaniia v oblasti mifopoeticheskogo* (Moscow: Progress—Kul'tura, 1995), 197–99.
44. Donald Fanger unites Balzac and Dostoevsky (together with Gogol and Dickens) under the literary historical category of "romantic realism." The point here is that certain "unreformed idealists" treated reality as visionaries, infusing their novels with a great deal of condensation and heightening and thus emerging as somehow transitional between the Romantics of the beginning of the century and the "reformed idealists," that is to say, the true realists, such as Tolstoy and Flaubert. See *Dostoevsky and Romantic Realism: A Study of Dostoevsky in Relation to Balzac, Dickens, and Gogol* (Cambridge: Harvard University Press, 1965), 3–27. In the chapter on Balzac, I outlined a distinction between the Romantic—that is, subjectivist, ironic, and indeed visionary—novel and the kind of novel that, by internalizing the modern logic of temporal acceleration, partakes of and renders immanent an older romance idealism. It can thus go without saying that throughout this book "romance" means something different from, though in some respects not entirely unrelated to, what it means for Fanger.
45. The original Russian lacks a copula, thus effecting a more determinate collapse of the past onto the present in the person of Raskolnikov.
46. Michael Holquist notes the relevance here of St. Augustine's *Confessions*, with its transition after book 10 from autobiographical chronology to a timeless meditation on ultimate beginnings. See Holquist, 95.
47. In a recent essay, Gary Saul Morson suggests that many readers feel dissatisfied with the novel's epilogue because while the novel as a whole tends to align itself with Razumikhin's "prosaic practical goodness," the final passages are "cast wholly in Sonya's terms." As a result, we find an inconsistency between the novel's privileging of "practical reason and small acts of [prosaic] goodness" on the one hand and its celebration of religious faith on the other. From the perspective adopted here, however—namely that of

viewing character not as a set of psychological traits adding up to a "moral temperament" but as a historically determinate and historiographically fruitful temporal shape or zone of emplotment—the place of both Razumikhin and the epilogue in the novel appears in a different light.

Though as a moral-psychological type Razumikhin is indeed no more than "a decent fellow," in anchoring a temporal trajectory, he is consistently associated with the ideology of organic historiography and the generic aura of a *Bildungsroman*. In fact, his very name presupposes a higher reason (*razum*) than the one associated with practical activity and good sense (*rassudok*). As a zone of emplotment for his enigmatic friend (and, with him, for Russia), Razumikhin comes to represent more than a potentially infinite series of prosaic little acts, he represents a global—and thoroughly "theoretical"—conception of both universal history and individual biography as involving the gradual unfolding or fruition of the organic spirit of a human being or a nation. The reinsertion of Razumikhin's temperament into the temporal (historiographic and generic) shape with which it is associated makes it clear that the ideology of small prosaic acts (good or bad) is more properly associated in Dostoevsky with the petit bourgeois historiography of a Luzhin than with that of the hero of a possible national epic (*bogatyr'*), Razumikhin. In fact it might be this very heightening of the pathos of the gradual that allows Razumikhin's zone of emplotment to be reactivated alongside Sonya's in the last words of the novel, with the triple insistence on the slowness of the hero's regeneration. See Morson, "The God of Onions: *The Brothers Karamazov* and the Mythic Prosaic," in *The New Word on The Brothers Karamazov*, ed. Robert Louis Jackson, (Evanston: Northwestern University Press, 2004).

48. We do find similar formulations in Dostoevsky, especially in *The Brothers Karamazov*, with the Elder Zosima's paradoxical principle of the "lasting deed" (*podvig*) of active love and of the "great [monastic] obedience in the world" (*velikoe poslushanie v miru*). See Fyodor Dostoevsky, *The Brothers Karamazov*, 58.

49. No other novel by Dostoevsky presents us with such an insistent thematization of the accidental, but most of them, and especially the novels of the post-Reform period, rely on this structure for veridictory effects. Accidentally, characters bump into one another, hear about one another, see one another's portraits, remember one another; emplotment zones cross, sparking temporalized insight into the enigma of the self.

Chapter 4

1. Lev Tolstoy, *Polnoe sobranie sochinenii*, 90 vols. (Moscow: Khudozhestvennaia literatura, 1928–1964), 62:413–14. Subsequently, references to this edition will be provided in the text. Here and below translation from this edition is mine.

2. Nikolai Strakhov, *Mir kak tseloe: Cherty iz nauki o prirode* (St. Petersburg: Tipografiia brat'ev Panteleevykh, 1892), 93. Strakhov's conviction is in fact so solid that he dares to challenge Alexander Herzen's by then paradigmatic doubts about historical progress in a tone of unmistakable condescension: "Recall the words of our remarkable thinker and artist, Herzen: 'Why did everyone decide,' he says, 'that children exist only in order to become adults? They exist for the sake of themselves, they have their own distinct life.' Everyone decided this, we might answer, because it is better to be an adult than a child, because becoming adults is a necessity contained in the very nature of children" (94).

Herzen's defense of childhood against teleological sublation into maturity appears in *From the Other Shore* (*S Togo berega*, 1848–1849) as an analogical counterpart to his objections against a rigidly progressive Hegelian philosophy of history. To Herzen, the debacle of the 1848 revolutions in Europe has revealed that history may possess a trajectory neither developmental nor even linear. There is no guarantee, it turns out, that either an isolated human being or humanity as a whole has maturation as its proper path and adulthood as its *telos*. Still more astutely, Herzen implies that even if such a guarantee did exist, adulthood, which he associates with the triumph of petit bourgeois European philistinism (*meshchanstvo*), would not necessarily be a worthy goal. Herzen perceives the existing, post-1848, order of things as proclaiming itself to be the world of responsible maturity, the standard of wisdom, to which any self-respecting bourgeois must ascend, tracing the predictable generic trajectory of a successful *Bildungsroman*. In a single gesture, then, Herzen rejects history as progress and life as adequation to the way of the world. His own ideal, opposing that of maturity, emerges through the paradoxical metaphor of gray-haired youth (*sedaia iunost'*), an intractable, anarchic idealism preserved and tempered in (but not destroyed by) experience. See Alexander Herzen, *Polnoe sobranie sochinenii v tridtsati tomakh,* ed. V. Volgin (Moscow: Akademiia nauk, 1956), 8:11.

Strakhov refuses to sympathize with Herzen's reservations about biographical and historical teleology. But his treatment of the "remarkable thinker" is less rudimentary than might initially appear. Like Tolstoy's supposed incomprehension of Hegelian Spirit, Strakhov's rejection of the defense of childhood is shrewder than it would seem. He recognizes that behind Herzen's biographical metaphor lurks not only a rejection of progressive universal history but also a protest against the current state of affairs, the world as it is, with its claim of superiority over humanity's past. Thus, his dismissal of Herzen's misgivings rejects not only the apparently silly suggestion that adulthood might not be the sole and proper *telos* of a child but also the equally "infantile" protests against the present order of things.

3. Strakhov, *Mir kak tseloe,* ix–x.

4. For the original elaboration of the concept of "estrangement," with special attention to the use of this technique in Tolstoy, see Viktor Shklovsky, *Theory of Prose,* trans. Benjamin Sher (Normal, Ill: Dalkey Archive Press, 1998), 1–14.

5. Jürgen Habermas, *The Philosophical Discourse of Modernity,* trans. Frederick G. Lawrence (Cambridge: MIT Press, 1990), 16.

6. Elsewhere of course Tolstoy speaks with approval about the notion of personal development as moral improvement. But improvement itself is never conceived as dependent on an accumulation of experience; rather it is a matter of closer and closer approximation to eternal principles inscribed in our hearts. Thus: "Moral laws already exist; humanity is only clarifying them for itself" (*PSS,* 25:226).

7. Lev Tolstoy, *Anna Karenina,* trans. Richard Pevear and Larissa Volokhonsky (New York: Penguin Classics, 2002), 525. Subsequently, references to this edition will be provided in the text. Here the translation departs from the original, which reads, more literally: "suddenly *being* an attribute of the manner of action" (*PSS,* 19:96).

8. Habermas, *Philosophical Discourse of Modernity,* 42.

9. See, for example, Lotman, "Puti razvitiia russkoi prosvetitel'skoi prozy XVIII veka," 93–95.

10. Discussions of the science of war in *War and Peace* repeatedly juxtapose these two conceptions of the relation between truth and system. In one of the most explicit instances, General Pfühl's views are juxtaposed to those of Prince Andrei. First: "Pfühl was one of those inordinately, unshakably self-assured men—self-assured to the point of martyrdom, as only a German can be, because only a German bases his self-assurance on an abstract idea: science, that is the supposed knowledge of absolute truth" (770). Then, several pages later: "A thought that had early and often occurred to [Prince Andrei] during his military activities—the idea that there was not and could not be a science of war . . . —now appeared to him as an absolute self-evident truth." See Tolstoy, *War and Peace,* trans. Ann Dunnigan (New York: Signet Classics, 1968), 775. Subsequent references to this edition will be given parenthetically in the text.

11. For an account of Tolstoy's relationship with Chicherin, see Boris Eikhenbaum, "Tolstoy: Shestidesiatye gody," in *Lev Tolstoy* (Munich: Wilhelm Fink Verlag, 1968), 27–37.

12. Vasily Zelinsky, *Russkaia kriticheskaia literatura o proizvedeniiakh L. N. Tolstogo* (Moscow, 1902), 8:17.

13. For an overview of the critical tradition linking Tolstoy with Stendhal, see Isabelle Naginski's dissertation, *Stendhal and Tolstoy: A Study in Literary Kinship* (Ph.D. diss., Columbia University, 1982), 12–18.

14. Eikhenbaum, "Molodoi Tolstoi," in *Lev Tolstoy,* 97.

15. Lev Tolstoy, *The Death of Ivan Ilych,* in *Tolstoy's Short Fiction,* ed. and rev. trans. Michael R. Katz (New York: W. W. Norton, 1991), 167.

16. N. M. Mendel'son, ed., *Pis'ma Tolstogo i k Tolstomu* (Moscow: Gosudarstvennoe izdatel'stvo, 1928), 223.

17. The term "situation rhyme" is used by R. F. Christian to refer to Tolstoy's tendency to introduce "constant repetition of identical or closely related situations" in *War and Peace,* but it is of course just as applicable to *Anna Karenina.* See Christian, *Tolstoy: A Critical Introduction* (Cambridge: Cambridge University Press, 1969), 132.

18. Elizabeth Stenbock-Fermor's book on the novel is largely dedicated to an exhaustive account of the novel's "architectural" elegance. See *The Architecture of "Anna Karenina": A History of Its Writing, Structure, and Message* (Lisse: Peter de Ridder Press, 1975).

19. Frye, *Anatomy of Criticism*, 33.

20. A curious parallel can be found in Stendhal's *La Chartreuse de Parme*, where the youthful hero, Fabrice, is granted an early understanding of this dynamic: "'I haven't changed one bit,' he said to himself, 'all those fine resolutions I made at our lake shore when I was looking at life so philosophically have evaporated. My soul was wandering at the time; it was all a dream and dissolves at the touch of real life.'" See Stendhal, *The Charterhouse of Parma*, trans. Richard Howard (New York: The Modern Library, 2000), 175.

21. This reading of the two plotlines contests Gary Saul Morson's influential formulation of the central opposition of the novel as essentially moral-characterological. According to Morson, the trouble with Anna is that she is too much of a determinist; the good thing about Levin is that he lives in the present. Anna believes in fate; Levin believes in himself. Commenting on a series of dreams, premonitions, omens that appear to overdetermine Anna's suicidal trajectory, Morson argues that these are nothing in themselves, that they acquire a force only because Anna allows them to do so. Anna is not, in other words, condemned to death under a train from the beginning, but is rather nudged toward this death by a kind of literary superstition. Her future is predetermined and hastened by her idea of what that future must be; her prophecies are self-fulfilling. In short, Anna's story is not that "of a fated woman but that of a woman who imagines she is one." By contrast, Levin and Kitty allow their lives to unfold within a temporality that is not foreclosed. Their focus is on the present; they let the future take care of itself. And in this way, they stage the key lesson of the novel: "Life as Tolstoy imagines it does not fit a pattern as art does. Our lives tend to no goal, nor are they destined to be shaped into a story." See Morson, "Anna Karenina's Omens," in *Freedom and Responsibility in Russian Literature: Essays in Honor of Robert Louis Jackson*, ed. Elizabeth Cheresh Allen and Gary Soul Morson (Evanston: Northwestern University Press, 1995), 142–44. In a recent book on *Anna Karenina*, Morson does not appear to have significantly revised his views. See his *Anna Karenina in Our Time: Seeing More Wisely* (New Haven: Yale University Press, 2007). See especially chapter 3, "Anna's Suicide and the Totalism of Meaning," 118–39.

Left in this form, Morson's distinction is confronted with a number of counterexamples in the text. To begin with, Anna's death-prefiguring dreams are not just her own, but are uncannily shared by Vronsky. The famous scene of the horse race, culminating with the death of Frou-Frou and, if read closely, foreshadowing Anna's own end, as well as the earlier narratorial references to death in the seduction scene, are certainly not attributable to Anna's own fatalistically inclined consciousness. And if Anna's story is indeed of Anna's own making, why does she not, as she believes she will, die at childbirth?

No less problematic is the reading of Levin as a devotee of the prose of life. First, there is Levin's obsession with grand theorizing. Throughout the novel he is at least as concerned with philosophical questions on a large scale as with the immediate problems of his everyday life. Is there a soul? Is there immortality? Is there a God? Levin's main mode of projecting himself into the future is theoretical: he decides (at the moment of more or less unexpected enlightenment) on a particular way of leading his life and tries to adjust his behavior accordingly. Even at the moment when he appears to have been disappointed by every philosophical system he has encountered, he is capable of formulating general principles of behavior: "He knew that he had to hire workers as cheaply as possible, but that he should not put them in bondage by paying them in advance at a cheaper rate than they were worth, though it was very profitable" (791). To be sure, Levin does quarrel with theory when it loses all traction with experience, but he is just as unwilling to engage with experience in an altogether untheoretical way.

Like Anna, Levin is occasionally susceptible to moments of spontaneous premonition. The reader, attuned to the kind of aesthetics (subsisting within Anna's narrative) in which an accidental and dangerous gunshot is an omen of an approaching disaster, becomes suspicious at the moment when Vasen'ka Veslovsky's rifle accidentally fires (579). Several pages later, during a hunt, finding himself side by side with Vasen'ka by a swamp, Levin himself begins to put past events and words into a whole spreading out to include the future. The earlier accidental gunshot, together with the recollection of Kitty's words—"See that you don't shoot each other" (582)—make him momentarily fear the worst. At an earlier point in the novel, he responds rather readily to the changes he observes in the sky, reading the appearance and disappearance of a shell-shaped cloud as a sign for the direction his own life will take (276). Much of chapter 14 in part 5 of the novel is dedicated to the frustration of Levin's *preconceived* ideas and images of family bliss. In short, when it comes to the need for mastery over time, the two protagonists are not very different. The differences between them are more readily available when they are understood as anchors of distinct and differently shaped plotlines.

22. For an account of the temporal unevenness in the novel, see Vladimir E. Alexandrov, "Relative Time in *Anna Karenina*," *Russian Review* 41, no. 2 (1982): 159–68.

23. Goethe, *Wilhelm Meister's Apprenticeship*, 309.

24. In this connection, Pierre's encounter with the Mason Bazdeev in *War and Peace* is telling as well. Here, as in the *Lehrjahre*, the Masons are associated with the capacity to look back on one's life and evaluate it from the perspective of what has been achieved. Just as the Society of the Tower presents Wilhelm with a scroll narrating his "apprenticeship," Bazdeev is somehow able to recount to Pierre all the significant events of his life. But in Tolstoy this encounter takes place not at the end, but at the middle of the journey; and the authority of this holistic narrative—or at least of those who purvey it—is undermined all-too-quickly. See Tolstoy, *War and Peace*, 430.

25. Here, Pevear and Volokhonsky's translation is somewhat misleadingly inconsistent. On page 794, they render *po pravde* more literally as "by the truth," while here they choose to translate *sluzhenie pravde* as "serving the good."

26. Of course, the import of the ideological message of the revelation is undeniable. But as such, the acceptance of the teachings of Orthodox Christianity is bound, by the logic of this narrative as well as more generally by the logic of Tolstoy's biography and art, to be short lived.

27. It is yet another instance of the novel's architectonic perfection that each plotline contains a reverberation of the weightiest intrusion of death into the other. In the end, Anna commits suicide and Levin contemplates it. In the middle, Levin witnesses his brother's death while Anna comes close to dying in childbirth. A decisive event in one—in the other, its fleeting echo. It is as if these parallel paths suddenly intersect—not diegetically, as they do when Levin and Anna actually meet, but structurally—and each character is momentarily tempted by the narrative trajectory of the other.

Levin's suicide would mean that after all there is no way out, that the world is complete, that, with his happy marriage, his story has come to an end. But this meaning would have been inimical to the very formal principle of his narrative, which repeatedly and to the end posits him as still outside, unfinished, straining for more. Anna's near-death at childbirth represents the only significant moment in her narrative when her own expectations are frustrated. She has been told in her dream that she will die at childbirth, and yet she survives. This moment posits precisely the sort of gap between "thought" and "life" that structures Levin's entire narrative. And into that gap the experience of death is inserted. Anna is tempted, it seems, to make death immanent to her life, to link it, in other words, to the necessary rift between her forward-looking emplotment of her own life and that life as it actually unfolds in the narrative. But just as Levin is only tempted by but does not choose suicide, so Anna's experience of death leaves no permanent mark on the shape of her story.

28. Stendhal, *Red and Black*, 69.

29. The situation in *War and Peace* is somewhat more complicated. There, alongside the narrator's debunking of the characters' modes of binding events, we find prolonged narratorial interventions of the kind we might find in an eighteenth-century philosophical novel. Here, the narrator emerges as a much more prominent and more legitimately truth-purveying function. Tolstoy's move to *Anna Karenina* has been characterized as, among other things, involving an increasingly subjectivized mode of narration. See, for example, Donna Tussing Orwin's discussion of this aspect of the transition in *Tolstoy's Life and Thought: 1847–1880* (Princeton: Princeton University Press, 1993).

30. The passage is indeed so difficult to follow that even the novel's latest translators seem to have made a mistake. Instead of "Don't count the marshal, he's no one to give orders . . . ," the translation should read: "Don't doubt (suspect) the marshal, he is not a manager (a steward) . . ."

31. A similar and even more radical annexation occurs earlier in the novel vis-à-vis Kitty's perspective when the narrator speaks a certain truth through Kitty, this time in her direct discourse but in words and categories that are difficult to attribute to Kitty herself, especially in the state of despair in which she finds herself at the moment. See Tolstoy, *Anna Karenina*, 83.

32. Lotman, *Struktura,* 291.

33. See Lukács, "Tolstoy i razvitie realizma," in *Literaturnoe nasledstvo* 35/36 (Moscow: Pushkinskii dom, 1939), 66.

34. See Lotman, "Puti razvitiia russkoi prosvetitel'skoi prozy XVIII veka," 93.

35. Bakhtin, *The Dialogic Imagination,* 84.

36. In his essay on "Forms of Time and Chronotope in the Novel," Bakhtin draws on narrative genres dating from the Hellenistic period to the age of the realist novel. It is not surprising, then, that *the railroad* does not make it into his (in any case rather provisional) classification of novelistic chronotopes. After all, the railroad figures a very modern, and one might even say, a protomodernist time shape, and the essay, with its historical center of gravity in Rabelais, never quite gets to it. It is also perhaps not surprising, given what we have already seen about the somewhat archaist tendencies of Levin's narrative, that its chronotope will be more easily identifiable among the options suggested by Bakhtin.

37. For a brief account of Tolstoy's own attitudes toward the railroad, see Stenbock-Fermor, *Architecture of "Anna Karenina,"* 66–68.

38. In fact, as Henry Pickford points out, the word rail [*rels*] is etymologically related to the word "rule." See Henry Pickford III, "The Sense of Semblance: Modern German and Russian Literature After Adorno" (Ph.D. diss., Yale University, 2001), 197.

39. On Stiva as the social animal *par excellence,* see Caryl Emerson, "Prosaics in *Anna Karenina*: Pro and Con," *Tolstoy Studies Journal* 8 (1995–96): 150–76.

40. Leo Tolstoy, *The Kreutzer Sonata,* in *Great Short Works of Leo Tolstoy,* intro. and append. John Bayley, trans. Louise and Aylmer Maude (New York: Perennial Classics, 2004), 414.

41. This very logic, only in reverse, is briefly visible in *Anna Karenina* as well when, returning from Moscow to his estate after Kitty rejects his proposal of marriage, Levin fails to let go of this memory until he is off the train (92).

42. For a brief account of the role of railways in transforming the Europeans' experience of time and distance at the end of the nineteenth century, see Stephen Kern, *The Culture of Time and Space: 1880–1918* (Cambridge: Harvard University Press, 2003), 213–15.

43. The railroad is perhaps the most forceful image of that frantic pace with which the Anna-Vronsky plotline develops.

44. Bakhtin, *The Dialogic Imagination,* 111–29.

45. Ibid., 113. As examples of this sort of narrative, Bakhtin adduces a number of works from the eighteenth century. Novels by Diderot, Smollett, Defoe, Fielding are all mentioned in connection with this chronotope. But perhaps the most relevant one for Tolstoy is the life of Jean-Jacques in Rousseau's *Confessions.* In the course of the book, Jean-Jacques is an apprentice to an engraver, a music copyist, a Calvinist, then a Catholic and, later, a Calvinist again, a secretary to a French ambassador, a political philosopher, a friend and then an enemy of the *philosophes,* a convert, by the roadside, to the religion of natural goodness, a successful novelist, a composer, a theorist of education, an exile. All this and more can be said about him precisely because he is so open to change, an infinitely convertible hero, proclaiming himself again and again to be a new Jean-Jacques. Not development to be sure, not a biographical progression from childhood to maturity, but a crisis-ridden path traversed by someone who is eternally a child.

46. Bakhtin, *The Dialogic Imagination,* 121.

47. For a convincing characterization of Tolstoy as a *frondeur* and an archaist, see Boris Eikhenbaum, "*Tolstoy: Shestidesiatye gody.*"

48. Bakhtin, *The Dialogic Imagination,* 249.

49. Ibid., 230.

Conclusion

1. Thus Heidegger, for example, explicitly acknowledges the debt of *Being and Time* to Kant's elaboration of the transcendental schematism. See Martin Heidegger, *Kant and the Problem of Metaphysics,*

trans. Richard Taft (Bloomington: Indiana University Press, 1997), 141. Sartre does not conceal his dependence on a certain (perhaps Kojèvian) Hegel in matters pertaining to truth's relation to time. See Jean-Paul Sartre, *Truth and Existence,* trans. Adrian van den Hoven (Chicago: University of Chicago Press, 1992). For Husserl's complicated "dialogue" with Kant on the subject of time and perception, see Paul Ricoeur, *Time and Narrative,* trans. Kathleen Blamey and David Pellauer (Chicago: University of Chicago Press, 1988), 3:23–59.

2. Henri Bergson, *Creative Evolution,* trans. Arthur Mitchell (Mineola, N.Y.: Dover, 1998), 344. Cited below and in the text as *CE.*

3. In *Creative Evolution,* Bergson prefers to speak of the "cinematographical mechanism" (*le mécanisme cinématographique*) rather than of spatialization. I use "spatialization" throughout, however, both because it is Bergson's metaphor of choice in most of his writings and because it allows us to sidestep the less relevant discussion of whether or not Bergson had an adequate understanding of cinematic effects.

4. It is worth noting that when Bergson turns to the analysis of the philosophies of time of seventeenth- and early eighteenth-century philosophers, he ends up concluding that they, too, like their ancient forebears, regard "reality as well as truth" as "integrally given in eternity" (*CE,* 354). According to him, it is not until the late eighteenth and nineteenth centuries, with Kant and Spencer, that we find a genuinely serious, though still mistaken, philosophical attitude to time.

5. Henri Bergson, *Time and Free Will: An Essay on the Immediate Data of Consciousness,* trans. F. L. Pogson (New York: Cosimo Classics, 2008), 104. Cited henceforth in the text and below as *TFW.*

6. Henri Bergson, *Matter and Memory,* trans. N. M. Paul and W. S. Palmer (New York: Zone Books, 1991), 32. Cited henceforth in the text as *MM.*

7. Rafael Winkler, "Husserl and Bergson on Time and Consciousness," in *Analecta Husserliana: The Yearbook of Phenomenological Research,* ed. Anna-Teresa Tymieniecka (Dordrecht, The Netherlands: Springler, 2006), 90:110.

8. Thus, Gilles Deleuze comments in *Bergsonism*: "The past . . . has ceased to act or to be useful. But it has not ceased to be. Useless and inactive, impassive, it IS, in the full sense of the word: It is identical with being in itself." See Deleuze, *Bergsonism,* trans. Hugh Tomlinson and Barbara Habberjam (New York: Zone Books, 1988), 55.

9. For a brief but astute discussion of the phrase as it relates to Kant's transcendental deduction, see Leonard Lawlor, *The Challenge of Bergsonism: Phenomenology, Ontology, Ethics* (New York: Continuum, 2003), 54.

10. Walter Benjamin, "On Some Motifs in Baudelaire," in *Charles Baudelaire: A Lyric Poet in the Era of High Capitalism,* trans. Harry Zohn (London: Verso, 1992), 111.

11. Ibid., 117.

12. Susan Buck-Morss, *The Origin of Negative Dialectics: Theodor W. Adorno, Walter Benjamin, and the Frankfurt Institute* (New York: The Free Press, 1977), 160.

13. See Kant, *Critique of Pure Reason,* 183. Of course, what is perpetually "lost" in Kant is the notorious *Ding an sich,* and it should not come as a surprise that Bergson refuses to accept this loss as anything but a surplus of spatialized perception, available to more intuitive grasp. See *CE,* 230. This attempt to name and render accessible the Kantian thing in itself is, incidentally, one of the many convergences between Bergson and the other major theorist of unconscious experience, Sigmund Freud, who implies in his paper "The Unconscious" that the eponymous phenomenon possesses the characteristics of the Kantian thing in itself, with the qualification that it is more knowable. See Freud, "The Unconscious," in *The Freud Reader,* ed. Peter Gay (New York: W. W. Norton, 1995), 577.

14. In the concluding sections of *Time and Free Will,* Bergson criticizes Kant for maintaining a spatialized conception of time (232–33). In a sense, I am arguing here that this reading is anachronistic. Spatialization is an obscuring of experience while the schematism is its necessary condition of possibility. It is even unfair to call Kantian time homogeneous; time in Kant is always already schematized, shaped to fit experience and endow it with coherence. In other words, Bergson's accusation seems to depend on the (specifically modernist?) bias that all ordering is spatialization.

15. Benjamin, "On Some Motifs in Baudelaire," 145.

16. Ibid., 144.

17. Max Horkheimer, "On Bergson's Metaphysics of Time," *Radical Philosophy* 131 (2005): 15.

18. Walter Benjamin, *The Arcades Project*, trans. Howard Eiland and Kevin McLaughlin (Cambridge: Belknap Press of Harvard University Press, 2002), 463.

19. Benjamin, "Theses on the Philosophy of History," in *Illuminations: Essay and Reflections*, trans. Harry Zohn (New York: Shocken Books, 1968), 255.

20. Ibid., 257.

21. Ibid., 254.

22. Benjamin, *Arcades Project*, 471.

23. Ibid.

24. For Bergson's discussion of the durational exemplarity of melody, see *TFW*, 100.

25. Benjamin, *Arcades Project*, 481.

26. See, for example, Georg Lukács, *Essays on Thomas Mann*, trans. Stanley Mitchell (New York: Grosset and Dunlap, 1965), 79–80; and Georg Lukács, *The Meaning of Contemporary Realism*, trans. John and Necke Mander (London: Merlin Press, 1962), 37. The more specific charge that Bergson's *durée* privileges inner over outer or historical experience rings truer perhaps when raised against *Time and Free Will* than against *Matter and Memory*, where an effort is evident to think these two sides of experience together in terms of a durational conception of time. I don't dwell here on differences in emphasis among Bergson's metaphysical works and read them instead as informing one another while privileging, for reasons having to do with the subject matter at hand, the more synthetic *Matter and Memory*.

27. From this point of view, it is possible to see Bergson's dual temporality of spatialization and *durée* as participating in what Fredric Jameson describes in "The End of Temporality" as the modernist "sensitivity to deep time," which results from the situation of uneven development wherein highly modernized parts of the world, such as Western industrial cities, coexist with premodern villages or colonies. This is in fact not the reading of Bergson that Jameson himself appears to endorse later in this essay, in large part perhaps because he reads him, together with Deleuze, and to my mind mistakenly, as a proto-postmodernist, whose theories of time reach their dead end in a conception of a kind of perpetual present or eternity. See Jameson, "The End of Temporality," *Critical Inquiry* 29, no. 4 (2003): 699, 712.

28. Benjamin, *Arcades Project*, 463.

29. Gustave Flaubert, *Sentimental Education*, trans. Robert Baldick (New York: Penguin, 2004), 459–60.

30. Ibid., 455.

31. Ibid., 454.

32. Marcel Proust, *Remembrance of Things Past*, trans. C. K. Scott Moncrieff, Terence Kilmartin, and Andreas Mayor (New York: Vintage Books, 1982), 3:1106. Henceforth cited in the text by volume and page number.

33. Genette, *Narrative Discourse*, 85.

34. A classic counterexample to the eighteenth century use of discourse in the novel is of course Laurence Sterne's *Tristram Shandy* (1859–1869), which was, as is well known, extraordinarily influential for both modernist novelistic practice and theory. See David Pierce and Peter Jan de Voogd, eds., *Laurence Sterne in Modernism and Postmodernism* (Amsterdam: Rodopi, 1996).

35. I will not explicitly address the question of the similarities and differences between Bergson's and Proust's theories of time and memory. These debates have been going on for a very long time; Proust himself took part in them. Scholarship on the question includes Joyce N. Megay, *Bergson et Proust: Essai de mise au point de la question de l'influence de Bergson sur Proust* (Paris: Librairie philosophique J. Vrin, 1976); A. E. Pilkington, *Bergson and His Influence: A Reassessment* (Cambridge: Cambridge University Press, 1976), 146–77; Georges Poulet, *Studies in Human Time*, trans. Elliott Coleman (New York: Harper Torchbooks, 1956), 316–18; Robert Champigny, "Proust, Bergson, and Other Philosophers," in *Proust: A Collection of Critical Essays*, ed. René Girard (Englewood Cliffs: Prentice Hall, 1962), 122–31; Deleuze, *Proust and Signs*, trans. Richard Howard (Minneapolis: University of Minnesota Press, 2000), 58–59.

36. For Benjamin on "convoluted time" in Proust, see "The Image of Proust" in *Illuminations*, 211.

37. Benjamin, "Theses on the Philosophy of History," in *Illuminations*, 256.

38. Ibid., 263.

39. Andrei Bely, *Peterburg* (St. Petersburg: Nauka, 2004), 238. I am using the fuller Russian original from 1913 for this citation; elsewhere, I use the only existing English translation, which relies on the 1922 edition revised and abridged by Bely himself.

40. Andrei Bely, *Petersburg*, trans. Robert A. Maguire and John E. Malmstad (Bloomington: Indiana University Press, 1978), 11. Henceforth, references to this edition are made in the body of the text.

41. See Vladimir Papernyi, "Poetika russkogo simvolizma: Personologicheskii aspect," in *Andrei Belyi. Publikatsii. Issledovaniia* (Moscow: Institut mirovoi literatury, 2002), 165.

42. Joseph Frank, "Spatial Form in Modern Literature," in *The Widening Gyre: Crisis and Mastery in Modern Literature* (New Brunswick: Rutgers University Press, 1963), 57.

43. A similar point is made more recently, and with Bely among others in mind, by Anne Banfield in "Remembrance and Tense Past," in *The Cambridge Companion to the Modernist Novel*, ed. Moragh Shiach (Cambridge: Cambridge University Press, 2007), 54.

44. Hegel, *Phenomenology*, 27

45. Theodor Adorno, *In Search of Wagner*, trans. Rodney Livingstone (London: Verso, 2005), 30.

46. Frank, "Spatial Form in Modern Literature," 60.

47. Adorno, *In Search of Wagner*, 51, 52.

48. Ibid., 56.

49. Ibid., 55.

50. On the ways the railroad, the telegraph, the telephone, the automobile, the electric tram, etc. exercised the spatiotemporal imaginations of contemporaries, see Kern, *The Culture of Time and Space*, 65–88.

51. This is where we are perhaps best positioned to understand Bakhtin's reading of Dostoevsky, one that radically devalues plot in favor of polyphonic discourse, as precisely a "modernist" reading, or a reading of Dostoevsky as a modernist. As such, it repeats the gesture, one that we find in Bergson, Benjamin, and Adorno, of linking plotted coherence to the degraded category of spatialization and seeking to understand the crucial features of an author's poetics in nonnarrative terms. Bakhtin's polyphony, then, emerges as a metaphor serving a function quite similar to Adorno's sonority.

52. For a comparison between Bergson's and Husserl's conceptions of time, see Winkler. For a relevant discussion of Heidegger, see Piotr Hoffman, "Death, Time, and History: Division II of *Being and Time*" in *The Cambridge Companion to Heidegger*, ed. Charles Guignon (Cambridge: Cambridge University Press, 1997), 195–214.

53. Yuri Tynianov, *Arakhaisty i novatory* (Moscow: Priboi, 1929), 558–59.

Bibliography

Adorno, Theodor. *In Search of Wagner.* Translated by Rodney Livingstone. London: Verso, 2005.
———. *Minima Moralia: Reflections on a Damaged Life.* Translated by E. F. N. Jephcott. London: Verso, 2005.
Alexandrov, Vladimir E. "Relative Time in *Anna Karenina.*" *Russian Review* 41, no. 2 (1982): 159–68.
Allison, Henry E. *Kant's Transcendental Idealism: An Interpretation and Defense.* New Haven: Yale University Press, 1983.
Althusser, Louis, and Étienne Balibar. *Reading Capital.* Translated by Ben Brewster. London: Verso, 1979.
Ansel, Yves. *Stendhal: Le Temps et l'histoire.* Toulouse: Presses Universitaires du Mirail, 2000.
Appel, Toby A. *Cuvier-Geoffroy Debate: French Biology in the Decades Before Darwin.* New York: Oxford University Press, 1987.
Auerbach, Erich. *Mimesis: The Representation of Reality in Western Literature.* Translated by Willard R. Trask. Princeton: Princeton University Press, 1953.
Augustine. *Confessions.* Translated by R. S. Pine-Coffin. New York: Penguin, 1961.
Bacon, Francis. *The New Organon.* Edited by Lisa Jardine and Michael Silverthorne. Cambridge: Cambridge University Press, 2000.
Baer, Brian. "Translating the Transition: The Translator-Detective in Post-Soviet Fiction." *Linguistica Antverpiensia NS—Themes in Translation Studies* 4 (2005): 243–54.
Bakhtin, Mikhail. *The Dialogic Imagination: Four Essays.* Translated by Caryl Emerson and Michael Holquist. Austin: University of Texas Press, 1981.
———. *Problems of Dostoevsky's Poetics.* Translated and edited by Caryl Emerson. Minneapolis: University of Minnesota Press, 1984.
———. *Sobranie sochinenii.* Edited by S. Bocharev and V. Kozhinov. 6 vols. Moscow: Iazyki slavianskoi kul'tury, 2002.
———. *Speech Genres and Other Essays.* Translated by Vern W. McGee. Edited by Caryl Emerson and Michael Holquist. Austin: University of Texas Press, 1996.
Balzac, Honoré de. *"La Comédie Humaine" of Honoré de Balzac.* 7 vols. New York: The Century, 1906.
———. *La Cousin Bette.* Translated by Kathleen Raine. New York: The Modern Library, 2002.
———. *Écrits sur le roman: Anthologie.* Paris: Librairie générale française, 2000.
———. *Eugénie Grandet.* Translated by Sylvia Raphael. Oxford: Oxford University Press, 1990.
———. *The Girl with the Golden Eyes.* Translated by Carol Cosman. New York: Carroll and Graf, 1998.

———. *Lost Illusions*. Translated by Herbert J. Hunt. New York: Penguin Classics, 1971.
———. *The Magic Skin*. Translated by Ellen Marriage. Gainesville: Blue Unicorn Editions, 2005.
———. *Oeuvres complètes de Honoré de Balzac*. Revised and annotated by Marcel Bouteron and Henri Longon. 40 vols. Paris: L. Conard, 1912–1940.
———. *La Peau de chagrin*. Paris: G. F. Flammarion, 1971.
———. *Le Père Goriot*. Translated by Burton Raffel. New York: W. W. Norton, 1998.
———. *The Quest of the Absolute and Other Stories*. Philadelphia: Gebbie Publishing, 1899.
———. *The Works of Honoré de Balzac*. Vol. 2, *Louis Lambert*. Boston: Dana Estes, 1901.
Banfield, Anne. "Remembrance and Tense Past." In *The Cambridge Companion to the Modernist Novel*, edited by Moragh Shiach. Cambridge: Cambridge University Press, 2007.
Barthes, Roland. *S/Z*. Translated by Richard Miller. New York: Farrar, Straus and Giroux, 1974.
Beiser, Frederick C. *The Romantic Imperative: The Concept of Early German Romanticism*. Cambridge: Harvard University Press, 2003.
Bely, Andrei. *Peterburg*. St. Petersburg: Nauka, 2004.
———. *Petersburg*. Translated by Robert A. Maguire and John E. Malmstad. Bloomington: Indiana University Press, 1978.
Benjamin, Walter. *The Arcades Project*. Translated by Howard Eiland and Kevin McLaughlin. Cambridge: Belknap Press of Harvard University Press, 2002.
———. *Charles Baudelaire: A Lyric Poet in the Era of High Capitalism*. Translated by Harry Zohn. London: Verso, 1992.
———. "The Concept of Criticism in German Romanticism." In *Walter Benjamin: Selected Writings*, vol. 1, *1913–1926*, edited by Marcus Bullock and Michael W. Jennings. Cambridge: Belknap Press of Harvard University Press, 1996.
———. *Illuminations: Essays and Reflections*. Translated by Harry Zohn. New York: Shocken Books, 1968.
Bergson, Henry. *Creative Evolution*. Translated by Arthur Mitchell. Mineola, N.Y.: Dover, 1998.
———. *Matter and Memory*. Translated by N. M. Paul and W. S. Palmer. New York: Zone Books, 1991.
———. *Time and Free Will: An Essay on the Immediate Data of Consciousness*. Translated by F. L. Pogson. New York: Cosimo Classics, 2008.
Bernstein, J. M. *The Philosophy of the Novel: Lukács, Marxism, and the Dialectics of Form*. Minneapolis: University of Minnesota Press, 1984.
Bloch, Ernst. *The Heritage of Our Times*. Translated by Neville Plaice and Stephen Plaice. Berkeley and Los Angeles: University of California Press, 1990.
Brombert, Victor. *Stendhal: Fiction and the Themes of Freedom*. New York: Random House, 1968.
Brooks, Peter. *The Melodramatic Imagination: Balzac, Henry James, Melodrama, and the Mode of Excess*. New Haven: Yale University Press, 1995.
———. *Reading for the Plot: Design and Intention in Narrative*. Cambridge: Harvard University Press, 2000.
Buck-Morss, Susan. *The Origin of Negative Dialectics: Theodor W. Adorno, Walter Benjamin, and the Frankfurt Institute*. New York: The Free Press, 1977.
Campbell, Richard. *Truth and Historicity*. Oxford: Clarendon Press, 1992.
Champigny, Robert. "Proust, Bergson, and Other Philosophers." In *Proust: A Collection of Critical Essays*, edited by René Girard. Englewood Cliffs, N.J.: Prentice Hall, 1962.
Charlton, D. G. "Prose Fiction." In *The French Romantics*, edited by D. G. Charlton. 2 vols. Cambridge: Cambridge University Press, 1984.

Chateaubriand, François-René. *Political Reflections on the True Interests of the French Nation.* London: Schulze and Dean, 1814.
Christian, R. F. *Tolstoy: A Critical Introduction.* Cambridge: Cambridge University Press, 1969.
Chulkov, Mikhail. *Prigozhaia povarikha.* Moscow: EKSMO, 2008.
Cohen, Margaret. *The Sentimental Education of the Novel.* Princeton: Princeton University Press, 1999.
Constant, Benjamin. *Adolphe.* Translated by Margaret Mauldon. Oxford: Oxford University Press, 2001.
———. *De la Liberté chez les modernes.* Paris: Le Livre de Poche, 1980.
Corneille, Pierre. *Théâtre 2.* Paris: G. F. Flammarion, 1980.
Cousin, M. Victor. *Course of the History of Modern Philosophy.* Translated by O. W. Wright. 2 vols. New York: D. Appleton, 1857.
de Bertier de Sauvigny, Guillaume. *The Bourbon Restoration.* Philadelphia: University of Pennsylvania Press, 1966.
de Bonald, Louis. *On Divorce.* Translated and edited by Nicholas Davidson. New Brunswick: Transaction, 1992.
Debord, Guy. *The Society of the Spectacle.* Translated by Donald Nicholson-Smith. New York: Zone Books, 1995.
Deleuze, Gilles. *Bergsonism.* Translated by Hugh Tomlinson and Barbara Habberjam. New York: Zone Books, 1988.
———. *Proust and Signs.* Translated by Richard Howard. Minneapolis: University of Minnesota Press, 2000.
de Maistre, Joseph. "The Saint Petersburg Dialogues." In *The Works of Joseph de Maistre,* translated by Jack Lively. New York: Macmillan, 1965.
Dostoevsky, Fyodor. *The Brothers Karamazov.* Translated by Richard Pevear and Larissa Volokhonsky. New York: Vintage Classics, 1990.
———. *Crime and Punishment.* Translated by Richard Pevear and Larissa Volokhonsky. New York: Vintage Classics, 1992.
———. *The Eternal Husband and Other Stories.* Translated by Richard Pevear and Larissa Volokhonsky. New York: Bantam, 1997.
———. *The Idiot.* Translated by Richard Pevear and Larissa Volokhonsky. New York: Vintage Classics, 2001.
———. *Polnoe sobranie sochinenii v tridtsati tomakh.* Edited and annotated by G. M. Fridlender et al. 30 vols. Leningrad: Nauka, 1972–1990.
Eikhenbaum, Boris. *Lev Tolstoy.* Munich: Wilhelm Fink Verlag, 1968.
Emerson, Caryl. "Prosaics in *Anna Karenina:* Pro and Con." *Tolstoy Studies Journal* 8 (1995–1996): 150–76.
Fanger, Donald. *Dostoevsky and Romantic Realism: A Study of Dostoevsky in Relation to Balzac, Dickens, and Gogol.* Cambridge: Harvard University Press, 1965.
Fénelon, François. *Aventure de Télémaque.* Paris: Honoré Champion, 2009.
Fichte, Johann Gottlieb. *Fichte: Early Philosophical Writings.* Translated and edited by Daniel Breazeale. Ithaca: Cornell University Press, 1988.
———. *Science of Knowledge (Wissenschaftslehre).* Translated and edited by Peter Heath and John Lachs. New York: Meredith, 1970.
Fielding, Henry. *The History of Tom Jones.* Edited by R. P. C. Mutter. London: Penguin, 1966.
Flaubert, Gustave. *Sentimental Education.* Translated by Robert Baldick. New York: Penguin, 2004.

Foucault, Michel. *The Order of Things: An Archaeology of the Human Sciences.* New York: Random House, 1970.
Frank, Joseph. *Dostoevsky: The Miraculous Years, 1865–1871.* Princeton: Princeton University Press, 1995.
———. "Spatial Form in Modern Literature." In *The Widening Gyre: Crisis and Mastery in Modern Literature.* New Brunswick: Rutgers University Press, 1963.
Freud, Sigmund. "The Unconscious." In *The Freud Reader,* edited by Peter Gay. New York: W. W. Norton, 1995.
Frye, Northrop. *Anatomy of Criticism: Four Essays.* Princeton: Princeton University Press, 1957.
———. *The Secular Scripture: A Study of the Structure of Romance.* Cambridge: Harvard University Press, 1976.
Gasché, Rodolphe. "Foreword: Ideality in Fragmentation." In *Friedrich Schlegel, Philosophical Fragments,* translated by Peter Firchow. Minneapolis: University of Minnesota Press, 1991.
Genette, Gérard. *Figures, essais.* 4 vols. Paris: Éditions du seuil, 1966.
———. *Figures of Literary Discourse.* Translated by Alan Sheridan. New York: Columbia University Press, 1982.
———. *Narrative Discourse: An Essay in Method.* Translated by Jane E. Lewin. Ithaca: Cornell University Press, 1980.
Girard, René. *Deceit, Desire, and the Novel: Self and Other in Literary Structure.* Translated by Yvonne Freccero. Baltimore: Johns Hopkins University Press, 1990.
Goethe, Johann Wolfgang. *Wilhelm Meister's Apprenticeship.* Translated and edited by Eric A. Blackall. Princeton: Princeton University Press, 1995.
Grossman, Leonid. *Dostoevskii: Put', poetika, tvorchestva.* Moscow: Sovremennye problemy, 1928.
Habermas, Jürgen. *The Philosophical Discourse of Modernity.* Translated by Frederick G. Lawrence. Cambridge: MIT Press, 1990.
Hegel, Georg Wilhelm Friedrich. *Hegel's Aesthetics: Lectures on Fine Art.* Translated by T. M. Knox. 2 vols. Oxford: Clarendon Press, 1975.
———. *Lectures on the History of Philosophy.* Translated by E. S. Haldane and Frances H. Simson. 3 vols. Lincoln: University of Nebraska Press, 1995.
———. *Phenomenology of Spirit.* Translated by A. V. Miller. Oxford: Oxford University Press, 1977.
Heidegger, Martin. *Kant and the Problem of Metaphysics.* Translated by Richard Taft. Bloomington: Indiana University Press, 1997.
Herder, Johann Gottfried. *On Social and Political Culture.* Translated and edited by F. M. Barnard. Cambridge: Cambridge University Press, 1969.
Herzen, Alexander. *Polnoe sobranie sochinenii v tridtsati tomakh.* Edited by V. Volgin. 30 vols. Moscow: Akademiia nauk, 1956.
Hoffman, Piotr. "Death, Time, and History: Division II of *Being and Time.*" In *The Cambridge Companion to Heidegger,* edited by Charles Guignon. Cambridge: Cambridge University Press, 1997.
Holquist, Michael. *Dostoevsky and the Novel.* Princeton: Princeton University Press, 1977.
Horkheimer, Max. "On Bergson's Metaphysics of Time." *Radical Philosophy* 131 (2005).
Horowitz, Louise K. "Pastoral Fiction." In *A New History of French Literature,* edited by Denis Hollier. Cambridge: Harvard University Press, 1989.
Huet, Pierre-Daniel. *The History of Romances: An Enquiry into Their Original; Instructions for Composing Them; An Account of the Most Eminent Authors.* Translated by Stephen Lewis. London, 1715.

Hyppolite, Jean. *Genesis and Structure of Hegel's "Phenomenology of Spirit."* Translated by Samuel Cherniak and John Heckman. Evanston: Northwestern University Press, 1974.
Jakobson, Roman. *Language in Literature.* Cambridge: Harvard University Press, 1987.
Jameson, Fredric. "*La Cousine Bette* and Allegorical Realism." *PMLA* 86, no. 2 (1971): 241–54.
———. "The End of Temporality." *Critical Inquiry* 29, no. 4 (2003): 695–718.
———. *The Hegel Variations on the Phenomenology of Spirit.* New York: Verso, 2010.
———. *The Ideologies of Theory: Essays (1971–1986).* Vol. 2, *The Syntax of History.* Minneapolis: University of Minnesota Press, 1988.
Jauss, Hans Robert. "Modernity and Literary Tradition." *Critical Inquiry* 31, no. 2 (2005): 329–64.
———. *Toward an Aesthetic of Reception.* Translated by Timothy Bahti. Minneapolis: University of Minnesota Press, 1982.
Johnson, Leslie. *The Experience of Time in "Crime and Punishment."* Columbus: Slavica, 1984.
Kabat, Geoffrey. *Ideology and Imagination: The Image of Society in Dostoevsky.* New York: Columbia University Press, 1978.
Kale, Steven. *French Salons: High Society and Political Sociability from the Old Regime to the Revolution of 1848.* Baltimore: Johns Hopkins University Press, 2004.
Kant, Immanuel. *The Critique of Pure Reason.* Translated by Norman Kemp Smith. New York: St. Martin's Press, 1965.
———. *On History.* Translated by Lewis White Beck, Robert E. Anchor, and Emil L. Fackenheim. New York: Macmillan, 1963.
Karpachev, M. D. "Obshchestvenno-politicheskaia mysl' poreformennoi epokhi." In *Ocherki russkoi kul'tury XIX veka.* edited by L. D. Dergacheva et al., 4: 197–398. Moscow: Moscow State University Press, 2003.
Kern, Stephen. *The Culture of Time and Space: 1880–1918.* Cambridge: Harvard University Press, 2003.
Kheraskov, Mikhail. *Numa Pompilius, ili protsvetaiushchii Rim.* Moscow: Universitetskaia tipografiia, 1803.
Kliger, Ilya. "Anamorphic Realism: Veridictory Plots in Balzac, Dostoevsky, and Henry James." *Comparative Literature* 59, no. 4 (2007): 294–314.
Kliger, Ilya, and Nasser Zakariya. "Organic and Mechanistic Time and the Limits of Narrative," *Configurations* 15, no. 3 (2007): 331–53.
Kojève, Alexandre. *Introduction to the Reading of Hegel:ABlectures on the "Phenomenology of Spirit."* Translated by James H. Nichols Jr. Ithaca: Cornell University Press, 1969.
Koselleck, Reinhart. *The Practice of Conceptual History: Timing History, Spacing Concepts.* Translated by Todd Samuel Presner and others. Stanford: Stanford University Press, 2002.
Kracauer, Siegfried. *History: The Last Things Before the Last.* New York: Oxford University Press, 1969.
Kroen, Sheryl. *Politics and Theatre: The Crisis of Legitimacy in Restoration France, 1815–1830.* Berkeley and Los Angeles: University of California Press, 2000.
LaCapra, Dominick. *History, Politics, and the Novel.* Ithaca: Cornell University Press, 1987.
Lacoue-Labarthe, Philippe, and Jean-Luc Nancy. *The Literary Absolute: The Theory of Literature in German Romanticism.* Translated by Philip Barnard and Cheryl Lester. Albany: State University of New York Press, 1988.
Lawlor, Leonard. *The Challenge of Bergsonism: Phenomenology, Ontology, Ethics.* New York: Continuum, 2003.

Leibniz, Gottfried Wilhelm. *Theodicy: Essays on the Goodness of God, the Freedom of Man, and the Origin of Evil.* Translated by E. M. Huggard. La Salle, Ill.: Open Court, 1985.
Likhachev, Dmitry. *Izbrannye raboty v trekh tomakh.* 3 vols. Leningrad: Khudozhestvennaia literatura, 1987.
Lotman, Yuri. "Puti razvitiia russkoi prosvetitel'skoi prozy XVIII veka." In *Problemy russkogo prosveshcheniia v literature XVIII veka,* edited by Pavel Berkov. Moscow: Akademiia nauk, 1961.
———. *Struktura khudozhestvennogo teksta.* Providence: Brown University Press, 1971.
Lukács, Georg. *Essays on Thomas Mann.* Translated by Stanley Mitchell. New York: Grosset and Dunlap, 1965.
———. *History and Class Consciousness: Studies in Marxist Dialectics.* Translated by Rodney Livingstone. Cambridge: MIT Press, 1971.
———. *The Meaning of Contemporary Realism.* Translated by John and Necke Mander. London: Merlin Press, 1962.
———. *Studies in European Realism.* Translated by Edith Bone. New York: Grosset and Dunlap, 1964.
———. *Theory of the Novel.* Translated by Anna Bostock. Cambridge: MIT Press, 1971.
———. "Tolstoy i razvitie realizma," *Literaturnoe nasledstvo* 35/36. Moscow: Pushkinskii dom, 1939.
McKeon, Michael. "Generic Transformations and Social Change: Rethinking the Rise of the Novel." In *Theory of the Novel: A Historical Approach,* edited by Michael McKeon. Baltimore: Johns Hopkins University Press, 2000.
———. *Origins of the English Novel, 1600–1740.* Baltimore: Johns Hopkins University Press, 2002.
McReynolds, Susan. *Redemption and the Merchant God: Dostoevsky's Economy of Salvation and Antisemitism.* Evanston: Northwestern University Press, 2008.
Medvedev, Pavel. *The Formal Method in Literary Scholarship.* Translated by Albert J. Wehrle. Baltimore: Johns Hopkins University Press, 1978.
Megay, Joyce N. *Bergson et Proust: Essai de mise au point de la question de l'influence de Bergson sur Proust.* Paris: Librairie philosophique J. Vrin, 1976.
Mendel'son, N. M., ed. *Pis'ma Tolstogo i k Tolstomu.* Moscow: Gosudarstvennoe izdatel'stvo, 1928.
Miller, D. A. "Balzac's Illusions Lost and Found." *Yale French Studies* 67 (1984): 164–81.
———. "Narrative 'Uncontrol' in Stendhal." In *Modern Critical Interpretations: Stendhal's "The Red and the Black,"* edited by Harold Bloom. New York: Chelsea House, 1988.
Milton, John. *Complete Poems and Major Prose.* Edited by Merritt Y. Hughes. Upper Saddle River: Prentice Hall, 1957.
Moretti, Franco. "The Moment of Truth." *New Left Review* 159 (September–October 1986): 39–48.
———. *The Way of the World: The Bildungsroman in European Culture.* Translated by Albert Sbragia. London: Verso, 1987.
Morson, Gary Saul. *"Anna Karenina" in Our Time: Seeing More Wisely.* New Haven: Yale University Press, 2007.
———. "Anna Karenina's Omens." In *Freedom and Responsibility in Russian Literature: Essays in Honor of Robert Louis Jackson,* edited by Elizabeth Cheresh Allen and Gary Soul Morson. Evanston: Northwestern University Press, 1995.
———. "The God of Onions: *The Brothers Karamazov* and the Mythic Prosaic." In *The New*

Word on The Brothers Karamazov, edited by Robert Louis Jackson. Evanston: Northwestern University Press, 2004.
———. "Introductory Study." In *Fyodor Dostoevsky, A Writer's Diary*, vol. 1, *1873–1876*. Translated by Kenneth Lanz. Edited by Gary Saul Morson. Evanston: Northwestern University Press, 1994.
Morson, Gary Saul, and Caryl Emerson. *Mikhail Bakhtin: Creation of a Prosaics*. Stanford: Stanford University Press, 1990.
Mylne, Vivienne. *The Eighteenth-Century French Novel: Techniques of Illusion*. Cambridge: Cambridge University Press, 1981.
Naginski, Isabelle. *Stendhal and Tolstoy: A Study in Literary Kinship*. Ph.D. diss., Columbia University, 1982.
Nancy, Jean-Luc. *Hegel: The Restlessness of the Negative*. Translated by Jason Smith and Steven Miller. Minneapolis: University of Minnesota Press, 2002.
Nietzsche, Friedrich. *The Birth of Tragedy and The Case of Wagner*. Translated by Walter Kaufmann. New York: Vintage, 1967.
Novalis. *Henry von Ofterdingen*. Trans. by Palmer Hilty. Prospect Heights, Ill.: Waveland Press, 1964.
Orwin, Donna Tussing. *Tolstoy's Life and Thought: 1847–1880*. Princeton: Princeton University Press, 1993.
Paperno, Vladimir. "Poetika russkogo simvolizma: Personologicheskii aspect." In *Andrei Belyi. Publikatsii. Issledovaniia*, edited by A. G. Boichuk. Moscow: Institut mirovoi literatury, 2002.
Pickford, Henry, III. "The Sense of Semblance: Modern German and Russian Literature After Adorno." Ph.D. diss., Yale University, 2001.
Pierce, David and Peter Jan de Voogd, eds. *Laurence Sterne in Modernism and Postmodernism*. Amsterdam: Rodopi, 1996.
Pilkington, A. E. *Bergson and His Influence: A Reassessment*. Cambridge: Cambridge University Press, 1976.
Plato, *Timaeus*. In *The Dialogues of Plato*, vol. 3, translated by B. Jowett. New York: Random House, 1892.
Poulet, George. *Studies in Human Time*. Translated by Elliott Coleman. New York: Harper Torchbooks, 1956.
Prendergast, Christopher. *Balzac: Fiction and Melodrama*. London: Arnold Press, 1978.
———. *The Order of Mimesis: Balzac, Stendhal, Nerval, Flaubert*. Cambridge: Cambridge University Press, 1986.
Prévost, abbé. Manon Lescaut. Paris: Presses universitaires de France, 1995.
Prévost, Antoine François. *The Story of the Chevalier Des Grieux and Manon Lescaut*. Translated by Angela Scholar. Oxford: Oxford University Press, 2004.
Proust, Marcel. *Remembrance of Things Past*. Translated by C. K. Scott Moncrieff, Terence Kilmartin, and Andreas Mayor. 3 vols. New York: Vintage Books, 1982.
Rahv, Philip. "Dostoevsky in *Crime and Punishment*." In *Dostoevsky: A Collection of Critical Essays*, edited by René Wellek. Englewood Cliffs, N.J.: Prentice Hall, 1962.
Richardson, Samuel. *Clarissa Harlowe*. 9 vols. London: Chapman and Hall, 1902.
Ricoeur, Paul. *Time and Narrative*. Translated by Kathleen Blamey and David Pellauer. 3 vols. Chicago: University of Chicago Press, 1988.
Robb, Graham. *Balzac: A Biography*. New York: W. W. Norton, 1994.
Rousseau, Jean-Jacques. *Julie or the New Heloise: Letters of Two Lovers Who Live in a Small Town*

at the Foot of the Alps. Translated and annotated by Philip Stewart and Jean Vaché. Hanover: Dartmouth College Press, 1997.
Rudé, Fernand. *Stendhal et la pensée sociale de son temps.* Brionne: G. Monfort, 1983.
Sainte-Beuve, Charles Augustin. *Tableau historique et critique de la poésie français au XVIe siècle.* Coeuvres-et-Valsery: Ressouvenances, 1999.
Sartre, Jean-Paul. *Truth and Existence.* Translated by Adrian van den Hoven. Chicago: University of Chicago Press, 1992.
Schiller, Friedrich. "Letters on the Aesthetic Education of Man." Translated by Elizabeth Wilkinson and L. A. Willoughby. In *Friedrich Schiller, Essays,* edited by Walter Hinderer and Daniel O. Dahlstrom. New York: Continuum, 1993.
Schlegel, Friedrich. *Lucinde and the Fragments.* Translated by Peter Firchow. Minneapolis: University of Minnesota Press, 1971.
———. *Philosophical Fragments.* Translated by Peter Firchow. Foreword by Rodolphe Gasché. Minneapolis: University of Minnesota Press, 1991.
Shklovsky, Viktor. *Theory of Prose.* Translated by Benjamin Sher. Normal, Ill.: Dalkey Archive Press, 1998.
Stenbock-Fermor, Elizabeth. *The Architecture of "Anna Karenina": A History of Its Writing, Structure, and Message.* Lisse: Peter de Ridder Press, 1975.
Stendhal. *The Charterhouse of Parma.* Translated by Richard Howard. New York: The Modern Library, 2000.
———. *Correspondance (1830–1832).* 10 vols. Paris: Le Divan, 1968.
———. *Memoirs of an Egotist.* Translated by Andrew Brown. London: Hesperus Press, 2003.
———. *On Love.* Translated by H. B. V. under the direction of C. K. Scott Moncrieff. Garden City: Doubleday, 1957.
———. *Racine and Shakespeare.* Translated by Guy Daniels. New York: Crowell-Collier Press, 1962.
———. *Red and Black.* Translated and edited by Robert M. Adams. New York: W. W. Norton, 1969.
———. *Le Rouge et le noir.* Paris: Gallimard, 1951.
———. *Short Novels of Stendhal.* Translated by C. K. Scott Moncrieff. New York: Liveright, 1946.
Strakhov, Nikolai. *Mir kak tseloe: Cherty iz nauki o prirode.* St. Petersburg: Tipografiia brat'ev Panteleevykh, 1892.
Taine, Hippolyte Adolphe. *Balzac: A Critical Study.* Translated by Lorenzo O'Rourke. New York: Funk and Wagnalls, 1906.
Tobin, Patricia. *Time and the Novel: The Genealogical Imperative.* Princeton: Princeton University Press, 1978.
Todorov, Tzvetan. *Genres in Discourse.* Translated by Catherine Porter. Cambridge: Cambridge University Press, 1990.
———. *Passion for Democracy: Benjamin Constant.* Translated by Alice Seberry. New York: Algora, 1999.
———. *The Poetics of Prose.* Translated by Richard Howard. Ithaca: Cornell University Press, 1977.
Tolstoy, Lev. *Anna Karenina.* Translated by Richard Pevear and Larissa Volokhonsky. New York: Penguin Classics, 2002.
———. *The Death of Ivan Ilych.* In *Tolstoy's Short Fiction,* edited and with revised translations by Michael R. Katz. New York: W. W. Norton, 1991.

———. *The Kreutzer Sonata*. In *Great Short Works of Leo Tolstoy*, introduction and appendices by John Bayley, translations by Louise and Aylmer Maude, J. D. Duff, and Sam A. Carmack II. New York: Perennial Classics, 2004.
———. *Polnoe sobranie sochinenii*. 90 vols. Moscow: Khudozhestvennaia Literatura, 1928–1964.
———. *War and Peace*. Translated by Ann Dunnigan. New York: Signet Classics, 1968.
Toporov, Viktor. *Mif, ritual, simvol, obraz: Issledovaniia v oblasti mifopoeticheskogo*. Moscow: Progress—Kul'tura, 1995.
Torop, Peeter. *Dostoevskii—Istoriia i ideologiia*. Tartu: Tartu University Press, 1997.
Tynianov, Yuri. *Arakhaisty i novatory*. Moscow: Priboi, 1929.
Wachtel, Andrew. *An Obsession with History: Russian Writers Confront the Past*. Stanford: Stanford University Press, 1994.
Watt, Ian. *The Rise of the Novel: Studies in Defoe, Richardson, and Fielding*. London: Chatto and Windus, 1957.
Weber, Samuel. *Unwrapping Balzac: A Reading of "La Peau de chagrin."* Toronto: University of Toronto Press, 1979.
Wellek, René. *A History of Modern Criticism 1750–1950*. Vol. 2, *The Romantic Age*. New Haven: Yale University Press, 1992.
White, Hayden. *Metahistory: The Historical Imagination in Nineteenth-Century Europe*. Baltimore: Johns Hopkins University Press, 1973.
Williams, Ioan. *The Idea of the Novel in Europe: 1600–1800*. New York: New York University Press, 1979.
Winkler, Rafael. "Husserl and Bergson on Time and Consciousness." In *Analecta Husserliana: The Yearbook of Phenomenological Research*, edited by Anna-Teresa Tymieniecka. 90 vols. Dordrecht, The Netherlands: Springer, 2006.
Zelinsky, Vasily. *Russkaia kriticheskaia literatura o proizvedeniiakh L. N. Tolstogo*. 8 vols. Moscow, 1902.

Index

Auerbach, Erich, 210n40, 218n40
Augustine, 210n35
Adorno, Theodor, 199–201, 232n51

Bacon, Francis, 4–5
Bakhtin, Mikhail, 2, 125, 172–73, 214nn108–9, 111, 215n30, 222n29, 232n51
Balzac, Honoré de, 36, 38, 39, 41, 43–76, 77, 78, 89, 119, 126, 143, 151–52, 177, 180, 203, 216n43
  authorial discourse in, 46–47, 49 161, 163, 166
  Avant-propos to the *Comédie humaine*, 45, 51
  La Cousine Bette, 46, 47, 49, 58, 89
  Eugénie Grandet, 47–48, 58
  La Fille aux yeux d'or, 58, 75
  Gobseck, 65, 71
  Illusions perdues, 49, 62, 75
  Louis Lambert, 31, 37–38, 50–61, 61–64, 67, 68, 70, 74, 80, 116, 132, 138, 216n43
  metaphor in, 37, 50–61, 62, 63, 64, 70–71, 73, 74, 116, 126, 132
  La Peau de chagrin, 37–38, 55, 61–76, 77, 93, 111–13, 116, 126, 132, 138, 166, 167, 170, 202, 217nn51–52, 219n53
  Le Père Goriot, 48, 49, 55 121, 125–26, 215n24
  La Recherche de l'Absolu, 48–49, 55
  Sarrasine, 47, 55
  wager in, 66–68, 69, 72, 82, 93–94
Barthes, Roland, 47, 209n30
Bely, Andrei, 179, 195–200, 201–2, 204–5
Benjamin, Walter, 178, 184–90, 191, 195, 203, 205, 212n77
Bergson, Henri, 178, 179–83, 184–86, 188, 189–90, 191, 199, 200, 202, 203, 205, 230nn3–4, 13–14, 231n26
  Creative Evolution, 179–80, 230n3
  Matter and Memory, 181–83
  Time and Free Will, 180–81, 230n14
Bildung. See *Bildungsroman*

Bildungsroman, 20, 29, 30, 40, 59, 68, 94, 125, 126, 135, 136, 137, 142–44, 169, 173, 174–75, 177, 187, 197, 213n97, 225n47
Brooks, Peter, 54, 63
Buck-Morss, Susan, 185

Chateaubriand, François-René, 38, 43, 101
Chulkov, Mikhail, 8
Cohen, Margaret, 95
Constant, Benjamin, 38–39, 83–84, 86–87, 89
  Adolphe, 38–39, 86–89, 90
  "On the Liberty of the Ancients Compared to That of the Moderns," 83–84
Cousin, M. Victor, 44, 101, 151

Davin, Felix, 53
de Bonald, Louis, 38, 79, 89
Debord, Guy, 93
de Maistre, Joseph, 38, 85, 86, 89
Descartes, René, 10, 14, 210n36
Dostoevsky, Fedor, 39, 40, 41, 114–44, 161–62, 164, 166, 175, 177, 180, 191, 193, 197, 220n1, 221nn8, 15, 223nn31, 36, 232n51
  accident in, 39–40, 116–17, 126–31,132, 138–39, 142, 143, 197, 223n31, 225n49
  The Adolescent, 118, 161
  The Brothers Karamazov, 118, 137, 225n48
  Crime and Punishment, 39, 117–18, 121–25, 126–44, 159, 161, 166, 167, 169, 170, 174–75, 176, 197, 203, 222nn25, 27, 223nn33, 35, 224n42, 225n47
  Diary of a Writer, 114
  emplotment in, 40, 120–21, 121–25, 126–28, 133–37, 138–39, 140–44
  gospel truth in, 131–33, 137–38, 224n40
  The Idiot, 118, 136, 161, 220n4, 223n34
  "The Meek One," 114–17, 118, 129, 130, 132, 220n3
  Notes from Underground, 161, 221n17
  The Possessed, 118, 137, 161
  Winter Notes on Summer Impressions, 123

fabula, 69–71, 72–74, 75, 82, 86, 93, 98, 101, 110, 112, 128, 143, 157, 161, 172, 203, 216n47
Fénelon, François, 8
Fichte, Johann Gottlieb, 24–28, 29, 213n86
Fielding, Henry, 9, 11
   Tom Jones, 7, 8–10, 21, 23–24, 30, 46, 49, 94, 193, 208n27, 211n70, 212n76
Flaubert, Gustave, 84, 192, 195, 199
Foucault, Michel, 13, 14, 210n47
fragment, 37, 60–61, 62, 64–66, 137–38, 198–99, 204
Frank, Joseph, 199–200, 201
Frye, Northrop, 29, 208n22

Geoffroy Saint-Hilaire, Étienne, 45, 51, 57
Genette, Gérard, 46–47, 70, 110, 194
Goethe, Johann Wolfgang, 4, 20–25, 28, 29, 45, 124, 175, 202
   Wilhelm Meister's Apprenticeship, 20–24, 29–30, 46–47, 94, 124, 135, 143, 159, 175, 177, 212nn73, 76, 213n97, 216n46, 219n53, 228n24
   Wilhelm Meister's Theatrical Mission, 20–21, 30, 177
Goncharov, Ivan, 143

Habermas, Jürgen, 12, 149–50
Hegel, Georg Wilhelm Friedrich, 14, 17–24, 26, 28, 29–30, 33, 35, 44, 45, 47, 60, 83, 93, 132, 148, 149, 152, 157, 158, 174, 178, 183, 189, 190, 199, 210n44, 211nn66, 68
Heidegger, Martin, 178, 189, 203, 230n1
Herder, Johann Gottfried, 12, 13, 35
Herzen, Alexander, 225n2
Horkheimer, Max, 186, 188–89
Huet, Pierre-Daniel, 5–6
Husserl, Edmund, 178, 189, 203

Jakobson, Roman, 58
James, Henry, 9
Jameson, Fredric, 89, 213n98, 231n27
Jauss, Hans Robert, 80–81, 100, 214n104
Jena Romanticism, 25, 28, 33, 64, 212n77, 213n93, 216n43
Jetztzeit. See time of the now

Kant, Immanuel, 12, 14–17, 24–25, 28, 30, 32, 33, 148, 178, 183, 185–86, 190, 196–97, 211n53, 212n77, 230nn4, 13–14
Kheraskov, Mikhail, 8
Kojève, Alexandre, 16, 17–18
Koselleck, Reinhart, 4–5, 12

Lacoue-Labarthe, Philippe, 64, 212n77
Leibniz, Gottfried Wilhelm, 3–4, 12–13, 210n44
Lotman, Yuri, 7, 223n31
Lukács, Georg, 1, 45, 169, 189, 211n58, 213n97, 231n26

McKeon, Michael, 3–4, 32
Moretti, Franco, 2, 46–47, 75, 112, 135
Milton, John, 208n25

Nancy, Jean-Luc, 64, 212n77
narrative discourse, 8–9, 41, 46–47, 49, 70, 161–66, 177, 193. *See also* Genette, Gerard
Nietzsche, Friedrich, 207n18
nonsynchronicity, 35–36, 43, 100–101, 119–21, 214n104
Novalis, 29, 213n93

picaresque, 7–8, 20, 22, 30, 31, 178
Poulet, George, 84, 210n36
Prévost, Antoine François, 6–7
Proust, Marcel, 178, 191–96, 199, 200, 201, 204–5

realism, 32, 33, 38, 39, 44, 62–63, 75, 89, 152, 213n98, 218n40, 223n31
Richardson, Samuel, 11, 209n33
romance, 3–4, 6, 12–13, 24–25, 27–29, 31, 37–38, 61, 81, 104–5, 138, 166–67, 207n8, 209n33, 210n44, 212n73, 213n93, 217nn51–52
Romance idealism, 4, 5, 7, 11, 16, 29, 32, 75–76, 106, 154, 167, 168, 224n44
Rousseau, Jean-Jacques, 7, 11, 44, 229n45

Schema. See schematism
schematism, 16–17, 25, 33, 183, 185, 190, 205, 211n53, 214n110, 221n16, 230nn1, 14
Schlegel, Friedrich, 24, 26–30, 37, 60–61
Schopenhauer, Arthur, 166
Shklovsky, Viktor, 69
sjuzhet, 69–71, 72–74, 75, 82, 83, 93, 98, 101, 109–10, 112, 128, 143, 154, 157, 158, 161, 172, 202, 203, 216n47
sonority, 201–2, 204, 205, 232n51
Stendhal, 30, 38–39, 40–42, 43, 77–113, 119, 131, 150–51, 162, 163, 164, 166, 177, 191, 203–4, 217n19
   Armance, 38, 85, 91, 95–6, 97, 98, 101
   La Chartreuse de Parme, 43, 227n20
   De l'Amour, 85
   duty in, 38–39, 90–93, 95–99, 99–101, 103, 105–6, 108–9, 110, 111, 116, 131, 170, 218nn38, 47

pastoral in, 95–98, 102, 108
Racine et Shakespeare, 78–81, 82–83, 85–86, 89, 102, 104
Le Rouge et le noir, 38, 39, 77–78, 90–113, 116, 154–55, 162–64, 167, 168, 170, 204, 219nn57, 59
Souvenirs d'égotisme, 81, 82, 84, 86, 89, 101
the whole in, 38, 89, 95, 111, 168
Strakhov, Nikolai, 145–49, 151, 152, 154, 158, 161, 225n2
The World as a Whole, 146–47, 158

Taine, Hippolyte Adolphe, 45
Tobin, Patricia, 10
Todorov, Tzvetan, 9, 49, 83, 213n93
time, 5, 10, 12, 13, 15–18, 26, 67, 80, 123, 157, 172, 177–205, 208nn25, 27, 209n33, 211n53, 223n36, 230n4
 acceleration of, 4–5, 11, 31, 34–36, 37, 38, 40, 58, 68, 73, 76, 80, 83, 93, 102, 112, 205
 intimate, 87, 98, 101, 109
 of modernity, 5, 11, 16, 34–36, 58, 75–76, 105, 169–70, 179, 186, 219n53
 of the now, 184–85, 189, 194, 202
 and spatialization, 180–83, 184, 190–91, 196, 199, 203, 205, 230n14, 231n27
 truth and, 9–10, 11, 13, 14, 16–17, 19–20, 22–24, 30–31, 33–37, 44, 49, 68, 76, 85–86, 101, 114, 146, 157–58, 161–66, 174–76, 177–79, 185, 193, 204
 of the wager, 66–68, 82, 93

Tolstoy, Lev, 30, 40–42, 84, 145–76, 177, 178, 180, 191, 198, 202, 203, 204, 226n6, 229n45
 Anna Karenina, 40, 145, 147, 148, 149, 151, 152–56, 157–61, 162–76, 177–78, 202, 203–4, 227n21, 228nn27, 29, 31, 41, 43
 correspondence with Strakhov, 145–47, 154
 The Death of Ivan Ilych, 152, 160
 epigraph in, 157, 166–67
 estrangement in, 150, 164–65, 173, 174, 175, 203, 226n4
 The Kreutzer Sonata, 40, 171
 opinions of Hegel, 146–150, 225n2
 Strider, 147
 totality in, 40, 147–48, 150, 151–52, 153–54, 157–58, 161, 165, 172, 174, 175, 202
 War and Peace, 145, 147, 156, 226n10, 228nn24, 29
 What then Must we Do?, 148

veridiction, 2–3, 7, 9, 11, 14, 24, 30, 33–34, 36, 38–39, 40–42, 47, 49, 50–51, 61–63, 70, 84, 88–89, 93, 105, 106, 107, 110–11, 118, 120–21, 130, 131, 139, 143–44, 150, 151, 157–58, 164, 166, 167, 170, 175–76, 177–79, 180, 187, 190, 193, 198–200, 201, 203–5, 208n27, 209n30, 214nn110–11
Voltaire, 3–4

Watt, Ian, 3, 5
White, Hayden, 13, 214n102
Wissenschaftslehre. See Fichte

www.ingramcontent.com/pod-product-compliance
Lightning Source LLC
Chambersburg PA
CBHW021400290426
44108CB00010B/316